Justice, Crime, and Citizenship in Eurasia

What role does law play in post-communist societies? This book examines the law as a social institution in Eurasia, exploring how it is shaped in everyday interactions between state and society, organisations and individuals, and between law enforcement and other government entities. It bridges the gap between theoretically rich work on law-in-action and the empirical reality of Eurasia.

The contributions in this volume include research on policing, the legal profession, public attitudes towards law, regime support and oppositional mobilisation, crime policy, and property rights, among others. The studies shift away from the common perception that, in Eurasia, the law exists only as a tool for the state to enforce order and suppress dissent. Instead, they show, through empirical analyses, that citizens evade, use, reinterpret and shape the law even in authoritarian contexts—sometimes containing state violence and challenging the regime, and other times reinforcing state capture from below.

The chapters in this book were originally published as a special issue of the journal *Europe-Asia Studies.*

Erica Marat is Associate Professor at the College of International Security Affairs of the National Defence University, USA. She specialises in violence, mobilisation and security institutions.

Lauren A. McCarthy is Associate Professor of Legal Studies and Political Science at the University of Massachusetts Amherst, USA. Her research focuses on the relationship between law and society in Russia, police and law enforcement institutions, civilian oversight and the issue of human trafficking.

Justice, Crime, and Citizenship in Eurasia

A Sociolegal Perspective

Edited by
Erica Marat and Lauren A. McCarthy

Routledge
Taylor & Francis Group
LONDON AND NEW YORK

First published 2023
by Routledge
4 Park Square, Milton Park, Abingdon, Oxon, OX14 4RN

and by Routledge
605 Third Avenue, New York, NY 10158

Routledge is an imprint of the Taylor & Francis Group, an informa business

British Library Cataloguing-in-Publication Data
A catalogue record for this book is available from the British Library

ISBN13: 978-1-032-31207-1 (hbk)
ISBN13: 978-1-032-31208-8 (pbk)
ISBN13: 978-1-003-30860-7 (ebk)

DOI: 10.4324/9781003308607

Typeset in Times New Roman
by codeMantra

Publisher's Note
The publisher accepts responsibility for any inconsistencies that may have arisen during the conversion of this book from journal articles to book chapters, namely the inclusion of journal terminology.

Contents

Citation Information

The chapters in this book were originally published in the *Europe-Asia Studies*, volume 73, issue 1 (2021). When citing this material, please use the original page numbering for each article, as follows:

Introduction

Justice, Crime and Citizenship in Eurasia: A Socio-legal Perspective
Erica Marat and Lauren A. McCarthy
Europe-Asia Studies, volume 73, issue 1 (2021) pp. 1–7

Chapter 1

Who Reports Crime? Citizen Engagement with the Police in Russia and Georgia
Lauren A. McCarthy, Scott Gehlbach, Timothy Frye and Noah Buckley
Europe-Asia Studies, volume 73, issue 1 (2021) pp. 8–35

Chapter 2

Popular Legal Attitudes and the Political Order: Comparative Evidence from Georgia, Russia and Ukraine
William M. Reisinger, Marina Zaloznaya and Vicki Hesli Claypool
Europe-Asia Studies, volume 73, issue 1 (2021) pp. 36–59

Chapter 3

Transcending Illegality in Kyrgyzstan: The Case of a Squatter Settlement in Bishkek
Eliza Isabaeva
Europe-Asia Studies, volume 73, issue 1 (2021) pp. 60–80

Chapter 4

Negotiating the Right to Information: Citizen–Government Interactions in the Implementation of the Regulations on Open Government Information in China
Yiyi Lu
Europe-Asia Studies, volume 73, issue 1 (2021) pp. 81–100

Chapter 5

Between Human Rights and Transitional Justice: The Dilemma of Constitutional Courts in Post-Communist Central Europe
Katarína Šipulová and Hubert Smekal
Europe-Asia Studies, volume 73, issue 1 (2021) pp. 101–130

Chapter 6

Becoming a Judge in Russia: An Analysis of Judicial Biographies
Aryna Dzmitryieva
Europe-Asia Studies, volume 73, issue 1 (2021) pp. 131–156

Chapter 7

Building Socialist Legality: Political Order and Institutional Development in the Soviet and Chinese Procuracies
Margaret Hanson and Michael Thompson-Brusstar
Europe-Asia Studies, volume 73, issue 1 (2021) pp. 157–177

Chapter 8

The Limits of Authoritarian Modernisation: Zero Tolerance Policing in Kazakhstan
Gavin Slade, Alexei Trochev and Malika Talgatova
Europe-Asia Studies, volume 73, issue 1 (2021) pp. 178–199

Chapter 9

Propaganda and the Police: The Softer Side of State Control in China
Suzanne E. Scoggins
Europe-Asia Studies, volume 73, issue 1 (2021) pp. 200–220

Chapter 10

'Vigilante Shows' and Law Enforcement in Russia
Gilles Favarel-Garrigues
Europe-Asia Studies, volume 73, issue 1 (2021) pp. 221–242

Chapter 11

Technological Solutions for Complex Problems: Emerging Electronic Surveillance Regimes in Eurasian Cities
Erica Marat and Deborah Sutton
Europe-Asia Studies, volume 73, issue 1 (2021) pp. 243–267

Notes on Contributors

Noah Buckley is Assistant Professor in the Department of Political Science at Trinity College Dublin, Ireland, and Research Fellow at the International Centre for the Study of Institutions and Development at the Higher School of Economics in Moscow. His research interests include authoritarian politics, public opinion, and Russian and postcommunist politics.

Vicki Hesli Claypool is Professor Emerita of Political Science at the University of Iowa, USA. She was Co-principal Investigator on National Science Foundation and Department of Defense grants and Principal Investigator on partnership programme grants funded by the US Department of State. She has authored, co-authored and co-edited six books, fifteen book chapters, and fifty journal articles. She publishes in the fields of Russian and Ukrainian voting behaviour, health care reform, nationalism, and separatism.

Aryna Dzmitryieva is Researcher at the Institute for the Rule of Law at the European University at St Petersburg, Russia, and Doctoral Candidate at the University of Eastern Finland, Finland. Her research interests include the sociology of the legal profession, judicial reform and policing in post-socialist countries. She co-authored the monographs *Rossiiskie sud'i: sotsiologicheskoe issledovanie professii* (2016) and *Legal Education in Russia: Between University, Profession, State and Market* (2021).

Gilles Favarel-Garrigues is National Centre for Scientific Research Professor at Sciences Po-CERI, France. He holds a PhD in Political Science from Sciences Po. He has published widely on policing in contemporary Russia and on international mobilisations against transnational criminal threats. His current works are devoted to vigilantism, especially in post-Soviet societies.

Timothy Frye is Marshall D. Shulman Professor of Post-Soviet Foreign Policy at Columbia University, USA, and Research Director at the International Center for the Study of Institutions and Development at the Higher School of Economics in Moscow. He is the author of *Weak Strongman: The Limits of Power in Putin's Russia* (2021) and the editor of *Post-Soviet Affairs*.

Scott Gehlbach is Professor in the Department of Political Science and Harris School of Public Policy at the University of Chicago, USA. A political economist and comparativist, his work is motivated by the contemporary and historical experience of Russia, Ukraine, and other post-communist states. He has made numerous contributions to the study of autocracy, economic reform, political connections and other important topics in political economy. He is the author most recently of *Reform and Rebellion in Weak States* (2020).

Margaret Hanson is Assistant Professor of Political Science in the School of Politics and Global Studies at Arizona State University, Tempe, USA. Her research focuses on authoritarian politics and factors that stabilise or, conversely, undermine the control of dictators and of aspiring dictators, with particular emphasis on the former Soviet Union. More specifically, she is interested in how formal and informal institutions interact to shape governance in autocracies and her work centres on the role of law, courts and corruption.

Eliza Isabaeva defended her PhD thesis in the field of Social Anthropology at the University of Zurich, Switzerland. Her dissertation examined the dynamic relationship between state and society on the example of internal migrants who reside in an illegal settlement in the outskirts of Bishkek. She has published articles on migration, remittances, urbanisation and the state in contemporary Kyrgyzstan.

Yiyi Lu is Lecturer at the College of Politics and Public Administration at Tianjin Normal University, China. She is the author of *Non-governmental Organisations in China: The Rise of Dependent Autonomy* (Routledge, 2008) and co-editor of *China's Soft Power and International Relations* (Routledge, 2012). Her research has appeared in *Public Policy and Administration*, *China: An International Journal* and *International Journal of Environmental Studies*. She was previously Columnist for *The Wall Street Journal*'s China Real Time Report.

Erica Marat is Associate Professor at the College of International Security Affairs at the National Defense University, USA. Her research focuses on violence, mobilisation and security institutions in Eurasia, India and Mexico. Her most recent book, *The Politics of Police Reform: Society against the State in Post-Soviet Countries* (2018), explores conditions in which police reform projects succeed and why they fail in countries with recent authoritarian past. She is currently engaged in a research project on China's and Russia's provision of public services for illiberal governances in 15 countries across 5 continents.

Lauren A. McCarthy is Associate Professor of Legal Studies and Political Science at the University of Massachusetts Amherst, USA, and Director of Legal Studies. Her research focuses on the relationship between law and society in Russia, police and law enforcement institutions, civilian oversight and the issue of human trafficking. Her book *Trafficking Justice: How Russian Police Enforce New Laws, from Crime to Courtroom* (2015) explored how Russian law enforcement agencies have implemented laws on human trafficking. She is currently working on a project focusing on citizen oversight of the legal system in Russia.

William M. Reisinger is Professor of Political Science at the University of Iowa, USA. His research concerns authoritarianism and democracy in the former communist states, especially Russia. He has written or edited eight books, including *The Regional Roots of Russia's Political Regime*, co-authored with Bryon Moraski (2017), as well as numerous articles and book chapters. His research has been supported by Fulbright-Hays Fellowship and grants from the National Science Foundation, the US Army Research Office and the Minerva Initiative.

Suzanne E. Scoggins is Associate Professor of Political Science at Clark University, Worcester, USA. Her work focuses on policing in reform-era China, exploring themes of local governance, state legitimacy and authoritarian control. She is the author of *Policing China: Street-Level Cops in the Shadow of Protest* (2021).

Katarína Šipulová is the Head of the Judicial Studies Institute at Masaryk University, Czechia. She earned her PhD in European Studies at Masaryk University, and an MSt degree in Socio-Legal Research at the University of Oxford. Her research activities are centred on courts, judicial independence, transitional justice and democratization of the Central and Eastern European countries. She currently participates on the research project INFINITY: Informal Judicial Institutions and Democratic Decay. Katarína is a member of the Oxford Global Society, the Czech government's Committee for Fundamental Rights and Prevention of Discrimination, and the ECPR Law and Courts Steering Committee.

Gavin Slade is Associate Professor of Sociology and Chair of the Sociology and Anthropology Department at Nazarbayev University, Nur-Sultan, Kazakhstan. His research focuses on the criminal justice systems of the countries of the former Soviet Union, in particular on prisons, policing and organised forms of crime. He is the author of *Reorganizing Crime: Mafia and Anti-Mafia in Post-Soviet Georgia* (2013).

Hubert Smekal is Assistant Professor at Maynooth University, Ireland and Senior Researcher at the Judicial Studies Institute Masaryk University, Czechia, Czech Republic. He spent a year (2010–2011) as Fulbright–Masaryk Scholar at the Center for the Study of Law and Society, UC Berkeley. He co-founded the Czech Centre for Human Rights and Democratization and served as Member of the Czech Government Human Rights Council. His academic interests include human rights and judicialisation of (international) politics. He has published articles in *European Constitutional Law Review*, *German Law Journal*, *Netherlands Quarterly of Human Rights* and *Journal of Mixed Methods Research*.

Deborah Sutton holds a master's degree from the School of Slavonic and East European Studies at University College London, UK, where she also served as Managing Editor of *Slovo*, the school's peer-reviewed journal. As Independent Researcher, she has investigated money laundering in the Baltics and women's security in Central Asia. Sutton has also contributed to several research projects, focusing on Central Asia and post-Soviet politics and affairs. She currently lives in Washington, DC.

Malika Talgatova is Doctoral Student at the University of California San Diego, USA. She also holds an MA in Political Science and International Relations from Nazarbayev University, Nur-Sultan, Kazakhstan, and an MA in Political Science from University of California San Diego. Her research interests include authoritarian regimes, political violence and repression in autocracies, and media control.

Michael Thompson-Brusstar is Doctoral Candidate in Political Science at the University of Michigan, USA, where he also received an MA in Chinese Studies. His research focuses on party discipline, state control and policy change in China and Taiwan, where his fieldwork was supported by a Fulbright Student Fellowship.

Alexei Trochev is Associate Professor of Political Science at Nazarbayev University, Nur-Sultan, Kazakhstan. He is the author of *Judging Russia: The Constitutional Court in*

Russian Politics, 1990–2006 (2008). His numerous articles on post-communist law and politics have appeared in the *Journal of Law and Courts, American Journal of Comparative Law, Communist and Post-Communist Studies* and *International Political Science Review*. He is the editor of the journal *Statutes and Decisions: The Laws of the USSR and its Successor States*.

Marina Zaloznaya is Associate Professor at the Department of Sociology and Criminology at the University of Iowa, USA. Her research explores public sector corruption, political behaviour and gender in non-democratic regimes from a range of methodological perspectives, including ethnography, survey methods, comparative historical inquiry and network analysis. She is the author of *The Politics of Bureaucratic Corruption in Post-Transitional Eastern Europe* (2017).

Introduction
Justice, Crime and Citizenship in Eurasia: A Socio-legal Perspective

ERICA MARAT & LAUREN A. MCCARTHY

WHAT ROLE DOES LAW PLAY IN POST-COMMUNIST SOCIETIES? The common perception is that the police are predatory (Gerber & Mendelson 2008; Zernova 2012), state officials are corrupt (Holmes 2012; Reisinger *et al.* 2017) and the population is a passive observer of law-making by the elites (Way & Levitsky 2006; Fortin-Rittberger 2014). The existing literature in area studies offers a simplistic picture of law—it is either obeyed or evaded by state and society. The few true socio-legal studies of the region focus mainly on Russia (McCarthy 2015; Hendley 2017) and use a state-centric perspective (Taylor 2011). In contrast, the socio-legal field has made considerable contributions through investigating the limits of the law in both democratic and non-democratic countries of the former communist bloc, the role of bureaucrats in shaping the law, citizens' ability to use the law to fight injustice, and the impact of law, legal processes and law-breaking by citizens on patterns of political and economic governance. These studies have appeared mostly in disciplinary journals with limited area studies audiences (Slade 2012; Zaloznaya 2012, 2015; Light 2014; Buckley *et al.* 2016; Marat 2016, 2019).

This Special Issue continues to bridge the gap between theoretically rich work on law-in-action and the empirical reality of the post-communist bloc. Along with recent journal volumes edited by Zaloznaya (2020) and Solomon and Gadowska (2018), the contributions in this issue cover a broad range of empirical topics, ranging from research on policing to the legal profession, public attitudes towards law, regime support and oppositional mobilisation, crime policy, and property rights, among others. The issue examines the law as a social institution, shedding light on how it is negotiated and shaped in everyday interactions between state and society, organisations and individuals, and between law enforcement and other government entities. The studies shift away from the common perception that, in Eurasia, the law exists only as a tool for the state to enforce order and suppress dissent. Instead, they show through empirical analyses that citizens evade, use, reinterpret and shape the law even in authoritarian contexts—sometimes containing state violence and challenging the regime, and, other times, reinforcing state capture from below.

In curating the 11 essays featured in this Special Issue, we hope to show the value of incorporating socio-legal perspectives into studies of protests, state coercion, civil society and electoral politics, among other themes. The essays cover eight countries, with a geographic reach of all of Eurasia—from the Czech Republic to China. We have also made a special effort to include contributions from regional scholars, whose rich insights are often missing from these discussions. In this Introduction, we highlight several important themes: the importance of methodological diversity in investigating socio-legal phenomena in the region; the varied impacts of institutional legacies; the ongoing dualism of the law for political/non-political cases and for elites/ordinary citizens; the creative methods people in authoritarian settings use to legally mobilise; and the limits of using the law to create change, particularly in authoritarian regimes.

Diversity in methodological approaches

The authors in our Special Issue draw on interdisciplinary and methodologically diverse perspectives ranging from cross-national surveys to media analyses and ethnographic studies. In two cross-national surveys, Lauren McCarthy, Scott Gehlbach, Timothy Frye and Noah Buckley, and William Reisinger, Vicki Hesli Claypool and Marina Zaloznaya showcase the advantages that can be gained by combining large-*n* statistical analysis with nuanced questions aimed at probing the complexities of attitudes towards the law. Through survey experiments, McCarthy and her colleagues find that citizens in Russia and Georgia are willing to cooperate with the state in reporting crimes depending on the nature of the crime and their ability to remain anonymous. Likewise, by analysing national surveys in Georgia, Russia and Ukraine, Reisinger and his co-authors show that there are important differences in citizens' respect for the law, measured as willingness to participate in corruption, based on their attitudes toward and experiences of the country's political and legal institutions.

This Special Issue also contains exciting qualitative and ethnographic studies of law as a social institution. Eliza Isabaeva's close examination of the ways that informal settlers outside of Bishkek talk about and strategise to legalise their status, demonstrates their simultaneous belief in the power of law—using legal language and creating informal legal institutions for self-governance—while at the same time holding deeply conflicting beliefs about the law's neutrality and ability to solve their problems. Using two case studies, Yiyi Lu exposes creative strategies used by ordinary citizens who 'communicate, negotiate, cooperate or collide in every request for government information'. She demonstrates that, despite the limitations of the law, citizens are still able to use it to hold the government accountable.

Particularly in the more authoritarian contexts, where interviews may be harder to conduct, many of the essays included here demonstrate the value of examining less-traditional sources like government policy statements, case law and statutes to trace the historical development of legal institutions and outcomes that we see today. Katarina Šipulová and Hubert Smekal analyse legislation and case law, while conducting a series of interviews, to show the Czech Constitutional Court's critical role in mediating the demands of international human rights institutions like the European Court of Human Rights and the domestic demands for post-communist transitional justice. Aryna Dzmitryieva's essay on judicial selection in Russia demonstrates how the creation of new quantitative data from judicial biographies, alongside government documents and interviews, can teach us about the inner workings of the justice system in Russia. Margaret Hanson and Michael Thompson-Brusstar use comparative historical analysis to conduct a controlled comparison of the formation of procuracies in the Soviet Union and China.

Alongside documentary evidence, we also see the exciting possibilities that social media has given us to examine the happenings in authoritarian regimes. Gavin Slade, Alexei Trochev and Malika Talgatova compare government reports with public surveys and analysis of social media apps to measure the effectiveness of Kazakhstan's efforts to reform policing. Suzanne Scoggins also examines both government documents and social media to reveal how China's police have undertaken an active public relations campaign to gain support and empathy from the public. Like Slade and his colleagues, she notes how police in autocratic countries cannot simply achieve their goals through coercion alone but need to convince the public of the legitimacy and usefulness of their innovations. Gilles Favarel-Garrigues analyses YouTube videos that Russian vigilante groups have posted to explain the ways that these groups attempt to legitimise their activities and attract commercial sponsors.

Institutional legacies

The essays also help us to recognise the variety of legal pathways that the countries under study have taken in the post-communist period. While in some Eurasian countries the legacy of the communist past is undeniable, in others, their post-communist trajectories have had a greater impact on the law, legal systems and legal attitudes. The development of legal institutions is an important theme in many of the essays in this issue. Hanson and Thompson-Brusstar's historical analysis of the institutionalisation of the procuracy in Russia and China reveals the difference in outcomes between two similar institutional contexts, demonstrating how bottom-up pressures from workers in China weakened the procuracy, whereas in the Soviet Union, the procuracy was able to outcompete its popular rivals and emerge as a powerful agency. Dzmitryieva's examination of judicial selection in Russia also demonstrates that, despite the post-Soviet Russian state's attempts to create an independent judiciary, legacies of cronyism and patronage relations still prevail over professional experience when Russian judges are selected.

Conversely, Reisinger and his co-authors argue that post-Soviet developments have had a more important impact on citizen legal attitudes and willingness to engage in corrupt behaviour than their common legacies. Erica Marat and Deborah Sutton show that despite the common heritage of a surveillance state, the differences in economic development in post-Soviet Eurasia have meant that wealthier cities can afford a greater variety of electronic surveillance technologies. Likewise, Šipulová and Smekal demonstrate the ways that the prospects of joining the EU and other Western human rights institutions have shaped the Czech Republic's post-communist transitional justice policy, and continue to do so today.

Dualism of law

One of the most important insights from socio-legal research has been showing the ways that law works differently for differently situated people. In the Eurasian region, the focus is often on political or non-political cases and legal outcomes and their corrosive effects on the legitimacy of the legal system (Ledeneva 2008). Two of our essays demonstrate this phenomenon. Reisinger and his colleagues show that reminding people that 'the authorities' evade the law, not an infrequent occurrence in the region, made people express more willingness to do so themselves. This was consistently the case in all three countries they studied—Georgia, Ukraine and Russia. Likewise, Dzmitryieva demonstrates that people who are already connected with the court and government apparatus are more likely to be considered for judicial positions than lawyers who have worked in other sectors, limiting the perspectives of judges throughout Russia and undermining faith in the system. Two other essays focus on another area of unequal outcomes—economic marginalisation and privilege. By researching new settlements in the outskirts of Bishkek, Isabaeva shows how the law can be simultaneously delegitimising and offer the promise of future legal status. Residents of the settlement strive to gain a legal status that would afford them equal rights to the city. They engage with the local bureaucrats they know are corrupt and elected city officials who only pay attention to their needs during elections. At the same time, the rise of an urban middle class in Ukraine and Kazakhstan shows that requests for the expansion of control of public spaces tend to come from more affluent groups at the expense of more marginalised ones. Marat and Sutton's essay demonstrates how smart city technologies installed to assist law enforcement agencies in large cities tend to over-police marginalised groups. Marat and Sutton, as well as Isabaeva, also show that, even within the limits of one city, the law offers different opportunities and restrictions for individuals, often depending on their legal status and economic wealth.

Legal mobilisation

The predominant narrative is that legal mobilisation in authoritarian regimes is limited because of constraints imposed on civil society by the state and by the politicisation of law by incumbent political regimes. But even in most autocratic systems, like China and Kazakhstan, the law can serve as a powerful tool in the hands of activists seeking to establish legal precedents in courts or by regular citizens trying to protect their rights to property or to exercise political freedoms. As Lu demonstrates while observing the case of China, open government laws allow citizens to request information from the government. However, when trying to claim these rights, citizens encounter ineffective or intransigent bureaucracies which fail to actually provide the information. Instead, they turn to creative solutions like filing repeated requests, holding online campaigns in support of their appeals and challenging government decisions in courts. Isabaeva investigates the variety of ways whereby Kyrgyz informal settlers have mobilised to convince the city of Bishkek that they deserve incorporation and residence permits.

However, legal mobilisation is not always so benevolent. It can just as easily be used to enforce an illiberal legal and political regime, as Favarel-Garrigues shows in his essay on the rise of vigilante groups in Russia. These groups independently, and often with the support of the state, mobilise to enforce existing law through shaming and physical violence. They justify their 'raids' as contributing to a purer, more moral and healthier Russian society, while at the same time targeting marginalised groups like migrants or gay men. They do so to profit from the online content filmed during their raids, while also often acting to contribute to policing. But instead of demonstrating the weakness of the state in enforcing the laws it creates, these groups actually strengthen the reach of the state.

Limitations on the use of law

While the law offers many possibilities for mobilisation from below, states also use the law to create societal and behavioural change, particularly in sophisticated authoritarian regimes. Many of the essays in this Special Issue offer new insights on how the law is used in authoritarian regimes and the limitations of using the law to create change. In their exploration of the oft-overlooked procuracy and its power of general supervision, Hanson and Thompson-Brusstar highlight the importance of administrative institutions for solidifying authoritarian power. Equally important, however, is the design of those institutions and their comparison of China and the USSR show how even the smallest difference—in the Soviet Union, the procuracy was subordinated only to national authorities while in China it was subordinated to national and local authorities—can impact the institution's efficacy.

As authoritarian regimes become more stable, they also feel pressure to modernise and become more responsive to citizen demands, particularly in the area of public order and security. As several of the essays show, however, striking a balance between regime continuance and public satisfaction can be tricky. Marat and Sutton's essay shows how regimes have responded to citizen demands for increased safety by introducing 'smart' surveillance technology for order maintenance, yet there are significant concerns over where those data are stored and how they are used, since China and Russia are the primary purveyors of these technological innovations. Scoggins demonstrates that, even in powerful regimes like China's, the government still feels it needs to use propaganda campaigns like reality shows, social media engagement and cartoons to reinforce the police's legitimacy even while suppressing the population through force and coercion.

Gavin Slade and his colleagues, in turn, unveil the difficult balance that authoritarian countries must strike in balancing police loyalty against public demand for better, less corrupt policing. Their exploration of Kazakhstan's attempt to implement zero tolerance policing demonstrates that, at best, these modernisation attempts lead to performative changes rather than real ones, and very little change in the public's behaviour in reporting disorderly and criminal behaviour. Similarly, the survey experiments operationalised by McCarthy and her co-authors test various policy changes that the state could make to encourage the public's cooperation in reporting crimes that they had experienced or witnessed—easing the burden of reporting, appealing to social norms, anonymous reporting and providing financial rewards—finding that in Russia and Georgia, at least, only the possibility of anonymous reporting had any effect on stated public willingness to report. Together these essays show the uphill battle that authoritarian and non-authoritarian regimes face in trying to make changes in the areas of security and public order. On the other hand, as Favarel-Garrigues suggests, a lack of reform can create the conditions for vigilante groups to arise to enforce laws themselves.

Conclusion

We hope this Special Issue will encourage more research on law as a fluid social institution in Eurasia. The themes in the field are limitless. Future studies can continue comparing the capabilities of autocratic and democratic systems to use the law to achieve social and political results across diverse populations. How does the law limit or expand autocratic countries' efforts to control populations? Why are laws that limit civil liberties supported by the public in democracies? What broad political and social changes prompt governments to expand citizens' rights? In 2020, widespread post-electoral protests in Belarus indicated that the public can mobilise against a long-term autocrat with a robust coercive apparatus. The public defied government orders and punitive action banning political protest, perhaps expanding its rights to gather. How will this be reflected in the law, whether President Alyaksandr Lukashenka's regime succeeds or fails? On the contrary, why does seemingly free political competition in countries like Kyrgyzstan and Armenia still lead to laws that limit civic participation and freedom of the press?

On a local level, many social groups experience the unequal effects of the law. Migrants, ethnic, racial and sexual minorities, and economically disenfranchised groups may inadvertently be more marginalised by new policing methods or regulations on social and political behaviour. Some individuals and groups may be resilient even when faced with unfair circumstances. Both human vulnerability and resilience against the law are fascinating research topics from a socio-legal perspective. Such research can further contribute to our understanding of how laws originate and what their consequences are, whether they are products of the imagination of political elites or rooted in bottom-up legal mobilisation. Ultimately, a socio-legal lens can be adapted by any discipline focusing on the interaction of state and society and we encourage future scholars to work more in this area.

References

Buckley, N., Frye, T., Gehlbach, S. & McCarthy, L. (2016) 'Cooperating with the State: Evidence from a Survey Experiment on Policing in Moscow', *Journal of Experimental Political Science*, 3, 2.

Favarel-Garrigues, G. (2015) 'A Power Horizontal. The Public–Private Enforcement of Judicial Decisions in Russia', *Europe-Asia Studies*, 67, 4.

Fortin-Rittberger, J. (2014) 'Exploring the Relationship Between Infrastructural and Coercive State Capacity', *Democratization*, 21, 7.

Gerber, T. & Mendelson, S. (2008) 'Public Experiences of Police Violence and Corruption in Contemporary Russia: a Case of Predatory Policing?', *Law & Society Review*, 42, 1.

Hein, M. (2015) 'The Fight Against Government Corruption in Romania: Irreversible Results or Sisyphean Challenge?', *Europe-Asia Studies*, 67, 5.

Hendley, K. (2017) *Everyday Law in Russia* (Ithaca, NY, Cornell University Press).

Hensell, S. (2012) 'The Patrimonial Logic of the Police in Eastern Europe', *Europe-Asia Studies*, 64, 5.

Holmes, L. (2012) 'Corruption in Post-Soviet Russia', *Global Change, Peace & Security*, 24, 2.

Ledeneva, A. (2008) 'Telephone Justice in Russia', *Post-Soviet Affairs*, 24, 4.
Light, M. (2014) 'Police Reforms in the Republic of Georgia: The Convergence of Domestic and Foreign Policy in an Anti-Corruption Drive', *Policing and Society*, 24, 3.
Marat, E. (2016) 'Reforming Police in Post-Communist Countries: International Efforts, Domestic Heroes', *Comparative Politics*, 48, 3.
Marat, E. (2019) 'Mimicking "Broken Windows" Policing in Post-Soviet Cities: Expanding Social Control in Uncertain Times', *Policing and Society*, 29, 9.
McCarthy, L. (2015) *Trafficking Justice: How Russian Police Enforce New Laws, from Crime to Courtroom* (Ithaca, NY, Cornell University Press).
Muravyeva, M. (2017) 'Conservative Jurisprudence and the Russian State', *Europe-Asia Studies*, 69, 8.
Reisinger, W. M., Zaloznaya, M. & Claypool, V. L. H. (2017) 'Does Everyday Corruption Affect how Russians View their Political Leadership?', *Post-Soviet Affairs*, 33, 4.
Slade, G. (2012) 'No Country for Made Men: The Decline of the Mafia in Post-Soviet Georgia', *Law & Society Review*, 46, 3.
Solomon Jr, P. H. & Gadowska, K. (2018) 'Legal Change in Post-communist States: Contradictions and Explanations. Introduction', *Communist and Post-Communist Studies*, 51, 3.
Taylor, B. D. (2011) *State Building in Putin's Russia: Policing and Coercion After Communism* (Cambridge, Cambridge University Press).
Way, L. & Levitsky, S. (2006) 'The Dynamics of Autocratic Coercion After the Cold War', *Communist and Post-Communist Studies*, 39, 3.
Zaloznaya, M. (2012) 'Organizational Cultures as Agents of Differential Association: Explaining the Variation in Bribery Practices in Ukrainian Universities', *Crime, Law and Social Change*, 58, 3.
Zaloznaya, M. (2015) 'Does Authoritarianism Breed Corruption? Reconsidering the Relationship Between Authoritarian Governance and Corrupt Exchanges in Bureaucracies', *Law & Social Inquiry*, 40, 2.
Zaloznaya, M. (2020) 'Former Soviet Union: An Introduction to the Special Issue', *Demokratizatsiya: The Journal of Post-Soviet Democratization*, 28, 1.
Zernova, M. (2012) 'Coping with the Failure of the Police in Post-Soviet Russia: Findings from One Empirical Study', *Police Practice and Research,* 13, 6.

Who Reports Crime? Citizen Engagement with the Police in Russia and Georgia

LAUREN A. MCCARTHY, SCOTT GEHLBACH,
TIMOTHY FRYE & NOAH BUCKLEY

Abstract

What factors affect citizens' engagement with the state? We explore this question through a study of victims' and bystanders' willingness to report crimes to the police, using data from survey experiments conducted in Russia and Georgia. We find that citizens' willingness to report in both countries is strongly influenced by the nature of the crime, but not generally by instruments that the state might use to encourage greater reporting. Our results recommend scepticism about the ability of governments to easily engineer citizens' engagement with the state.

GOVERNMENTS OFTEN DEPEND ON CITIZEN ENGAGEMENT with the state to perform core functions, including revenue extraction, national defence, and the preservation of social order (Weber 1978; North 1990; Tilly 2005). Rather than bearing the expense of universally assessing and enforcing tax obligations, states assume that many citizens will report their income honestly (Levi 1988). To avoid the costs of establishing and administering conscription, governments often operate volunteer armies (Mulligan & Shleifer 2005). Instead of monitoring everyone at all times, states rely on citizens to obey the law and maintain social order even when the possibility of punishment by the state is remote (McCubbins & Schwartz 1984; Tyler 1990; Ellickson 1991).

Prior research suggests that states that rely on cooperation to tax, conscript, and monitor their citizens have significant advantages over those that do not (North 1981; Levi 1988; Root 1994; Mulligan & Shleifer 2005; Gehlbach 2008; Besley & Persson 2011). There is less consensus, however, on the particular determinants of such cooperation. When are citizens most likely to engage with the state? To what extent does cooperation depend on incentives provided by state authorities and on the broader institutional environment?

At the time the research was conducted, Scott Gehlbach was at the University of Wisconsin-Madison and an affiliate of the International Centre for the Study of Institutions and Development at the Higher School of Economics in Moscow; Noah Buckley was at Columbia University. We gratefully acknowledge financial support for this project from the Basic Research Programme of the National Research University—Higher School of Economics. Additional materials are available in the online Appendix.

We address these questions through a study of a central form of engagement: the willingness of citizens to report crimes to the police. A citizen's decision to inform the police of crimes they have witnessed or experienced is a critical juncture in the criminal justice process. As Tyler observes, 'crime and problems of community disorder are difficult to solve without the active involvement of community residents' (Tyler 2012, p. 77). Absent such participation, states are often forced into more resource-intensive strategies of proactive enforcement and surveillance. Yet cross-country studies of crime victimisation suggest a widespread failure of citizens to cooperate with the police in this way. As many as half of all crimes in industrialised countries go unreported (Bouten *et al.* 2002; Torrente *et al.* 2017), with higher rates in many developing and transition countries (Estienne & Morabito 2016). The stakes involved in solving this problem are high: beyond the impact on everyday welfare, a failure to provide basic law and order can depress economic activity and raise questions about the quality of governance, particularly in low- and middle-income countries (Brinks 2007; North *et al.* 2009). Other consequences of non-reporting include the misallocation of police resources due to inaccurate crime information and the inability of crime victims to access needed services and protect themselves from future victimisation (Ranapurwala *et al.* 2016).

We use a series of survey experiments to identify determinants of citizens' propensity to report crimes to the police. In line with the existing literature, we examine factors having to do with the crime itself (its severity and the stakes involved); we also focus on variables infrequently explored but important for many developing and transition countries. We ask, for example, whether citizens are more or less likely to report crimes to the police when the perpetrator is in fact a police officer—a situation that involves both cooperating with the state and holding the state accountable for its actions. Additionally, we explore the impact of various institutional factors: the ease and anonymity of reporting, appeals to social norms, and the provision of financial incentives. These factors are more under the control of the state than the characteristics of the crime, the victim, and the bystander, which are the focus of much prior work.

Our survey experiments are situated in two post-Soviet states, Russia and Georgia, that share a number of institutional features. In both countries, any decision to cooperate with the state is freighted with meaning, given the Soviet legacy of using citizens as informants. This is especially true of the behaviour that we study: providing information to law enforcement, which in the recent past would have been associated at least as much with regime survival as public order. More generally, Russia and Georgia share a common history of communist rule and the subsequent transition from state socialism during the 1990s.

At the same time, there are important differences between Russia and Georgia, including in their histories of police reform and cultures of reporting. In Russia, the public remains wary of a police force that displays predatory behaviour towards the citizens it is supposed to protect, whereas in Georgia, there is widespread public approval of a police force that underwent deep reforms in the mid-2000s. At the same time, various observational studies suggest that Georgians are generally less likely to report crimes to the police than are citizens of other postcommunist countries, including Russia. Our goal is not necessarily to explain these differences in levels of cooperation with the police, which may have deep roots beyond the focus of our study. We are, however, attentive to the possibility that institutional and cultural variation may be reflected in differences in the effects of treatments manipulated in our survey experiments.

In fact, and somewhat against our expectations, we find few systematic cross-country differences in treatment effects. In both countries, a key determinant of citizen engagement with the police is the severity of the crime. In contrast, instruments that are more under the direct control of the state generally have a negligible impact on stated willingness to report crimes to the police—this notwithstanding a successful history of police reform in one of the two countries we examine. The sole exception to this general conclusion is that citizens in both Russia and Georgia appear far more likely to report crimes when guaranteed anonymity, a mechanism that in principle is available to state authorities. As we discuss below, this finding contrasts sharply with results from observational data from countries in other political environments, reinforcing the value of our research design and setting.

Our essay makes two broad contributions to the existing literature. First, a rich and vast body of work, which we summarise below, has attempted to identify demographic and contextual covariates of the decision to report a crime. Most of these studies are based on observational data, raising the possibility that unobserved factors drive observed correlations. Our study, in contrast, randomly assigns contextual variables across respondents to measure their influence on reporting behaviour. Relative to other experimental methods, our approach comes with obvious trade-offs. On the one hand, we cannot directly test the assumption that respondents would behave in practice as they state that they would in response to survey questions. On the other hand, we are able to explore contextual variables (such as the perpetrator and severity of a crime) that could not be easily or ethically manipulated in a field experiment.[1]

Second, existing studies of crime reporting have been mostly conducted in democratic and wealthy countries with relatively good legal and law-enforcement institutions.[2] Our research setting of Russia and Georgia allows us to extend this work to more weakly institutionalised environments. In so doing, we broaden the focus of existing work to include variables such as whether the crime is committed by a police officer, which may be more relevant in countries with a history of weak rule of law.

The continuing relevance of this study is underlined by slow but ongoing processes of reform in the post-Soviet region. As countries throughout the region propose and implement various police reform programmes (Marat 2018; Trochev & Slade 2019), they each must confront the quandary of how to encourage cooperation from the public in reporting and investigating crime. Our findings suggest that, while the state may try to

[1]A small experimental literature on crime reporting generally focuses on instruments different from those we explore. See Lasley and Palombo (1995), Goudriaan and Nieuwbeerta (2007), Aviram and Persinger (2012), Kivivuori *et al.* (2012), Tolsma *et al.* (2012), and Buckley *et al.* (2016).

[2]For exceptions, see Birkbeck *et al.* (1993), who compare the United States and Venezuela; Bennett and Wiegand (1994) on Belize; Zhang *et al.* (2007) on China; Tankebe (2009) on Ghana; Sheu and Chiu (2012) on Taiwan; Kochel *et al.* (2013) on Trinidad and Tobago; Sidebottom (2015) on Malawi; Buckley *et al.* (2016) on Russia; Boateng (2018) on Ghana; and Gingerich and Oliveros (2018) on Costa Rica. Also see Estienne and Morabito (2016), who use ICVS data to look at determinants of reporting robbery and assault in 23 developing and transition countries.

introduce various reforms that could encourage reporting, thereby boosting police efficacy, cooperation from the public is not so easily gained.

The essay proceeds as follows. In the next section, we summarise the existing literature, identifying a number of factors that may influence citizens' willingness to report crimes to the police. Following this, we describe our data. We then discuss the design of our four survey experiments and our results. In the final section, we offer concluding thoughts.

Motivations for engaging with the police

When might a crime victim or a witness to a crime decide to contact the police? In the tradition of economic analyses of crime and punishment (Becker & Landes 1974), scholars have explored numerous factors that might influence reporting. Here we focus on two broad categories of factors that we can manipulate using survey experiments. The first group of variables examines features of the crime, such as its severity and the identity of the perpetrator, whereas the second focuses on institutional factors, including the presence of financial incentives, the ease of reporting, the possibility of anonymous reporting, and the presence of social norms.[3]

Features of the crime

The severity of the crime may be a prime motivator for reporting.[4] In fact, studies that use observational data from international crime-victim surveys typically find that the most common reason given for not reporting is that the crime is not serious enough to do so (Skogan 1984; Carcach 1997; Bureau of Justice Statistics 2003; Goudriaan *et al.* 2004; van Kesteren & van Dijk 2010). That said, perceptions of severity can be quite individual. In the case of theft of a family heirloom, for example, there may be a strong emotional attachment to the item, which can increase the perceived severity of the crime beyond that implied by the item's material value (Bowles *et al.* 2009). Severity can also

[3]There is a vast literature on determinants of crime reporting; for overviews, see Skogan (1984), Tarling and Morris (2010), and Xie and Baumer (2019). Among the many considerations that we do not examine are victim or witness characteristics; community features, such as the location of the crime or local crime rates; the belief that information about the crime is useful; citizens' past experiences with crime, crime reporting, or the police (Conaway & Lohr 1994; Goudriaan *et al.* 2004); the psychological costs of reporting (for example, self-blame and social stigma in cases of sexual violence); and the possibility of recovering property or compensation from an insurance company (not a common scenario in our research setting). We also do not engage with the impact of victim/witness perceptions of police legitimacy, procedural justice, trust in the police (Tyler 1990; Sunshine & Tyler 2003), or corruption (Soares 2004). Instead, the experimental design we employ in this essay allows us to focus on concrete crime-related and institutional factors driving engagement with the police rather than demographic and attitudinal determinants of crime reporting, which are more often the focus in existing observational literature.

[4]The number of offenders as well as relations between the victim and the perpetrator may shape perceptions of severity (Block 1974; Lynch & Danner 1993). In particular, if offenders are friends, neighbours, or family members, the victim may attempt to solve the problem on her own rather than involving the police (Felson *et al.* 1999). Looking beyond immediate relations, crime victims may be afraid of retaliation by the perpetrator or anticipate being intimidated into not participating in the criminal justice process.

be measured in terms of violence, and indeed, various studies find that respondents are more likely to report violent crimes (Skogan 1984).

Features specific to the perpetrator of the crime may also shape incentives to report. One such characteristic, largely ignored in the literature (perhaps because most studies of crime reporting take place in well-institutionalised settings), is whether the perpetrator is himself an officer of the state. In countries with weak institutions, police officers often use their authority to break the law as well as to enforce it (Ivkovic 2005; Brinks 2007; Gerber & Mendelson 2008). Citizens of such countries who report crimes committed by the police to the police may bear a direct cost of reprisal.[5] Anticipating this threat, victims or witnesses may be reluctant to report, thus failing both to cooperate with the state and to hold the state accountable for its actions. This is particularly true for those who may have directly witnessed police violence (Gingerich & Oliveros 2018). Further, fear of retaliation may also be greater in countries where the police generate additional income by selling information about criminal investigations (Taylor 2011). Alternatively, and not mutually exclusively, potential reporters may expect that the police will fail to act on reports of crimes committed by one of their own, or otherwise abuse their powers in the investigation process for personal gain (Semukhina 2016).

Institutional context

While features of the crime and perpetrator may be important, reporting rates may also depend on the nature of formal institutions. Among these is the institution of the police, as previously discussed in the context of police officers who commit crimes. Generalising from this particular scenario, citizens who believe that the police are ineffective, incompetent, or corrupt may not bother reporting a crime. In cross-national surveys, Skogan (1984) and Estienne and Morabito (2016) find that such perceptions are less important predictors of reporting than the seriousness of the crime, though others conclude that perceptions of police effectiveness matter more for reporting some crimes than for others (Goudriaan *et al.* 2004; Boateng 2018) or when perceptions of effectiveness are particularly high or low (Torrente *et al.* 2017). Citizens may also be more motivated to report if the police are viewed as legitimate, as when police procedure is judged to be fair (Sunshine & Tyler 2003).

Other features of the institutional environment may also play a role. In principle, monetary rewards may encourage victims and bystanders to report crimes.[6] On the other hand, such rewards may have the perverse effect of externalising intrinsic motivations, making it less likely that citizens will report crimes to the police (Bickman & Helwig 1979).[7] Payment for information may also make citizens feel like police informants rather than good citizens. Research that has examined reward mechanisms in more strongly

[5]Although fear of retaliation is rarely mentioned in crime-victim surveys as a reason for not reporting, we do not know how or if that relates to bystanders' decisions (van Kesteren & van Dijk 2010).

[6]See, for example, the recommendations of the National Crime Prevention Council, available at: https://www.ncpc.org/resources/home-neighborhood-safety/strategies/strategy-crime-tip-rewards/, accessed 26 October 2020.

[7]This view is similar to that of Titmuss (1970), who argues that paying people to donate blood would reduce the supply of blood.

institutionalised settings has found mixed results, reinforcing the value of examining this policy mechanism (Challinger 2004).

Because the decision to cooperate is not costless, one might expect reporting to be less likely when the costs of doing so are high. Typically, the largest such cost is the opportunity cost of time spent reporting a crime to the police. This includes the time needed to go to the police station or phone the police to file a report, which in turn depends on the time spent by the police officer taking the report.[8] If the case does go forward, additional time may be spent during the investigation process and at trial. Beyond the opportunity cost of time spent, there is also the emotional cost that may come with a long and drawn-out process or, for the victim, the process of reliving the crime each time it is described. In multiple other contexts, time and emotional costs are cited as primary reasons for not pursuing a claim in civil court (Felstiner *et al.* 1980–1981; Engel 2005; Hendley 2010), and it seems plausible that these factors would also play a role in criminal cases.

Some of the costs described here may be lower if reporting can be done anonymously. Programmes that use anonymity to encourage crime reporting are employed widely, but there is still much to learn about their effectiveness. Although the existing literature suggests that anonymous reporting plays little role in encouraging crime reporting (Bickman & Helwig 1979; Tolsma *et al.* 2012), the observational nature of such studies and their focus on developed democracies leave open the possibility of an effect with our research design and setting.[9]

Finally, informal institutions such as social norms may influence reporting rates. A crime victim or witness may feel a sense of civic duty that compels them to cooperate; they may report the crime because they hope that others would do the same in their position or because they do not want the same thing to happen to others. Indeed, respondents in (observational) studies of crime-victim reporting in wealthy democratic countries often attribute their behaviour to a feeling of civic duty, broadly conceived (Smith & Maness 1976; Goudriaan *et al.* 2004; Tarling & Morris 2010).

Of course, not all social norms encourage reporting. In many cultures, there is a stigma that accompanies cooperation with the police, including reporting crimes (Ruback *et al.* 1999). This may be particularly true in the post-Soviet context, where there is a long history of the state's using citizens as informants (Kelly 2005).[10] That said, even residents of post-authoritarian states may share a desire for basic law and order, which is difficult to achieve without some cooperation with the police.[11] Our focus on

[8]In a survey-experimental design set in the Netherlands, Tolsma *et al.* (2012) find that changing the accessibility of the police and the reporting method does not make much difference in stated willingness to report, whereas reducing the time spent reporting does. Lasley and Palombo (1995), in turn, find in a lab experiment that being able to use the internet rather than the telephone encourages more reporting.

[9]See Gingerich and Oliveros (2018) who advocate for this policy change in Costa Rica.

[10]That said, informers sometimes served to hold state officials, including enterprise managers, accountable for their actions; see Lampert (1985).

[11]Using data from a survey of Moscow residents, McCarthy (2014) documents strong support for local patrol officers (*uchastkovyi*) who would be responsible for addressing crimes like those described in our vignettes.

non-political crimes may thus minimise the impact of Soviet legacies on the incentive to report.

Research setting

Our research settings are Russia and Georgia, two postcommunist countries that share a number of similarities yet have pursued markedly different policies of police reform. Russia and Georgia emerged from the socialist period with similar policing organisations and histories of institutional change. Police forces in both countries were seen as ineffective and corrupt, and they were generally distrusted in the early postcommunist years (Taylor 2006). Both countries experienced a period of institutional collapse following the breakup of the Communist Party and the Soviet Union, and both pursued the standard set of postcommunist reforms such as liberalisation and privatisation (Papava 2005).

At the same time, the two countries differ in obvious ways, such as their economic scale, industrial structure, and integration into the global economy. In addition, and notwithstanding the general tendency of state socialism to generate informal practices to solve everyday problems (Bunce 1999; Ledeneva 2006; Burakova 2011; Kakachia & O'Shea 2012; Light 2013a), Georgia had a larger second economy and an arguably stronger reliance on informal institutions during the Soviet period (Mars & Altman 1983).[12] These practices, as well as numerous other historical and cultural factors that are beyond our control, may affect general tendencies to cooperate with the police. We are much less interested in accounting for any differences in these baseline levels than in how subjects respond to the treatment conditions in each country.

More importantly for our study, Russia and Georgia also engaged in markedly different strategies of police reform in the decade prior to our survey, with potentially important consequences for citizens' willingness to engage with the police. After the Rose Revolution in 2003, President Mikheil Saakashvili of Georgia swiftly introduced wide-ranging and deep reforms of nearly the entire Georgian police system, with the goal of eradicating systemic corruption.

The police force was downsized and police officers were dismissed *en masse*, including almost all traffic police officers; according to Light, 'of the approximately 25,000 employees serving in the Ministry of Internal Affairs, some 16,000 were dismissed within two years of the Rose Revolution' (Light 2013a, p. 7). There was also significant structural reorganisation, with the police limited to tasks that focused on enforcing laws while their previous authority to issue passports and registration documents was moved to a newly created civilian agency. Finally, the reform significantly increased police salaries and instituted new training programmes and competitive entry requirements. The police now earn substantially more than the average wage in Georgia, and the status of the profession has increased (Kakachia & O'Shea 2012; Light 2013a).

[12] 'Already during Soviet times, the Georgian economy was notorious for its vast informal sector and its many networks of political patronage, greased by corruption and associated practices' (Kupatadze 2018, p. 5).

The results of Georgia's reform were impressive. Low-level bribery, which was previously commonplace, has virtually disappeared; links between the police and organised crime were largely eliminated; major crime has declined. For the average Georgian citizen at the time of our survey in 2013, the police had become a dependable, effective force that they trusted and could call on in times of need (Kakachia & O'Shea 2012; IRI 2013; Light 2013a). Residents also ranked the police highly for their readiness to help and their ability to fight crime (Bonvin 2006).[13]

Meanwhile, Russia's police reforms have been limited both in scope and in impact on real-world police operations and police–society interactions. The most recent reform effort in 2011 involved renaming the police, introducing new behaviour codes for personnel, reducing the size of the force by 22% through a recertification process, and raising the salaries of those who remained (Solomon 2014; Taylor 2014). In addition, the local police are now required to hold quarterly meetings with the public.

These reforms appear to have had little impact on citizen–police relations or the efficacy of the police in preventing and fighting crime. Police work remains a low-status job, and there has been little effort to professionalise the force, as in Georgia, through stricter training requirements or a more competitive entrance exam (Taylor 2014). Problems with corruption, abuse, and the commercialisation of police functions remain rampant; despite rhetoric to the contrary, there appears to be little political will to address these issues (Gilinsky 2011; Kosals & Dubova 2012; Taubina 2012; Solomon 2014). The mandatory quarterly meetings with the public, if they happen at all, are usually formal affairs (for example, an accounting of local crime statistics) that afford little opportunity for dialogue with citizens. Finally, the slimming-down process appears to have increased corruption, created personnel shortages, and driven out many good police officers.[14] Although trust in the police has increased somewhat in recent years, the police remain mostly unreformed in their everyday practices and patterns of behaviour (McCarthy 2015; Levada Centre 2017, 2018; Paneyakh *et al.* 2018).

These contrasting experiences with police reform are reflected in very different attitudes towards the police. In the surveys we describe below, conducted in 2012 and 2013, we asked respondents in Russia and Georgia to assess the degree to which they trust the police in their country on a five-point scale. The mean response in Russia was 2.9 ($SD = 1.0$), compared to 3.9 in Georgia ($SD = 1.0$). Other contemporaneous surveys conducted in these countries provide such telling figures as 86% favourability ratings for the police in Georgia (IRI 2013) and 34% satisfaction with and trust in local police in Russia (Levada Centre 2012).

Somewhat paradoxically, crime reporting has historically been lower in Georgia than in Russia, even after Saakashvili's reforms. Although the data are not fully comparable, various rounds of the International Crime Victim Surveys (ICVS) suggest that Georgians are among

[13]Recent research has revealed a more mixed record of the Georgian police reform programme, as concerns about high-level corruption, lack of civilian oversight, abuse of detainees, violent crackdowns on protests, and overzealous enforcement of drug laws have driven down trust in the police (Lehmbruch & Sanikidze 2014; Asatiani & Coalson 2015; Nasuti 2016; Fuller 2018; di Puppo 2019). According to a 2018 public opinion poll, favourable opinion of the police had fallen from a high of 90% in 2012 to 50% (IRI 2018).

[14]'Glava Fonda "Obshchestvennyi verdikt": Pereattestatsiya lishila politsiyu luchshikh sotrudnikov', 25 April 2012, available at: http://publicverdict.org/topics/lib_experts/10214.html, accessed 26 October 2020.

the least likely to report crimes among respondents in 12 democratic and postcommunist countries (van Dijk 2012, Table 5). Data from the 1992, 1996, 2010, and 2011 rounds of the ICVS suggest a reporting rate of roughly 40–48% for burglary in Georgia, compared to 61–63% in Russia in 1992 and 1996 (Zvekic 1996, Table 5; Van Dijk & Chanturia 2012). In a similar survey that we conducted in 2011 with Moscow residents, 60% of respondents who had experienced a crime stated that they had reported it to the police.[15] Again, however, our main goal is not to explain baseline levels of reporting between Russia and Georgia, but to explore differences in response to our experimental treatments.

Methodology

To understand the impact of institutional and crime-related factors on willingness to report crime to the police, we conducted surveys of the general population in both Russia and Georgia to explore the determinants of citizen engagement with the police. This empirical approach offers substantial strengths, even as we also acknowledge its limitations. Survey experiments such as those we conducted in Russia and Georgia allow us to manipulate the empirical context in ways that would be unethical in a field experiment and impractical otherwise. The method also allows us to precisely control the composition of our survey samples, the treatments being delivered, and the measurement of outcomes. Such conditions are difficult to satisfy, for example, in settings characterised by natural experiments, though the latter may offer the advantage of studying real-world outcomes. Our approach also stands in contrast to more qualitative work, with the typical trade-off between inference from a large sample and the rich ethnographic detail that can be obtained from more targeted inquiries. While we seek to obtain an accurate, comprehensive view of the forest, much work remains to be done on examining the trees.

Within Russia, we hired the Levada Centre, a leading polling firm based in Moscow, to conduct a nationally representative survey of 1,601 adult residents of Russia in late 2012. After having previously piloted three of the survey experiments that we describe below in a Moscow-only survey in late 2011, we added a series of questions to the firm's monthly nationally representative survey of the population, known as the Courier (*Kur'er*), which took place from 10–20 December.[16] The survey includes 128 sampling points drawn from 46 of Russia's 83 regions. The Courier uses a four-stage stratified sample with strata at the level of community, electoral district, household, and individual. Interviewers spoke with respondents face-to-face at their homes. Only one respondent per household was selected for participation in the survey, with quotas for gender-age and gender-education. The response rate of those who were contacted was 48%, for a final sample of 1,601 respondents. Twenty percent of those who took part in the survey were telephoned to

[15]The figures for all types of crime reporting in the ICVS for Russian and Georgia are much lower than those for more established democracies, see *International Crime Victim Survey*, available at: http://wp.unil.ch/icvs, accessed 29 October 2020. For further estimates from survey data of crime-reporting rates in Russia, see http://publicverdict.org/articles_images/11491_59458_index1113.pdf, accessed 26 October 2020.

[16]Although there are subtle differences in question wording, the results from this pilot survey are qualitatively similar to those that we report below (Buckley *et al.* 2016).

check the accuracy of their responses as reported by the interviewers. With this sample design, the margin of error in the survey is less than 3%.

We subsequently contracted with the All-Russia Centre for the Study of Public Opinion (VTsIOM) to put an identical survey in the field in Georgia in mid-2013.[17] The utmost effort was taken to ensure that the survey questionnaire, sampling methodology, and survey implementation process in Georgia matched those in Russia to the greatest degree possible. To verify the accuracy of the Georgian questionnaire, we translated the survey instrument from Russian into Georgian and then back into Russian. A nationally representative sample of 1,601 adults from 40 sampling points was interviewed between 2 and 19 June 2013. Of these sampling points, 20 were in urban centres and 20 were in rural areas. As Russian is still widely spoken in some Georgian regions, we offered our respondents the choice of having the survey administered in either Russian or Georgian. Survey implementation included standard monitoring and control procedures, including repeat control visits to 15% of households. Of the individuals contacted and requested to participate in the survey, 30% assented and were successfully interviewed.

To check for egregious administrative error, we conducted balance tests on the 11 covariates used in the regressions reported above. Figures A5 and A6 in the online Appendix report results for Russia and Georgia, respectively. In both countries, the number of significant results is approximately what we would expect by chance: 11 out of 132 *p*-values significant at 0.10 in the Russian sample, nine out of 132 in the Georgian sample. Relative to the Russian survey, there were unexpectedly high rates of item non-response for the potentially sensitive survey experiments in Georgia. To check that this was not the consequence of some failure in survey implementation, we worked with VTsIOM to verify that proper interview procedures were taken and that the data were recorded correctly. Our results are unchanged when controlling for demographic characteristics that may be correlated with non-response, as shown in Tables A1–A4 as well as when we replace missing values through multiple imputation.

Within each survey, we embedded four survey experiments that manipulated contextual and institutional variables that may influence reporting a crime to the police; the pre-translation wording of the experiments was identical in the two surveys (other than a currency difference, which we describe below). Randomised assignment of treatment in these survey experiments allows us to identify the impact of specific variables on the probability of reporting a crime to the police, independent of other variables discussed in the literature.

In each of the four experiments, we provided vignettes that placed citizens in hypothetical scenarios; for obvious reasons, it is usually impractical to directly test citizens' reactions to such events.[18] Three of the four experiments ask our respondents to put themselves in the shoes of a bystander witnessing a crime, the fourth asks respondents to put themselves in the shoes of a victim.

[17]Bidding procedures mandated by Russian law (the Georgian survey was bid in Russia, where our funding was located) prevented us from choosing the same survey firm for both countries.

[18]One study in the United States did so. Bickman and Helwig (1979) first surveyed subjects about the likelihood they would report shoplifting and then staged multiple instances of shoplifting at a supermarket to see if intent matched behaviour. It did: 78% of those who said they would report did so, whereas most of those who said they would not, did not.

Survey experiments and results

Experiment 1

In the first question, we vary the severity of the crime and the identity of the perpetrator, as follows:

Survey experiment 1
Treatments:

1. Suppose you saw a police officer taking a wallet and mobile phone from a drunk person lying near a bus stop.
2. Suppose you saw a police officer beating a defenceless person.
3. Suppose you saw someone taking a wallet and mobile phone from a drunk person lying near a bus stop.
4. Suppose you saw someone beating a defenceless person.

Would you report this to the police?
Responses: certainly not; probably not; maybe, maybe not; probably; certainly

We anticipate that most respondents, regardless of country, would view beating a defenceless person as a more severe crime than theft, potentially increasing the benefits from reporting it (for example, public safety is increased if a violent offender is taken off the street). With respect to the identity of the offender, the costs of cooperation may be higher if reporting on a police officer, as a police officer may have greater ability to retaliate. Negative perceptions of the police—that they protect their own, rather than protecting the public—also imply that there may be a higher perceived likelihood that the offence will go uninvestigated or unpunished, thereby lowering the willingness to report because it would be seen as a waste of time with little chance of a successful resolution.

Our results from the first survey experiment are strongly consistent with the first of these predictions. As shown in Table 1, which, for each country, averages across all possible responses (on a five-point scale) for each of the four treatment groups, citizens in both Russia and Georgia are significantly more likely to report a crime that involves beating a defenceless person. (In the online Appendix, we provide the full distribution of responses to this and the subsequent survey experiments for each of the various experimental groups.) In contrast, there is only limited evidence in support of the second prediction. Russian respondents who receive the 'beating' treatment are significantly less likely to say that they would report a crime perpetrated by a police officer than by a stranger, but there is no significant difference for those who receive the 'stealing' treatment, and no difference for either group among Georgian respondents.

Given differences in the comprehensiveness and effectiveness of police reform in Russia and Georgia we might expect to find differences across the two countries. What do the data say? Table 1 reveals two sizable cross-country differences: averaging across all four treatment groups, respondents in Georgia are less likely to report crimes to the police, and the severity of the crime (beating relative to petty theft) matters somewhat less in Georgia than in Russia. To formally test for the significance of these differences, we pool the Russia and Georgia samples and reproduce the 2×2 tables reported above in a regression framework. Figure 1 illustrates the resulting coefficient estimates. On average, the baseline response is a full half-point lower in Georgia than in Russia (2.84 compared to 3.37 on a five-point scale), and the difference in the magnitude of the 'beating' treatment between the two countries is significantly different from zero.

TABLE 1

DIFFERENCE-IN-MEANS RESULTS FROM RUSSIA AND GEORGIA: CRIME SEVERITY AND PERPETRATOR IDENTITY

	Russia			*Georgia*		
	Police officer	*Stranger*	*Difference in means*	*Police officer*	*Stranger*	*Difference in means*
Stealing	3.28 (1.18)	3.37 (1.14)	0.09 (0.09)	2.79 (1.51)	2.84 (1.42)	0.05 (0.12)
Beating	3.78 (1.10)	4.01 (0.98)	0.23*** (0.08)	3.10 (1.49)	3.09 (1.45)	−0.01 (0.12)
Difference in means	0.50*** (0.08)	0.64*** (0.08)	0.73*** (0.08)	0.32*** (0.12)	0.26*** (0.11)	0.30*** (0.12)

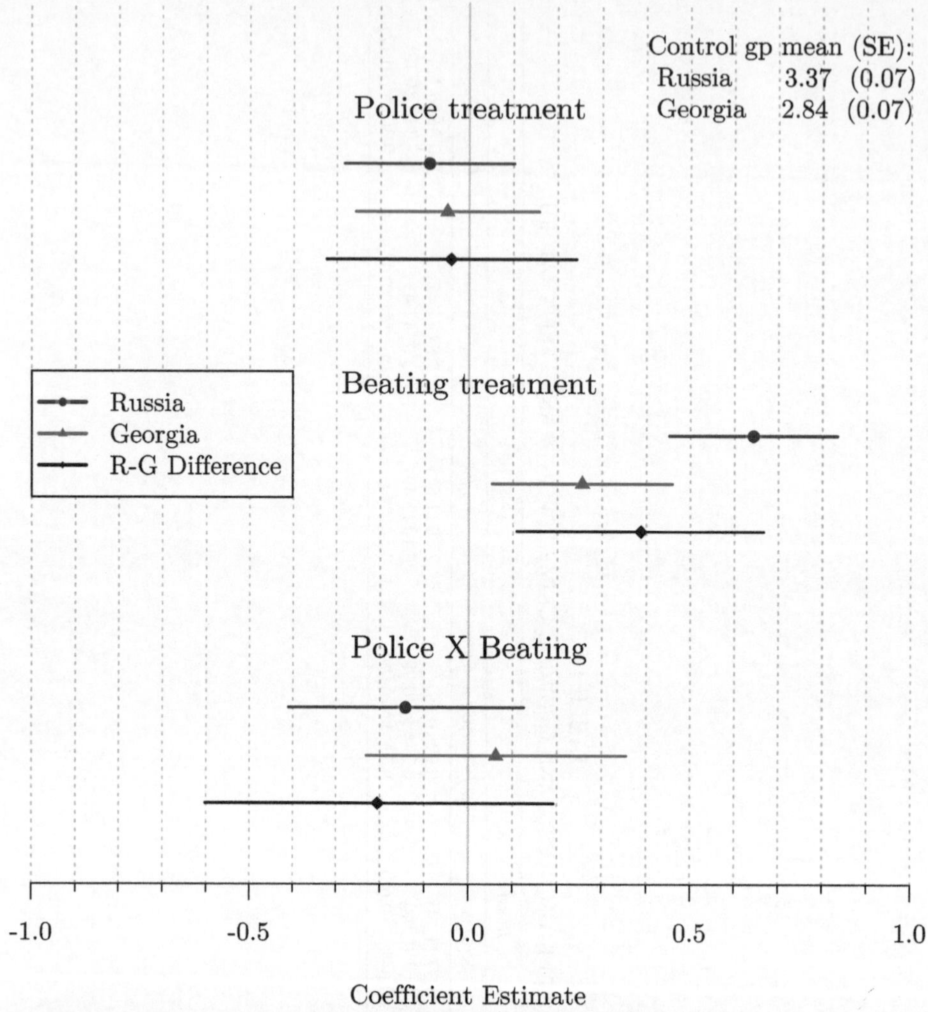

FIGURE 1. COEFFICIENT PLOTS OF SURVEY EXPERIMENT RESULTS: CRIME SEVERITY AND PERPETRATOR IDENTITY

As we show below, the difference in baseline responses between Russians and Georgians on their propensity to report generally holds across all of our four survey experiments. Further, as we demonstrate in the online Appendix, the estimated difference is largely unaffected by controlling for demographic characteristics, which are distributed somewhat differently across the two samples, or by accounting for differences across countries in the willingness of various subgroups to report.[19] Although surprising, given

[19]In principle, young respondents in Georgia but not in Russia might be disproportionately inclined to report crimes to the police, given that young Georgians but not young Russians have experienced good policing for most of their adult lives. In practice, as shown in Tables A1–A4 in the online Appendix, there is no significant interaction between age and country for any of our four survey experiments.

differences in police reform in the two countries, the greater willingness of Russians to report crimes is consistent with other survey evidence from the two countries, as discussed above, and may reflect underlying cultural characteristics not captured by our demographic controls. These results suggest that even where police reforms have been effective, as in Georgia, it may be difficult to quickly engineer high levels of engagement with the police. For the remainder of the essay, we focus on the effects of our various experiments in each country.

Experiment 2

In the second survey experiment, we vary the identity of the offender and the anonymity of reporting, as follows:

Survey experiment 2
Treatments:

1. If you knew about a crime committed by a police officer, and if it was not necessary to leave your personal information to report this crime …
2. If you knew about a crime committed by a police officer, and if it was necessary to leave your personal information to report this crime …
3. If you knew about a crime committed by a stranger, and if it was not necessary to leave your personal information to report this crime …
4. If you knew about a crime committed by a stranger, and if it was necessary to leave your personal information to report this crime …

… would you report it to the police?
Responses: certainly not; probably not; maybe, maybe not; probably; certainly

---

One oft-discussed way to promote crime reporting is to promise witnesses some degree of anonymity should they turn to the police. For respondents who fear reprisals or the social costs of reporting, anonymous reporting may give them sufficient confidence to come forward. Thus, we expect that citizens would be more willing to engage with the police if they were not required to provide personal information when reporting a crime, unless there was some sort of benefit to them (for example, a reward) for being identifiable. For reasons just discussed, we also anticipate that the costs of reporting would be greater when a crime is committed by a police officer rather than a stranger, though this may be attenuated when anonymous reporting is allowed. Anonymous reporting is not currently allowed under Russian law (and thus not possible to explore through a field experiment), which requires name and passport information to file an official crime report, though it is possible this is unknown to many respondents. In Georgia, anonymous reporting of crimes is allowed, though this is a recent change, so knowledge of the possibility may be limited (Light 2013b).

Our second survey experiment retains the police officer/stranger contrast but manipulates the anonymity of reporting rather than the nature of the crime. As Table 2 illustrates, in both Russia and Georgia, respondents who are told that it is not necessary to leave personal information to report a crime are far more likely to say that they would do so than those who are told that reporting is not anonymous. Looking across the full distribution of responses, the anonymity treatment produces an increase of 11.1 percentage points (in Russia) and 4.5 percentage points (in Georgia) in the percent of individuals who say that

TABLE 2

DIFFERENCE-IN-MEANS RESULTS FROM RUSSIA AND GEORGIA: ANONYMITY OF REPORTING AND PERPETRATOR IDENTITY

	Russia			*Georgia*		
	Police officer	*Stranger*	*Difference in means*	*Police officer*	*Stranger*	*Difference in means*
Anonymous	3.65 (1.20)	3.67 (1.16)	0.01 (0.08)	2.77 (1.49)	2.74 (1.39)	−0.04 (0.12)
Not anonymous	3.23 (1.30)	3.27 (1.19)	0.04 (0.10)	2.64 (1.39)	2.44 (1.36)	−0.20* (0.11)
Difference in means	−0.43*** (0.09)	−0.40*** (0.09)	−0.39*** (0.09)	−0.14 (0.11)	−0.30*** (0.11)	−0.33*** (0.12)

TABLE 3

DIFFERENCE-IN-MEANS RESULTS FROM RUSSIA AND GEORGIA: CIVIC DUTY AND MONETARY REWARD

	Russia			*Georgia*		
	No reward	*Reward*	*Difference in means*	*No reward*	*Reward*	*Difference in means*
No civic-duty frame	3.72 (1.07)	3.74 (1.12)	0.02 (0.08)	2.91 (1.43)	2.44 (1.38)	−0.47*** (0.11)
Civic-duty frame	3.66 (1.14)	3.68 (1.18)	0.02 (0.08)	2.97 (1.41)	2.49 (1.26)	−0.48*** (0.10)
Difference in means	−0.06 (0.08)	−0.06 (0.08)	−0.04 (0.08)	0.06 (0.11)	0.05 (0.10)	−0.42*** (0.10)

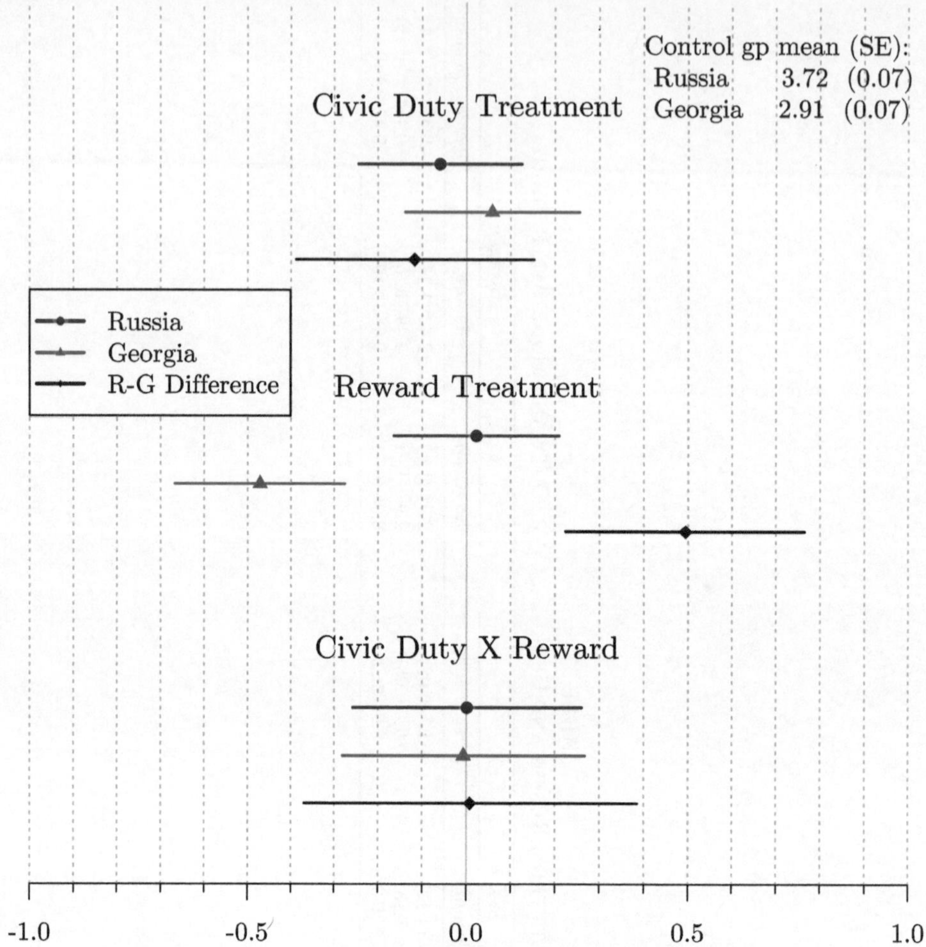

FIGURE 3. COEFFICIENT PLOTS OF SURVEY EXPERIMENT RESULTS: CIVIC DUTY AND MONETARY REWARD

ineffective. The difference between the two national responses is statistically significant, as shown by Figure 3.

Experiment 4

Our first three survey experiments focus on crime reporting by bystanders. What about when the potential cooperator is the victim? In this question, we vary the severity of the crime and the opportunity cost of time, as follows:

Survey experiment 4
Treatments:

1. Suppose some thieves broke into your apartment and stole some not very valuable items, and suppose that reporting this crime to the police would take about two hours.
2. Suppose some thieves broke into your apartment and stole some not very valuable items, and suppose that reporting this crime to the police would take about six hours.
3. Suppose some thieves broke into your apartment and stole some very valuable items, and suppose that reporting this crime to the police would take about two hours.
4. Suppose some thieves broke into your apartment and stole some very valuable items, and suppose that reporting this crime to the police would take about six hours.

Would you report this crime to the police?
Responses: certainly not; probably not; maybe, maybe not; probably; certainly

---

The phrasing '(not) very valuable' is intended to capture both the physical and sentimental value of the stolen objects. We anticipate that respondents would be more willing to report a crime if the value of stolen objects was high, as well as if reporting the crime took only two rather than six hours. We do not have strong prior expectations about the likely interaction between these two treatments.

As Table 4 demonstrates, respondents in both Russia and Georgia are far more likely to say that they would report a crime if 'very valuable' rather than 'not very valuable' items were stolen from them. Figure A4 in the online Appendix illustrates that this difference is driven by a sharp increase in the percentage of respondents who say they would 'certainly' report the crime, with approximately 40% and 50% of Russian and Georgian respondents, respectively, who received the 'very valuable' treatment indicating that they would do so. The average effect of high-value theft is approximately twice as large in Georgia as in Russia.

In contrast, there is no evidence that the opportunity cost of time plays a strong role in explaining variation in engagement with the police in either country. Regardless of the severity of the crime, the results reported in Table 4 indicate that individuals who are told that it would take about six hours to report a crime are no less likely to say that they would cooperate with the police than those who are told that it would take about two hours. Differences in the severity of the crime seem to matter much more than do differences in the time it takes to report it (see Figure 4).

Robustness

Our research design, in which respondents are randomly assigned to various treatment conditions, suggests that demographic characteristics are unlikely to drive our qualitative results. Tables A1–A4 in the online Appendix show this to be the case. Across all four survey experiments, both the direction and magnitude of our treatment effects are robust to controlling for a host of demographic characteristics, including age, gender, education, and material wealth.

TABLE 4

Difference-in-Means Results from Russia and Georgia: Opportunity Cost of Time and Crime Severity

	Russia			Georgia		
	Low-value robbery	*High-value robbery*	*Difference in means*	*Low-value robbery*	*High-value robbery*	*Difference in means*
Two hours to file report	3.50 (1.18)	3.91 (1.17)	0.41*** (0.09)	3.23 (1.48)	4.04 (1.36)	0.81*** (0.11)
Six hours to file report	3.46 (1.21)	3.91 (1.10)	0.45*** (0.08)	3.37 (1.51)	3.90 (1.35)	0.53*** (0.11)
Difference in means	−0.04 (0.09)	0.00 (0.08)	0.41*** (0.08)	0.13 (0.11)	−0.14 (0.10)	0.67*** (0.11)

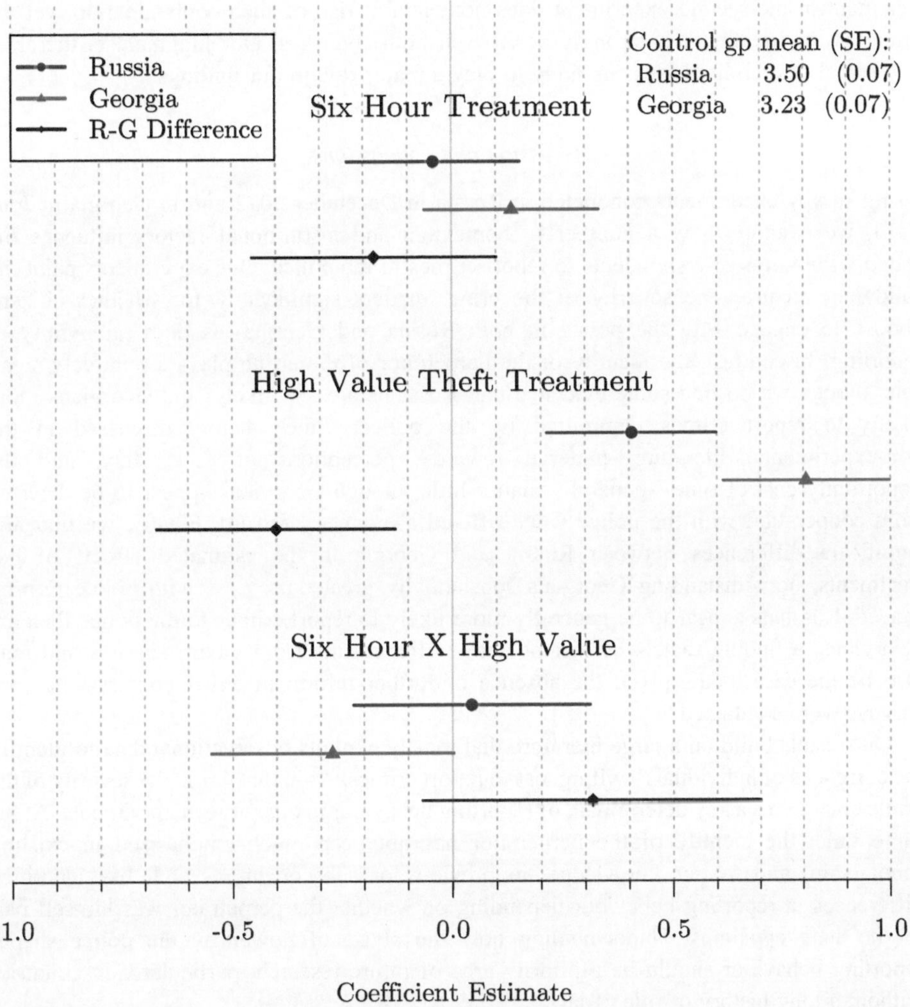

FIGURE 4. COEFFICIENT PLOTS OF SURVEY EXPERIMENT RESULTS: OPPORTUNITY COST OF TIME AND CRIME SEVERITY

One possible concern with our results is that responses could be driven by social desirability bias. In principle, for example, respondents might worry that interviewers would view them as callous if they did not say they would report the beating of a defenceless person, whereas petty theft would not provoke the same response. Although we cannot rule out such considerations completely, the framing of the civic-duty treatment in our third survey experiment ('Many people consider it their civic duty … ') seems most likely to provoke the social desirability bias, yet as shown, there is no significant effect of this treatment in either Russia or Georgia. Conversely, the anonymity treatment in the second experiment does not seem at risk of such contamination, yet the effect of this treatment is strongly positive in both countries. Our judgment is therefore that social desirability bias is unlikely to play a major role in our findings.

Discussion and conclusions

Using survey experiments conducted in Russia in December 2012 and in Georgia in June 2013, we examine how a number of contextual and institutional factors influence the stated willingness of respondents to report crimes to the police. Our experiments paint the following picture. The severity of the crime matters significantly for whether citizens choose to engage with the police in both Russia and Georgia, as does anonymity of reporting. In contrast, the identity of the perpetrator of the crime plays a relatively small role, though we do find some evidence that Russians are less likely, and Georgians more likely, to report crimes committed by the police. Other factors discussed in the non-experimental literature—material rewards, perceptions of civic duty, and the opportunity cost of time—generally matter little, though Georgians appear to be deterred from cooperation with the police when offered a monetary reward. Finally, we find few significant differences between Russia and Georgia in the estimated effects of our treatments, notwithstanding Georgia's substantially greater progress with police reform. Indeed, Russians appear to be generally more likely to report crimes to the police than are Georgians, a finding that is consistent with earlier results from victim surveys and may also be the case today, given the absence of further reform in either country since our surveys were conducted.

Our results build on a large literature that mostly exploits observational data to identify the correlates of individuals' willingness to report crimes. As in that work, the severity of the crime emerges as a key determinant of reporting behaviour in our survey experiments. At the same time, the identity of the perpetrator has not been much emphasised in existing scholarship, and to our knowledge no previous or subsequent research has identified differences in reporting behaviour depending on whether the perpetrator was himself part of the state apparatus. Understanding how the abuse of power by the police shapes reporting behaviour should be a priority area of future research, particularly in countries without a long history of rule of law.

Most striking, however, is what does not matter for individuals' stated willingness to report crimes. Among the various factors that we study, it is generally those that might be manipulated by the state to encourage greater reporting—material rewards, appeals to civic duty, or the time required to report a crime—that show the least effect (with the caveat that monetary rewards appear to actually deter reporting among Georgian respondents).

Our findings do, however, suggest a narrow opening through which citizens might be encouraged to report crimes to the police. Given that respondents in both countries are substantially more likely to report crimes when guaranteed anonymity, greater attention might be given to ensuring that citizens who do report crimes are protected. That said, it is important to remember the pernicious role that anonymous reporting played in supporting authoritarian rule during the Soviet period in Russia and Georgia. Any debate about the reintroduction of anonymous reporting in these countries would need to carefully weigh the benefits that we identify against the costs of more negative forms of engagement with the state.

Overall, these experimental findings reinforce a central lesson from the study of cooperation with the state in realms such as taxation and conscription. Engagement with the state is not achieved easily but, rather, is the outcome of a slowly evolving social contract between citizens and the state, an ongoing process in the majority of the world's countries, including Russia and Georgia. As other post-Soviet countries consider how best to reform their police forces, particularly those that look to Georgia's 'shock therapy' approach as a model to be emulated, our results should serve as a cautionary tale. Even where comprehensive institutional reform is feasible and largely viewed as successful in increasing institutional effectiveness and lowering corruption, as in the Georgian case, there should be no expectation that citizens' behaviour will quickly adapt to being more cooperative as a result.

Beyond these normative considerations, our work illustrates the value of using survey experiments to complement observational studies of topics such as crime reporting. Both the similarities and differences from previous work that we find are given greater credence by the knowledge that unobserved characteristics are unlikely to drive our results. At the same time, we hope that the findings we describe here open the door to future scholarship, be it qualitative, focus group-based, large-*N* observational, or experimental. The ability to easily manipulate various features of the crime and institutional context through vignettes is an additional advantage of survey experiments—one that can be profitably employed in future experimental work or built upon by scholars working with other methodologies.

References

Asatiani, S. & Coalson, R. (2015) 'Specter of Police Abuse Still Haunting Georgia', *Radio Free Europe/Radio Liberty*, 5 February.

Aviram, H. & Persinger, A. (2012) 'Perceiving and Reporting Domestic Violence Incidents in Unconventional Settings: A Vignette Survey Study', *Hastings Women's Law Journal*, 23, 2.

Becker, G. S. & Landes, W. M. (eds) (1974) *Essays in the Economics of Crime and Punishment* (New York, NY, Columbia University Press).

Bennett, R. R. & Wiegand, R. B. (1994) 'Observations on Crime Reporting in a Developing Nation', *Criminology*, 32, 1.

Besley, T. & Persson, T. (2011) *Pillars of Prosperity: The Political Economics of Development Clusters* (Princeton, NJ, Princeton University Press).

Bickman, L. & Helwig, H. (1979) 'Bystander Reporting of a Crime', *Criminology*, 17, 3.

Birkbeck, C., Gabaldon, L. G. & LaFree, G. (1993) 'The Decision to Call the Police: A Comparative Study of the US and Venezuela', *International Criminal Justice Review*, 3, 1.

Block, R. (1974) 'Why Notify the Police: The Victim's Decision to Notify the Police of an Assault', *Criminology*, 11, 4.

Boateng, F. D. (2018) 'Crime Reporting Behavior: Do Attitudes Toward the Police Matter?', *Journal of Interpersonal Violence*, 33, 18.

Bonvin, B. (2006) *Public Security in Georgia and the Region Bordering Abkhazia: Revisiting Some Received Ideas* (Geneva, Transnational Crime and Corruption Center, Caucasus Office).

Bouten, E., Goudriaan, H. & Nieuwbeerta, P. (2002) 'Criminal Victimization in Seventeen Industrialized Countries', in Nieuwbeerta, P. (ed.) *Crime Victimization in Comparative Perspective: Results from the International Crime Victims Survey, 1989–2000* (The Hague, Boom Legal Publishers).

Bowles, R., Garcia Reyes, M. & Garoupa, N. (2009) 'Crime Reporting Decisions and the Cost of Crime', *European Journal of Criminal Policy Research*, 15, 4.

Brinks, D. (2007) *The Judicial Response to Police Killings in Latin America* (New York, NY, Cambridge University Press).

Buckley, N., Frye, T., Gehlbach, S. & McCarthy, L. (2016) 'Cooperating with the State: Evidence from Survey Experiments on Policing', *Journal of Experimental Political Science*, 3, 2.

Bunce, V. (1999) 'The Political Economy of Postsocialism', *Slavic Review*, 58, 4.

Burakova, L. (2011) *Pochemu v Gruzii Poluchilos'* (Moscow, Alpine Business Books).

Bureau of Justice Statistics (2003) *Reporting Crime to the Police, 1992–2000* (Washington, DC, US Department of Justice).

Carcach, C. (1997) *Reporting Crime to the Police* (Canberra, Australian Institute of Criminology).

Challinger, D. (2004) *Crime Stopper Victoria: An Evaluation*, Technical and Background Paper No. 8 (Canberra, Australian Institute of Criminology).

Conaway, M. R. & Lohr, S. L. (1994) 'A Longitudinal Analysis of Factors Associated with Reporting Violent Crimes to the Police', *Journal of Quantitative Criminology*, 10, 1.

di Puppo, L. (2019) *Policing as Spectacle in Georgia: The Creation of Boundaries in a Post-Soviet Revolutionary Country*, Basic Research Programme Working Papers WP BRP 85/SOC/2019 (Moscow, Higher School of Economics).

Ellickson, R. C. (1991) *Order Without Law: How Neighbors Settle Disputes* (Cambridge, MA, Harvard University Press).

Engel, D. M. (2005) 'Globalization and the Decline of Legal Consciousness: Torts, Ghosts, and Karma in Thailand', *Law and Social Inquiry*, 30, 3.

Estienne, E. & Morabito, M. (2016) 'Understanding Differences in Crime Reporting Practices: A Comparative Approach', *International Journal of Comparative and Applied Criminal Justice*, 40, 2.

Felson, R. B., Messner, S. F. & Hoskin, A. W. (1999) 'The Victim–Offender Relationship and Calling the Police in Assaults', *Criminology*, 37, 4.

Felstiner, W. L. F., Abel, R. L. & Sarat, A. (1980–1981) 'The Emergence and Transformation of Disputes: Naming, Blaming, Claiming?', *Law and Society Review*, 15, 3/4.

Fuller, L. (2018) 'Can Planned Reforms Restore Public Confidence in Georgia's Police?', *Radio Free Europe/Radio Liberty*, 12 March.

Gehlbach, S. (2008) *Representation Through Taxation: Revenue, Politics, and Development in Postcommunist States* (New York, NY, Cambridge University Press).

Gerber, T. & Mendelson, S. (2008) 'Public Experiences of Police Violence and Corruption in Contemporary Russia: A Case of Predatory Policing?', *Law & Society Review*, 42, 1.

Gilinsky, Y. (2011) 'Torture by the Russian Police: An Empirical Study', *Police Practice and Research: An International Journal*, 12, 2.

Gingerich, D. W. & Oliveros, V. (2018) 'Police Violence and the Underreporting of Crime', *Economics & Politics*, 30, 1.

Goudriaan, H., Lynch, J. P. & Nieuwbeerta, P. (2004) 'Reporting to the Police in Western Nations: A Theoretical Analysis of the Effect of Social Context', *Justice Quarterly*, 21, 4.

Goudriaan, H. & Nieuwbeerta, P. (2007) 'Contextual Determinants of Juveniles' Willingness to Report Crimes: A Vignette Experiment', *Journal of Experimental Criminology*, 3, 2.

Hendley, K. (2010) 'Mobilizing Law in Contemporary Russia: The Evolution of Disputes Over Home Repair Projects', *American Journal of Comparative Law*, 58, 4.

Igorev, A. (2012) 'Pomoshch' politsii okazhetsya ochen' v kassu', *Kommersant"*, 24 August, available at: http://www.kommersant.ru/doc/2007246, accessed 26 October 2020.

IRI (2013) 'Georgian National Study, February 18–27, 2013', International Republican Institute, available at: http://www.iri.org/sites/default/files/2013_May_16_Survey_of_Georgian_Public_Opinion_February_18-27_2013.pdf, accessed 26 October 2020.

IRI (2018) 'Public Opinion Survey: Residents of Georgia, April 10–22, 2018', International Republican Institute, available at: http://www.iri.org/sites/default/files/2018-5-29_georgia_poll_presentation.pdf, accessed 26 October 2020.

Ivkovic, S. K. (2005) 'Police (Mis)Behavior: A Cross-Cultural Study of Corruption Seriousness', *Policing: An International Journal of Police Strategies & Management*, 28, 3.

Kakachia, K. & O'Shea, L. (2012) 'Why does Police Reform Appear to have been more Successful in Georgia than in Kyrgyzstan or Russia?', *The Journal of Power Institutions in Post-Soviet Societies*, 13.

Kelly, C. (2005) *Comrade Pavlik: The Rise and Fall of a Soviet Boy Hero* (London, Granta Books).

Kivivuori, J., Sirén, R. & Danielsson, P. (2012) 'Gender Framing Effects in Victim Surveys', *European Journal of Criminology*, 9, 2.

Kochel, T. R., Parks, R. & Mastrofski, S. D. (2013) 'Examining Police Effectiveness as a Precursor to Legitimacy and Cooperation with Police', *Justice Quarterly*, 30, 5.

Kosals, L. & Dubova, A. (2012) 'Commercialization of Police and Shadow Economy: The Russian Case', *Economic Sociology: The European Electronic Newsletter*, 13, 2.

Kupatadze, A. (2018) *Informal Governance and Corruption: Transcending the Principal Agent and Collective Action Paradigms in Georgia* (Basel, Basel Institute on Governance), available at: https://baselgovernance.org/publications/informal-governance-and-corruption-transcending-principal-agent-and-collective-4, accessed 29 October 2020.

Lampert, N. (1985) *Whistleblowing in the Soviet Union: Complaints and Abuses Under State Socialism* (New York, NY, Schocken Books).

Lasley, J. R. & Jones Palombo, B. (1995) 'When Crime Reporting Goes High-Tech: An Experimental Test of Computerized Citizen Response to Crime', *Journal of Criminal Justice*, 23, 6.

Ledeneva, A. (2006) *How Russia Really Works: The Informal Practices That Shaped Post-Soviet Politics and Business* (Ithaca, NY, Cornell University Press).

Lehmbruch, B. & Sanikidze, L. (2014) 'Soviet Legacies, New Public Management and Bureaucratic Entrepreneurship in the Georgian Protection Police. Agencifying the Police?', *Europe-Asia Studies*, 66, 1.

Levada Centre (2012) 'Rossiyane o politsii', 4 May, available at: https://www.levada.ru/2012/05/04/rossiyane-o-politsii/, accessed 25 November 2020.

Levada Centre (2017) 'Otnoshenie k politsii', 7 November, available at: https://www.levada.ru/2017/11/07/otnoshenie-k-politsii/, accessed 29 October 2020.

Levada Centre (2018) 'Institutsional'noe doverie', 4 October, available at: https://www.levada.ru/2018/10/04/institutsionalnoe-doverie-4/, accessed 29 October 2020.

Levi, M. (1988) *Of Rule and Revenue* (Berkeley, CA, University of California Press).

Light, M. (2013a) 'Police Reforms in the Republic of Georgia: The Convergence of Domestic and Foreign Policy in an Anti-Corruption Drive', *Policing & Society*, 24, 3.

Light, M. (2013b) 'To Know the City: Urban Policing Innovations in the Post-Soviet Republic of Georgia', in Lippert, R. K. & Walby, K. (eds) *Policing Cities: Urban Securitization and Regulation in a 21st Century World* (New York, NY, Routledge).

Lynch, J. P. & Danner, M. J. E. (1993) 'Offense Seriousness Scaling: An Alternative to Scenario Methods', *Journal of Quantitative Criminology*, 9, 3.

Marat, E. (2018) *The Politics of Police Reform: Society Against the State in Post-Soviet Countries* (New York, NY, Oxford University Press).

Mars, G. & Altman, Y. (1983) 'The Cultural Bases of Soviet Georgia's Second Economy', *Soviet Studies*, 35, 4.

McCarthy, L. A. (2014) 'Local-Level Law Enforcement: Muscovites and Their Uchastkovyy', *Post-Soviet Affairs*, 30, 2–3.

McCarthy, L. A. (2015) *Trafficking Justice: How Russian Police Enforce New Laws, from Crime to Courtroom* (Ithaca, NY, Cornell University Press).

McCubbins, M. D. & Schwartz, T. (1984) 'Congressional Oversight Overlooked: Police Patrols Versus Fire Alarms', *American Journal of Political Science*, 28, 1.

Mulligan, C. B. & Shleifer, A. (2005) 'Conscription as Regulation', *American Law and Economics Review*, 7, 1.

Nasuti, P. (2016) 'Administrative Cohesion and Anti-Corruption Reforms in Georgia and Ukraine', *Europe-Asia Studies*, 68, 5.

North, D. C. (1981) *Structure and Change in Economic History* (New York, NY, Norton).

North, D. C. (1990) *Institutions, Institutional Change, and Economic Performance* (New York, NY, Cambridge University Press).

North, D. C., Wallis, J. J. & Weingast, B. R. (2009) *Violence and Social Orders: A Conceptual Framework for Interpreting Recorded Human History* (New York, NY, Cambridge University Press).

Paneyakh, E., Titaev, K. & Shklyaruk, M. (2018) *Traektoria Ugolovnogo Dela: Institutsional'nyi Analiz* (St Petersburg, European University at St Petersburg Press).

Papava, V. (2005) *Necroeconomics: The Political Economy of Post-Communist Capitalism* (New York, NY, iUniverse).

Ranapurnwala, S., Berg, M. T. & Casteel, C. (2016) 'Reporting Crime Victimizations to the Police and the Incidence of Future Victimizations: A Longitudinal Study', *PLoS ONE*, 11, 7.

Root, H. (1994) *The Fountain of Privilege: Political Foundations of Markets in Old Regime France and England* (Berkeley, CA, University of California Press).

Ruback, R. B., Barry, K. S., Outlaw, M. C. & Shaffer, J. N. (1999) 'Normative Advice to Campus Crime Victims: Effects of Gender, Age, and Alcohol', *Violence and Victims*, 14, 4.

Rubnikovich, O. & Barinov, V. (2018) 'MVD razreshil platit informatoram?', *Kommersant"*, 21 August.

Semukhina, O. (2016) 'Public Assistance of Police During Criminal Investigations: Russian Experience?', *Police Practice and Research*, 17, 3.

Sheu, C.-J. & Chiu, S.-P. (2012) 'Determinants of Property Crime Victims to Report to the Police in Taiwan', *International Review of Victimology*, 18, 3.

Sidebottom, A. (2015) 'On the Correlates of Reporting Assault to the Police in Malawi', *British Journal of Criminology*, 55, 2.

Skogan, W. G. (1984) 'Reporting Crimes to the Police: The Status of World Research', *Journal of Research in Crime and Delinquency*, 21, 2.

Smith, A. E. & Maness, D. (1976) 'The Decision to Call the Police: Reactions to Burglary', in McDonald, W. (ed.) *Criminal Justice and the Victim* (Beverly Hills, CA, Sage).

Soares, R. (2004) 'Crime Reporting as a Measure of Institutional Development', *Economic Development and Cultural Change*, 52, 4.

Solomon Jr, P. H. (2014) 'Courts, Law and Policing Under Medvedev: Many Reforms, Modest Change, New Voices', in Black, J. L. & Johns, M. (eds) *Russia After 2012: From Putin to Medvedev to Putin—Continuity, Change, or Revolution?* (New York, NY, Routledge).

Sunshine, J. & Tyler, T. R. (2003) 'The Role of Procedural Justice and Legitimacy in Shaping Public Support for Policing', *Law & Society Review*, 37, 3.

Tankebe, J. (2009) 'Public Cooperation with the Police in Ghana: Does Procedural Fairness Matter?', *Criminology; An interdisciplinary Journal*, 47, 4.

Tarling, R. & Morris, K. (2010) 'Reporting Crime to the Police', *British Journal of Criminology*, 50, 3.

Taubina, N. (2012) 'Reforma: chto sdelano i chego ne khvataet', *Obshchestvennyi verdikt*, 1 March.

Taylor, B. (2006) 'Law Enforcement and Civil Society in Russia', *Europe-Asia Studies*, 58, 2.

Taylor, B. (2011) *State Building in Putin's Russia: Policing and Coercion After Communism* (New York, NY, Cambridge University Press).

Taylor, B. (2014) 'Police Reform in Russia: The Policy Process in a Hybrid Regime', *Post-Soviet Affairs*, 30, 2–3.

Tilly, C. (2005) *Trust and Rule* (New York, NY, Cambridge University Press).

Titmuss, R. M. (1970) *The Gift Relationship* (London, Allen and Unwin).

Tolsma, J., Blaauw, J. & te Grotenhuis, M. (2012) 'When do People Report Crime to the Police? Results from a Factorial Survey Design in the Netherlands, 2010', *Journal of Experimental Criminology*, 8, 2.

Torrente, D., Gallo, P. & Oltra, C. (2017) 'Comparing Crime Reporting Factors in EU Countries', *European Journal on Criminal Policy and Research*, 23, 2.

Trochev, A. & Slade, G. (2019) 'Trials and Tribulations: Kazakhstan's Criminal Justice Reforms', in Caron, J. F. (ed.) *Kazakhstan and the Soviet Legacy: Between Continuity and Rupture* (Singapore, Palgrave Macmillan).
Tyler, T. (1990) *Why People Obey the Law* (Princeton, NJ, Princeton University Press).
Tyler, T. (2012) 'The Psychology of Cooperation: Implications for Public Policy', in Shaffer, E. (ed.) *The Behavioral Foundations of Public Policy* (Princeton, NJ, Princeton University Press).
van Dijk, J. (2012) 'The International Crime Victims Survey: Latest Results and Prospects', *Criminology in Europe*, 3, 11.
van Dijk, J. & Chanturia, T. (2012) *The Remarkable Case of Georgia* (Tbilisi, Gorbi Institute, Ministry of Justice, Georgia).
van Kesteren, J. & van Dijk, J. (2010) 'Key Victimological Findings from ICVS', in Shoham, S. G., Knepper, P. & Kett, M. (eds) *International Handbook of Victimology* (New York, NY, Routledge).
Weber, M. (1978) *Economy and Society* (Berkeley, CA, University of California Press).
Xie, M. & Baumer, E. P. (2019) 'Crime Victims' Decisions to Call the Police: Past Research and New Directions', *Annual Review of Criminology*, 2.
Zhang, L., Messner, S. F. & Liu, J. (2007) 'An Exploration of the Determinants of Reporting Crime to the Police in the City of Tianjin, China', *Criminology*, 45, 4.
Zvekic, U. (1996) 'Policing and Attitudes Towards Police Private in Countries in Transition: Preliminary Results of the International Crime (Victim) Survey', in Pagon, M. (ed.) *Policing in Central and Eastern Europe: Comparing Firsthand Knowledge with Experience from the West* (Ljubljana, College of Police and Security Studies).

Popular Legal Attitudes and the Political Order: Comparative Evidence from Georgia, Russia and Ukraine

WILLIAM M. REISINGER, MARINA ZALOZNAYA & VICKI HESLI CLAYPOOL

Abstract

Using data from nationally representative surveys in 2015 in Georgia, Russia and Ukraine, we show that legal attitudes are shaped by experiences within a country's specific political-legal order. Many who expressed support for legality when their own needs were at stake became more willing to evade the law when reminded of elites doing so. And, in an authoritarian, rule-by-law setting, expressed respect for legality correlates negatively with support for democracy. Whether a country's most democracy-supporting citizens more strongly support legality will depend on whether the legal system is a fair and neutral arena or a tool of undemocratic political authorities.

THE LEGAL ATTITUDES THAT PREVAIL AMONG A COUNTRY'S citizens shape the functioning not only of legal institutions *per se* but of governance more generally. The extent to which citizens believe they should obey laws and judicial rulings influences how easily a regime can secure the public compliance it needs. Principled support for legality, as opposed to obedience because of possible consequences, has generally been treated as a type of pro-democratic value. Since a liberal democratic polity must include such rule-of-law elements as equality before the law and protection of individual rights, a democratic public should value legality and demand it from those who govern. In authoritarian settings or societies with an authoritarian legacy, principled support for legality may be at a lower level than elsewhere, but it is expected that people who express stronger support for democratic government will tend to be more supportive of legality as well. However, using data from 2015 surveys in three Eurasian countries—Georgia, Russia, Ukraine—we show that citizens' support for legality does not match this common expectation. The patterns of legal attitudes vary among these countries based on how political and legal

This essay is based upon work supported in part under grant number W911NF-14-1-0541 from the US Army Research Office/Army Research Laboratory. The views expressed are those of the authors and should not be attributed to the Army Research Office/Army Research Laboratory. We are grateful for research assistance provided by Yooneui Kim and to Lauren McCarthy and the anonymous referees for valuable suggestions.

institutions operate and, in an authoritarian context, citizens who are more supportive of democracy are less, not more, likely to be committed to following the law.

The literature on legal attitudes in the Soviet successor countries is not large, and most research has examined Russia alone (Reisinger *et al.* 1997; Gibson 2003; Baird & Javeline 2007; Gerber & Mendelson 2008; Kozyreva 2008; Hendley 2012a, 2017b; McCarthy 2014, p. 196; Andrianova 2018).[1] A central theme in this literature is ascertaining whether or not citizen attitudes and behaviours will support efforts to strengthen the rule of law. Combining individual-level results with comparisons among three countries allows us to shed new light on how citizens' attitudes and behaviours are influenced by the legacy of the Soviet period and contemporary social and political realities. Georgia, Russia and Ukraine vary in the extent to which the state is democratically controlled and the legal system approximates rule-of-law ideals or, in contrast, their legal systems give special advantages to officials. Most theories about public attitudes towards the law were developed in settings close to the former pole. Citizens in the countries closer to the latter pole, Russia and, to a lesser extent, Ukraine, are more likely than Georgians to view the law in utilitarian rather than principled terms and to turn to it when necessary even without granting it strong legitimacy.

Popular legal consciousness and the debate over nihilism

We seek to understand the distributions, within and among the three societies, of individuals' attitudes to the law and their relationship to the legal system—what is often termed these citizens' legal consciousness (Merry 2010, p. 44).[2] This is a complicated object of study. Kurkchiyan describes a consensus among scholars of legal consciousness that 'the way in which people perceive law and legality is a multilayered and dynamic construct, responsive to their surrounding social situation' (Kurkchiyan 2011, p. 372).[3]

We are particularly interested in respect for legality as an element of legal consciousness. Respect for legality refers to the belief that oneself and others like oneself are obliged to follow public legal rules and procedures. Communist and now postcommunist societies are often depicted as only weakly possessing respect for the law. They exhibit, in other words, 'legal nihilism', a form of 'condescension toward the law' (Hendley 2012b, p. 160) that condones fudging, evading or disobeying the law when meeting one's needs requires it. Legal nihilism has been posited as a key residue of the Soviet period in Russia and the other successor states (Alexeyev 1991; Huskey 1991; Sakwa 2000; Kurkchiyan 2003).[4] While Soviet citizens were obliged to obey the law, the inefficiencies of central planning and the challenges of dealing with a complex bureaucracy meant that most people

[1]Studies of other postcommunist countries include Galligan (2003), Kurkchiyan (2003), Trochev (2012), and Hertogh and Kurkchiyan (2016).

[2]We are not seeking to depict or compare these countries' legal cultures in their entirety. While legal culture is an important concept in comparative sociolegal studies, it poses challenges to define and measure. An influential early treatment is Friedman (1975). For debates on the concept's utility, see Nelken (1997, 2010), Merry (2010), Von Benda-Beckmann and Von Benda-Beckmann (2010).

[3]See also Nielsen (2000), Silbey (2005).

[4]Or, in the case of Russia, the Soviet experience may have reinforced an older tradition of legal nihilism (Wortman 1976).

adjusted to evading legal requirements to achieve their needs. They were also well aware that the law did not constrain the political elite in the same way that it constrained them (Quigley 1990; Sharlet 1990; Berman 1992; Huskey 1992). It would seem natural for attitudes of disregard or disdain towards the law to emerge in that context.

Other evidence, though, suggests that legal nihilism is not the best way to understand the Soviet legacy. For one thing, as soon as Soviet citizens gained the opportunity to protest in the late 1980s, a prominent demand was that officials respect the law. Also, survey evidence from Russia in the 1990s showed more support for legality among the public than the term nihilism suggests (Reisinger *et al.* 1997; Gibson 2003). Hendley (2012b) confirmed these findings using data from the mid-2000s, even though her informal conversations indicated that most Russians believed legal nihilism to be rampant in their society.

We argue that differing conclusions about legal nihilism highlight the complexities in citizens' legal consciousness. We present a different way to explain individual-level legal views, seeing them as shaped by their country's political order and how, in the given political context, individuals interact with the legal system. Our ability to compare legal views in three post-Soviet countries helps reveal these complexities.

The role of the political-legal context

For many years, studies of ordinary citizens' relations to and use of the law were mostly based on evidence from democratic societies, which are characterised by comparatively strong commitment to the rule of law. Although the rule of law is a much debated term,[5] its core meaning is widely shared. It connotes a setting in which citizens are, to a relatively high degree, equal before the law, and in which legal institutions function fairly and predictably. In such societies, elites find it more difficult to use their power in self-serving ways, and citizens have greater possibilities to use legal institutions to pursue their needs.

In non-democratic societies, however, rule-of-law principles are weakly observed.[6] Recent empirical work shows that citizens' attitudes and behaviours towards the legal system are quite different in autocracies.[7] For instance, writing about China, Lei and Zhou argue that national 'government is above the law' and 'law is a tool in the government's hands' (Lei & Zhou 2015, p. 588). Scholars describe such societies as having 'rule by law' (Ginsburg & Moustafa 2008) or 'authoritarian rule of law' (Rajah 2012). In rule-by-law countries, ruling regimes structure legal institutions and deploy the law 'to better institutionalise their rule and to strengthen discipline within their states' burgeoning administrative hierarchies' (Ginsburg & Moustafa 2008, pp. 7–8). Rather than constraining the politically powerful, in other words, legality in such systems primarily extends their control.

[5]See, for example, Shapiro (1994), Zywicki (2003), Krygier (2012).

[6]The World Justice Project's (2018) rule-of-law index for 2015, the year our surveys were conducted, assesses over 100 countries. It correlates with those countries' scores on the V-Dem Project's (2019) measure of liberal democracy at 0.77 (0.000). The rule-of-law measure in the World Governance Indicators (2016) similarly correlates with democracy at 0.76 (0.000) across an even larger sample of countries.

[7]See, for example, Gallagher (2006, 2017), Moustafa (2007), Hendley (2017b), Kurkchiyan and Kubal (2018).

This basic difference in the relationship between the political regime and how the legal system operates has several implications for citizens' attitudes and behaviours. The typical approach to analysing individuals' legal attitudes assumes democratic citizens should accept the legal system as an impartial arbiter of societal disputes—a means for the state to enforce fairly enacted laws (Shapiro 1981). Accepting judicial and other legal procedures and decisions is necessary for the larger good, yet this assumes that legal procedures and decisions bind the powerful as well. When citizens understand their country's courts and other legal actors to operate not impartially but in the service of the regime, when extensive bureaucratic corruption allows state officials to profit from citizens, then citizens lose the sense that their own respect for the law is ultimately beneficial even if it requires a self-abnegating choice in the present. Citizens instead come to see interactions with the state as prisoners' dilemmas in which those who obey the letter of the law are losing out to others who do not. Moreover, authoritarian regimes inherently undercut citizens' view that the system is impartial because their institutions are, by definition, intended to shield those in power from recourse by citizens who have been poorly treated. They prevent the operation of a political opposition that can act as a watchdog over the operation of courts and other state institutions. The higher the degree of authoritarianism, the more citizens come to understand the law as a tool for the regime and that they must approach the legal system pragmatically, not idealistically.

For these reasons, respect for legality and support for democracy, which correlate among citizens in democratic societies, can be weakly related or even reversed in authoritarian, rule-by-law societies. The citizens who most support democracy will more strongly view the law as an instrument of control in the hands of the undemocratic state. Because they want the law to play a different role, to keep the powerful in check, they will express less support for the law as it stands.

Why, then, do ordinary people obey the law in non-democratic societies? Most of what we know about the reasons for compliance with the law is based on empirical research conducted in the United States and Western Europe. This research finds that people are more likely to comply with the law when they believe the legal system is legitimate, in particular, that it is impartial and fair (Tyler 1990, 2006; Jackson *et al.* 2012; Tyler & Jackson 2014). The more the legal system generally is viewed as being unfair, the less we should expect to find that relationship. Instead, a substantial proportion of compliance with the law in non-democratic societies will stem from the benefits of complying rather than normative considerations.

In line with this expectation, recent work on legal views in rule-by-law settings found that even though few citizens in rule-by-law societies view legal institutions as imbued with impartiality and fairness, they often rely on them in their everyday lives. Hendley (2017b, p. 4) for instances, argues that, despite prevailing stereotypes, Russia is not a lawless state. Rather, 'Russians routinely negotiate resolutions to their problems with others in the shadow of the law or, when informal efforts prove futile, take their problems to courts and have them resolved in accordance with the law'. Similarly, Gallagher (2006, p. 785) finds that, despite 'negative evaluations/perceptions of the legal system in terms of its fairness and effectiveness', Chinese citizens exhibit growing feelings of personal efficacy in using the legal system. In both societies, high demand for legal remedies exists alongside nihilistic views about the law.[8]

Legal attitudes and behaviours should thus differ across our three countries in accord with differences among their political and legal regimes. Of our three post-Soviet societies, Georgia became the most democratic from the Rose Revolution of 2003 through the peaceful turnover of executive power in 2012. During the same period Georgia's courts achieved more significant independence than those in Ukraine and Russia (Kaufmann & Kraay 2016; World Justice Project 2018). It is also the only post-Soviet country to have substantially reduced its level of corruption (IBRD 2012; Aliyev 2017, pp. 105–19). This effort included programmes designed to build 'lawfulness' among citizens (Godson *et al.* 2003). Ukraine, like Georgia, is judged to be substantially democratic since 2014 following the Euromaidan protests and the flight from the country of then-president Viktor Yanukovych, although the stability of those democratic elements remains unclear. Widespread agreement has emerged over the last decade that Russia's regime is fully authoritarian, not a hybrid (Levitsky & Way 2010; Gel'man 2014, p. 518). The Varieties of Democracy project's polyarchy score, which captures the level of adherence to liberal democracy for 178 countries, ranked Georgia 56th in the world in 2015 while Ukraine ranked 119th, and Russia ranked 141st (Coppedge *et al.* 2019).

In addition to testing for cross-national patterns consistent with the differences among the countries in their legal-political environment, we will go beyond the common, usually implicit assumption that an individual's legal consciousness flows from a single underlying mental orientation.[9] Scholars who measure support for legality, whether *via* surveys, focus groups or interviews, treat the responses as imperfect glimpses of the underlying dimension. Most of them, therefore, ask multiple questions to probe the underlying dimension of interest in different ways before combining the answers into a single index variable. The index variable stands in for the unmeasurable, or latent, variable.

We must be careful, though, about interpreting a person's responses to measurement questions as flowing from an ingrained position on a single dimension of respect for legality. Social psychology research indicates that people do not have rigid, pre-formed attitudes that can be cleanly invoked by survey questions. Instead, people draw on multiple memories and considerations as they respond to the prompts in a particular question (Zaller & Feldman 1992; Lodge & Taber 2013). A country's laws and legal actors intersect with citizens' lives in multiple ways. For most people, reaching a conclusion about when the legal system deserves their support will be influenced by which of the dimensions of the legal system a question invokes. In comparing a country that more strongly provides rule of law to one with rule by law, we should expect that

[8]This combination should not be seen as occurring only in non-democratic societies. In fact, this way of relating to law is one of three common types of the legal consciousness—the 'with the law' type—in Ewick and Silbey's (1998) canonical study of legal consciousness in the United States. Other researchers have documented similar attitudes to law among working-class citizens, minorities and women in the United States (Merry 1990; Nielsen 2000). Gallagher (2006, pp. 787–88) suggests that it may be how citizens who experience structural disadvantage—in democratic as well as non-democratic settings—cope with systems that are unfavourable to them.

[9]Orientations, in this sense, are 'general dispositions that pattern sets of actions and sets of specific attitudes' (Eckstein 1988, p. 791).

respect for legality will be higher in the former when the question deals only with the law itself. But when a question also invokes the legal system, we should expect those who have found ways to benefit from engaging with the legal system to express support for it even though they are aware it is not impartial, resulting in higher support for legality in the rule-by-law society.

In addition, efforts to identify the sources of legal attitudes should be sensitive to the array of considerations that can influence those attitudes. As Taber and Young (2013, p. 525, citing Eysenck & Keane 2010) put it, individuals are 'embedded within an information environment, and their mental processing is interactive between environmental and internally stored information'. Socialisation during youth matters, and demographics can capture some common differences. Yet people continuously update their understanding of the relationship between the legal system and themselves (or those close to them) with new information from multiple channels, including their experiences (Nelken 2010, p. 19). We should expect that citizens' encounters with state officials will be particularly relevant to their evolving judgments about whether the legal system serves people like them, how they can use the legal system to protect themselves or advance their interests, and to what extent the legal system provides broader societal goods worthy of their respect. As people update their views of the legal system, they will more readily accept stimuli that accord with previously held positions (Redlawsk 2002; Nyhan & Reifler 2010; Lodge & Taber 2013). The attitudes people express about the law and legality will therefore be related to emotionally powerful outlooks such as partisanship, social identity and, as Hendley's (2017b) recent work has proposed, the sense of personal control over one's life.

Patterns of legal attitudes and behaviours

To test our expectations, we use data from representative national surveys conducted in Georgia, Russia and Ukraine in the summer and early autumn of 2015. The surveys involved face-to-face interviews with 1,208 people in Georgia, 2,000 in Russia and 1,535 in Ukraine. We begin by examining the nationwide distributions for five types of legal attitudes. Table 1 shows distributional information on the responses to these questions in each country. Two questions asked respondents to absolutely disagree, disagree, agree or absolutely agree with two statements, one expressing respect for the law, the other willingness to disobey it, each providing a different possible rationale.[10] One asked if the law must be obeyed even if it interferes with citizens' ability to resolve their problems. The other suggested obeying the law was not mandatory given that 'the authorities' do not always obey it.

Although these two questions about respect for the law were formulated to capture the same latent concept—what Tyler and Huo (2002, pp. 108–11) call 'obligation to obey the law'—we cannot combine them into a single index variable. Tests such as Cronbach's alpha and confirmatory factor analysis indicate that they do not relate to the same

[10]We have recoded the questions so that higher scores indicate more support for legality. The wording of these and other questions are provided in the Appendix.

TABLE 1
PRO-LEGAL ATTITUDES IN GEORGIA, RUSSIA AND UKRAINE

	Georgia	*Russia*	*Ukraine*
Must observe the law even when:			
—the law interferes with one's ability to resolve problems			
Mean: 1 (Absolutely disagree)–4 (Absolutely agree)	2.78	2.56	2.66
Proportion agreeing or absolutely agreeing must obey law	58%	51%	55%
	n=1,078	*n*=1,818	*n*=1,263
—the authorities do not obey the law			
Mean	2.08	2.20	2.15
Proportion agreeing or absolutely agreeing that one must obey law	35%	36%	35%
	n=1,141	*n*=1,870	*n*=1,327
Anti-corruption views:			
—opposition to corrupt behaviour			
Mean: 1 (all 4 always acceptable)–3 (None of 4 ever acceptable)	2.59	2.26	2.41
Mode	2.75	2	3
	n=1,198	*n*=1,940	*n*=1,464
—prefers complete absence of corruption	89.6%	71.9%	88.8%
Standard deviation	0.31	0.45	0.32
	n=1,117	*n*=1,735	*n*=1,339
Behaviour with regard to the legal system:			
—in response to a dispute, turned to the legal system	35%	51%	49%
	n=206	*n*=610	*n*=315
—turned to connections	14%	50%	42%
In addition to the legal system	12%	34%	22%
Without using the legal system	15%	66%	60%
—turned to a spiritual or religious mentor	50%	20%	21%
In addition to the legal system	19%	14%	10%
Without using the legal system	67%	27%	32%

Source: Reisinger *et al.* (2015).

underlying orientation. They differ cross-nationally and have different individual-level correlates. We therefore present them separately.

Two other measures capture attitudes towards engaging in bureaucratic corruption. These provide another look at an individual's commitment to legality. Although taking part in bureaucratic corruption depends on more than a person's attitudes towards the law in general, it involves doing something extra-legal to incentivise a bureaucrat to benefit an individual by departing from the specified procedures. We asked respondents whether they considered it always acceptable (scored as 1), sometimes acceptable (2) or never acceptable (3) to do each of four things: give a bribe, provide a gift, do a favour or use one's connections. Our index measure of opposition to corrupt actions is the average across these four variables, with a score of three being the most supportive of legality in the sense that the person considers none of the four actions acceptable.[11]

We also posed a hypothetical question relating to bureaucratic corruption. Would the person prefer to live in a society where all officials strictly obeyed the law when dealing with citizens or one in which officials sometimes accepted bribes, presents or favours in

[11]The Cronbach's alpha scores for the four variables are 0.73 in Georgia, 0.83 in Russia and 0.89 in Ukraine.

exchange for special treatment? This is another measure of abstract respect for the law, albeit one that may be only weakly related to citizen behaviour. Someone who prefers the corruption-free scenario may assume that 'everyone else ignores the law, so they have to do the same' (Kurkchiyan 2003, pp. 26–7). It nonetheless deserves examining since, as Hendley (2012b) argues, Russians tend to believe the worst about their fellow citizens even as they themselves express their support for legality.

The final measure indicates the person's propensity to turn to the legal system for help in dealing with a serious dispute rather than to seek out other options, such as a religious figure, a politician, an NGO or an influential friend. Respondents, it ought to be noted, could mention more than one option. Those who had been involved in what they considered a serious dispute were a small minority in each country: 17% in Georgia, 31% in Russia and 21% in Ukraine. From among that group, those who indicated they had contacted a lawyer, legal consultancy or legal-defence organisation, or who had gone to the police, a court or other law-enforcement agency were scored as one. Those who turned elsewhere are scored as zero.

Differences across questions

Before discussing the cross-national results, we should note that individuals' responses about their legal values depended strongly on the prompts used in each question and what associations they produced. The first measure of respect for the law, framed in terms of obeying the law when it poses a barrier to resolving one's own problems, produced a majority in all three countries who indicated that the law should outweigh personal considerations. On the other hand, these majorities were not overwhelming; sizeable minorities in each country indicated they were not committed to obeying all laws.

The second measure, which reminded respondents of the possibility that their country's authorities did not obey the law, produced significantly lower respect for legality in all three countries. Each country produced a nearly identical proportion willing to support legality in the face of a law-abusing power structure: just over one third.[12] Few Georgians, Russians or Ukrainians felt obliged to respect the law when the law did not similarly constrain elites. Many who expressed support for observing the law even when it interfered with meeting their own needs rejected legality when it favoured the powerful. People in these societies, it seems fair to conclude, view law as part of a social compact that requires individual sacrifice at times for a larger good but can also be evaded or opposed when its results are perceived to be unfair as or when those in power violate the compact. In line with this, Grødeland and Miller (2015) found that only 45% of Ukrainians believed that normally law-abiding people would disobey the law when obeying was troublesome, but 85% would do so if an official pressured them for a bribe. This pattern also fits with results from a number of studies conducted outside the former

[12]Hendley (2017b, pp. 25–6) provides results for Russia from a similar agree–disagree statement posed in 2004, 2006 and 2012: ordinary citizens can disobey the law if officials do not obey it. Instead of the four options in our question, Hendley's respondents could only choose 'agree', 'disagree' or 'ambivalent'. Our result for Russia, 36% selecting the pro-legality position, is slightly above her 2004 findings of 33% selecting the pro-legality position and below her results of 42% in 2006 and 49% in 2012.

Soviet Union (Tyler 1990; Tyler & Huo 2002; Grimes 2006; Jackson *et al.* 2012; Trinkner & Cohn 2014).

In none of the three countries do corrupt transactions with bureaucratic officials find high levels of public support. On the one–three index scale, all three societies' average is above the midpoint, and the modal response in Georgia and Ukraine is highly disapproving. Also, in all three countries large majorities indicated they would prefer never to deal with corruption when interacting with officials, even if that would preclude them from 'working the system' to their own benefit. When asked in the abstract, then, citizens in our three countries would prefer their bureaucracies to work without what many posited as the social 'grease' of corruption (Key 1949; Nye 1967; Scott 1969; Becquart-Leclercq 1989).

Of those who had faced a serious dispute in the preceding year, the level of recourse to the legal system was middling in Russia and Ukraine and low in Georgia. These levels do not directly indicate how these citizens viewed their countries' courts.[13] We find, for example, no statistically significant difference in responses to a question about trusting the judiciary between those who had turned to the legal system and those who did not. These levels do, though, provide insight into the extent to which expressed respect for legality commitment translates into actually using legal mechanisms for problem resolution. Table 1 also shows the percentages of respondents who said they had used connections or turned to a religious adviser. In all three countries, nearly as many citizens reported turning to one of these alternatives as those who had used the legal system.

The picture produced of post-Soviet citizens' legal attitudes varies quite a bit, then, depending on how the question is framed. Support for legality was strong when citizens were asked about corrupt exchanges with bureaucratic officials. Behavioural support in the form of using the legal system was lower. Support for abiding by the law differed significantly depending on what obstacle to legality was mentioned. Majorities supported legality when the obstacle was their personal needs, while almost two thirds felt less bound by the law when primed with the suggestion that those with power do not obey the law.

Differences across countries

In rough terms, as described above, Georgia is the most democratic, rule-of-law-oriented of the three societies, with Russia the least. Ukraine is in the middle, closer to Russia in some ways and to Georgia in others. We can expect that frequency of respect for legality, when the question is posed in terms of satisfying one's personal needs, will be in the same rank order across the countries: Georgia, then Ukraine, then Russia. The responses to the first question in Table 1 bear this out. The average scores place Georgia highest, Ukraine second and Russia lowest. The proportions who fall into the supportive side of the scale also follow that order.[14]

The average responses to the next question, about respect for legality when the authorities do not obey the law, rank in the opposite order: Russians show the highest average level of support, Georgians the least and Ukrainians are in the middle. This reversal of cross-national

[13]On Russians' attitudes towards the courts, see Hendley (2012a, 2017a, 2018).

[14]For all the measures in Table 1, the differences between the country means are statistically significant using the Kruskal–Wallis equality-of-populations rank test and Dunn's test.

ordering would be surprising if both this and the preceding question were measuring the same underlying dimension of respect for legality. By drawing the respondent's attention to potential unfairness, this question does nevertheless depress principled considerations of legality and raises the salience of viewing the legal system as a vehicle for personal gain: 'if others are disobeying the law, I must as well'. Although this effect occurs in all three countries, it plays the strongest role in the society where elite lawlessness is the least widespread: Georgia. Russians and, to almost the same extent, Ukrainians are somewhat more inured to this aspect of their legal-political context. This pattern suggests that Georgians are less likely to expect the law to be subservient to political interests, giving them a more principled view of legality than Ukrainians and, especially, Russians, who see political manipulation of the law as more or less routine, and for whom the question evokes the possibility of reaping individual gains.

Following the thinking that a more strongly authoritarian setting will promote viewing the law as a vehicle for personal benefit, we also expect that Russians will hold the most permissive attitudes towards bureaucratic corruption, which implies breaking the law for personal gain. Ukrainians will appear in the middle, and Georgians will be most opposed to it. Our results show this to be the case. Opposition to corrupt behaviour in Russia is substantially below that in Georgia or Ukraine. So also is the percentage of Russians who prefer a corruption-free state: compared to almost three quarters of Russians surveyed, almost nine out of ten Georgian and Ukrainian citizens expressed that preference. Ukraine's modal score on opposition to corrupt behaviours is actually higher than Georgia's, even though Georgians score one step higher on the scale overall. Ukraine's higher level of opposition to corrupt behaviours primarily stems from elderly Ukrainians being sharply more anti-corruption than their younger fellow citizens. Georgians are more consistently hostile to corrupt behaviour across age groups. As we discuss in the next section, age differences are relevant to legal attitudes in Russia and Ukraine but not in Georgia.

With regard to differences in turning to the legal system for assistance addressing a dispute, Table 1 shows that this behaviour is much more frequent in Russia and Ukraine than in Georgia. As noted above, lower attitudinal respect for legality in an authoritarian context need not translate into lower usage of legal institutions. Supporting our expectation that citizens in rule-by-law societies are more apt to see legal institutions as only one possible resource to pursue their ends is how frequently Russians, in particular, and Ukrainians supplement their appeals to the legal system with the use of personal connections. Of Russians with a dispute who turned to the legal system, fully one third also reported seeking help from acquaintances with influence. That number for Ukrainians is about one fifth. In Georgia, though, only one out of eight reported seeking to use both tools. Among Russians and Ukrainians who skipped the legal route, the majority sought to use connections to help resolve the matter, while only 15% did so in Georgia.

Georgians used a third avenue for dispute resolution even more often than turning either to the legal system or to connected acquaintances. Fifty percent reported having sought assistance from a priest or other religious figure. One out of five who did seek help from the legal system turned to a priest as well. For those who did not turn to legal institutions, two thirds sought help from a priest. The corresponding figures for Russia and Ukraine are 27% and 32%. Georgians hold more traditional values than do Russians and Ukrainians.[15] Their level of religiosity is significantly higher: when asked whether they would obey the law or their religion if some legal provision contradicted their beliefs, 69% of our Georgian respondents chose their religion, in contrast to 19% of the Russians and 22% of the Ukrainians.

Responses to these three measures, then, support our argument that contemporary legal attitudes are shaped in important ways by citizens' ongoing judgments about the experiences they and others like them have had interacting with their country's legal and political institutions. Georgia, which leads the other two countries in its level of democracy, in the extent to which the rule of law prevails and in its success at reducing bureaucratic corruption, evinces the highest level of support for legality. Support for legality is lowest in Russia, where citizen–state interactions are most authoritarian. Pro-legal attitudes and behaviours in Ukraine come mid-way between the other two countries, reflecting that citizen–state relations are in some ways closer to those of Georgia and in other ways closer to those of Russia.

Individual-level patterns

The measures of nationwide central tendencies shown in Table 1 cannot clarify another important dimension of these countries' legal attitudes: the variation between citizens within each country. We turn now to an examination of how individuals' demographic characteristics, attitudes and experiences influence their respect for legality. We do this only for the first two measures in Table 1, those concerning attitudinal respect for legality. The individual factors we include in our model are of three types.

We incorporate basic demographic categories found to influence legal attitudes in comparative research: gender, education, age, family finances and religiosity. For Ukraine, we also include a variable to capture that country's continuing cultural divide between more Western-oriented and more Russian-oriented citizens. In Ukraine, respondents were given the option of answering either a Ukrainian or Russian version of the questionnaire. Although language is an important marker for ethnic and cultural differences, bilingualism is common in Ukraine, and answers to questions about fluency or language use were not necessarily reflected in the choice they made about taking the survey.

Our model also includes four individual political attitudes. The first concerns an individual's emphasis on the importance of fighting crime. This captures those who have a strong law-and-order orientation. Even though law-enforcement agencies are part of a country's legal system, strong concern about crime makes people more likely to endorse tough measures that disregard formal legal procedures. We thus expect those who prioritise stopping crime to less frequently express respect for legality. The second is a measure of attachment to democratic politics. It asks people whether they agree that

[15]On Inglehart and Welzel's scale of traditional/secular-rational values, which runs from -1 to $+1$, with lower scores indicating more traditional values, Russia and Ukraine score 0.5, while Georgia's score is -0.6 (Inglehart *et al.* 2014).

democratic freedoms are more important than strong leadership. Also included is the standard question testing interpersonal trust: whether the person believes that people generally can be trusted. The work of Uslaner (2008) and You (2018) has shown that interpersonal trust levels in a society influence and are influenced by the frequency of corruption and other forms of illegality. Trust should be particularly relevant to the question about respect for legality when it interferes with meeting an individual's needs. Respecting the law at personal cost requires accepting that others will also do their part to support legality. Those lacking interpersonal trust are less likely to believe others will do their part. The final attitudinal variable in the model is a question about the extent to which a respondent trusted their country's judiciary. Such trust, naturally, makes it easier to believe that legality is worthy of respect.

Finally, we look for relationships between legal attitudes and an individual's recent experiences. In particular, we expected interactions with state and judicial officials to be associated with an individual's views on the law. We included a variable distinguishing those who reported having given a bribe, gift or favour to an official over the preceding year from those who had not.[16] Also, for Russia and Ukraine, we include a variable distinguishing those who live in or adjacent to an area currently experiencing or recently having experienced military conflict.[17] All of Georgia would count as a conflict zone in this sense, so we could not employ it as a separate variable. Military conflicts increase out-migration, create chaos and detract resources from public infrastructure, all of which upset institutional stability (Bellows & Miguel 2006). Less stable conflict areas also have higher rates of corrupt engagement than other regions (Zaloznaya *et al.* 2018).

Table 2 presents multivariate analyses of respect for the law when it interferes with meeting an individual's needs. Because the measures of respect for legality have only four ordered possible responses, from 'strongly disagree' to 'strongly agree', we use ordinal logistic regression to estimate the relationships. In all cases, positive coefficients

[16]We took steps to encourage honesty in answering this question. All respondents were promised anonymity; interviewers were instructed to ensure that respondents had privacy; and the study was described as focusing on political and economic developments in the country. The questions on corruption were embedded in a series of questions focusing on the quality of interactions with bureaucratic officials. In addition, we included in the questionnaire a list experiment to test for respondents misreporting their actions (on list experiments, see, Blair & Imai 2012; Glynn 2013; Rosenfeld *et al.* 2016). This procedure involves randomly assigning respondents to one of two groups. Both groups are presented with a list of statements and asked to indicate how many of the statements they agree with, but not to indicate which ones. The first group's list has four items; the second group's has the same four plus the statement, 'Over the last year, I gave or accepted a bribe'. Because people are placed into the two groups randomly, the increase in the number of statements agreed with can be used to estimate how many respondents agreed with the bribery statement. Among both Russians and Georgians, the estimated experience with bribery was only slightly higher than the proportion indicating directly that they had given a bribe in the previous year: 17.6% compared to 14.7% in Russia, and 4.5% compared to 3.4% in Georgia. In Ukraine, the 22.5% who directly reported bribe-giving was actually higher than the experimental estimate of 10.5%.

[17]Four distinct conflicts have destabilised specific Russian and Ukrainian regions: ethnic and territorial disputes in Russia's North Caucasus region as well as two periods of active combat by Russia's own military; the 2008 Russian–Georgian conflict; Russia's annexation of the Crimean Peninsula in March 2014; and the military conflict with Russia-backed separatists in eastern Ukraine. Our survey included respondents from the following conflict-affected regions: in Russia, Dagestan, Krasnodar, Stavropol, Belgorod, Voronezh, Kursk, Rostov and Kabardino-Balkaria; and in Ukraine, Dnipropetrovsk, Donetsk, Zaporizka, Luhansk, Sumsk, Kharkiv and Kherson.

TABLE 2
MULTIVARIATE ANALYSES OF RESPECT FOR LEGALITY WHEN IT INTERFERES WITH MEETING NEEDS

	If law interferes with meeting individual needs					
	Georgia		*Russia*		*Ukraine*	
	1	*2*	*1*	*2*	*1*	*2*
Female	0.145	0.144	−0.030	−0.040	−0.010	0.008
	(0.128)	(0.128)	(0.105)	(0.105)	(0.134)	(0.134)
Complete higher education	0.078	0.068	0.275**	0.291***	0.339**	0.367**
	(0.147)	(0.148)	(0.110)	(0.112)	(0.141)	(0.142)
Age 30–55	0.145	–	−0.035	–	−0.184	–
	(0.173)		(0.127)		(0.195)	
56 and up	0.110	–	0.142	–	−0.078	–
	(0.186)		(0.151)		(0.201)	
Age by generation:						
1941–1950	–	−0.299	–	−0.723**	–	−0.050
		(0.310)		(0.313)		(0.259)
1951–1969	–	−0.410	–	−0.810***	–	0.055
		(0.262)		(0.272)		(0.234)
1970–1976	–	−0.136	–	−0.734**	–	−0.135
		(0.318)		(0.290)		(0.283)
1977–1987	–	−0.297	–	−0.743***	–	−0.202
		(0.280)		(0.279)		(0.255)
1988–	–	−0.453	–	−0.674**	–	0.150
		(0.293)		(0.285)		(0.290)
Financial situation	0.071	0.075	0.014	0.021	−0.033	−0.046
	(0.066)	(0.067)	(0.071)	(0.071)	(0.089)	(0.090)
Religious believer	0.038	0.047	0.141	0.129	0.209	0.196
	(0.291)	(0.292)	(0.120)	(0.120)	(0.166)	(0.167)
Language of questionnaire was Ukrainian	–	–	–	–	0.178	0.172
					(0.158)	(0.159)
Prioritises stopping crime	−0.283***	−0.282***	−0.264***	−0.270***	−0.353***	−0.358***
	(0.054)	(0.054)	(0.057)	(0.057)	(0.072)	(0.072)
Democratic freedoms outweigh need for strong leadership	−0.083	−0.087	−0.528***	−0.529***	−0.357***	−0.353***
	(0.055)	(0.055)	(0.057)	(0.057)	(0.066)	(0.067)
Most people can be trusted	−0.041	−0.033	0.218**	0.210*	−0.307**	−0.308**
	(0.280)	(0.281)	(0.108)	(0.108)	(0.130)	(0.130)
Trusts judiciary	0.108	0.110	0.141**	0.131**	0.132	0.132
	(0.068)	(0.069)	(0.063)	(0.063)	(0.089)	(0.089)
Lives in a conflict zone	–	–	0.026	0.028	−0.243	−0.250
			(0.134)	(0.134)	(0.167)	(0.167)
Gave a bribe, gift or favour to any official	−0.254	−0.228	−0.391**	−0.409***	−0.234	−0.231
	(0.369)	(0.369)	(0.141)	(0.141)	(0.143)	(0.143)
Chi-square:	36.78***	40.13***	144.99***	152.20***	87.14***	89.29***
Pseudo-R^2:	0.02	0.02	0.04	0.04	0.04	0.04
Valid *N*:	862	862	1,334	1,334	883	883

Notes: Estimation was done by ordinal logistic regression using Stata's ologit command. * Significant at <0.10; ** significant at <0.05; *** significant at <0.01.

indicate an association with stronger legal values and negative coefficients with weaker legal values. For each country, two models are presented, in order to allow us to examine age differences in two different ways. The first model incorporates dummy variables for middle-aged (age 30–55) and older (56 and above) respondents that contrast attitudes among those cohorts with younger (18–29) respondents. The second model replaces those with a series of dummy variables that follow the Soviet-era generations shown by Hendley (2017b, pp. 29–30) to produce meaningful differences in legal attitudes in Russia. Incorporating age in these different ways does not substantially alter any of the other results in the Table.

First, we note that few variables in this model explain the variation in Georgians' attitudes. The exception is that Georgians who are concerned with fighting crime express significantly less respect for legality. This variable has the same strong impact in all three countries, matching expectations from other analyses.

For Russia and Ukraine, more factors emerge as significant, and the models do a somewhat better job of explaining the patterns in each country. With a couple of noteworthy exceptions, our explanatory variables work the same way in both countries. Looking first at demographics, we find that they play a relatively small role when individual attitudes and experiences are taken into account. Both Russians and Ukrainians with higher education express more respect for legality than those without. Women are not significantly different from men in any of the countries. Neither a person's financial situation nor their religious beliefs (or lack thereof) had a significant impact.

Distinguishing age between young, middle-aged and older respondents—model 1 for each country—has no effect. The generational variables shown in model 2 for each country reach statistical significance only in Russia. This partly replicates Hendley's (2017b, pp. 29–30) finding; we nonetheless caution against treating age differences as important. The coefficients for the generations included in the model are contrasting that age group with those born prior to or in 1940. In our 2015 survey, that means respondents 75 years of age and older, a small group given the low life expectancy of Russians (and a small portion of those we label 'older' in model 1, only 4% of our sample). Our data reinforce Hendley's surprising finding that Russians socialised under Stalin are the most supportive of legality. Yet the coefficients for the generations shown are quite similar in their magnitude. This indicates that, while each of those cohorts differs significantly from the 75-plus cohort, they differ little from each other. Using the youngest generation as the omitted referent variable instead of the oldest confirms this small inter-generational difference. Even in Russia, then, neither place in the life cycle nor age *per se* has an important independent impact when controlling for the other factors.

We find additional similarities between Russia and Ukraine in the impact of attitudes and experiences. In these societies, as in Georgia and elsewhere, people who worry most about crime express lower respect for legality. In Russia, those with greater faith in the judiciary are more willing to comply with legal requirements, even at a personal cost. The same positive relationship holds in Ukraine, although somewhat less strongly and without reaching statistical significance in this model. The lack of statistical significance is partly due to the fact that only 11% of our respondents expressed trust in Ukraine's judiciary whereas a much higher level (52%) did so in Russia.

In all three countries, those who reported giving a bribe, gift or favour to a bureaucratic official over the preceding year expressed lower respect for legality. This effect is stronger and statistically significant only in Russia. As expected, having recently engaged in an extra-legal activity influences an individual's view of the legal system and the state. The negative coefficient supports the argument that engaging in corruption reinforces an understanding of the state and its legal system as based not on universal principles but particularistic ones. To the extent that this viewpoint is activated, it makes less sense to comply with formal law at a cost to meeting one's own needs.

The final variable that has a similar impact in both Russia and Ukraine is particularly intriguing. As we posited above, in an authoritarian, rule-by-law society, respect for legality might correlate negatively with support for democratic values. Our measure of support for democratic freedoms in Table 2 has a significantly negative impact in both Russia and Ukraine, most strongly in the former. That is, those expressing more support for democracy are likely to express less respect for legality. In Georgia, the least authoritarian polity, the relationship is small and does not reach statistical significance, indicating that pro-democracy Georgians tend to view legality neutrally or positively.

Two factors in this model influence Russian and Ukrainian views significantly but in different directions. Russians who indicated interpersonal trust in other citizens expressed greater respect for legality. This relationship fits with our expectation that interpersonal trust is necessary for an individual to accept the strictures of abiding by the law. The significant negative coefficient for Ukrainians is thus surprising and is related to the strong cultural divide across Ukrainian territory. Those living in the western areas of the country had significantly lower levels of interpersonal trust compared to other Ukrainians, and also tended to express greater respect for legality.

In Table 3, we present the results of running the same models on the other measure of respect for legality: the need to obey the law even if the authorities are not. Some of the patterns are the same as in Table 2; those that differ deserve note. Having higher education or not no longer distinguishes Russians and Ukrainians who express more respect for the law. To the extent that higher education in these countries cultivates a modern outlook on the law, as Table 2 suggests, the question invoking a scenario of elite advantage overshadows that effect. At the same time, a higher level of respect for the law among retirement-aged Russians and Ukrainians reaches significance. The fall-off in support from the previous question to this one (and shown in Table 1), occurs most strongly among working-age citizens. A final difference in the demographic influences between Tables 2 and 3 is that family financial situation has a strong positive effect in both Georgia and Ukraine. Those who were better off financially expressed greater willingness to obey the law even when elites did not.

In Ukraine, those who took the survey in Ukrainian rather than Russian were more inclined to support obeying the law even if elites did not. The relationship was also positive in Table 2, but it is more strongly and significantly so here. The Ukrainian speakers, concentrated in Ukraine's western regions, were less likely to abandon their respect for law given the prompt about elite advantages.

Of the attitudinal influences, it again turns out that concern about the need to stop crime has a strong and significant negative impact on respect for the law in all three countries. In Russia, the negative correlation between respect for the law and democratic values is

TABLE 3
MULTIVARIATE ANALYSES OF RESPECT FOR LEGALITY WHEN AUTHORITIES ARE NOT LAW-ABIDING

	If authorities do not obey the law					
	Georgia		*Russia*		*Ukraine*	
	1	*2*	*1*	*2*	*1*	*2*
Female	−0.024 (0.132)	−0.036 (0.132)	−0.019 (0.104)	−0.020 (0.104)	0.224* (0.132)	0.223* (0.133)
Complete higher education	0.134 (0.152)	0.169 (0.153)	0.126 (0.109)	0.131 (0.111)	0.206 (0.141)	0.195 (0.142)
Age 30–55	−0.114 (0.177)	–	0.182 (0.127)	–	−0.007 (0.190)	–
56 and up	−0.165 (0.190)	–	0.365** (0.149)	–	0.343* (0.195)	–
Age by generation:						
1941–1950	–	−0.448 (0.319)	–	−0.323 (0.312)	–	−0.195 (0.252)
1951–1969	–	−0.469* (0.266)	–	−0.344 (0.275)	–	−0.392* (0.230)
1970–1976	–	−0.445 (0.317)	–	−0.397 (0.296)	–	−0.481* (0.278)
1977–1987	–	−0.281 (0.283)	–	−0.462 (0.282)	–	−0.510** (0.251)
1988–	–	−0.134 (0.294)	–	−0.607** (0.289)	–	−0.494* (0.286)
Financial situation	0.242*** (0.068)	0.243*** (0.068)	−0.035 (0.071)	−0.039 (0.071)	0.251*** (0.087)	0.254*** (0.088)
Religious believer	−0.188 (0.303)	−0.177 (0.305)	−0.096 (0.119)	−0.096 (0.120)	−0.253 (0.163)	−0.249 (0.164)
Language of questionnaire was Ukrainian	–	–	–	–	0.543*** (0.158)	0.534*** (0.158)
Prioritises stopping crime	−0.146*** (0.054)	−0.139** (0.055)	−0.190*** (0.055)	−0.192*** (0.056)	−0.304*** (0.068)	−0.302*** (0.069)
Democratic freedoms outweigh need for strong leadership	0.012 (0.056)	0.008 (0.056)	−0.247*** (0.054)	−0.247*** (0.054)	0.060 (0.064)	0.054 (0.065)
Most people can be trusted	0.594** (0.266)	0.625** (0.267)	0.098 (0.108)	0.099 (0.108)	−0.050 (0.128)	−0.065 (0.129)
Trusts judiciary	0.124* (0.071)	0.137* (0.071)	0.113* (0.062)	0.112* (0.062)	0.222** (0.089)	0.214** (0.089)
Lives in a conflict zone	–	–	0.016 (0.134)	0.018 (0.134)	−0.174 (0.165)	−0.199 (0.166)
Gave a bribe, gift or favour to any official	−0.360 (0.406)	−0.333 (0.408)	−0.365** (0.142)	−0.371*** (0.142)	−0.211 (0.141)	−0.211 (0.142)
Chi-square:	40.12***	44.94***	56.62***	56.62***	67.96***	66.52***
Pseudo-R^2:	0.02	0.02	0.02	0.02	0.03	0.03
Valid *N*:	883	883	1,348	1,348	920	920

Notes: Estimation was done by ordinal logistic regression using Stata's ologit command. * Significant at <0.10; ** significant at <0.05; *** significant at <0.01.

again robust. That relationship no longer emerges in Ukraine, however. Interpersonal trust, which has no impact on Georgians' respect for the law, has a strong influence here: because the question suggests that elites disobey the law, it divided the Georgian respondents in a significant way. Those with lower interpersonal trust expressed less willingness to respect the law, while those with higher interpersonal trust, for whom the possibility of elites breaking the social compact was less compelling, expressed more willingness. Similarly, in all three countries, citizens with higher trust in the country's judiciary saw less need to evade the law even if the elite held legal advantages. As with the other measure, having been involved in a corrupt exchange in the past year lowered the level of expressed respect for the law, with the relationship being strongest in Russia.

Discussion

These findings highlight that a country's state-legal structures and political regime influence its citizens' legal attitudes. Kurkchiyan (2003, p. 26) is no doubt correct to point to 'the homogenizing impact of the Soviet period, with its single body of law, identical administrative structures and common indoctrination'.[18] Yet if the Soviet experience were still casting a heavy shadow on citizens' legal attitudes, the cross-national differences we find would be absent. The sole significant relationship shared across all three countries is that those more concerned about crime expressed lower respect for legality, and this relationship has been found in comparative work outside the postcommunist setting. The Soviet-era legacy is best seen as only one strand in explaining contemporary legal consciousness.

A much more important characteristic is the extent to which state bodies are democratically controlled and the legal system approximates rule-of-law ideals. Where democracy and the rule of law are strong, principled approaches to legality will be more prevalent. To the extent that a country's legal system operates to advantage officials of a state the citizens cannot control, then utilitarian approaches dominate. As Baekken (2019) describes, Russian elites have worked since 2000 to construct a highly centralised political regime, a key component of which is a legal system that can operate autonomously in routine matters while supporting the regime's efforts to prevent political challenges. In this context, utilitarian rather than principled views of the law are more prevalent in Russia than in the other two countries. By contrast, in Georgia, widespread public demands for reform in the early 2000s allowed a new administration to take strides in strengthening the rule of law, and principled legal views are most common there. Ukraine's postcommunist political and legal changes have been less clear-cut in either direction.[19] It makes sense, then, that Ukrainians' legal views and behaviour are in between those of Russian and Georgian citizens.

Obeying the law when it is framed in terms of the powerful abusing the system finds many fewer supporters and reverses the cross-national order. Here the order is Russia, Ukraine, Georgia. In the rule-by-law context of Russia, fewer citizens have faith in the principled

[18]On how the legacy of Soviet or varieties of communist rule influence postcommunist countries beyond the legal sphere, see *inter alia* Jowitt (1992), Hanson (1995), Munro (2006), Ishiyama (2015), Carter *et al.* (2016), Pop-Eleches and Tucker (2017).

[19]See, for example, Kuzio (2015).

position, so their willingness to obey the law is comparatively less affected by introducing the qualifier. Russians are also much more willing to condone corruption when interacting with officials, an important resource for those with little faith in the legal system. Russians in our study who had actually engaged in corruption over the preceding year expressed significantly lower levels of respect for legality, in both Tables 2 and 3.

Despite their more negative attitudes towards legality, Russians and Ukrainians make use of the legal system to help with a dispute at a substantially higher rate than Georgians. At the same time, they more frequently seek to use their personal connections to help them, often in tandem with pursuing a legal case. To varying extents, in each of the countries surveyed there are citizens who consider the law wholly or partially illegitimate and do not connect it to democratic principles, yet who regularly resort to it in their everyday lives.

Thus, scholars analysing legal attitudes must attend to the state-legal context of the countries under study. Doing so helps make sense of otherwise puzzling differences among our three post-Soviet countries and is even more vital for more diverse comparisons. Georgia, Russia and Ukraine are not at the extremes of this distinction globally. They differ sufficiently from each other, though, to help understand the differences in how their citizens assess and interact with the legal system. Grødeland and Miller (2015) reach the same conclusion—citizens' views of the law are importantly conditioned by how they assess their country's political-legal context—by comparing five European countries, one of which is Ukraine.

In addition, our findings suggest that legal attitudes can relate to other political and social orientations in surprising ways. We find that in the less democratic settings, respect for legality correlates not with higher support for democratic values but with lower. This holds for both Russia and Ukraine in Table 2 and for Russia alone in Table 3. In these countries, those who see stronger democracy as a priority are more likely to view laws and legal institutions as tools of autocracy and be less committed to following them. Widespread public support for legality or, more broadly, the rule of law, may indeed be a requisite for democratic development. In many societies, however, expressing support for legality is not necessarily connected to support for democracy or other Western or modern values. Scholars must measure the citizens' legal attitudes carefully and examine how those views flow from different experiences with political and legal institutions.

Conclusion

We have used data from nationally representative surveys to examine popular attitudes towards the law in Georgia, Russia and Ukraine and to compare across the three countries. Most studies of post-Soviet legal attitudes have drawn evidence from Russia alone. Incorporating data from two additional countries allows a comparative perspective and more reliable conclusions about the nature of the Soviet-era legacy in attitudes towards the law.

The divergent legal attitudes in these three countries show that prevalent Soviet-era outlooks have been retained or replaced to different degrees, as a function of the political and legal contexts that emerged after 1991. The extent to which citizens express respect or disregard for the law corresponds to how their country's legal system operates. Also, in all three countries, the way a question frames a citizen's relationship to the law influences the answers given. In every context surveyed here, many people who expressed support for legality when their own needs were at stake became more willing to evade the law when reminded of elites doing so. We also demonstrate that expressed respect for legality does not always correlate with support for democracy, one of the political attitudes often assumed to be held by those with respect for legality. Whether a country's most pro-democracy citizens more strongly support legality depends on whether the legal system is a fair and neutral arena or a tool of undemocratic political authorities.

Legal institutions are important elements of contemporary authoritarian and hybrid regimes. The roles these institutions play in democracies are valuable to the leaders of autocracies as well: keeping disputes away from overtly political channels, for instance. At the same time, autocratic legal systems must not allow outcomes that challenge the political leadership or its members' perquisites. Our findings indicate that the citizens of these countries do understand the extent to which their legal system is neutral, transparent and binds elites as well as non-elites to the law, and that they view the law and interact with legal institutions accordingly.

References

Alexeyev, S. (1991) *Law and Legal Culture in Soviet Society* (Moscow, Progress Publishers).

Aliyev, H. (2017) *When Informal Institutions Change: Institutional Reforms and Informal Practices in the Former Soviet Union* (Ann Arbor, MI, University of Michigan Press).

Andrianova, V. (2018) 'The Everyday Experiences of Russian Citizens in Justice of the Peace Courts', in Kurkchiyan, M. & Kubal, A. (eds).

Baekken, H. (2019) *Law and Power in Russia: Making Sense of Quasi-Legal Practices* (New York, NY, Routledge).

Baird, V. A. & Javeline, D. (2007) 'The Persuasive Power of Russian Courts', *Political Research Quarterly*, 60, 3.

Becquart-Leclercq, J. (1989) 'Paradoxes of Political Corruption: A French View', in Heidenheimer, A. J., LeVine, V. T. & Johnston, M. (eds) *Political Corruption: A Handbook* (New Brunswick, NJ, Transaction).

Bellows, J. & Miguel, E. (2006) 'War and Institutions: New Evidence from Sierra Leone', *American Economic Review*, 96, 2.

Berman, H. J. (1992) 'The Rule of Law and the Law-Based State (Rechtsstaat)', in Barry, D. D. (ed.) *Toward the 'Rule of Law' in Russia? Political and Legal Reform in the Transition Period* (Armonk, NY, M.E. Sharpe).

Blair, G. & Imai, K. (2012) 'Statistical Analysis of List Experiments', *Political Analysis*, 20, 1.

Carter, J., Bernhard, M. H. & Nordstrom, T. (2016) 'Communist Legacies and Democratic Survival in a Comparative Perspective: Liability or Advantage', *East European Politics and Societies*, 30, 4.

Coppedge, M., Gerring, J., Knutsen, C. H., Lindberg, S. I., Teorell, J., Altman, D., Bernhard, M., Fish, M. S., Glynn, A., Hicken, A., Lührmann, A., Marquardt, K. L., McMann, K., Paxton, P., Pemstein, D., Seim, B., Sigman, R., Skaaning, S.-E., Staton, J., Wilson, S., Cornell, A., Gastaldi, L., Gjerløw, H., Ilchenko, N., Krusell, J., Maxwell, L., Mechkova, V., Medzihorsky, J., Pernes, J., von Römer, J., Stepanova, N., Sundström, A., Tzelgov, E., Wang, Y.-T., Wig, T. & Ziblatt, D. (2019) *Varieties of Democracy* [Dataset], available at: https://doi.org/10.23696/vdemcy19, accessed 12 April 2019.

Di Franceisco, W. & Gitelman, Z. (1984) 'Soviet Political Culture and "Covert Participation" in Policy Implementation', *American Political Science Review*, 78, 3.

Eckstein, H. (1988) 'A Culturalist Theory of Political Change', *American Political Science Review*, 82, 3.

Ewick, P. & Silbey, S. S. (1998) *The Common Place of Law: Stories from Everyday Life* (Chicago, IL, University of Chicago Press).

Eysenck, M. W. & Keane, M. T. (2010) *Cognitive Psychology: A Student's Handbook* (6th edn) (New York, NY, Psychology Press).

Friedman, L. M. (1975) *The Legal System: A Social Science Perspective* (New York, NY, Russell Sage Foundation).

Gallagher, M. E. (2006) 'Mobilizing the Law in China: "Informed Disenchantment" and the Development of Legal Consciousness', *Law & Society Review*, 40, 4.

Gallagher, M. E. (2017) *Authoritarian Legality in China: Law, Workers, and the State* (New York, NY, Cambridge University Press).

Galligan, D. J. (2003) 'Legal Failure: Laws and Social Norms in Post-Communist Europe', in Galligan, D. J. & Kurkchiyan, M. (eds) *Law and Informal Practices: The Post-Communist Experience* (Oxford, Oxford University Press).

Gel'man, V. (2014) 'The Rise and Decline of Electoral Authoritarianism in Russia', *Demokratizatsiya: The Journal of Post-Soviet Democratization*, 22, 4.

Gerber, T. P. & Mendelson, S. E. (2008) 'Public Experiences of Police Violence and Corruption in Contemporary Russia: A Case of Predatory Policing?', *Law & Society Review*, 42, 1.

Gibson, J. L. (2003) 'Russian Attitudes Towards the Rule of Law: An Analysis of Survey Data', in Galligan, D. J. & Kurkchiyan, M. (eds) *Law and Informal Practices: The Post-Communist Experience* (Oxford, Oxford University Press).

Ginsburg, T. & Moustafa, T. (eds) (2008) *Rule by Law: The Politics of Courts in Authoritarian Regimes* (New York, NY, Cambridge University Press).

Glynn, A. N. (2013) 'What Can We Learn with Statistical Truth Serum? Design and Analysis of the List Experiment', *Public Opinion Quarterly*, 77, S1.

Godson, R., Kenney, D. J., Litvin, M. & Tevzadze, G. (2003) *Building Societal Support for the Rule of Law in Georgia* (Washington, DC, National Strategy Information Center).

Grimes, M. (2006) 'Organizing Consent: The Role of Procedural Fairness in Political Trust and Compliance', *European Journal of Political Research*, 45, 2.

Grødeland, A. B. & Miller, W. L. (2015) *European Legal Cultures in Transition* (New York, NY, Cambridge University Press).

Hanson, S. E. (1995) 'The Leninist Legacy and Institutional Change', *Comparative Political Studies*, 28, 2.

Hendley, K. (2012a) 'The Puzzling Non-Consequences of Societal Distrust of Courts: Explaining the Use of Russian Courts', *Cornell International Law Journal*, 45, 3.

Hendley, K. (2012b) 'Who Are the Legal Nihilists in Russia?', *Post-Soviet Affairs*, 28, 2.

Hendley, K. (2017a) 'Contempt for Court in Russia: The Impact of Litigation Experience', *Review of Central and East European Law*, 42, 2–3.

Hendley, K. (2017b) *Everyday Law in Russia* (Ithaca, NY, Cornell University Press).

Hendley, K. (2018) 'To Go to Court or Not? The Evolution of Disputes in Russia', in Kurkchiyan, M. & Kubal, A. (eds).

Hertogh, M. & Kurkchiyan, M. (2016) '"When Politics Comes Into Play, Law is no Longer Law": Images of Collective Legal Consciousness in the UK, Poland and Bulgaria', *International Journal of Law in Context*, 12, 4.

Huskey, E. (1991) 'A Framework for the Analysis of Soviet Law', *Russian Review*, 50, 1.

Huskey, E. (1992) 'From Legal Nihilism to Pravovoe Gosudarstvo', in Barry, D. D. (ed.) *Toward the 'Rule of Law' in Russia?* (Armonk, NY, M.E. Sharpe).

IBRD (2012) *Fighting Corruption in Public Services: Chronicling Georgia's Reforms*, International Bank for Reconstruction and Development (Washington, DC, World Bank).

Inglehart, R., Haerpfer, C., Moreno, A., Welzel, C., Kizilova, K., Diez-Medrano, J., Lagos, M., Norris, P., Ponarin, E. & Puranen, B. (2014) *World Values Survey: Round Six—Country-Pooled Datafile*

[Dataset], available at: http://www.worldvaluessurvey.org/WVSDocumentationWV6.jsp, accessed 12 March 2019.

Ishiyama, J. T. (2015) 'Regime Legacies and Governance in Post-Communist States', *Taiwan Journal of Democracy*, 11, 2.

Jackson, J., Bradford, B., Hough, M., Myhill, A., Quinton, P. & Tyler, T. R. (2012) 'Why do People Comply with the Law?: Legitimacy and the Influence of Legal Institutions', *British Journal of Criminology*, 52, 6.

Jowitt, K. (1992) *New World Disorder: The Leninist Extinction* (Berkeley, CA, University of California Press).

Kaufmann, D. & Kraay, A. (2016) *World Governance Indicators* [Dataset], available at: http://info.worldbank.org/governance/wgi/index.aspx, accessed 10 July 2016.

Key, V. O. (1949) *Southern Politics in State and Nation* (New York, NY, A. A. Knopf).

Kozyreva, P. M. (2008) 'Pravovoe Soznanie i doverie', *POLIS: Politicheskie Issledovaniya*, 4.

Krygier, M. (2012) 'Rule of Law', in Rosenfeld, M. & Sajo, A. (eds) *The Oxford Handbook of Comparative Constitutional Law* (New York, NY, Oxford University Press).

Kurkchiyan, M. (2003) 'The Illegitimacy of Law in Post-Soviet Societies', in Galligan, D. J. & Kurkchiyan, M. (eds) *Law and Informal Practices: The Post-Communist Experience* (Oxford, Oxford University Press).

Kurkchiyan, M. (2011) 'Perceptions of Law and Social Order: A Cross-National Comparison of Collective Legal Consciousness', *Wisconsin International Law Journal*, 29, 2.

Kurkchiyan, M. & Kubal, A. (eds) (2018) *A Sociology of Justice in Russia* (New York, NY, Cambridge University Press).

Kuzio, T. (2015) 'Ukraine: Leaving the Crossroads', in Wolchik, S. L. & Curry, J. L. (eds) *Central and East European Politics: From Communism to Democracy* (3rd edn) (Lanham, MD, Rowman & Littlefield).

Lei, Y.-W. & Zhou, D. X. (2015) 'Contesting Legality in Authoritarian Contexts: Food Safety, Rule of Law and China's Networked Public Sphere', *Law and Society Review*, 49, 3.

Levitsky, S. & Way, L. (2010) *Competitive Authoritarianism: Hybrid Regimes After the Cold War* (New York, NY, Cambridge University Press).

Lodge, M. & Taber, C. S. (2013) *The Rationalizing Voter* (New York, NY, Cambridge University Press).

McCarthy, L. A. (2014) 'Local-Level Law Enforcement: Muscovites and Their Uchastkovyy', *Post-Soviet Affairs*, 30, 2–3.

Merry, S. E. (1990) *Getting Justice and Getting Even: Legal Consciousness Among Working-Class Americans* (Chicago, IL, University of Chicago Press).

Merry, S. E. (2010) 'What is Legal Culture—an Anthropological Perspective', *Journal of Comparative Law*, 5, 2.

Moustafa, T. (2007) 'Mobilising the Law in an Authoritarian State: The Legal Complex in Contemporary Egypt', in Halliday, T. C., Karpik, L. & Feeley, M. M. (eds) *Fighting for Political Freedom: Comparative Studies of the Legal Complex and Political Liberalism* (Portland, OR, Hart).

Munro, N. (2006) 'Russia's Persistent Communist Legacy: Nostalgia, Reaction, and Reactionary Expectations', *Post-Soviet Affairs*, 22, 4.

Nelken, D. (1997) *Comparing Legal Cultures* (Aldershot, Dartmouth).

Nelken, D. (2010) 'Using Legal Culture: Purposes and Problems', *Journal of Comparative Law*, 5, 2.

Nielsen, L. B. (2000) 'Situating Legal Consciousness: Experiences and Attitudes of Ordinary Citizens About Law and Street Harassment', *Law & Society Review*, 34, 4.

Nye, J. S. (1967) 'Corruption and Political Development: A Cost–Benefit Analysis', *American Political Science Review*, 61, 2.

Nyhan, B. & Reifler, J. (2010) 'When Corrections Fail: The Persistence of Political Misperceptions', *Political Behavior*, 32, 2.

Pop-Eleches, G. & Tucker, J. (2017) *Communism's Shadow: Historical Legacies and Contemporary Political Attitudes* (Princeton, NJ, Princeton University Press).

Quigley, J. (1990) 'The Soviet Union as a State Under the Rule of Law: An Overview', *Cornell International Law Journal*, 23, 2.

Rajah, J. (2012) *Authoritarian Rule of Law: Legislation, Discourse, and Legitimacy in Singapore* (New York, NY, Cambridge University Press).

Redlawsk, D. P. (2002) 'Hot Cognition or Cool Consideration? Testing the Effects of Motivated Reasoning on Political Decision Making', *Journal of Politics*, 64, 4.

Reisinger, W. M., Hesli Claypool, V. L. & Zaloznaya, M. (2015) *Surveys on Political Causes and Consequences of Bureaucratic Corruption in the Post-Soviet Region* (Iowa City, IA, University of Iowa).

Reisinger, W. M., Miller, A. H. & Hesli, V. L. (1997) 'Russians and the Legal System: Mass Views and Behavior in the 1990s', *Journal of Communist Studies and Transition Politics*, 13, 3.

Rosenfeld, B., Imai, K. & Shapiro, J. N. (2016) 'An Empirical Validation Study of Popular Survey Methodologies for Sensitive Questions', *American Journal of Political Science*, 60, 3.

Sakwa, R. (2000) 'Russia: From a Corrupt System to a System with Corruption', in William, R. (ed.) *Party Finance and Political Corruption* (New York, NY, St. Martin's Press).
Scott, J. C. (1969) 'Corruption, Machine Politics, and Political Change', *American Political Science Review*, 63, 4.
Shapiro, I. (1994) *The Rule of Law* (New York, NY, New York University Press).
Shapiro, M. (1981) *Courts: A Comparative and Political Analysis* (Chicago, IL, University of Chicago Press).
Sharlet, R. (1990) 'Soviet Legal Reform in Historical Context', *Columbia Journal of Transnational Law*, 28.
Silbey, S. S. (2005) 'After Legal Consciousness', *Annual Review of Law and Social Science*, 1.
Taber, C. S. & Young, E. (2013) 'Political Information Processing', in Huddy, L., Sears, D. O. & Levy, J. S. (eds) *The Oxford Handbook of Political Psychology* (2nd edn) (New York, NY, Oxford University Press).
Trinkner, R. & Cohn, E. (2014) 'Putting the "Social" Back in Legal Socialization: Procedural Justice, Legitimacy, and Cynicism in Legal and Nonlegal Authorities', *Law and Human Behavior*, 38, 6.
Trochev, A. (2012) 'Suing Russia at Home', *Problems of Post-Communism*, 59, 5.
Tyler, T. R. (1990) *Why People Obey the Law* (New Haven, CT, Yale University Press).
Tyler, T. R. (2006) 'Psychological Perspectives on Legitimacy and Legitimation', *Annual Review of Psychology*, 57.
Tyler, T. R. & Huo, Y. J. (2002) *Trust in the Law: Encouraging Public Cooperation with the Police and Courts* (New York, NY, Russell Sage Foundation).
Tyler, T. R. & Jackson, J. (2014) 'Popular Legitimacy and the Exercise of Legal Authority: Motivating Compliance, Cooperation, and Engagement', *Psychology, Public Policy, and Law*, 20, 1.
Uslaner, E. M. (2008) *Corruption, Inequality, and the Rule of Law: The Bulging Pocket Makes Life Easy* (New York, NY, Cambridge University Press).
Von Benda-Beckmann, F. & Von Benda-Beckmann, K. (2010) 'Why Not Legal Culture?', *Journal of Comparative Law*, 5, 2.
World Justice Project (2018) *Rule of Law Index* 2019 (Washington, DC, World Justice Project), available at: https://worldjusticeproject.org/sites/default/files/documents/ROLI-2019-Reduced.pdf, accessed 5 August 2020.
Wortman, R. S. (1976) *The Development of a Russian Legal Consciousness* (Chicago, IL, University of Chicago Press).
You, J.-S. (2018) 'Trust and Corruption', in Uslaner, E. M. (ed.) *The Oxford Handbook of Social and Political Trust* (New York, NY, Oxford University Press).
Zaller, J. & Feldman, S. (1992) 'A Simple Theory of the Survey Response: Answering Questions Versus Revealing Preferences', *American Journal of Political Science*, 36, 3.
Zaloznaya, M., Hesli Claypool, V. L. & Reisinger, W. M. (2018) 'Pathways to Corruption: Institutional Context and Citizen Participation in Bureaucratic Corruption', *Social Forces*, 96, 4.
Zywicki, T. J. (2003) 'The Rule of Law, Freedom, and Prosperity', *Supreme Court Economic Review*, 10.

Appendix Wording of questions used in measures

Legal attitudes.

- If a law interferes with citizens' ability to resolve their problems, then it is sometimes okay not to observe that law: absolutely agree (1), somewhat agree (2), somewhat disagree (3) or absolutely disagree (4).
- It makes no sense to obey the laws when the authorities are not doing so: absolutely agree (1), somewhat agree (2), somewhat disagree (3) or absolutely disagree (4).
- If you wanted to receive a faster or higher quality service from any of the aforementioned officials, to what extent do you think it is acceptable to do any of the following as an incentive: always (1), sometimes (2) or never (3)?
  - Give money, 1–3
  - Give a gift, 1–3

- Do a favour, 1–3
- Use connections, 1–3

The index variable 'Anti-Corruption Views' can range from one to three, with three indicating all four activities are seen as never permissible; a score of one means the respondent sees all four as always permissible.

- Would you prefer a system where officials never accept bribes, presents or favours and never give special treatment in return, or sometimes accept bribes, presents or favours and in return give people special treatment? Our measure is the percent selecting the former alternative, with no bribe-taking officials.
- People often turn to others for help in resolving serious disputes. For each item I read, please tell me if during the past year you have taken this action to help resolve such a dispute.
  - Contacted a lawyer, legal consultancy or legal defence organisation.
  - Discussed the problem with a deputy or their office.
  - Turned to police, a court or other law-enforcement agency.
  - Discussed the problem with a spiritual/religious mentor.
  - Turned to someone with connections.
  - Sought help from an NGO.

Respondents were coded as turning to the legal system if they selected the first or third option.

Financial situation.

- Which of the following statements most closely corresponds to the financial situation of your family?
  - We do not have enough money, even for food.
  - We have enough money for food, but it is difficult to buy clothes.
  - We have enough money for food and clothes, and we can save something, but not enough to buy expensive things (such as a TV or refrigerator).
  - We can afford to buy some expensive things (such as a TV or refrigerator).
  - We can afford anything we want.

Prioritises stopping crime.
Absolutely agree, somewhat agree, somewhat disagree or absolutely disagree:

- It is very important to stop crime, even if it means violating the rights of the accused.

Democratic freedoms vs leadership.
Absolutely agree, somewhat agree, somewhat disagree or absolutely disagree:

- Democratic freedoms are more important than strong leadership for [country] right now.

Interpersonal trust.

- Speaking generally, do you think that most people can be trusted, or that one needs to be careful in dealings with other people?

Trust in judiciary.

- Please tell me, how much do you trust the judicial powers in [country]: you trust them fully, you trust them mostly, you mostly don't trust them or you don't trust them at all?

Corruption engagement.

- Now I want to talk to you about different types of officials that you receive services from in the course of your daily life. On this card are listed various categories of such officials. Over the last 12 months, have you had any contact with any of these officials?
  - Officials of the judicial system (judges, clerks, justice department officials, attorneys prosecutors and other officials).
  - Doctors, nurses, medical workers or hospital administrators.
  - Inspectors (in health, construction, food quality, sanitary control and licensing).
  - Officials issuing certificates and permits (marriage/death/birth certificates; construction permits).
  - Officials in housing and communal services.
  - Officials who issue governmental tenders.
  - Politicians at the local level (mayors, local executive heads/heads of *raiony*).
  - Professors/instructors in higher educational institutions.
  - Police officers.
  - Tax officials.
  - Teachers and school administrators.
  - Traffic police.
  - Other ____________
- Now, please tell me, of the officials with whom you had contact, which ones, if any, asked you for a bribe (extra money), a present or a favour in exchange for their services?
- Some people say that offering officials additional incentives is the only way to get decent services in contemporary [country]. To which of these officials did you give a bribe (extra money), a present or do a favour in exchange for a service?

Transcending Illegality in Kyrgyzstan: The Case of a Squatter Settlement in Bishkek

ELIZA ISABAEVA

Abstract

Governments are reluctant to acknowledge illegal settlements. Ak Jar is an illegal settlement on the outskirts of Bishkek. If the settlement were formally legalised, its residents would receive property documents as well as recognition and inclusion. They have thus developed strategies to achieve the legalisation of Ak Jar. Although the settlement is technically illegal, by behaving 'legally' (that is, following legal norms and practices), the residents and community leaders generate the appearance and even some of the effects of legality (such as, legitimate power supply, recognition by politicians). This creates a halfway space between 'legal' and 'illegal' that moves the settlement away from 'full' illegality and closer to legalisation.

EMPIRICAL STUDIES SHOW THAT THE LINE BETWEEN LEGAL and illegal activities in everyday life can be ambiguous and blurred (Heyman & Smart 1999; Van Gelder 2010; Botoeva 2019). Therefore, any sharp distinction between 'authorised' and 'non-authorised' appears to be overly simplistic. To unveil the complexity around this dichotomy, scholars suggest studying the involvement of state agencies and authorities in so-called illegal activities (Heyman & Smart 1999; Azuela & Meneses-Reyes 2014; Polese *et al.* 2019). With regard to research in urban settings, we are often confronted with the legal–illegal dichotomy in informal settlements because the inhabitants are perceived as having broken formal state laws (Al Sayyad 1993; Fernandes & Varley 1998; Fernandes 2011). For example, some illegal settlements may have been formed through the practice of squatting or they might be located on hazardous grounds unsuitable for residential use or the dwellers might have ignored building regulations by relevant state agencies.

Needless to say, in the context of state-defined illegality, legalisation—a 'process by which extra-legal tenure is integrated into the national legal system' (Ubink *et al.* 2009, p. 12)—becomes an important issue. Security of tenure is believed to encourage people to invest in their housing and in the infrastructure of their settlements (Ubink *et al.* 2009, p. 7).

The author wishes to thank the Humer Foundation for Academic Talent for PhD funding. The author would also like to thank Erica Marat, Lauren McCarthy, Peter Finke, Melissa Burn, Ulrich Brandenburg, Madeleine Reeves, Aida Alymbaeva, Yasmine Berriane, and the participants of the working group 'Forschungswerkstatt' for their invaluable input and constructive comments. Research for this essay was conducted when the author was a PhD candidate at the doctoral programme URPP Asia & Europe, University of Zurich, 2011–2014.

However, this hypothesis can be challenged when we consider the viewpoint that 'informal neighborhoods in cities throughout the developing world have been found to enjoy reasonable degrees of (*de facto*) security of tenure' (Van Gelder 2010, p. 240). Thus, Van Gelder advocates going beyond the legal–illegal dichotomy and paying attention to various strategies by which the illegal becomes legal (Van Gelder 2010, p. 243). Such a shift in status tells us about the fluid nature of law, which is a dynamic process of negotiation between authorities and the subjects of the law rather than something static imposed by the state (Hatcher 2015; Polese *et al.* 2019). On the contrary, the law is actively constructed, imbued with meaning and shaped by social relations (Varley 2002; Blomley 2003).

It is in the context of such legal fluidity that I analyse empirical data on the illegal settlement Ak Jar, located on the outskirts of Kyrgyzstan's capital city Bishkek. Ak Jar emerged as a result of squatting and consequently came to be identified as illegal by the state agencies. Correspondingly, Ak Jar dwellers have also been viewed and treated as law breakers by the state and the wider public alike. Enduring the hardship of state neglect of their settlement for many years, the dwellers have gradually developed a number of strategies to achieve formal legalisation, obtain property documents, and include themselves and Ak Jar in official state structures. As an unacknowledged settlement on public land that has been deemed unsuitable for housing construction, Ak Jar has 'fundamental problems of illegality' (Fernandes 2011, p. 5). As Azuela and Meneses-Reyes also show for Mexico City, definitions of illegality are not straightforward but emerge out of social interactions in a particular social context (Azuela & Meneses-Reyes 2014, p. 176). As a result, we can only understand the lines between 'formal and informal, public and private, legal and illegal, acceptable and unacceptable' by observing how they come into play in different localities (Polese *et al.* 2019, p. 4).

In this essay, I will discuss negotiations and strategies implemented by Ak Jar's community leaders to transcend illegality and achieve formal legalisation. To do so, I build on Van Gelder's (2010) insight that the legal–illegal dichotomy lacks nuance and that we need to dig deeper to reveal what lies behind that dichotomy. I further adopt a relational perspective on informal space, focusing not on territory *per se* but on the dynamic interactions within the Ak Jar community itself and between Ak Jar residents and external stakeholders (Braverman *et al.* 2014, pp. 17–8). In the following, I first address the conditions that led to the emergence of Ak Jar and subsequent public reactions to squatting. Afterwards, I introduce Ak Jar as a place where different claims to property or usage rights have clashed. The main part of the essay is dedicated to Ak Jar dwellers' strategies and negotiations with state authorities. Here, I address the informal administration and mechanisms of discipline in Ak Jar, the strategies that were employed to make public demands and, finally, the blurring of Ak Jar's illegal status as part of the process of moving towards formal legalisation. The essay is based on extensive anthropological research in Ak Jar during January–August 2012 by means of approximately 50 semi-structured interviews, informal talks, expert interviews and participant observation. I returned to Ak Jar twice for a month-long follow-up research in January and July 2013. I closely observed the work of Ak Jar's community leaders and accompanied them to various meetings with state officials and agencies and participated in community meetings.

The conditions for squatting and public reactions to it

Ak Jar popped up on a previously uninhabited vast area on the northern edge of Bishkek after the Tulip Revolution and the ensuing change of political regime in March 2005. Although pre-revolutionary unrest had been happening in other parts of the country for a while (Bukasheva 2005), it peaked on 24 March in Bishkek when the angry masses stormed into the presidential palace ('White House') and President Askar Akaev fled the country. The events of 24 March created a political vacuum that fostered a chaotic situation of illegal activities such as looting and land squatting. It took several days for the interim government to appoint Kurmanbek Bakiev as acting president. During that time, a new wave of squatters established themselves as residents in Ak Jar.

In Ak Jar, the residents refer to these first squatters as *top bashylar* (pl. of *top bashy*), a term that translates as 'head(s) of a group'. When I asked residents during interviews how they obtained a land plot or a house in the settlement, many said they had bought from *top bashylar*. According to my informants, *top bashylar* were a group of people formed from the top, that is, people with links to politicians and other state officials. The state authorities had allegedly given *top bashylar* information about which land plots were 'vacant' in the city or adjacent areas. Since *top bashylar* were linked to powerful authorities, they were not prevented from squatting and could escape legal punishment. In the beginning, there were 28 *top bashylar* who came to the empty territory of today's Ak Jar. Without consulting relevant state agencies, they measured out plots which varied in size, from 0.04 to 0.06 hectares, and allocated them first to themselves and their immediate family members for free, then to other relatives, fellow villagers and friends for a relatively cheap price. Any remaining plots were sold to people who approached them for a piece of land.

Unauthorised squatting was a consequence of an inadequate supply of public and affordable housing for rent or purchase in the context of rising internal migration to Bishkek. Most of the Soviet-era public housing in the city had been privatised by 2005. Incoming migrants who could not afford to buy private housing of their own lived as tenants in 'small, poorly furnished rooms … struggling to pay exorbitant rent' (Sanghera & Satybaldieva 2012, p. 102). Because there was no culture of regulated private renting, home ownership was seen as the only way to live securely and decently. Other factors that made squatting an attractive option were the fragile rural economy and the limited capacity of the state to enforce laws (Sanghera *et al.* 2011).

Squatting on Bishkek's peripheral lands continued beyond the immediate chaos of regime change, producing a number of settlements on the city fringes. The state authorities and security forces under new interim president Bakiev did little to stop the mass squatting. Some public figures indicated that state agencies and officials were involved in the squatting by either giving information on where to squat and how to proceed afterwards, or simply turning a blind eye to squatting (Avdeeva 2005; Soltoeva 2005). Others highlighted Bakiev's attempts to stabilise the tense situation around housing, referencing his inaugural speech in summer 2005 when he promised to resolve people's social needs.[1] Nevertheless, there were loud critical voices from both ordinary Bishkek residents and

[1]'Sostoyalas' inauguratsiya prezidenta Kyrgyzstana Kurmanbeka Bakieva', *Radio Azattyk*, 14 August 2005, available at: https://rus.azattyk.org/a/2429372.html, accessed 26 November 2020.

prominent politicians who condemned land squatting. They emphasised the illegality (Russian: *nezakonnost'*) of squatting practices and the need to uphold the law above all else (Fedorova 2005; Sorokina 2005). Moreover, they noted that squatting was largely a well-organised action. For instance, the leader of the political party *Ar-Namys* (Dignity), Felix Kulov, referred to the squatters as counterrevolutionary forces who sought to enrich themselves by grabbing the property of others (Panfilova 2005). Another political leader, Kubatbek Baibolov, called for the prosecution and punishment of squatting organisers (Maratova 2005). Then Minister of Foreign Affairs Rosa Otunbaeva had a similarly critical opinion of squatters, identifying people among them who already owned property in Bishkek or elsewhere and thus were not in desperate need of housing (Panfilova 2005). In the same manner, the leader of the NGO 'Civil Society against Corruption' (Russian: *Grazhdanskoe obschestvo protiv korruptsii*) Tolekan Ismailova categorised several groups of people who had squatted on land in Bishkek: local residents who lived together with adult children, requiring a house of their own; internal migrants who lived and worked in Bishkek but did not have their own property; residents of Bishkek's adjacent regions who had housing but needed extra housing for their adult children; residents of different Kyrgyz provinces who did not have access to their own homes in the capital city (Maratova 2005; Panfilova 2005).

When mass land squatting occurred in the outskirts of Bishkek, the city authorities admitted publicly that they were unable to stop it. A representative of the city council, Nurzhamal Baibolova, stated:

> Illegal land squatting is a problem not only for the leadership in Bishkek but also for the entire government. As opposed to the government, the city authorities do not have the power to influence the law-breakers. According to the master plan of the city, the land that has been squatted is designated for another type of construction. For instance, a construction of multistorey high-rise building has been planned. Thus, the construction of individual houses is not justified. (Maratova 2005)

Bishkek's long-term residents also made themselves heard in the popular daily newspaper *Vechernii Bishkek*. Throughout 2005, *Vechernii Bishkek* frequently published complaints by both regular residents and public figures. For example, on 19 April 2005, the newspaper featured the opinions of two prominent Kyrgyzstani figures in an article titled 'Aksakaly perezhivayut za stolitsu' ('Respected elders worried about the capital city') (Fedorova 2005). The first, Kuluipa Konduchalova, a former politician and culture minister, was quoted as saying that the city needed to grow, but not in the form of primitive shacks. The second, Mirsaid Mirrakhimov, a widely respected doctor, pointed out that the authorities should first and foremost adhere to the regulations in the 'Declaration of City Development', a public document defining future development goals for Bishkek (Fedorova 2005). With their statements, both Konduchalova and Mirrakhimov demonstrated their position against squatters and squatting, thereby hoping to sway public opinion against illegal settlers.

According to another article published by *Vechernii Bishkek* on 5 July 2005, ordinary Bishkek residents were reportedly worried that land squatting was causing chaos in the city because the squatters occupied land plots without permission to do so. The residents requested that the city authorities protect the interests of the city so that its residents could live a 'normal' life, and thus called on the authorities to punish self-styled leaders of the squatter settlements (Sorokina 2005). In November 2005, 234 Bishkek residents of diverse backgrounds (teachers, doctors, pensioners) wrote an open letter to the public titled *Zakon—dlya vsekh* (Law—For All), which was published in *Vechernii Bishkek*:

> We feel deeply outraged by the illegal demands of squatters who have grabbed city lands. Why turning the capital city into a big village?[2] We, the residents of Bishkek, have been tolerant. Many Bishkek residents do not have comfortable housing of their own either. Some of us live together with relatives because we cannot afford to buy a separate property. Others rent accommodation but we do not organise pickets and demonstrations in front of the parliament or the city hall. We call on the authorities to not solve the housing problems of recent migrants at the expense of city lands. We ask the authorities to punish those who organise squatting and systematically destabilise the situation to the full extent of the law.[3]

In opposition to such outspoken criticism of illegal settlements from ordinary Bishkek residents, a number of journalists, NGO activists and scholars addressed issues that had a direct impact on the everyday life of the population in illegal settlements. For instance, NGOs Arysh (Godwill), the Children's Protection Centre (Russian: *Tsentr Zashity Detei*) and the Red Cross (Russian: *Krasnyi Krest*) focused on practical ways to assist residents: arranging meetings between state authorities and settlement residents, helping them to enrol their children in city schools, and teaching residents about family planning and reproductive health. Journalists, in their turn, reported widely in the media about the existence of these settlements and the hardships faced by the people living there (Akaev 2010; Shambetov 2015; Ivashenko 2016). The Kyrgyzstani scholarly community also made its contribution by unravelling common misperceptions about illegal settlements. For example, Nasritdinov and his colleagues (2015) deconstructed several myths about the number of illegal settlements in Bishkek, the people who inhabit these settlements, and the burden they present to the city of Bishkek, contradicting the alarming pictures created by the media about illegal settlements in Bishkek. Similarly, Cramer (2018) argued against the negative perception of illegal settlements as a site of criminality and chaos by introducing the concept of *yntymak* (Kyrgyz: unity) as a vital force of organising everyday life as well as politics. Balihar Sanghera (2010a, 2010b) reviewed squatting from the perspective of the illegal residents, specifically, from the position of their moral reasoning. He lists five justifications offered by the settlement population, ranging from their moral right to basic goods and land to their views on the property-owning class and the looting of national assets by the elites in post-revolutionary Kyrgyzstan.

Various pro and contra opinions notwithstanding, Ak Jar was not demolished. At the time of writing, it remains tolerated by the authorities, if not the locals, and the first steps towards

[2]In the understanding of people, there was a sharp distinction between urban and rural settings whereby the former was a place of prosperity and modernity, and the latter—a place of destitution.

[3]'Zakon—dlya vsekh!', *Vechernii Bishkek*, 8 November 2005, available at: https://vecherka.kg/2005/11/08/actualno/3.html, accessed 26 November2020.

its formal legalisation (that is, delivery of drinking water and electricity, raising funds to finance architects who would prepare the master plan) have been taken.

Contested claims to property

Ak Jar is located to the north of Bishkek, just outside official city borders. The settlement is thus part not of the city of Bishkek but is located in Chui *Oblast'*. Neither the administration of Chui *Oblast'* nor Bishkek City, however, were keen on having the settlement as their administrative entity after it developed in the aftermath of the Tulip Revolution. The administration of Chui *Oblast'* justified its reluctance to accept Ak Jar by citing a lack of finances for newly emerging settlements.[4] Furthermore, Ak Jar developed on formerly agricultural land without prior infrastructure, adjacent to Bishkek and distant from other villages and settlements in Chui *Oblast'*. Therefore, the *oblast'* authorities argued that the construction of infrastructural facilities—electricity, water, roads—serving Ak Jar would create an unacceptable burden on the province's administration.[5]

In response to the position of Chui *Oblast*', the Bishkek administration also disavowed responsibility for Ak Jar, arguing that the settlement's territory lay beyond the city's official borders and administrative control. When residents approached state officials to determine in which administrative unit Ak Jar was located so that they could discuss the process of legalisation, they felt as if they were being kicked back and forth.[6] Consequently, Ak Jar has remained in an ambiguous situation, acknowledged neither by Chui *Oblast'* nor by the city of Bishkek.

Meanwhile the settlement has grown bigger. The first residents recall a few scattered houses in the early days of the settlement in the spring of 2005; however, during my research in Ak Jar in 2012–2013, the population numbers cited by Ak Jar's community leader Kuban[7] were over 7,200 households. Geographically, Ak Jar resembles a US city because its central street is 1.8 km long and crossed by 40 streets that branch out on both sides (see Figure 1).

Before the emergence of Ak Jar in the spring of 2005, its vast and empty territory was leased by a member of the Kyrgyz Parliament, Aslanbek Maliev (Mitenko 2011). Maliev had long wanted to build a large market complex on the territory.[8] However, when Ak Jar was squatted, Maliev started a legal case to have the land returned to him. The case first went to the regional court, then to the *oblast'* court. Maliev lost both court cases. The courts ruled the case in favour of Ak Jar residents, even though the settlement was illegal (Mitenko 2011). According to Ak Jar residents, the court ruling was based on Maliev's failure to pay land tax for leasing the land plot. There is, however, a tacit understanding among Ak Jar dwellers that the state authorities at that time were cautious not to make ordinary—often economically deprived—people angry.[9] On the basis of these court

[4]Interview with Kuban, Ak Jar's community leader, Ak Jar settlement, Bishkek, 17 February 2012.
[5]Interview with Kuban, Ak Jar's community leader, Ak Jar settlement, Bishkek, 17 February 2012.
[6]Interview with Kuban, Ak Jar's community leader, Ak Jar settlement, Bishkek, 17 February 2012.
[7]For reasons of confidentiality, all the names of Ak Jar residents have been anonymised. The names of public figures remain real unless anonymity was explicitly requested during the interview.
[8]Interview with Kuban, Ak Jar's community leader, Ak Jar settlement, Bishkek, 17 February 2012.
[9]Interview with Kuban, Ak Jar's community leader, Ak Jar settlement, Bishkek, 17 February 2012.

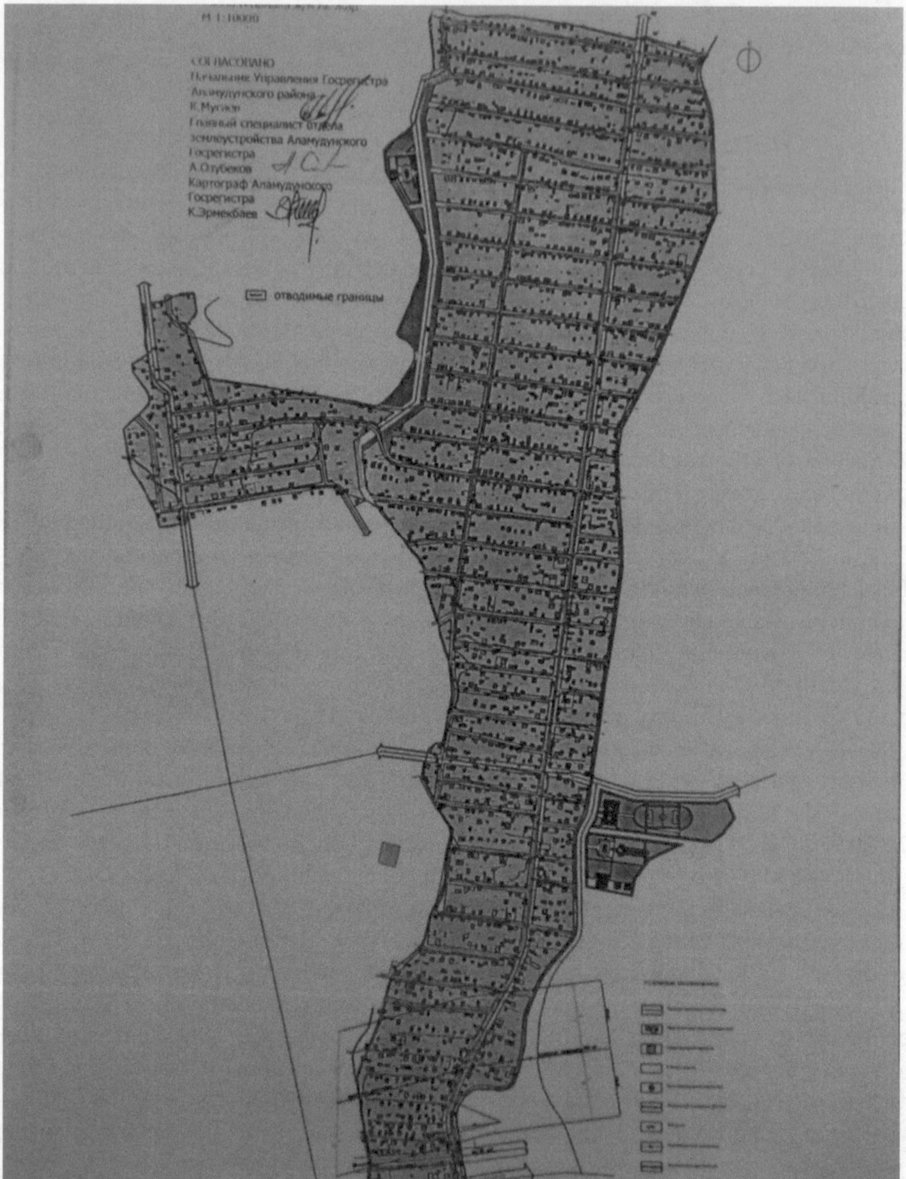

FIGURE 1. Map of Ak Jar

Source: Copy received from staff at the Kyrgyz Scientific Institute for City Planning (Russian: *Kyrgyzskii Nauchno-Issledovatel'skii Proektnyi Institut po Gradostroitel'stvu*), 26 July 2012. Reproduced with permission.

rulings, Ak Jar survived despite its officially illegal status. After the first land-rush in 2005, more people moved into the settlement, turning it into the largest illegal settlement in Bishkek.

A significant number of Ak Jar residents had already been living in Bishkek for several years as tenants (*kvartiranty*). Life as a *kvartirant*, however, was prohibitively expensive. Many wanted to own their own home, to be free from the 'watchful eye' of the landlord and high rental costs.[10] Furthermore, owning a home enables an individual to obtain city registration (*propiska*), a document that grants access to a variety of social services and is bound to a person's official place of residence. Most residents of Ak Jar could not obtain a *propiska* because their residence in the settlement was illegal. Only a few were able to procure registration through relatives in Bishkek who owned property.

Another group of Ak Jar dwellers were recent migrants who had moved to the city from the provinces. A few of them purchased a land plot in Ak Jar from *top bashylar*. Many were given land by relatives who were already there. When I asked Tolkun, a woman in her thirties and mother of two, how she had come to Ak Jar, she told me that one day her husband had received a telephone call from his brother informing him that he had a shack in Ak Jar that needed to be occupied. He asked his brother to come with his family to live in the shack as its guardians. Left uninhabited, the shack was in danger of being occupied by other squatters. Tolkun and her husband were then living in a village in southern Kyrgyzstan and were unemployed. Therefore, moving to Bishkek, where there were more job opportunities and the promise of free housing, was beneficial for them. So, they locked up their house and moved to Bishkek.[11]

Although the land in Ak Jar was illegal, the *top bashylar* managed to sell plots in the settlement through deceitful means. For a potential client, a *top bashy* would say that the legalisation of Ak Jar was soon to be completed and the homeowners would receive property documents. When the client agreed, the *top bashy* would draft a letter, confirming the receipt of the requested sum of money from the client. This self-drafted letter was known as *raspiska* among Ak Jar residents. Both the client and *top bashy* then signed the *raspiska*, which however did not have any juridical power because no state agency could recognise it as an official document. Moreover, responding to the high demand for land at that time, *top bashylar* sometimes sold the same plot to several people. Therefore, the *top bashylar* were always blamed for frequent land conflicts in the settlement when several families fought for establishing ownership over a contested plot. Among the residents of Ak Jar, rumour has it that most of the *top bashylar* earned a good deal of money from land sales and then disappeared. Some of my informants told me that the *top bashy* who sold them land had died. The implication was that profiting from such dishonest deals had ended badly for those responsible. Ak Jar dwellers told me that the *top bashylar* had been cursed by the people they had wronged. On the one hand, this explanation implied that the *top bashylar* deserved punishment for what they did;[12] on the other, the settlement residents seemed to feel sorry for them. They thought that if the *top bashylar* had not been so greedy, perhaps people would not have cursed them to death. Because of the negative associations of *top bashylar*, residents in Ak Jar did not want to

[10]Interview with Karybek, Ak Jar resident, Ak Jar settlement, Bishkek, 19 February 2012.

[11]Interview with Tolkun, Ak Jar resident, Ak Jar settlement, Bishkek, 16 March 2012.

[12]Interview with Ermek, a claimant for a land plot in Ak Jar, Ak Jar settlement, Bishkek, 22 August 2012. At the time of the interview, Ermek lived with his family in another settlement in Bishkek as a tenant, as his house in Ak Jar was not yet habitable.

be identified as one of them, that is, as a law-breaking and greedy squatter. Although the reference to *top bashylar* is frequent and popular among Ak Jar residents, it is difficult to confirm whether *top bashylar* actually existed, but Ak Jar's current residents legitimised their own act of squatting by placing a part of the responsibility on the illegal deals made by the 'bad guys' soon after the 2005 political regime change.

Ak Jar's informal administration and the enforcement of discipline

At first glance, Ak Jar residents seem to perceive the law as 'a form of power, invested with particular forms of authority' (Merry & Canfield 2015, p. 535). As such, the law is supposed to regulate everyday life and provide order in the community. At the same time, residents are aware of the law's fluid and interpersonal side, speaking of it as resting 'in the hands of courts' (*sottun kolunda*) or 'in the hands of the wealthy/influential' (*akchasy bardyn kolunda*).[13] These two understandings coexist simultaneously, creating a tension between 'how the law is conceived and written, on the one hand, and how it is actually applied, on the other' (Polese *et al.* 2019, p. 4). In Ak Jar, this tension finds its expression in the establishment of an informal legal system, based on an effective internal administration of the settlement. This administration is ultimately independent of official structures but draws its legitimacy from claiming to act in the framework of state law.

Ak Jar's degree of internal organisation is impressive: the streets are clearly delineated, the provision of electricity and water is stable, and utility payments are made on time. Most of all, there is a clear administrative structure in Ak Jar. The settlement's chosen leader, Kuban, told me in an interview that his fellow residents chose him to be their leader in 2011 when the previous leader had to leave Ak Jar on the grounds of fraudulent land sale accusations and inactivity towards legalising the settlement.[14] Kuban organised a self-governance unit. As the head of the unit, Kuban appointed four assistants from among the residents of Ak Jar, based on their work experience, their reputation in the settlement and his personal rapport with them. At the time of my fieldwork, Kuban's team consisted of three women, Ainura, Chinara and Aigul, and one man, Maksat.

Before moving to Bishkek, Ainura had worked in the self-governance unit of her natal village and so had experience in administrative work. In Ak Jar, she was responsible for conducting the census of the settlement's population. Chinara was a middle-aged single mother; her age and motherhood secured her the respect of others. She was in charge of social and medical issues and had a list of Ak Jar dwellers who required social assistance. Maksat was known to be a loyal friend of Kuban and helped him with internal matters such as processing people's electricity payments for the local private energy company, Kyrgyz Energy. Finally, because Aigul had been living in Ak Jar from the earliest days of the settlement, she knew all the key community figures in Ak Jar. Aigul's knowledge was important to Kuban, especially when there were land conflicts in the settlement. In those instances, Kuban consulted with Aigul to decide the 'real' owner of a contested land plot. Residents accepted and submitted to the ruling of Kuban and his team. They turned to the

[13]Interview with Karybek, Ak Jar settlement, Bishkek, 19 February 2012.
[14]Interview with Kuban, Ak Jar's community leader, Ak Jar settlement, Bishkek, 17 February 2012.

community leaders for advice and supported their work with monthly payments of 20 KGS (US$0.4).

Conflicts frequently arose in the settlement, and the parties often invoked state law. Kuban used this word in his speeches to underscore his legitimacy as head of the settlement. He often claimed that he acted in the 'framework of the law' (Kyrgyz: *myizam cheginde*) or that his decisions were 'based on law' (Kyrgyz: *myizamdyn negizinde*).[15] When Ak Jar residents wanted to emphasise the authority of law, they referred to 'the courts' (Kyrgyz: *sot*). If the conflicting parties failed to find a consensus, negotiations stalled or they disagreed with Kuban, they said '*sot ele chechsin*' ('the court will decide')[16] or '*men sottun chechimi menen makulmun*' ('I agree with the verdict of a court').[17] These statements invoked official courts as a superior institution that could impose a just ruling. Paradoxically, however, the conflicting parties in Ak Jar also suspected that corrupt judges would side with the party that offered higher bribes (Russian: *vzyatka*) or that both parties would have to bribe the judges in order to have them even consider the case and work towards a resolution.[18] Taken together, the contradictions in their remarks highlighted residents' distance, in a context where law was administered informally, from a formal judicial system.

Nevertheless, the residents of Ak Jar invested their hopes in the judicial system because they associated courts with the state. Inclusion in the state was the ultimate goal that would put an end to their uncertainty. Most Ak Jar residents, especially those socialised and educated during the Soviet period, had a positive conception of the state, as a provider of social welfare, infrastructure and the necessities for living. Therefore, the residents of Ak Jar believed in and relied on the courts as they had once heavily relied on the state, even though the courts did not officially consider any cases from Ak Jar residents due to the illegal status of the settlement. In a way, the people's beliefs and hopes were metaphorical because they could not turn to the courts. In her study on the courts of elders in rural Kyrgyzstan, Judith Beyer (2016, p. 60) has shown that, although people may decry the lack of a state, they do their best to mimic state practices. In Ak Jar, too, the state was largely perceived as absent, yet the community leadership regularly invoked the state and its laws, copied official practices, and used bureaucratic language.

When the post-2005 expansion of Ak Jar grew, many residents upgraded their homes from small mud shacks to large and solid brick houses.[19] These upgrades were accompanied by gradual access to water and electricity on a collective basis. After a large street protest which Ak Jar residents staged in August 2011 demanding water and

[15]Interview with Kuban, Ak Jar's community leader, Ak Jar settlement, Bishkek, 25 July 2012.

[16]Interview with Gulzat and Bolot, formerly a wife and husband, who fought over a house they had built together, Ak Jar settlement, Bishkek, 12 August 2012.

[17]Interview with Ermek and Gulmira, two claimants of the same land plot, Ak Jar settlement, Bishkek, 20 August 2012.

[18]I heard this remark in different interviews with Kuban (Ak Jar's community leader, 17 February 2012), Ermek (a claimant for a land plot in Ak Jar, 20 August 2012) and Maksat (15 May 2012), Ak Jar settlement, Bishkek.

[19]The same strategies of building and beautifying a solid house (as opposed to a small mud shack) so that it cannot be demolished by authorities have been also noted by Sevim Aktaş (2013) in her work on Turkish informal settlements (*gecekondu*).

electricity (Kenenbaeva 2011), then president Atambaev tasked relevant private and state agencies to deliver these resources to the people of Ak Jar. By December 2011, electrical pylons had been installed along the main street of the settlement. However, only those households located along the main street or close to it could receive electricity directly from the pylons; other households had to negotiate with those on the main street in order to access the electricity grid. The typical agreement between households with a direct supply and 'dependent' ones was that the dependent households shared the electricity costs equally at the end of each month. These agreements were supervised by the informal administration which collected the payments. The community leader Kuban passed the payments on to the electricity company. Residents who did not pay their bills on time were pressured and punished. I witnessed a conflict involving Nazira, a woman in her early fifties, unemployed and the carer of her husband, who had special needs, and an infant grandchild. Due to her absence from Ak Jar for a while, Nazira failed to pay her electricity dues. Kyrgyz Energy ordered her electricity to be disconnected, but since Ak Jar has a system of collective connection and disconnection (Russ. *kollektivnoe podkyuchenie/otklyuchenie*) from the mains, her failure to pay the set share of the overall costs affected the energy supply of several households. Nazira's neighbours quickly gathered around her house and demanded that she come outside. When she did so, she was encircled by her angry neighbours who blamed her for their disconnection. She was publicly forced to admit her mistake and pay a fine to Kyrgyz Energy (see Figure 2).

Ak Jar's informal administration also had taken charge of resolving conflicts. In doing so, it was similar to the state-like organisations described by Jean-Louis Van Gelder (2010) in the *asentamientos* (informal settlements) of Buenos Aires. Van Gelder noted that the systems of self-governance in these illegal settlements simultaneously fulfilled the role of the executive, legislative and judicial branches (Van Gelder 2010, pp. 252–53). In the *asentamientos*, residents elected a neighbourhood administration to form an executive branch; the assemblies where *asentamiento* dwellers met for public discussions were termed the 'legislative branch'; and the neighbourhood administration ruled on matters related to the environment, infrastructure, service provision and disputes. According to Van Gelder, a strong internal organisation with a state-like structure fosters resilience and enables residents to respond to threats of eviction and police violence. Moreover, forming an administrative body and an internal legal order that mimics those of the state ensures the effective management of the occupied land. Van Gelder concludes that in order to legalise their tenure, settlement dwellers mimic the functions of the formal state, becoming 'conversant in its laws and policies', and thereby establish themselves discursively as a legal and valid entity (Van Gelder 2010, p. 251).

What do these internal efforts mean for the legal–illegal dichotomy? According to Van Gelder, an internal organisation that is capable of 'keeping conflict between settlers to a minimum, maintaining social cohesion, and establishing settlement organization and leadership' is essential to attain security of tenure and legalisation (Van Gelder 2010, p. 250). Building on this argument, I suggest that the informal administration of Ak Jar and efforts to maintain a legal order were aimed first at security of tenure (escaping demolition) and then at facilitating a process of legalisation. By enforcing internal discipline and resolving internal disputes, Kuban and his team were able to represent Ak Jar to outside stakeholders such as Kyrgyz Energy or state officials. Kuban and his

FIGURE 2. Nazira is Blamed Publicly by Her Neighbours for the Disconnection of the Communal Electricity Supply, March 2012
Source: Author's photo.

administration, although not unopposed internally, succeeded in creating a sort of 'associational power' (Braverman *et al.* 2014, p. 13) that transformed Ak Jar into a cohesive and reliable collective in negotiations with state authorities and utility companies.

I have described elsewhere (Isabaeva 2014) that, in some situations, residents of such settlements divide themselves into northerners and southerners and are distrustful of each other in certain situations. However, when it comes to the commonly agreed internal rules of Ak Jar, such differences are sidelined. Neighbours either pressure each other to follow the rules of the community or cooperate in order to help those in financial need. For example, during my period of fieldwork, a neighbour of Ainura Myrzabaeva wrote a letter (Kyrgyz: *koldoo barakchasy*) promising to pay her electricity bill if she was unable to make the payment on time. The letter was signed by residents of the same street whose power came from the common mains. However, it is unlikely that the letter would have received such support from Ainura's neighbours without the endorsement of the informal administration. After being drafted, the letter was exhibited in Kuban's offices for residents to sign. When I sighted the letter, not all the households concerned had signed it yet, and it is possible that some households ultimately did not sign it (see Figure 3). Nevertheless, the letter exemplifies the crucial role of the internal administration in building a community that could project unity to the outside. In a way, besides providing the tangible benefits of a stable electricity and water supply, Ak Jar's administrative structure conveyed a message of permanence and cohesiveness that empowered its residents in interactions with politicians, NGO representatives, researchers and journalists.

Negotiations and public attention

The formal legalisation of Ak Jar is a complex process and faces many obstacles. Some of these are related to specific local conditions; in particular, the soil has been assessed by geologists as unsuitable for housing. Experts fear that residential construction may lead to the ground sinking, with possible human and material damage.[20] Also, nearby high voltage powerlines and an underground gas pipeline were considered risks for a residential zone. Considering these environmental and technical hazards, Ak Jar's legalisation has proved to be highly problematic.

The Kyrgyz Scientific Institute for City Planning and the Department of Private Residential Construction have emphasised the illegality of Ak Jar by highlighting its emergence as a result of illegal land squatting and have opposed the settlement's legalisation.[21] In response, Ak Jar residents have employed different strategies to argue for legalisation. These included appeals to their rights as fellow-citizens and to a decent life. These different sets of appeals were important in asserting residents' right to stay permanently in Ak Jar. As various residents said to the author: 'Why are we called illegals? We are citizens of Kyrgyzstan and have a right to settle down wherever we want to'; 'Why do the people of other nationalities have comfortable housing in Bishkek and we, the Kyrgyz, do not?'; 'We want to live a normal life like human beings'; 'We want to belong to the state'; 'What are we supposed to do if there are no jobs for us in the villages and no housing in the city?'.[22] These appeals blend human rights arguments with nationalism and have a moralistic undertone. Even though residents knew that Ak Jar was considered an illegal settlement, they justified their squatting on the basis of a higher principle: that the state had an obligation to assist its underprivileged citizens. Van Gelder believes these kinds of appeals can be effective 'because the state needs some kind of normative framework to justify its interventions and tapping into official law opens up the road for a legal solution to the conflict' (Van Gelder 2010, p. 258).

Other tactics employed by Ak Jar residents to make themselves visible to the authorities and raise claims for social and material infrastructure included peaceful demonstrations in front of government buildings, letters addressed to high-ranking politicians and relevant state agencies, and meetings with lawmaker, NGOs and state officials. External outreach by Ak Jar dwellers was not only limited to contacts with politicians and state agencies. Residents have also actively used religion as a way to attract greater attention to their

[20]Interview with Melis, a worker of the Department of Private Residential Construction (Russian: *Departament Individual'nogo Zhilishnogo Stroitel'stva*), Bishkek, 14 March 2012. Also interview with Anarbek, a worker in the Kyrgyz Scientific Institute for City Planning, Bishkek, 26 July 2012.

[21]Interview with Melis, a worker of the Department of Private Residential Construction (Russian: *Departament Individual'nogo Zhilishnogo Stroitel'stva*), Bishkek, 14 March 2012. Also interview with Anarbek, a worker in the Kyrgyz Scientific Institute for City Planning, Bishkek, 26 July 2012.

[22]These questions and statements were uttered during an interview with four male Ak Jar residents: Kanybek, Avaz, Anarbek and Manas, Ak Jar settlement, Bishkek, 21 March 2012.

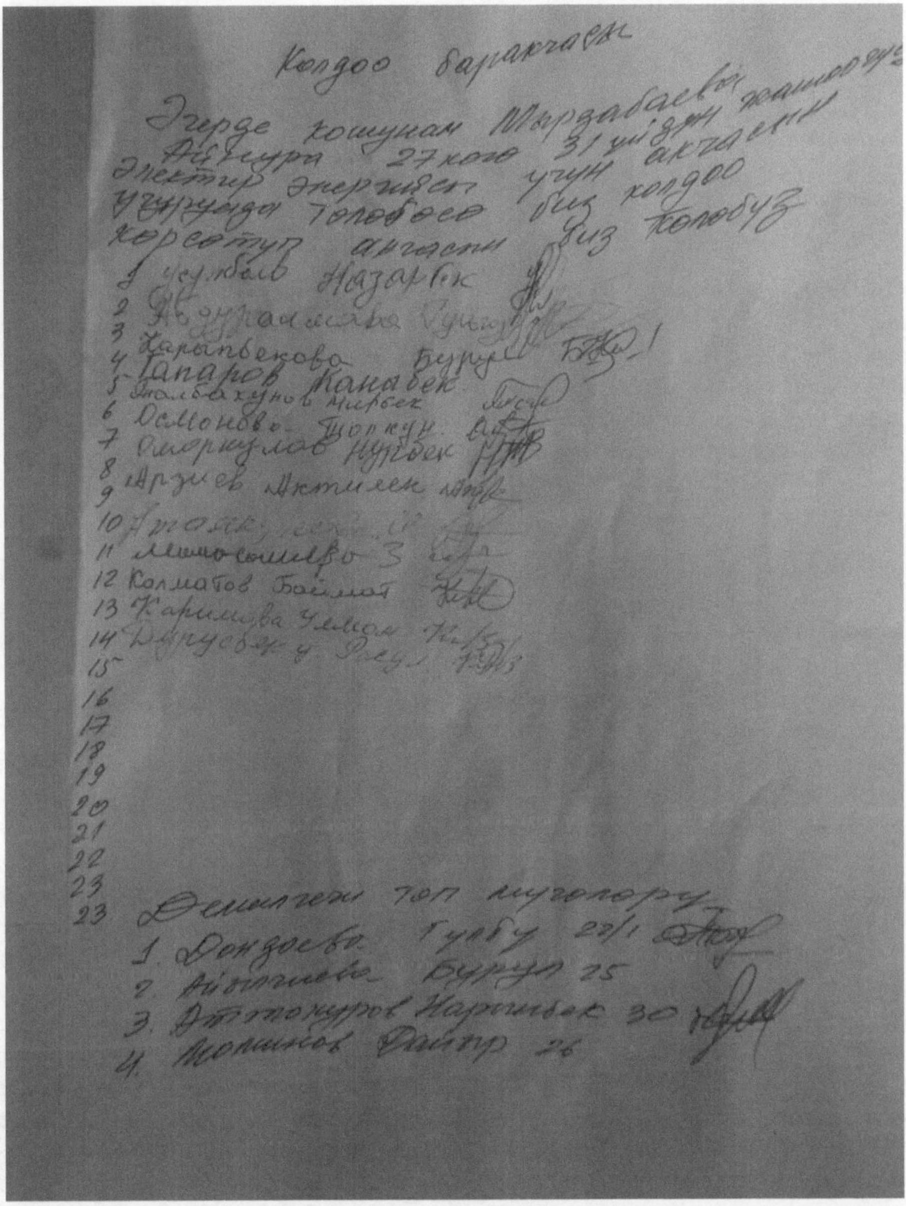

Колдоо баракчасы

Эгерде кошунам Мырзабаев [illegible] Айгуль 27 [illegible] 31 үйдүн актасын электр энергиясы үчүн актасын үчүрүүдө төлөбөсө биз колдоо көрсөтүп акчасын биз төлөбүз

1 [illegible] Назарбек
2 [illegible]
3 Карапбекова Бурул
4 Тапаров Канабек
5 [illegible]
6 Осмонова Торкун
7 [illegible] Нурбек
8 Арзиев Актилек
9
10 [illegible]
11 [illegible]
12 Колматов Баймат
13 Каримова [illegible]
14 [illegible]
15
16
17
18
19
20
21
22
23
23 [illegible]

1. [illegible] 22/1
2. [illegible] Бурул 25
3. [illegible] 30
4. [illegible] 26

FIGURE 3. The Letter of Support Composed by Neighbours on Behalf of a Needy Ak Jar Resident

Source: Copy received from Ak Jar's community leadership. Reproduced with permission.

cause. Chinara, for example, attended a weekly religious class for women called *baian*. The class included discussions of Islam, with an *imam* responding to questions from the public. The class was held in a private house in another part of Bishkek. At one class I attended with

Chinara, she asked all the *baian* attendees to pray for the legalisation of Ak Jar and the well-being of its residents. The *imam* responded:

> It is not the first time I have received this request and thus it is not the first time we are going to pray for Ak Jar. The author of the note[23] reports that the settlement Ak Jar, where she lives, is illegal and that there are many conflicts related to electricity and land. She asks us to pray collectively so that the settlement is legalised very soon and so that no conflicts take place there. So let us implement her request.[24]

Following this, the *imam* led the women in prayer, beseeching Allah that Ak Jar would obtain its long-awaited legalisation. By bringing Ak Jar's problems to the attention of an audience in Bishkek, Chinara raised awareness about her squatter settlement among Bishkek women who had no knowledge of conditions in Ak Jar and did not have such problems themselves. Her presence in a religious group also served to counter negative views of squatters among some Bishkek residents as anarchic and lawless.

Transcending illegality and becoming legal

As mentioned before, the legalisation of Ak Jar would necessarily involve the transfer of Ak Jar's territory from the jurisdiction of Chui *Oblast'* to that of Bishkek City and a redesignation of the previously agricultural land as a residential area, a process locally called *transformatsiya* (transformation). The completion of the process would then result in the incorporation of Ak Jar into Bishkek and the ensuing recognition of its dwellers as city residents.

The process of legalisation involves considerable costs, raising the question of whether informal dwellers are willing and able to pay part of the bill (Fernandes 2011, pp. 22–3). *Transformatsiya*, too, is a costly matter, requiring the drafting of a formal 'master plan' for Ak Jar, known in Russian as *gen plan* (*general'nyi plan*, general plan). A *gen plan* would map all housing in the settlement for the approval of Bishkek authorities, who would grant tenure rights to the residents. When the regional architecture office stated that it lacked financial means to draft the plan as a response to Ak Jar residents' repeated claims for property documents throughout the years 2006–2012, Ak Jar's community leader Kuban told me he had suggested collecting money from the residents to pay for the architects.[25] Kuban's suggestion was approved by the authorities and so he asked each household in Ak Jar to contribute 500 KGS (US$10) towards the *gen plan*.[26] The residents were told by the community leadership that, if legalisation proceeded successfully, their household would be granted legal property documents known locally as *krasnaya kniga* (in Russian) or *kyzyl kitep* (in Kyrgyz). Conversely, families who refused or were unable to pay 500 KGS were subjected to empty threats by being told that their properties would remain illegal. Although some Ak Jar residents were unhappy with

[23]After every class, attendees could write a question or a request on a piece of paper, which was then passed on to the *imam*. The *imam* would answer the question or implement the woman's request.
[24]*Baian* class, Kölmö settlement, Bishkek, 28 July 2012.
[25]Interview with Kuban, Ak Jar's community leader, Ak Jar settlement, Bishkek, 13 March 2012.
[26]Interview with Kuban, Ak Jar's community leader, Ak Jar settlement, Bishkek, 13 March 2012.

Kuban's aggressive way of collecting money,[27] he always used official language, saying that all the work he did for Ak Jar and for his fellow residents was within the framework of the law.[28]

I witnessed several times how Ak Jar residents made payments of 500 KGS to Kuban or his assistants. It usually happened in their office in the settlement. When the residents came to pay for electricity, the community leaders showed them a letter they had drafted themselves and which said that the person was ready to voluntarily contribute 500 KGS for the *gen plan*. The community leaders also explained verbally that paying 500 KGS would soon result in the granting of *krasnaya kniga/kyzyl kitep*. Urged by their leaders, the residents of Ak Jar made the payment and received a stamped receipt. When I asked Kuban what he would do with the collected money, he explained that he had opened a bank account in which to deposit it, and that he would transfer the money to the regional architecture office once everyone had paid.

In this case again, Kuban closely followed state practices such as handing out receipts, stamping them, and invoking notions such as law (*myizam*), state (*mamleket*), courts (*sot*) and rights (*ukuk*). Official terminology endowed Kuban and his words with legitimacy and demonstrated discursively that he was not a fraudster. Furthermore, he employed peer pressure to make people contribute to the *gen plan*. Many residents I talked to said that they had paid the requested money because Kuban told them that the others had paid as well. Not everyone agreed with Kuban's actions, though. No matter how diligently he tried to sound and act state-like, there was a group of women who resisted Kuban's aggressive and arbitrary collection of money and urged their neighbours to resist as well. Kuban referred to these women as *oppozitsiya* (opposition). They lived in Ak Jar and believed that the legalisation of the settlement was a task of the state (Kyrgyz: *mamlekettin ishi*). Further, they believed that Kuban was laundering money by making use of Ak Jar's docile population who were threatened and pressured by Kuban. 'He thinks we are fools and uneducated, but we are not', said Aijan about Kuban.[29] In order to verify whether Kuban's strategy to achieve Ak Jar's legalisation by raising funds from people was correct, Aijan and other *oppozitsiya* members held negotiations with state authorities on their own. Having received an official answer from the authorities that Kuban had no right to force people to collect money, Ak Jar's *oppozitsiya* members called upon their neighbours not to submit to the will of Kuban.[30]

While many of Kuban's fellow residents were keen to see Ak Jar legalised, he seemed to be more interested in other benefits such as maintaining his position as the head of the settlement and being in direct contact with the state and city authorities. In addition, as head of Ak Jar, Kuban was privy to valuable property information and could profit by selling land or giving it away to friends and family. In Kuban's interpretation, his term as head of the community would only end if the majority of his four assistants decided so. Since his assistants were loyal, a decision to remove him from leadership was unlikely. Legalisation of the settlement was not necessarily in Kuban's interests. As the leader of

[27]Interview with Nurgul, Aijan and Burul, Ak Jar settlement, Bishkek, 26 July 2012.
[28]Interview with Kuban, Ak Jar's community leader, Ak Jar settlement, Bishkek, 25 July 2012.
[29]Interview with Aijan, an Ak Jar resident, Ak Jar settlement, Bishkek, 25 July 2012.
[30]Interview with Aijan, an Ak Jar resident, Ak Jar settlement, Bishkek, 25 July 2012.

an illegal settlement, he could make and enforce his own rules and his position was secure; by contrast, legalisation would make him accountable to city authorities and entail the possibility of his replacement. Under the *status quo*, state and city officials as well as utility companies recognised Kuban as the legitimate spokesman for Ak Jar. In a certain sense, Ak Jar's informal administration was thus already embedded in formal state structures. This grey zone between legality and illegality was actually more favourable to the decision-makers in Ak Jar than formal legalisation, as they could benefit from many of the state's resources without being personally accountable.

Politicians also sought to benefit from Ak Jar's ambiguous situation and arrived in pre-election periods to solicit votes. One of these visitors was Nurbek Abdykeev, a member of Bishkek's City Council (see Figure 4). Nurbek's visit to Ak Jar on 27 June 2012 was organised by local NGO Arysh. While Nurbek was supposed to respond to residents' questions, he used the opportunity to canvas support for the upcoming elections:

> You need someone who understands your problems and who will take care of them. If you vote for a new person, that person will require time to get acquainted with your problems. By the time that person's term expires, your problems will be left unresolved. If you vote for a person of Russian, Dungan or Korean ethnicity, they will not understand your problems because they don't live in illegal settlements. If you vote for me, I will do everything in my capacity to ensure that Ak Jar is legalised.[31]

Although Ak Jar was labelled as an illegal settlement by state agencies, top and middle-ranked politicians actively sought votes there. For ambitious politicians, Ak Jar, with its roughly 15,000 inhabitants in 2012–2013, was an attractive reservoir of voters and supporters. Politicians' soliciting of electoral support reinforced the residents' perception that the state needed them as much as they needed the state, and that their illegal status would not be permanent. Why else would politicians be interested in them and their problems?[32] Most people attending the meeting with Nurbek believed that his intentions were sincere.[33] Other politicians, including Yrgal Kadyralieva, promised to work for the long-awaited legalisation of the settlement as well.[34]

Politicians' promises were not always empty slogans. Karybek summed up the collective feeling of Ak Jar residents: 'I wish we had elections every month because things get done only then'.[35] Similar attitudes to elections have also been observed in other contexts in Kyrgyzstan. Ismailbekova's interlocutors in the village of Vostok described the election campaigns in the autumn of 2007 as a 'short period during which people's concerns could be heard, taken into consideration, and realized in practice' (Ismailbekova 2014, p. 83).

[31]The meeting of Nurbek with the residents of Ak Jar took place in Kuban's office in Ak Jar, Bishkek, 27 June 2012.

[32]Interview with Kanybek, Avaz, Anarbek and Manas. The author encountered them in one of Ak Jar's side streets. Every time the electricity was switched off—a regular occurrence at Ak Jar—the men gathered outside to discuss everyday problems, Ak Jar settlement, Bishkek, 21 March 2012.

[33]Interview with Saltanat, Ak Jar settlement, Bishkek, 27 June 2012.

[34]Interview with Yrgal Kadyralieva, presidential palace and government house (White House), Bishkek, 15 August 2012.

[35]Interview with Karybek in his home, Ak Jar settlement, Bishkek, 19 February 2012.

FIGURE 4. MEETING OF AK JAR RESIDENTS WITH A REPRESENTATIVE OF THE BISHKEK CITY COUNCIL, AK JAR SETTLEMENT, JUNE 2012
Source: Author's photo.

While in comparable Latin American settlements, 'electoral promises to resolve the problems affecting informal settlements have tended to perpetuate informality' (Fernandes 2011, p. 7), Kyrgyz politicians followed up on their promises by taking concrete steps towards the legalisation of Ak Jar. In summer 2018, Dastan Jumabekov, the then speaker of the Kyrgyz parliament, announced that three important bills had been passed, including a bill to transform agricultural land plots around Bishkek into residential land. If signed by the president, the law would fulfil one of the important criteria of the legalisation process. Up to this moment, the law however has not been signed by the president.[36]

As of 2020, the legalisation process is not yet complete, nor is its outcome assured. When I conducted my fieldwork in Ak Jar, however, the general mood was decidedly positive. The steps towards legalisation—the delivery of electricity and water, fund raising to finance the settlement's master plan—had already created the expectation among residents that land plots in Ak Jar would soon become more valuable. While I did not observe any signs of land development or gentrification, as had happened in Latin American cases (Fernandes 2011, pp. 35–7), my interlocutors half-jokingly encouraged me to speculate in land and

[36]The bills had been passed when Sooronbai Jeenbekov was still in office. Following the controversial parliamentary elections of 4 October 2020, Jeenbekov resigned as the president of Kyrgyzstan on 15 October 2020.

buy a house in Ak Jar. Although I refrained from following this suggestion, Ak Jar's legalised future already seemed palpable.

Conclusion

After 15 years of tolerated illegality, Ak Jar may only be a few steps away from formal legalisation. When this happens, Ak Jar dwellers will receive their long-awaited property documents and gain a feeling of security and safety. In the context of this tolerated illegality, Ak Jar dwellers have made internal and external efforts to change the legal status of their settlement. By copying and reproducing state practices in Ak Jar's informal administration, the community leadership created an 'internal legality' (Van Gelder 2010, p. 242) that brought the 'absent' state into the settlement, enforcing collective action. External efforts demonstrated to the outside world that Ak Jar residents were not only a cohesive community but also law-abiding citizens who contributed to society. Although legalisation still faces significant obstacles, Ak Jar residents have succeeded in initiating and facilitating the process through collective action and financial contributions. The role of local and national politicians has likewise to be taken into account. While referring to the settlement as illegal, they visited the settlement to seek votes during campaign periods. Such political courting helped give Ak Jar dwellers a sense of agency. They negotiated with politicians and used election campaigns to trade their votes for promises of legalisation or infrastructure provision.

Ak Jar offers a Kyrgyz perspective on problems related to informal settlements that have, so far, been predominantly studied in Latin American contexts. Ak Jar confirms the insight drawn, for example, from *asentamientos* in Buenos Aires, that illegality is not a fixed status and that legality can be anticipated and negotiated through actions by those affected. Legality gives people security that they will not be evicted from homes and that they will be given property titles (Fernandes 2011, pp. 6–8). As shown in this essay, the case of Ak Jar can be distinguished from that of other illegal settlements: it has an effective internal administration and a strong capacity to negotiate demands with political decision-makers. These factors, as I have argued, have been instrumental in paving the way towards infrastructural upgrading and, possibly, legalisation.

References

Akaev, J. (2010) 'Jany konush: bolochok chempiondordun jaryksyz jashoosu', *RFL/RL Azattyk*, 6 July, available at: https://www.azattyk.org/a/Kyrgyzstan_Inhabited_Rights_Youth/2091894.html, accessed 18 November 2015.

Aktaş, S. (2013) 'The Urbanisation Issue and the Culture of Gecekondus in Turkey', *Oriente Moderno*, 93, 1.

Al-Sayyad, N. (1993) 'Informal Housing in a Comparative Perspective: On Squatting, Culture, and Development in a Latin American and a Middle Eastern Context', *Review of Urban and Regional Development Studies*, 5.

Avdeeva, E. (2005) 'Zemlya vse sterpit', *Vechernii Bishkek*, 12 July, available at: http://vecherka.kg/2005/07/12/panorama/6.html, accessed 8 August 2018.

Azuela, A. & Meneses-Reyes, R. (2014) 'The Everyday Formation of the Urban Space. Law and Poverty in Mexico City', in Braverman, I., Blomley, N., Delaney, D. & Kedar, A. (eds).

Beyer, J. (2016) *The Force of Custom: Law and the Ordering of Everyday Life in Kyrgyzstan* (Pittsburgh, PA, University of Pittsburgh Press).

Blomley, N. (2003) 'From "What?" to "So What?": Law and Geography in Retrospect', in Holder, J. & Harrison, C. (eds) *Law and Geography Current Legal Issues, 5* (Oxford, Oxford University Press).

Botoeva, G. (2019) 'Use of Language in Blurring the Lines between Legality and Illegality', in Polese, A., Russo, A. & Strazzari, F. (eds).

Braverman, I., Blomley, N., Delaney, D. & Kedar, A. (eds) (2014) *The Expanding Spaces of Law. A Timely Legal Geography* (Stanford, CA, Stanford University Press).

Bukasheva, B. (2005) 'Kto sdelal revolyutsyu i chto poluchil?', *TsentrAziya*, 8 April, available at: https://centrasia.org/newsA.php?st=1112978700, accessed 25 November 2018.

Cramer, B. (2018) 'Kyrgyzstan's Informal Settlements: *yntymak* and the Emergence of Politics in Place', *Central Asian Survey*, 37, 1.

Fedorova, Z. (2005) 'Aksakaly perezhivayut za stolitsu', *Vechernii Bishkek*, 19 April, available at: http://vecherka.kg/2005/04/19/ispytano/4.html, accessed 8 August 2018.

Fernandes, E. (2011) *Regularization of Informal Settlements in Latin America*, Policy Focus Report (Cambridge, MA, Lincoln Institute of Land Policy), available at: https://www.lincolninst.edu/sites/default/files/pubfiles/regularization-informal-settlements-latin-america-full_0.pdf, accessed 26 November 2020.

Fernandes, E. & Varley, A. (1998) *Illegal Cities: Law and Urban Change in Developing Countries* (London & New York, NY, Zed Books).

Hatcher, C. (2015) 'Illegal Geographies of the State: The Legalization of a "Squatter" Settlement in Bishkek, Kyrgyzstan', *International Journal of Law in the Built Environment*, 7, 1.

Heyman, J. & Smart, A. (1999) *States and Illegal Practices* (Oxford & New York, NY, Berg).

Isabaeva, E. (2014) 'Politicheskie predposylki dikhotomii "Sever-Yug" v Kyrgyzstane', *Ethnographicheskoe Obozrenie*, 4.

Ismailbekova, A. (2014) 'Performing Democracy: State-Making through Patronage in Kyrgyzstan', in Reeves, M., Rasanayagam, J. & Beyer, J. (eds) *Ethnographies of the State in Central Asia: Performing Politics* (Bloomington and Indianapolis, IN, Indiana University Press).

Ivashenko, E. (2016) 'Novostroiki Bishkeka: Zakhvatit' zemlyu, legalizovat'sya i zhit' vozle svalki', *Ferghana News Agency*, 25 February, available at: https://www.fergananews.com/articles/8896, accessed 10 March 2016.

Kenenbaeva, E. (2011) 'Ak Jarlyktar jaryk, suu ber dep, zhol buudu', *RFE/RL Azattyk*, 8 August, available at: https://www.azattyk.org/a/kyrgyzstan_society_ak_jar_rally/24290431.html, accessed 18 November 2015.

Maratova, M. (2005) 'Bishkek v panike—oruduyut tysyachi zemel'nykh maroderov', *TsentrAziya*, 16 April, available at: https://centrasia.org/newsA.php?st=1113618780, accessed 25 November 2018.

Merry, S. E. & Canfield, M. C. (2015) 'Law: Anthropological Aspects', in Wright, J. D. (ed.) *International Encyclopedia of the Social & Behavioral Science* (2nd edn) (Amsterdam, Elsevier).

Mitenko, P. (2011) 'Gde nochuet kirgizskaya revolyutsya', *Ferghana News Agency*, 11 March, available at: https://www.fergananews.com/articles/6917?&fromnews=1, accessed 15 March 2015.

Nasritdinov, E., Zhumakadyr kyzy, B. & Asanalieva, D. (2015) 'Myths and Realities of Bishkek's Novostroikas', in Laruelle, M. & Engval, J. (eds) *Kyrgyzstan Beyond 'Democracy Island' and 'Failing State'* (Lanham, MD, Lexington Books).

Panfilova, V. (2005) 'Kirgizskii peredel. Vokrug Bishkeka idet nastoyashchaya voina za zemel'nye uchastki', *TsentrAziya*, 15 April, available at: https://centrasia.org/newsA.php?st=1113550320, accessed 25 November 2018.

Polese, A., Russo, A. & Strazzari, F. (eds) (2019) *Governance Beyond the Law. The Immoral, the Illegal, the Criminal* (Cham, Palgrave Macmillan).

Sanghera, B. (2010a) 'Why are Kyrgyzstan's Slum Dwellers so Angry', *OpenDemocracy*, 15 June, available at: https://www.opendemocracy.net/en/odr/why-are-kyrgyzstans-slum-dwellers-so-angry/, accessed 20 June 2010.

Sanghera, B. (2010b) 'Wanted: Economic Equality to Mend Kyrgyzstan', *OpenDemocracy*, 27 August, available at: https://www.opendemocracy.net/en/odr/wanted-economic-equality-to-mend-kyrgyzstan/, accessed 30 August 2010.

Sanghera, B. & Satybaldieva, E. (2012) 'Ethics of Property, Illegal Settlements and the Right to Subsistence', *International Journal of Sociology and Social Policy*, 32, 96–114.

Sanghera, B., Satybaldieva, E., Rodionov, A., Serikzhanova, S., Choibekov, N. & Sultanmuratova, K. (2011) *Illegal Settlements and City Registration in Kyrgyzstan and Kazakhstan: Implications for Legal Empowerment, Politics and Ethnic Tensions*, OSI Occasional Paper (New York, NY, Open Society Foundations), available at: https://www.opensocietyfoundations.org/uploads/a1ac7588-f0e4-404a-9aae-07856fc82fa9/OPS-No-5-20120504.pdf, accessed 26 November 2020.

Shambetov, T. (2015) 'Zhany konushtardyn chechilbegen köigöiü', *RFE/RL Azattyk*, 18 June, available at: https://www.azattyk.org/a/kyrgyzstan_suburbs_around_bishkek/27078559.html, accessed 18 November 2015.

Soltoeva, A. (2005) 'Bishkek—zemlya obetovannaya', *Vechernii Bishkek*, 8 April, available at: http://vecherka.kg/2005/04/08/panorama/1.html, accessed 8 August 2018.

Sorokina, Z. (2005) 'Dovol'no beschinstvovat'!', *Vechernii Bishkek*, 5 July, available at: http://vecherka.kg/2005/07/05/panorama/9.html, accessed 8 August 2018.

Ubink, J. M., Hoekema, A. J. & Assies, W. J. (2009) *Legalising Land Rights: Local Practices, State Responses and Tenure Security in Africa, Asia and Latin America* (Leiden, Leiden University Press).

Van Gelder, J.-L. (2010) 'Tales of Deviance and Control: On Space, Rules, and Law in Squatter Settlements', *Law & Society Review*, 44, 2.

Varley, A. (2002) 'Private or Public: Debating the Meaning of Tenure Legalization', *International Journal of Urban and Regional Research*, 26, 3.

Negotiating the Right to Information: Citizen–Government Interactions in the Implementation of the Regulations on Open Government Information in China

YIYI LU

Abstract

This essay analyses the implementation of China's Regulations on Open Government Information (ROGI), an important piece of legislation that establishes Chinese citizens' right to information. By international standards, the ROGI only offers relatively weak protection for this right, but Chinese citizens and civil society organisations have used the ROGI creatively to pursue a variety of goals from private rights protection to public interest advocacy. Strong civic activism has been a major driving force behind the gradual progress in public access to government information that has been achieved since the ROGI came into effect in 2008.

CHINA'S REGULATIONS ON OPEN GOVERNMENT INFORMATION (ROGI) came into force on 1 May 2008. ROGI is China's equivalent to freedom of information (FOI) laws that affirm citizens' right to information and to demand government transparency. In addition to requiring government agencies to disseminate information proactively, the ROGI also allows citizens to file requests for government information and obligates government bodies to respond. Although the ROGI is recognised as an important piece of progressive legislation that constitutes a milestone in the development of rule of law in China, most assessments of the open government information (OGI) regime that has emerged since 2008 consider its success in protecting citizens' right to information[1] and enhancing government accountability to be limited (Yang 2013; Chen 2017; Distelhorst 2017; Duan 2017; Zhu & Fu 2017). By asking requesters of government information to demonstrate a

This work was supported by Ford Foundation: [Grant Number 0130-1388].

[1]It should be noted that although 'the right to know' is frequently mentioned in Chinese official documents and speeches as a basic right of Chinese citizens, the ROGI does not explicitly state that citizens have a 'right' to information. When a revised ROGI was promulgated in 2019, the 'right to information' was still not included in its text, despite the recommendation of many legal scholars (see, for example, 'Zhengfu ying Jiaqiang Zhengdichaiqian Xinxi Gongkai—Wang Youyin Lüshi Zhuanfang', Beijing Shengyun law firm's website, available at: http://www.bjsheng.cn/index.php?m=content&c=index&a=show&catid=109&id=3008, accessed 2 October 2020). However, it is generally recognised that the ROGI has in practice provided Chinese citizens with a legal foundation for asserting the right to information, despite its many limitations.

personal need for the information, China's OGI regime appeared to respect only the citizens' 'need to know' and not their 'right to know' (Chen 2017, p. 241).[2] By allowing too many exemptions to the information disclosure requirements and granting administrative agencies too much discretion in deciding whether particular information should be disclosed, key information that is essential in enabling the public to supervise the government and participate in decision-making is still kept secret, hence the saying that 'the disclosed information is not what the public is interested in, while information that the public is interested in is not disclosed' (Cheng *et al.* 2009).

Despite the many shortcomings of the OGI regime, it has opened up a new institutional channel for Chinese citizens to fight for their rights and interests and to influence government policies and practices. Given the dearth of institutional channels for political participation in China, the ROGI's impact on state–society relations should not be underestimated. Victims of illegal land confiscation and housing demolitions, environmental pollution and police abuse, disabled persons who have suffered discrimination, consumers who have been overcharged by state-owned monopoly companies—in all, individuals who previously had no means of challenging the illicit, wanton acts of the state and its agents, other than submitting petitions and staging unsanctioned protests—can now use the legal system to seek redress, starting by collecting evidence of government wrongdoing and irresponsibility through OGI requests. Civil society activists, from civic-minded university students who want to supervise government expenditures, to LGBT groups seeking more understanding and respect for gay rights, have tried to mobilise media attention and raise public awareness of the issues they champion by filing OGI requests.

The OGI regime has evolved over time. The ROGI has been a good example of how a piece of legislation can acquire its own dynamic once people start to use it. Initially, government agencies and officials were confused and overwhelmed by their new OGI duties (Piotrowski *et al.* 2009; Qin & Cheng 2009; Horsley 2016a) but they soon developed both formal and informal practices that helped them cope with the challenging transparency requirements. Citizens, on the other hand, have been pushing the boundaries from the beginning, searching constantly for new ways to exploit the ROGI's potential. In some cases, when government agencies refuse to release information which they believe should be available to them under the ROGI, requesters go on to file new requests concerning the individual officials they perceive to be obstructing, such as information on the officials' professional qualifications, their expenditures during business trips, or personal and family incomes and assets, as a way of putting pressure on the officials.[3]

[2]The revised ROGI that took effect in May 2019 has eliminated the 'needs test' for requesting government information, but OGI requesters complain that government agencies continue to use other provisions to deny their requests. See the section 'The ROGI and its Key Features' below for more discussion on the revision of the ROGI.

[3]For an example of such tactics by OGI requesters, see the Weibo account of user 'Bafen2009', available at: https://weibo.com/1210910084/GxY5a1hO9?from=page_1005051210910084_profile&wvr=6&mod=weibotime&type=comment#_rnd1556824501597, accessed 10 May 2019. Many OGI requesters post detailed information about their requests and government responses on Weibo, China's Twitter equivalent, to try to win the support of public opinion. 'Bafen2009' requested information on the travelling expenses of the head of a government agency with which he had a dispute and to which he had filed many unsuccessful OGI requests.

Such tactics triggered countertactics from government agencies—often in the form of more hurdles—to prevent requesters from 'abusing' their right to information. Requesters, in turn, would feel the need to intensify their efforts in order to break through government countertactics. Thus, government agencies and OGI requesters are engaged in an ongoing, double-sided process of learning and adaptation. As old practices change and new practices are introduced as a result, the OGI regime continues to evolve.

This essay examines the evolution of China's OGI regime, showing how it has been shaped by everyday interactions between citizens and government bodies as they communicate, negotiate, cooperate or collide in every request for government information. It argues that, despite the ROGI's limitations and the many problems with its implementation, it has still turned out to be a powerful tool for citizens to protect their rights and interests and to demand accountability from the government. This is not because the government designed the ROGI to be such a tool, but because citizens have assiduously explored the ROGI's potential. By continuing to file OGI requests, even when their requests are often denied, and by trying new approaches to get around government pretexts for withholding information, citizens have given the ROGI more substance than its makers intended.

The essay will use two in-depth case studies to illustrate how Chinese citizens and civil society organisations have exploited new opportunities for legal mobilisation offered by the ROGI. Zemans defines legal mobilisation as 'the act of invoking legal norms to regulate behaviour .... The law is ... mobilized when a desire or want is translated into a demand as an assertion of one's right' (Zemans 1983, p. 700). Legal mobilisation theory sees law as a resource that citizens can use to formulate rightful claims, advance goals in the public sphere, and negotiate disputes with the state and each other (McCann 2007). The case studies will show how Chinese OGI requesters have put the resources of the ROGI to such use. Both case studies are complex. Multiple requests were filed; dissatisfied with the results, the requesters took follow-up actions, including filing more requests, applying for administrative reconsideration and/or filing lawsuits. The case studies therefore do not just present OGI requests and their outcomes but describe the whole process of OGI requester–government interactions, including both the legal mobilisation tactics of the requesters and the counter-mobilisation tactics of the state.

The first study is a case of an individual citizen using the OGI mechanism to defend her rights and interests. It is based on extensive interviews with the requester and government and court documents provided by her. The second study shows how an NGO turned the ROGI into an effective tool for policy advocacy. It draws on a detailed written account of the events which a former staff member of the NGO, a central player in the story, provided to the author. Both case studies also used media reports as an additional source of information, as both cases have received media coverage, as a result of the conscious decision of the key parties involved to seek publicity.

The rest of the essay is divided into four sections. The first section below introduces the ROGI and describes some of its most important features. The second section discusses the evolution of the OGI regime since the ROGI took effect in 2008. This is followed by two exemplifying case studies. The final section further analyses the main issues explored in the essay and presents the conclusion.

The ROGI and its key features[4]

The ROGI came into force in May 2008 and was revised in 2019. The new version took effect in May 2019. As an administrative regulation promulgated by the State Council, the ROGI has less legal authority than a law. It does not apply to Chinese Communist Party organs, the People's Congress, the People's Political Consultative Conference, or judicial organs. Only government administrative organs and some quasi-administrative organisations are governed by the ROGI (Tang 2014).

Government agencies have the obligation to both disseminate information on their own initiative and disclose information in response to requests. The original ROGI required that government agencies reply to OGI requests within 15 business days. An extension of 15 business days was permitted if agencies felt they needed more time. The revised ROGI changes both the response time and the allowed extension to 20 business days. The revised ROGI also adds the following: if government organs consider the number or frequency of requests filed by a requester as 'exceeding reasonable limits', they may ask the requester to offer explanations. If they deem the explanations unreasonable, government organs can refuse to process the requests altogether. If they deem the explanations reasonable, then they may determine a 'reasonable extension of the response time' beyond 40 business days. The ROGI does not define what is reasonable or unreasonable, leaving it to the judgment of government agencies.

The original ROGI exempted some government information from disclosure, including state secrets, commercial secrets and private personal information. In addition, the General Office of the State Council (GOSC), the entity designated by the ROGI to oversee OGI work nationwide, issued a directive in 2010 stipulating that information arising from the government's internal management and information generated in the deliberative process preceding decision-making are 'not government information that should be disclosed' (General Office of the State Council 2010). Subsequently, many OGI requests were rejected on the grounds that they asked for information on government internal management and deliberative processes (Yang 2013; Fan 2017). The revised ROGI keeps the original exemptions and adds some more, listing not only internal management and deliberative process information but also administrative law enforcement case files, as exempt.

On top of the specific exemptions, the original ROGI provided a general rule that 'government information disclosed by administrative organs shall not endanger state security, public security, economic security or social stability'. This is often referred to as the 'three securities one stability' (*San Anquan Yi Wending*) provision. The revised ROGI has kept this rule. The ROGI does not define the 'three securities one stability', nor does it specify what kind of information might endanger them, leaving it to the discretion of administrative agencies. In practice, this has given administrative organs considerable latitude in using political excuses to shirk their disclosure obligations (Tang 2014; Chen Y. 2016; Shen 2016). Using the need to maintain social stability as a reason for withholding information is particularly problematic, and has resulted in many incidents of

[4]A comprehensive overview of the ROGI is beyond the scope of this essay. This section only describes the key aspects of the ROGI as pertinent to the discussion in subsequent sections.

local governments concealing critical information that has a direct impact on public health and safety; for example, information on a mining accident in Shanghang County, Fujian Province that polluted a nearby river (Chen Y. 2016).

Requesters who wish to challenge an administrative agency's decision regarding their OGI requests may apply for administrative reconsideration. If they are not satisfied with the administrative reconsideration decision, they may appeal it by filing an administrative lawsuit. Or, they may file a lawsuit directly.

While the ROGI has been hailed as a major step forward in promoting government transparency and citizens' right to information in China, it is not considered a strong piece of FOI legislation by international standards. One study that compares the original ROGI with international best practice identifies nine factors that significantly constrain Chinese OGI requesters' access to government information, including the ROGI's failure to define exemptions clearly and narrowly, the fact that it makes exemptions mandatory rather than discretionary, and the failure to establish an independent oversight body to mediate OGI disputes (Tang 2014). The revised ROGI does not render this observation invalid, as most of the factors that make the ROGI appear weak in international comparisons remain unchanged. The revised ROGI has removed one restriction on disclosure by request: requesters are no longer obligated to demonstrate a personal need for the information. However, the revision expands the scope of information that is exempt from disclosure and gives government organs more reasons to deny requests (for example, by proclaiming that the number or frequency of requests is unreasonable). As a result, the experience of many OGI requesters suggests that the removal of the 'needs test' has not made access to government information any easier.[5]

Evolution of OGI rules and practices

Using the ROGI is not easy. Both government agencies and OGI requesters have had much to learn. In the early days of the ROGI's implementation, after submitting requests, requesters sometimes found that staff in government offices had not even heard of the ROGI. Requesters had to explain to administrative organs what OGI was about and to 'teach' them how to reply to OGI requests. A law firm was even invited by a government agency that received its request—a first for them—to give them some training on processing OGI requests.[6]

Not fully understanding their obligations under the ROGI initially, many government organs simply ignored OGI requests or failed to observe the time limit for responding to requests. Both are clear violations of the ROGI and resulted in the defeat of many government organs in court when requesters sued them.[7] After the initial shock and

[5]Based on the author's communications with several OGI requesters and discussions in various social media groups in which the author is a member. Requesters generally complain that the revised ROGI is 'not as useful' as the old version for obtaining government information. There are more hurdles now than before, despite the removal of the needs test.

[6]Presentation by Wang Zhenyu, director of the Impact law firm, at a workshop organised by the firm in Beijing on 24 September 2014.

[7]Information on such cases can be found on the website China Judgements Online, available at: http://wenshu.court.gov.cn/Index, accessed 26 September 2020.

confusion, however, government agencies have adapted to the ROGI and are now much less likely to make simple mistakes, such as ignoring OGI requests altogether. They have also learned to standardise their replies to OGI requests. Requesters who applied for the same information from different government agencies used to receive very different replies. While one agency disclosed the information, another agency might claim the information did not exist, and a third agency might say the information involved state secrets and therefore could not be disclosed.[8] The discrepancies between the different replies would give requesters good grounds to challenge the non-disclosure decisions. As administrative organs learn to standardise and coordinate their replies to OGI requests, however, the occurrence of such discrepancies has been substantially reduced.

OGI rules and practices have evolved against the backdrop of the uneven development of rule of law in China. Amongst scholars of Chinese law, there has been a long-running debate on whether China has been gradually progressing towards rule of law since the start of its reform and opening era in 1978, or whether there can be no rule of law while it remains a one-party authoritarian state (Peerenboom 2002). In a major work on this subject, Peerenboom proposes drawing a distinction between 'thin' and 'thick' conceptions of rule of law. As he explains:

> A thin theory stresses the formal or instrumental aspects of rule of law—those features that any legal system allegedly must possess to function effectively as a system of laws, regardless of whether the legal system is part of a democratic or non-democratic society, capitalist or socialist, liberal or theocratic. (Peerenboom 2002, p. 3)

In contrast, thick conceptions of rule of law build on a thin conception of law, incorporating 'elements of political morality'. The dominant thick conception of rule of law in the West today is the liberal democratic version, which incorporates free market capitalism, multiparty democracy and a liberal interpretation of human rights.

While it is unclear if China will ever have the liberal democratic form of rule of law, Peerenboom suggests that it has been moving towards rule of law in the thin sense (Peerenboom 2002). Other scholars, including Minzner (2011), disagree with such views. In an extended commentary on the debate, Albert Chen persuasively argues that whether rule of law in the thin sense exists in China is a matter of degree:

> The nature and the structural or systemic characteristics of the contemporary Chinese party state are such that there are certain domains in which the rule of law is particularly weak, fragile, vulnerable, or even non-existent, while at the same time there exist other domains in which the rule of law is making progress or expanding. Similarly, there are certain types of court cases in which judicial professionalism, autonomy, and independence has developed considerably, while there are also 'political [*sic*] sensitive' cases in which the courts would defer to relevant party authorities. Thus, the concept of what I would call 'differential degrees of compliance with the rule of law in different domains and contexts of the Chinese state and society' should

[8] This was the experience of the environmental NGO Wuhu Ecology Centre (WEC) when it requested the same information from 31 provincial environmental protection bureaus in 2011. Information from a presentation by WEC member Ding Jie at a workshop organised by the author in Beijing, 29 September 2012.

> be introduced for the purpose of scholarly discourse and research on the rule of law. (Chen A.H.Y. 2016, p. 30)

The ROGI is a case that supports Chen's argument about varying degrees of rule of law in different domains and contexts. The ROGI is not an isolated piece of progressive legislation. Rather, it is part of a larger project to promote a 'rule of law government', a proclaimed goal of the Chinese state since the 1999 constitutional amendment that added a provision on 'ruling the country according to law' (Chen A.H.Y. 2016). Since 1999, there have been many important developments in the domain of administrative law, including the enactment of new laws on administrative reconsideration, the management of civil servants, administrative licensing and administrative coercion, and the revision of existing laws, notably the Administrative Litigation Law (Chen A.H.Y. 2016; Shen 2018). Together the new legislative developments have limited the power of administrative organs, regulated the exercise of their discretion, extended the range of areas wherein applications for judicial review may be brought, and strengthened the courts' power to deal with administrative organs that refuse to comply with court judgments in administrative litigation (Chen A.H.Y. 2016).

Thus, there has been progress towards a thin version of rule of law in the domain of public administration, with the enactment of the ROGI being one example of such progress. However, as discussed in the preceding section, the ROGI is by no means a strong piece of FOI legislation by international standards. Therefore, enactment of the ROGI itself is not sufficient proof of the realisation of 'rule of law government' with regard to the management of government information. The key test is how the ROGI has been implemented.

We can observe here what Albert Chen calls 'differential degrees of compliance with the rule of law in different domains and contexts'. The story is neither the triumph of rule of law nor the total disproof of it. Government implementation of the ROGI has displayed both positive and negative aspects. On the one hand, OGI work is increasingly regularised and standardised; government record management has improved; government agencies gradually disclose more information proactively. Regular OGI training for civil servants has been introduced; infrastructure to support OGI, such as e-government portals, has been upgraded; and OGI work has been included in performance evaluations of government agencies (Wang 2018).

On the other hand, the government has also issued supplementary rules or interpretations of the original ROGI that have narrowed the scope of information disclosure and made the application process more burdensome for requesters. These supplementary rules and interpretations have found their way into the revised ROGI. As mentioned above, a 2010 GOSC directive made information on government internal management exempt from disclosure, a principle that now constitutes a formal clause in the revised ROGI. The same directive also imposed a few other restrictions on information disclosure, including the stipulation that administrative organs should not be expected to 'consolidate, process or reformulate' information for requesters (General Office of the State Council 2010). 'The requested information is not in a readily available form and would need processing' has since become another excuse that enables government agencies to refuse OGI requests. This rule has also been written into the revised ROGI.

In addition to formal rules, government agencies have also developed many informal methods of responding to OGI requests that consist of negative, cynical moves to obstruct legitimate OGI requests (Lu 2011). One such method involves telling requesters that they have not described the requested information clearly enough, and that therefore it cannot be located. Unless requesters can produce the exact title or number of a government document, government agencies that have used the 'request unclear' excuse simply insist that they cannot tell what exactly is being requested.[9] This creates an impossible situation for requesters: without seeing the document, they cannot know its exact title and number; without knowing its exact title and number, they are not allowed to see the document.

On the civil society side, one clear trend since the ROGI came into force is that Chinese citizens and civil society organisations have enthusiastically used this new mechanism for rights protection and issue advocacy. The number of OGI requests has increased rapidly since 2008. In 2015, 57 central government departments received a total of nearly 150,000 OGI requests, compared with 3,000 recorded in 2011 (Horsley 2016b). The numbers of administrative appeals and lawsuits filed by dissatisfied requesters have also shown a corresponding rise. From 2011 to 2014, courts throughout China received a total of roughly 30,000 new OGI cases. In 2015, the number of OGI lawsuits more than tripled, to roughly 16,000, while 22,000 administrative appeals over OGI issues were filed (Horsley 2016b).

Although the government has won the majority of OGI administrative appeals and lawsuits, OGI requesters have continued to win some cases, proving Chen's thesis about differential degrees of compliance with the rule of law in different contexts in contemporary China. According to a report by OGICN, an NGO that has conducted extensive research on OGI issues, in 2015, OGI requesters won around 11.2% of administrative appeals and around 9.7% of lawsuits (OGICN 2016). The number of victories by OGI requesters has varied from year to year and from place to place. A report published by the Beijing First Intermediate People's Court shows that plaintiffs won 24.5% of the OGI cases it tried in 2012; however, in 2017 the figure was down to 7.8% (Lin & Jin 2017).

Another important trend related to the civil society side is that OGI requesters have continued to develop their skills in order to overcome the formal and informal hurdles created by government departments. Instead of accepting the government's rejections of their requests, determined requesters keep fishing for information by filing more requests. Many requesters have accumulated extensive knowledge of the organisational structure of the government bureaucracy, the functions of different departments, administrative procedures, and government policymaking and implementation processes:[10] such knowledge has ultimately enabled requesters to plan their 'campaign' more strategically.

[9]For example, at a forum organised by the China University of Political Science and Law to debate the proposed revision of the ROGI, several participants shared their experiences of having OGI requests rejected on this ground. The forum was held in Beijing on 29 July 2017.

[10]The author worked with or interviewed several such OGI requesters while leading a project that documented the Chinese public's use of the ROGI between 2013 and 2018. These requesters have typically filed hundreds or even thousands of OGI requests and lawsuits that concern many aspects of public administration.

For example, knowing that the decision to build a new road inevitably involves multiple agencies, they might first file a request with an agency that only has a peripheral role in the decision. Although it is not a central player in the decision, the agency may nevertheless have documents that mention the central role of other agencies and describe the decision. Once they have obtained these documents, requesters then move to demand information from the agencies that are central players in the decision. If these agencies deny that they have the information, the documents obtained through earlier requests prove that the agencies are lying.[11] In short, seasoned OGI requesters—individuals who have filed hundreds or even thousands of requests, administrative appeals and lawsuits—tend not to accept that the fortress of government secrecy is impregnable. They believe that if they are skilled and tenacious enough, they will be able to breach the fortress sooner or later.[12]

OGI requesters' development of skills has been aided by their extensive experience-sharing and networking *via* social media. On the popular Chinese social media app WeChat, for example, there are many active groups devoted to the discussion of OGI and administrative litigation. Members often share government agencies' replies to their OGI requests with the group and ask others for suggestions on how they might challenge 'no' decisions through administrative appeal or litigation, or how they might revise and resubmit their requests to make it harder for government agencies to say no.[13]

As OGI requesters continue to make more frequent and skilled use of the ROGI and the administrative appeal and litigation systems, rising user demand has played a key role in shaping the OGI regime's evolution. This will be further illustrated by the case studies below.

Case studies

The Gangzha District People's Court accuses Lu Hongxia of abusing her right to information and litigation

On 27 February 2015, OGI requester Lu Hongxia gained national notoriety when the Gangzha District People's Court in Nantong City, Jiangsu Province organised a press conference to present eight 'typical cases' of individuals 'abusing the right to file OGI lawsuits'.[14] Among the eight cases, that of Lu Hongxia was highlighted. Before the press conference, the Gangzha Court held a session to review Lu's OGI lawsuit against the Nantong Municipal Development and Reform Commission (DRC). Instead of hearing Lu's complaint against the DRC, the court dwelled on how Lu had 'abused' her

[11]Interviews with OGI requesters in Hunan Province, November 2016.

[12]Several seasoned OGI requesters with whom the author has collaborated on an OGI research project have expressed such a view, for example, Mr Xu in Tianjin, Mr Wang in Beijing and Mr Zhang in Guangzhou.

[13]The author is a member of several such groups and has run a WeChat public account that disseminates OGI information, including case studies of OGI requests and written judgements of OGI lawsuits.

[14]'Nantong Gangzha Court Takes the Lead in Reining in Abuse of OGI Litigation Right', *Chinadaily.com.cn*, 28 February 2015, available at: http://cnews.chinadaily.com.cn/2015-02/28/content_19675816.htm, accessed 7 December 2018.

right to information and litigation. It then ruled to dismiss Lu's lawsuit and further stated that:

> In future, if the plaintiff Lu Hongxia submitted similar OGI requests to administrative organs again, or filed similar lawsuits to the court again, her requests and lawsuits should be strictly scrutinised according to the stipulations of the ROGI.[15]

The Gangzha Court's ruling on *Lu Hongxia v. Nantong Municipal DRC* was the key message of its press conference. The ruling detailed Lu's 'abuse' of her right to information: between 2013 and January 2015, Lu, together with her relatives, filed at least 94 OGI requests to various Nantong government agencies, asking for information ranging from the municipal government's budget report, the number of cars owned by the municipal government, the licence numbers and brands of all government-owned cars, to the standards for detainee meals at Nantong Detention House in 2013.

According to the court ruling, Lu and her relatives filed at least 39 applications for administrative reconsideration to challenge some of the replies to their OGI requests. After the completion of the administrative reconsideration process, they were still not satisfied and filed at least 36 administrative lawsuits. The ruling gave some examples of Lu and her relatives' reasons for filing lawsuits: some OGI replies did not bear the logos of the administrative organs issuing them, or the document title was incomplete, or the document number was wrong. In short, the ruling implied that Lu and her relatives had filed frivolous lawsuits.

The court then charged that Lu's real purpose in filing OGI requests was not to obtain information, but to express discontent over the compensation she was offered for the demolition of her house and to 'exert pressure on the government and its relevant departments, in order to make them attach importance to and solve' her issue, so that she could 'maximise her interests in the demolition and relocation process'. It concluded that Lu's lawsuits 'lack interests in the litigation, have improper purposes, and are in bad faith. They have breached the necessity to exercise the right to litigation and have consequently forfeited the justification to exercise the right. They are typical actions that abuse the right to litigate'.[16]

While the Gangzha Court's ruling on *Lu Hongxia v. Nantong Municipal DRC* reads more like an indictment and condemnation of Lu's bad behaviour than a review of the dispute itself, before dismissing Lu's suit, the ruling does briefly outline her complaint against the Nantong DRC and the DRC's defence. On 26 November 2013, Lu submitted a request for 'the approval document for the greening project for Changping Road's western extension'. On 28 November, the DRC provided Lu with its document No. [2010]67 entitled 'The Municipal DRC's Written Reply Concerning the Changping Road Western Extension Project'. Lu contends that the information provided by the DRC is not what she requested. The Nantong DRC, on the other hand, maintains that it gave Lu the

[15] *Lu Hongxia v. Nantong Municipal Development and Reform Commission*, Jiangsu Province, Nantong City, Gangzha District People's Court Administrative Ruling, No. 00021, 27 February 2015, available at: http://bbs.0513.org/thread-2540947-1-1.html, accessed 7 December 2018.

[16] *Lu Hongxia v. Nantong Municipal Development and Reform Commission*, Jiangsu Province, Nantong City, Gangzha District People's Court Administrative Ruling, No. 00021, 27 February 2015, available at: http://bbs.0513.org/thread-2540947-1-1.html, accessed 7 December 2018.

approval document for the entire Changping Road western extension project, which covers road and bridge construction, pipe laying and greening. Therefore, the document contains the information that Lu requested. The DRC then accuses Lu of abusing her right to request government information and asks the court to dismiss her suit.[17]

The *Lu Hongxia v. Nantong Municipal DRC* case attracted considerable media attention and fuelled debates in the country's legal community, not only because it was the first time a court had dismissed an OGI lawsuit on the ground that the plaintiff had abused the right to information and litigation, but also because there is no mention of 'abusing the right to litigate' in existing Chinese laws. As one legal scholar told *China Youth Daily*, none of the reasons given by the Gangzha Court—Lu submitting a large number of OGI requests or creating pressure on the government with her OGI requests and lawsuits—justified its ruling. Whether Lu's lawsuits had put pressure on administrative agencies was not something that should concern the court. Since existing laws did not contain the concept of 'abusing the right to government information', the Gangzha Court's ruling violated the tenet of the ROGI (Cao & Wang 2015).

Despite the controversy, it appears that the judicial system supports the Gangzha Court's position. Lu appealed the ruling to the Nantong Intermediate People's Court, which affirmed the original ruling in July 2015. The case was then selected for publication in the November 2015 issue of the *Supreme People's Court Gazette*,[18] a sign of the endorsement of the Gangzha Court's ruling by the Supreme People's Court (SPC).

So far, this essay has presented the case of the Gangzha Court. It will now turn to Lu's side of the story. What drove her to file so many OGI requests and lawsuits? According to Lu, her dispute with the local government centred on the compensation plan for a demolished house which she and her ex-husband's family jointly owned. The local government followed the policy of still considering a divorced couple one household when offering compensation for their demolished house, if neither party has remarried (Lan 2015). The reason for this policy is this: if a divorced couple were recognised as forming two separate households, they would be entitled to more compensation for their jointly owned house than if they were still married and therefore formed one household. To prevent couples from arranging a fake divorce in order to claim more compensation, the local government decided to recognise only one household in the case of divorced couples for the purpose of allocating compensation, unless at least one of the parties had remarried, thus proving the divorce was not fake. Under this policy, Lu and her husband would have to claim compensation as one household first, then divide up the compensation themselves. However, Lu and her ex-husband had a very acrimonious divorce, and she did not wish to have any more dealings with him or his family. She objected to being forced to negotiate with his family about how to divide up the compensation. In addition to the emotional stress, dividing up the compensation with her ex-husband's family was also unacceptable to her because it would incur higher taxes.[19]

[17]*Lu Hongxia v. Nantong Municipal Development and Reform Commission*, Jiangsu Province, Nantong City, Gangzha District People's Court Administrative Ruling, No. 00021, 27 February 2015, available at: http://bbs.0513.org/thread-2540947-1-1.html, accessed 7 December 2018.

[18]'The Case of *Lu Hongxia v. Nantong Municipal Development and Reform Commission* regarding the Reply to An OGI Request', *Gazette of the Supreme People's Court of the People's Republic of China*, Issue No. 11, 2015, available at: http://gongbao.court.gov.cn/PeriodicalsDic.html, accessed 11 December 2018.

[19]Interview with Lu Hongxia, Nantong, 30 March 2017.

Thus, Lu tried to make the local government change its policy so it could offer her compensation directly. Contacting the government did not yield any result. She tried to file a lawsuit; the court refused to accept her suit. Lu then tried petitioning the government, but was put under administrative detention for ten days as punishment for 'illegal petitioning'.[20] As mentioned above, when the Gangzha Court accused Lu of abusing her right to information by requesting a wide range of government information, one example it gave was that Lu had requested information on the meal standards for detainees at Nantong Detention House in 2013. As Lu explains, she requested this information because she found the food offered to detainees to be of very poor quality when serving her time in the detention house. Detainees were forced to pay over the market price for better food if they did not want to eat meals provided. Lu maintains that she had a good reason for wanting to know the detention house's meal standards and that all her other OGI requests, while they covered a wide variety of issues, similarly served serious purposes.[21]

Lu met many other petitioners in the process of submitting her petitions all the way up to the central government in Beijing and in the detention house. From other petitioners Lu learned about the ROGI, which was how she started to file OGI requests. She also started to study laws, regulations and government policies. Since administrative organs often refused to disclose the information she requested, she had to apply for administrative reconsideration or file lawsuits to challenge the replies. In her lawsuit against the Nantong Municipal DRC that resulted in the above-mentioned Gangzha Court ruling, for example, Lu requested 'the approval document for the greening project for Changping Road's western extension'. The DRC claims that the document it gave Lu in November 2013 contains the requested information. However, Lu actually possesses another DRC document that discredits this claim. In another OGI request to the DRC in June 2014, Lu asked for 'the approval document for the greening project for Chengbei Avenue'. The DRC gave Lu a document that approved the greening projects for four roads together, including both Chengbei Avenue and, fortuitously, the Changping Road's western extension. In other words, the document which Lu obtained from the DRC through her June 2014 request is what the DRC should have given her in reply to her November 2013 request. The document which the DRC gave Lu in 2013 is the wrong document.[22] This supports Lu's argument that her suit against the Nantong DRC was for a good reason, despite the Gangzha Court's accusation that she did 'abuse' her right to sue.

[20]China has a petition system that allows citizens to contact government petition bureaus to lodge complaints, request assistance or seek resolutions to their problems. Petition bureaus do not have the power or resources to resolve issues themselves and can only refer petitions to relevant administrative organs for action. Once petitions have been processed by petition bureaus, even if relevant state organs fail to solve the issues to the satisfaction of the petitioners, the cases are considered closed from the government's point of view. However, when they are not satisfied, instead of giving up, many petitioners choose to take their petitions to higher level authorities or resubmit their petitions repeatedly. This is then considered 'illegal petitioning' by the state. Those who engage in 'illegal petitioning' may be accused of offences such as disrupting public order and punished by the government, typically in the form of administrative detention.

[21]Interview with Lu Hongxia, Nantong, 30 March 2017.

[22]During my interview with Lu Hongxia in Nantong on 30 March 2017, she allowed me to photograph documents related to her two requests to the Nantong DRC and her lawsuit against the DRC, including the two documents that the DRC disclosed to her, the two OGI request forms she submitted to the DRC, her statement of claim and the DRC's written defence submitted to the court. The documents appear to substantiate Lu's claim.

While Lu can produce many counterexamples to prove that her OGI requests and lawsuits were justified, she did follow a conscious strategy of using OGI requests to boost her bargaining position *vis-à-vis* the local government. A few years before her own partially owned house was demolished to provide land for a city development project, her parents' house was demolished to make way for the Chengbei Avenue project. Lu's OGI requests sought information on decision-making behind the two projects and the implementation processes, including how much money was spent, how much compensation was paid to affected households, whether adequate procedures were followed, whether legal requirements were satisfied, and the auditing reports for the projects.[23] As Lu told a *Global Times* journalist, 'the government work in both cases was a mess which is why I want to know the details of the two development projects and if it was legitimate for the government to do what it did' (Yuen 2015). The two projects hardly stood up to scrutiny in terms of complying with formal rules and procedures on paper. For example, Lu's father was forced to sign a blank sheet of paper indicating his acceptance of compensation, without being told how much the compensation would be, which violated relevant regulations.[24] By making OGI requests that could expose the 'messy' way the two projects were approved and implemented, Lu created pressure on the local government to satisfy her demand for proper compensation for her partially owned house.

Lu's decision to use OGI requests to probe not only the project that caused the demolition of her own house but also the project that demolished her parents' house was a strategic one. As she explains, her parents were entitled to more compensation for their house than they actually received. However, Lu says if the government could offer her an acceptable compensation deal on her own house, then she would give up the fight for her parents' compensation. Or, she would settle for a better deal for her parents' house and stop demanding a new compensation scheme for her own house. By making two demands but being prepared to settle if the government would meet either one, Lu made it easier for the local government to reach an agreement with her. In the end, the local government offered Lu a new deal for her own house. She stopped making OGI requests and withdrew her still-pending lawsuits. Thus, Lu's story ended well: she obtained what she wanted from the local government, and the local government no longer had a 'troublemaker' to worry about. It also resulted in a policy change. According to Lu, the local government stopped treating divorced couples with joint ownership of a house as still forming one household and now compensates the two parties separately.[25]

Li Jinsheng's OGI requests to the China Disabled Persons Federation (CDPF)[26]

As a blind person who was not proficient in Braille, Li Jinsheng felt disadvantaged when he took the national qualification examination for medical massage for blind people, which only

[23] Interview with Lu Hongxia, Nantong, 31 March 2017.
[24] Interview with Lu Hongxia, Nantong, 30 March 2017.
[25] Interview with Lu Hongxia, Nantong, 30 March 2017.
[26] This case study is based on a written account of the events by Yang Zhanqing, a former member of the NGO Yirenping who advised and supported Li Jinsheng in his efforts. Yang's account is therefore based on first-hand knowledge. Unless otherwise indicated, all information that is recounted in this case study comes from Yang's written account.

offered exam papers in Braille. Li checked The Law of the People's Republic of China on the Protection of the Disabled and found in Article 54 the following stipulation:

> In all kinds of entrance examinations, professional qualification examinations and occupational examinations held by the state with the participation of blind persons, Braille examination papers, electronic examination papers, or assistance from special staff shall be provided to blind persons.[27]

Li wanted to see options other than a Braille test paper made available to examinees like himself. He tried petitioning the government, with no result. Eventually he sought help from the anti-discrimination NGO Yirenping. The medical massage exam for blind people is administered by the CDPF. After studying the issue, Yirenping staff advised Li to try making the CDPF change its policy by filing OGI requests. In November 2011, Li sent a request to the CDPF asking for 'the reasons why the medical massage qualification examination for blind people does not provide an electronic examination paper or assistance from staff to examinees'.

The CDPF responded quickly, informing Li that an electronic examination paper or assistance from special staff did not meet the secrecy requirements of national examinations classified at the secret level, therefore it had not adopted such practices in examinations (Li 2013).

Li and Yirenping staff suspected that the CDPF simply made up this excuse. They noted that the National Self-Taught Higher Education Examination, which is taken by far more people and necessarily requires a higher level of security arrangements to keep the test papers secret, offers blind examinees both an electronic test paper and assistance by special staff. Li and Yirenping staff felt there was no reason for the medical massage examination to be administered in a more 'secret' fashion. Consequently, Li filed a second request, demanding that the CDPF disclose 'the legal justification' for its refusal to provide an electronic paper or assistance by staff for blind examinees in the medical massage qualification examination.

This time the CDPF replied that it was conducting a feasibility study of new examination methods, such as using computer-based or audio test papers: 'we will reform examination methods according to the results of the study, in order to better satisfy the needs of blind examinees'. The CDPF also promised: 'next year, we will make reform of the test method of the medical massage examination for blind people a key emphasis in our work' (Li 2013).

The CDPF reply did not address Li's question. Li and Yirenping staff speculated that the CDPF avoided the question because it could not justify its previous claim about 'secrecy requirements'. Although the CDPF's reply did not address Li's OGI request, he and Yirenping decided not to challenge it, because the CDPF did at least indicate willingness to change how the medical massage exam was administered, which was Li's real concern.

[27] *Zhonghua Renmin Gongheguo Canjiren Baozhang Fa 2008nian Xiudingban*, adopted 7 July 2008, available at: https://wenku.baidu.com/view/9386ce1b51e79b8969022677.html#, accessed 1 October 2020.

In view of this, Li and Yirenping felt it would be a good idea to give the CDPF some positive feedback and encouragement.

With Yirenping's help, Li drafted a letter to convey his excitement after receiving CDPF's promise to reform examination methods and posted it online to collect signatures in support of the reform. A total of 716 signatures were collected in 12 days. In January 2012, Li and another blind person travelled to the CDPF's headquarters in Beijing to hand-deliver the letter. They also presented the CDPF with a silk banner praising the CDPF's promise to introduce reforms. A CDPF official told Li and his companion that changing examination methods could not be accomplished overnight but promised to do their best to bring change as soon as possible (Li 2013).

However, when the next national medical massage qualification examination for blind people took place in September 2012, there was no change at all. Therefore, Li and Yirenping decided to submit a third OGI request to the CDPF. This time Li asked the CDPF to disclose, first, the content of the feasibility study of introducing an electronic exam paper or an audio version of exam questions and the study's findings in the past year; and second, whether an electronic exam paper or an audio version of exam questions was provided to examinees in the 2012 medical massage qualification examination for blind people in compliance with the Law on the Protection of the Disabled and the Regulations on the Construction of Barrier-Free Environments. If not, the CDPF was requested to explain why, and when such options would be made available to examinees.

When the CDPF failed to respond to the request in 15 business days, Li filed an application for administrative reconsideration to the Ministry of Civil Affairs (MCA), the CDPF's superior administrative organ, in January 2013. In February, the CDPF replied to Li, stating that 'because changing the examination method would involve multiple departments and multiple stages, the exact time of implementation cannot be determined at present'. The MCA did not respond to the administrative reconsideration application, which was in clear violation of the Administrative Reconsideration Law. However, since Li and Yirenping's main concern was to make the CDPF respond to Li's OGI request, once the CDPF replied, they decided not to pursue the MCA's failure to respond.

The CDPF's answer about the involvement of 'multiple departments and multiple stages' was vague and did not reflect what, if any, efforts had been made to bring about change. Li submitted a fourth OGI request, asking, 'What work is your organisation currently carrying out in reforming the examination method of the medical massage examination? What departments and stages are involved?'.

In May 2013, the CDPF provided Li with information on work that it had carried out month-by-month in 2013 to introduce electronic exam papers. It also stated that 'revamping of the examination system' would be initiated that same month and that an electronic exam paper would be piloted the following year.

When the annual medical massage qualification examination took place in September 2014, a computer-based audio version of the exam paper was indeed piloted in one of the 27 test centres. The CDPF also announced *via* the media that it would expand the pilot the following year (Yang 2014).

Discussion

The two cases above are not success stories from the point of view of the outcomes of the OGI requests: neither Lu Hongxia nor Li Jinsheng obtained most of the information they had requested. Lu was even labelled an abuser of the OGI system by the local government and court and had many of her OGI lawsuits dismissed. However, both were successful in the sense that they achieved their objectives. The cases demonstrate how Chinese citizens and civil society organisations have been able to use OGI requests to pursue a variety of goals, from private interest protection to public interest advocacy. Gaining access to government information was only one of their goals, and not even the primary one. In Li's case, he and Yirenping were clear from the beginning that they were interested in bringing about a policy change rather than obtaining any particular information. Many civil society organisations, such as LGBT groups, women's rights NGOs and environmental NGOs, have similarly used OGI requests as an advocacy tool. OGI requests provide an entry point for them to engage government agencies on policy issues. Requests can also generate newsworthy stories that attract media attention. Media coverage then helps to bring the issues into public view and may influence public opinion, which in turn may have some impact on government policy. For this reason, requesters who pursue advocacy goals often take other actions in parallel to their OGI requests, in order to make their actions more newsworthy. In Li's case, an online signature-collecting campaign was launched, and Li made a trip to Beijing to deliver the letter and silk banner to the CDPF in person. These activities were intended to provide journalists with additional copy, making Li's story more interesting and newsworthy.

Some requesters have also used OGI to gain legal standing to sue the government. In an article that analyses 'deviant OGI requests', three SPC judges describe a case in which a requester in a property dispute with a local government was not able to sue the government because the statute of limitations had expired. The requester found a solution by filing a large number of OGI requests for information related to his dispute with the local government, then sued local government departments over their replies to his OGI requests. The three judges caution that OGI lawsuits cannot resolve the requester's dispute with the government, but they acknowledge that some requesters have managed to exert pressure on government agencies by filing 'deviant OGI requests' followed by lawsuits. Taking advantage of some government agencies' aversion to losing in court, these 'deviant' requesters have managed to gain 'unjustifiable economic benefits' (Li *et al.* 2015). Lu Hongxia's case serves to illustrate this point. Although the local court accused her of abusing the OGI system, she succeeded in forcing the local government to offer her a better deal for her demolished house.

One important reason that Lu's requests created pressure on the local government seems to be that the two projects that led to the demolition of her own house and that of her parents had many flaws if measured against the high standards of 'law-based administration', a goal promoted by the central government that urges local governments to perform every administrative act strictly in accordance to laws and regulations. If scrutinised, the two projects were likely to reveal multiple violations of formal rules, as suggested by some documents Lu obtained through her OGI requests.[28] If the local government had not settled the dispute, Lu would have filed more requests for information about the two projects as well as other aspects of local administration, and she would have persisted in challenging non-disclosure decisions though administrative appeal and litigation.[29]

Although the local government could influence local courts to dismiss her lawsuits or rule against her, as it seems to have done, because Lu was very persistent and filed OGI requests and lawsuits non-stop, it was politically risky for the local government and court to blatantly violate the ROGI and legal norms in dealing with Lu's requests and lawsuits, given the party-state's promotion of 'ruling the country according to law'. As has been pointed out, in 'politically sensitive' domains where the Chinese party-state's key interests are at stake, rule of law does not appear to have been respected. However, in other domains, the party-state also sees benefit in promoting the rule of law, at least a thin version of rule of law that emphasises the formal and procedural aspects of the law and its enforcement (Chen A. 2016). Apparently political sensitivity did not apply in the case of Lu, who only had a small financial dispute with the local government. For the local government and court to bend the law in Lu's case, therefore, went against national policy and carried the risk of incurring political sanctions by higher authorities. Furthermore, Lu had appealed many of local courts' rulings to the provincial high court. To influence the high court's decisions illegally would entail further effort and risk on the part of the local government and court. This is why in Lu's case, as in many similar cases across the country, although OGI requesters may have their requests rejected and lose their administrative appeals and lawsuits, they may still force the government to meet their demands by filing more requests, administrative appeals and lawsuits. What really matters is not whether their OGI requests result in the disclosure of information, but whether they can create enough pressure on the government through their determined actions.

The ROGI's legislative aim is to promote government transparency and enable the public to supervise the government. It is meant to serve public interest by protecting citizens' right to know. However, in its actual application the ROGI appears to have largely been used as a tool for individuals to seek remedy for the infringements of their private rights and interests (Geng & Zhou 2016; Wang 2017), causing government entities major problems, as Lu's case illustrates. Citizen mobilisation of the ROGI as a strategic resource in negotiating disputes with the state is arguably the most unexpected outcome of the implementation of the ROGI. Apparently, the Chinese party-state did not fully anticipate such a development and has reacted by developing new OGI rules and practices to try to stem 'abuse' of the ROGI, culminating in the revision of the ROGI in 2019. Studies of legal mobilisation in other countries find that, in many cases, it has generated a backlash or counter-mobilisation from reactionary political forces (McCann 2007). In China, citizens' mobilisation of the ROGI has equally generated counter-mobilisation from political forces that feel threatened by citizen actions. The Gangzha Court's use of the charge of 'abusing the right to information and litigation' to dismiss Lu Hongxia's lawsuit is a vivid example of such

[28]Lu shared copies of some of the documents with the author.
[29]Interview with Lu Hongxia, Nantong, 30 March 2017.

counter-mobilisation. This approach has since been copied by other courts and endorsed by the SPC (Horsley 2016b).

Conclusion

This essay offers a socio-legal analysis of the development of China's OGI regime. It describes how the rules and practices of ROGI have been shaped by everyday interactions between OGI requesters and the government, as both sides constantly adapt to the way the other side applies the ROGI. At the outset, the ROGI raised many questions: what types of government information are subject to the disclosure requirement? What constitutes a legitimate OGI request? For what purposes can citizens apply for government information? How can requesters use the information obtained through OGI requests? What can be achieved by filing OGI requests other than obtaining information? The answers were not immediately clear to either requesters or government organs, nor have they been immutable since. Chinese citizens who use the OGI mechanism as a new avenue of political participation are constantly testing the limits of the system, while the government has reacted by continuously adjusting OGI rules and its practices in implementing the ROGI, in order to prevent what it sees as 'abuse' of the system.

Chinese citizens' use of the ROGI is a classic case of legal mobilisation. From the legal mobilisation perspective, the ROGI is a resource which Chinese citizens and civil society organisations have exploited very creatively, not only to assert their right to information, but also as a means to defend a range of other rights and interests, both private and public, and as a tool for issue advocacy. Researchers of the implementation of FOI laws globally have observed that 'the response from civil society needs to be energetic, committed, and long term .... Without a demand for information and vigorous monitoring of government implementation and enforcement efforts, the hard-won right to information can quickly atrophy' (Neuman & Calland 2007, p. 182). In China, strong societal demand has given substance to the ROGI and has been a major driving force behind the gradual progress of public access to government information that has been achieved since the ROGI came into effect.

The OGI regime's evolution in China is not only a story of legal mobilisation by civil society, but also a story of counter-mobilisation by the state. State counter-mobilisation has taken the form of both positive and negative measures with regard to the implementation of the ROGI. On the one hand, the Chinese state has promoted OGI out of pragmatic considerations, including the need to improve governance and public services, build trust in the government, curb rampant corruption and comply with international commitments (Horsley 2007; Wang 2018). It has taken some concrete steps to improve the ROGI's implementation in response to vigorous citizen demand. On the other hand, the state 'does not want to leave the door fully open, fearing that too much open government information might lead to more democratic demand' (Wang 2014, p. 193). At the level of individual government organs, there is also the fear that OGI might expose flawed administration, poor performance or malfeasance. Consequently, the state has developed both formal and informal rules and practices that limit citizens' utilisation of the OGI system when it finds legal mobilisation by citizens and civil society threatening.

Understanding the evolution of China's OGI regime is not possible without analysing law as practised by state actors, but it also needs the analysis of law as practised in society. By enacting the ROGI, the Chinese party-state made a commitment to government transparency, but the actual practices of government entities in implementing the ROGI suggest that they are as likely to obstruct the public's access to information as they are to facilitate it. Despite the obstacles, many OGI requesters have persisted in exercising their right to information, believing that the OGI regime can only improve through determined bottom-up mobilisation of the law. While rule of law is still far from being realised in China, there have been many cases in which OGI requesters have succeeded in having the non-disclosure decisions on their requests overturned by courts or through administrative appeals, forcing government agencies to change their practices. Therefore, civic activism to push the government to honour its OGI commitment is essential. It is the dynamic interactions of citizens and the state, their dialogues, battles and negotiations over each request for government information that have determined, and will continue to determine, the extent to which the right to information can be realised in China.

References

Cao, Y. & Wang, D. (2015) 'Foayuan Caiding Chaiqianhu "Lansu" Beizhi Quefa Falü Yiju', *Qingnian Bao*, 13 March, available at: http://zqb.cyol.com/html/2015-03/13/nw.D110000zgqnb_20150313_1-05.htm, accessed 10 November 2018.

Chen, A. H. Y. (2016) 'China's Long March Towards Rule of Law or China's Turn Against Law?', *The Chinese Journal of Comparative Law*, 4, 1.

Chen, Y. (2016) 'Transparency Versus Stability: The New Role of Chinese Courts in Upholding Freedom of Information', *Tsinghua China Law Review*, 9, 79.

Chen, Y. (2017) 'Taming the Right to Information: Motive Screening and the Public Interest Test Under China's FOI-Like Law', *Journal of Comparative Law*, 12, 2.

Cheng, Y., Qin, Y., Chen, J. & Yang, J. (2009) 'Zhengfu Xinxi Gongkai Yinian Guancha', *Liaowang*, No. 29, July, available at: http://news.sina.com.cn/c/sd/2009-07-20/095318256916.shtml, accessed 24 December 2018.

Distelhorst, G. (2017) 'The Power of Empty Promises: Quasi-Democratic Institutions and Activism in China', *Comparative Political Studies*, 50, 4.

Duan, H. (2017) 'Cong Zhengfu Xinxi Gongkai Tiaoli Kan Jishuhua Gaide de Kunjing', *FT Zongwenwang*, 15 August, available at: http://www.ftchinese.com/story/001073831?full=y&archive, accessed 24 December 2018.

Fan, C. (ed.) (2017) *Zhengfu Xinxi Gongkai Jiufen Susong Zhiyin yu Shiwu Jieda* (Beijing, Law Press).

General Office of the State Council (2008) 'Guowuyuan Bangongting guanyu Shixing Zhonghua Renmin Gongheguo Zhengfu Xinxi Gongkai Tiaoli Ruogan Wenti de Yijian', State Council, Document No. 36, 29 April, available at: http://www.gov.cn/zhengce/content/2008-04/30/content_1602.htm, accessed 18 April 2020.

General Office of the State Council (2010) 'Guowuyuan Bangongting guanyu Zuohao Zhengfu Xinxi Yishenqing Gongkai Gongzuo de Yijian', State Council, Document No. 5, 12 January, available at: http://www.gov.cn/xxgk/pub/govpublic/mrlm/201309/t20130913_66392.html, accessed 18 April 2020.

Geng, B. & Zhou, M. (2016) 'Zhengfu Xinxi Gongkai Lingyu Qisuquan de Lanyong he Xianzhi—Jiantan Lu Hongxia Su Nantongshi Fagaiwei Zhengfu Xinxi Gongkai An de Jiazhi', *Xingzheng Faxue Yanjiu*, 3.

Horsley, J. P. (2007) 'Toward a More Open China', in Florini, A. (ed.) *The Right to Know: Transparency for an Open World* (New York, NY, Columbia University Press).

Horsley, J. P. (2016a) 'China Promotes Open Government as it Seeks to Reinvent Its Governance Model', *Freedominfo.org*, 22 February, available at: http://www.freedominfo.org/2016/02/china-promotes-open-government-as-it-seeks-to-reinvent-its-governance-model, accessed 26 December 2018.

Horsley, J. P. (2016b) 'China's FOIA Turns Eight', *Freedominfo.org*, 28 April, available at: http://www.freedominfo.org/2016/04/chinas-foia-turns-eight/, accessed 17 December 2018.

Lan, T. (2015) 'Duihua "Jiangren" Lu Honhxia: Kandao Pingshi Buzhidao de Wenjian, jiu gen Fadacai Yiyang', *Pengpai Xinwen*, 4 March, available at: https://www.thepaper.cn/newsDetail_forward_1307627, accessed 7 December 2018.

Li, G., Geng, B. & Zhou, M. (2015) 'Zhengfu Xinxi Gongkai Feizhengchang Shenqing Anjian de Xianzhuang yu Duice', *Renmin Sifa*, 15, available at: http://www.360doc.com/content/17/0317/08/21727081_637551861.shtml, accessed 2 January 2019.

Li, Z. (2013) '5 Ci Shangshu Zhongcanlian, Mangren Qiulai Wuzhangai Kaoshi', *Dahe Bao*, 8 May, available at: http://newpaper.dahe.cn/dhb/html/2013-05/08/content_890394.htm?div=-1#, accessed 1 October 2020.

Lin, P. & Jin, Y. (2017) 'Beijing Yizhongyuan: Zhengfu Xinxi Gongkai Susong Zengduo,Zhengfu Baisulü Jiangzhi 7.8%', *Pengpai Xinwen*, 7 December, available at: https://www.thepaper.cn/newsDetail_forward_1896093, accessed 30 December 2018.

Lu, Y. (2011) 'Testing China's Government Transparency Sweet Talk', *Wall Street Journal*, 28 September, available at: https://blogs.wsj.com/chinarealtime/2011/09/28/testing-chinas-government-transparency-sweet-talk/, accessed 12 May 2019.

McCann, M. (2007) 'Law and Social Movements', in Sarat, A. (ed.) *The Blackwell Companion to Law and Society* (Oxford, Carldon, Blackwell).

Minzner, C. F. (2011) 'China's Turn Against Law', *American Journal of Comparative Law*, 59, 4.

Neuman, L. & Calland, R. (2007) 'Making the Law Work: The Challenges to Implementation', in Florini, A. (ed.) *The Right to Know: Transparency for an Open World* (New York, NY, Columbia University Press).

OGICN (2016) 'Zhongguo Zhengfu Xinxi Gongkai Jiuji Jizhi Guancha Baogao (2016)', available at: https://www.jianshu.com/p/ed3be8a51dbc, accessed 30 December 2018.

Peerenboom, R. (2002) *China's Long March Toward Rule of Law* (Cambridge, Cambridge University Press).

Piotrowski, S. J., Zhang, Y., Lin, W. & Yu, W. (2009) 'Key Issues for Implementation of Chinese Open Government Information Regulations', *Public Administration Review*, December.

Qin, Y. & Cheng, Y. (2009) '181 fen Shenqing yu 18 fen Huifu', *Liaowang*, No. 29, July, available at: http://news.sina.com.cn/c/sd/2009-07-20/095318256916_5.shtml, accessed 24 December 2018.

Shen, J. (2016) 'Zhengfu Xinxi Gongkai Liwai Guize Shijian Jianshi', *Renmin Luntan*, 18 October, available at: http://www.rmlt.com.cn/2016/1018/442426.shtml, accessed 18 December 2018.

Shen, K. (2018) 'Administrative Self-Regulation and the Rule of Administrative Law in China', *University of Pennsylvania Asian Law Review*, 13, 1.

Supreme People's Court (2011) 'Zuigao Renmin Fayuan guanyu Shenli Zhengfu Xinxi Gongkai Xingzheng Anjian Ruogan Wenti de Guiding', promulgated 29 July 2011, available at: http://www.china.com.cn/policy/txt/2011-08/16/content_23219028.htm, accessed 18 April 2020.

Tang, Y. (2014) '"Feeling for Rocks While Crossing the River": An Analysis of the Statutory Language of China's First Freedom of Information Law', *Journal of Information Policy*, 4.

Wang, G. (2017) 'Wang Guisong: Yi Gongmin de "Zhiqingquan" Shenshi "Xinxi Gongkai" de Zhidu Shijian', *Nandu Guancha de Boke*, 23 August, available at: http://nanduguancha.blog.caixin.com/archives/167573, accessed 4 January 2019.

Wang, X. (2014) *Open Environmental Information upon Disclosure Request in China: The Paradox of Legal Mobilization*, Doctoral thesis (Turku, University of Turku).

Wang, X. (2018) 'Zhengfu Xinxi Gongkai Zhidu Shinian: Maixiang Zhili Daoxiang de Gongkai', *Zhongguo Xingzheng Guanli*, 5.

Yang, L. (2014) 'Jisuanji Yuyinhua: Mangren Kaoshi de Xinbiange', *Zhongguo Canjirenwang*, 13 October, available at: http://www.chinadp.net.cn/datasearch_/journal/zc/2014-10/13-13768.html, accessed 11 December 2018.

Yang, W. (2013) *Zhengfu Xinxi Gongkai Zhuyao Wenti Yanjiu* (Beijing, Law Press).

Yuen, Y. (2015) 'Court Claims Family's Requests for Government Information is Abuse of Right', *Global Times*, 16 March, available at: http://www.globaltimes.cn/content/912281.shtml, accessed 7 December 2018.

Zemans, F. K. (1983) 'Legal Mobilization: The Neglected Role of the Law in the Political System', *American Political Science Review*, 77, 3.

Zhu, H. & Fu, H. (2017) 'Transparency as an Offence: Rights Lawyering for Open Government Information in China', *Journal of Comparative Law*, 12, 2.

Between Human Rights and Transitional Justice: The Dilemma of Constitutional Courts in Post-Communist Central Europe

KATARÍNA ŠIPULOVÁ & HUBERT SMEKAL

Abstract

The essay sheds light on the role of constitutional courts in transitional justice, focusing on their role in mitigating the conflicts between transitional justice and international human rights commitments. Through a study of the Czech Constitutional Court's case law, we demonstrate that international human rights work both as a constraint and a tool. Constitutional courts use international human rights law selectively, when it suits their reasoning and views on transition. Nevertheless, the influence of international human rights law strengthens over time, especially when supported by the adverse rulings of international bodies, and gradually prevails over transitional justice justifications.

COUNTRIES EXPERIENCING A TRANSITION TO DEMOCRACY FACE an uneasy challenge: how to reconcile transitional justice issues with their human rights commitments and aspirations. A first look at the issue might not indicate any trouble, as democratising countries strive to distinguish themselves from the previous regime by upholding principles of liberal democracy and human rights. Nevertheless, closer inspection reveals that, although transitional justice uses human rights language and builds on ideas shared by human rights movements, some of its principles can differ considerably. Transitional justice legislation introduces a different logic of punishment and reparations based on arbitrary baselines, time-limited provisions, values, and principles (Teitel 2000, pp. 285–87), which are often at odds with general conceptions of human rights and international human rights commitments (Whitehead 2009, p. 1). For example, lustration (the vetting of public officers for ties with the previous regime) can have consequences for passive voting rights and employment rights. Wide access to secret police files and archives interferes

This work was supported by the Czech Science Foundation (*Grantová agentura České republiky*) under Grant Agreement no. 16-09415S, Panel P408 ('Beyond Compliance—Domestic Implementation of International Human Rights Case Law'). The authors would like to express their gratitude to the anonymous reviewers, the editors of the special issue and to colleagues at JUSTIN Brno for their critical feedback. We are indebted to judges and ex-judges of Czech apex courts who found time to talk to us. Finally, audiences in Prague (JUSTIN—PluriCourts workshop) and Utrecht (AHRI conference) stimulated our further exploration of the issue.

with the right to privacy. Condemnation of political parties associated with the previous regime might have repercussions for free political competition and even the whole party system. Similarly, reparations are ordinarily organised around arbitrary policy lines, because new political elites decide who will benefit from reparations and under what conditions, thus potentially violating equality rights. Teitel therefore considers 'the transitional rule of law' an alternative model of principles, one that does not necessarily conform to the point of view of established liberal democracy (Teitel 2000).

We expose the apparent contradictions between human rights and transitional justice in the particularly compelling case of post-1989 Central and Eastern Europe (CEE). After more than four decades of communist dictatorships, countries from the CEE region turned to Western European democracies as a model, as they performed better both economically and in terms of human rights standards. The international context adds an important element because at that time, international human rights regimes had already existed for decades and international human rights bodies had developed rich jurisprudence. Moreover, newly established CEE constitutional courts with the power of constitutional review presented a well-tested institutional mechanism for putting checks on other branches of power. The transitioning CEE countries therefore had both rules (international human rights) and institutional templates (parliamentary democracies with constitutional courts) to emulate.

At the same time, all CEE countries had their own internal issues to resolve. Post-1989 transitional processes in the region revolved around communist parties and their repressive apparatuses, especially the secret state police and its numerous collaborators (David 2011). The new regimes sought to eliminate the old cadres from holding powerful positions in the political system (Welsh 1996; Stan 2009; Horne 2015) and compensate the victims of past injustices (Czarnota *et al.* 2005; Sadurski 2008; Stan & Nedelsky 2015, p. xli). Economic rebirth was no less important; privatisation schemes and plans for how to reintroduce private ownership opened up challenges regarding the return of forcibly nationalised properties to the rightful owners.

Despite the similarities between CEE communist regimes, the transitional justice choices adopted by individual countries varied greatly. The diversity of transitional justice decisions attracted the attention of political science scholarship (Huntington 1991; Moran 1994), which has long focused on decisions adopted by political actors (Welsch 1996; Kornai & Rose-Ackerman 2004; David 2011), or the impact of transnational human rights networks on political actors (Crocker 1998; Sikkink 2011). Beyond a few doctrinal studies, constitutional courts have been neglected by transitional justice scholarship, or at best, perceived as mere second-order agents implementing political actors' decisions regarding transitional justice.[1] Nevertheless, the evidence from CEE shows that constitutional courts played an important role in transitional justice processes, as the majority of CEE transitional justice legislation has been adjusted in constitutional review proceedings (Sólyom 2003; Sadurski 2008; Kosař & Petrov 2017).

We argue that not factoring constitutional courts into the analysis inevitably misses important restraints on the choices of other branches of government when deciding

[1]Exceptions include Ginsburg (2003, 2012), and Kopeček and Petrov (2016).

transitional policy issues. We draw on more recent scholarship researching the role of judiciaries in Latin American transitional processes (Hilbink 2007; Huneeus 2010; Ocantos 2018) and place constitutional courts among the significant actors of transitional justice. Exploring their case law and interviewing former judges helped us to open the 'black box' surrounding the process by which states decide on certain forms of transitional justice policies.

The newly (re)established constitutional courts in CEE countries experienced the contradiction between protecting human rights and dealing with the past. They were expected to contribute to safeguarding liberal values (Ferreres Comella 2004; Hirschl 2004, p. 31), as proclaimed both in national bills of rights and in international human rights treaties.[2] Moreover, bodies such as the European Court of Human Rights (ECtHR) or the UN Human Rights Committee (UN HRC) had developed rich case law that the parties to these treaties were supposed to follow. Constitutional courts thus had to think hard about how to reconcile international human rights requirements with domestic transitional justice processes. Using the example of the Czech Republic, we examine how CEE constitutional courts approached the dilemma between transitional justice policies and the requirements that stemmed from international human rights treaties in the period 1993–2018. Did they defer to the transitional justice solutions adopted by the political actors, or did they challenge them? Did they step into this sensitive arena and push for a human rights perspective?

The contribution of our essay is threefold. First, it illustrates the significance of constitutional courts in transitional justice. Second, the essay analyses the clash between human rights and transitional justice in constitutional case law. Third, we show to what extent and when the constitutional courts make use of international human rights law in transitional justice disputes.

The Czech Republic offers a compelling story in this regard.[3] The particularly severe and pervasive nature of the Czechoslovak police state in the 1950s and 1960s, together with weak communist political forces shortly after the transition, contributed to a very harsh approach to ridding the political system of its communist legacy. This translated into the implementation of the strictest and broadest lustration policies in the CEE region (Sadurski 2014, pp. 344–45). The range of lustration surprised early scholars working on CEE transitional justice rationales, given the peaceful Velvet Revolution of 1989 (Huntington 1991; Moran 1994). At the same time, the country signalled its allegiance to international standards of human rights protection, joining the Council of Europe (CoE) in 1991. This combination of factors, coupled with the strong position of the Czech Constitutional Court (CCC), makes the Czech Republic a suitable case for studying the clash between human rights and CCC case law on transitional justice. The case study will help in understanding the role of constitutional courts in transitional jurisprudence in similar configurations—namely, in a scenario of harsh transitional justice measures, a strong constitutional court, and international human rights constraints.

[2]After 1989, the CEE countries committed to the majority of then-existing HR treaties of the Council of Europe and to UN core HR treaties (Smekal *et al.* 2016). The European Convention on Human Rights represents the most important of these treaties.

[3]The Czech and Slovak Federal Republic split in the 'Velvet Divorce' shortly after the 1989 revolution. On 1 January 1993, the Czech Republic was established as an independent state.

The essay proceeds as follows. The next section introduces in more detail the post-communist form of transitional justice and the role played by CEE constitutional courts. This section also focuses on the obligations of CEE constitutional courts stemming from international human rights law. The following section is a prelude to the empirical part of the essay. It sets the stage, providing an overview of the Czechoslovak transition and of the transitional justice choices made by the Czech government, and describes our study design. Next, we present the quantitative data and broad patterns of the CCC's decision-making in transitional justice issues. The following section is composed of four individual transitional justice cases portraying different approaches of the CCC to clashes with ECtHR case law and the human rights commitments of the Czech Republic. The final section concludes.

Constitutional courts and international law in post-communist transitional justice processes

The term 'transitional justice' generally stands for judicial and non-judicial measures such as prosecution, truth and reconciliation commissions, and reintegration and reparation processes, used by states and social groups striving to come to terms with the crimes of previous regimes (Kritz 1995). In the post-communist environment, transitional justice measures typically revolved around various vetting mechanisms (Welsh 1996; Stan 2009; Horne 2015). Communist totalitarian regimes exhibited remarkably high degrees of public participation in their activities. Communist parties controlled enormous apparatuses; in 1989, the East German Stasi employed about 90,000 officers and a further 150,000 informers in a population of 17 million (Stan 2009, p. 6). The fragile new democracies sought to eliminate the networks of the communist elite. Lustration and the opening of secret police archives largely prevailed over attempts to prosecute the crimes of the communist era. This was also due to the significant period of time that had elapsed since the heaviest repression of the 1950s.

In addition to these important political choices, crucial decisions were made about how to deal with property issues (restitution) and how to compensate victims of past atrocities, political prisoners in particular (Sadurski 2008; Czarnota 2009; Stan & Nedelsky 2015). The CEE transitions thus consisted both of retributive and restorative streams of transitional justice policies,[4] because they engaged both in punishing the supporters of previous regimes (retribution) and in helping their victims (restoration). In short, CEE transitional justice policies included politically sensitive decisions on who should govern, how history would be written, and what the new distribution of significant assets would look like. At the same time, CEE states undergoing transition already faced a well-developed body of international human rights jurisprudence that constrained some of their transitional justice options.

[4]Restorative transitional justice measures aim to restore communities or relationships (Lambourne 2009, p. 30). They seek to reverse the results of the crimes to the situation before the crimes occurred, or compensate the victims of the past regime's crimes. Retributive justice involves punishment of the wrongdoer (Lambourne 2009, p. 30), which can range from criminal or administrative sanctions to punishment of a purely moral character, such as public condemnation.

However, the 1989 CEE transitional justice decisions were made amid political turmoil and somewhat chaotic institutional reconstructions (Pithart 1993; Grudzińska-Gross 1994). Given the compromised state institutions and low public trust, it was often left to constitutional courts, which represented a break with the past (Teitel 2000) and a disengagement from the previous regime (Grudzińska-Gross 1994; Teitel 2009; Uitz 2009, pp. 71–98), to intervene and articulate the values underlying the new democratic regimes (Sadurski 2008). Constitutional courts were expected to align the transitional justice policies with new rule of law standards, as well as with emerging international human rights commitments.

In the following section, we describe transitional justice policies typical for the CEE region and show how these were constrained by regional and international human rights commitments. Next, we formulate a series of research questions about how constitutional courts dealt with these constraints.

Post-communist transitional justice processes within the scope of international human rights commitments

Generally speaking, international bodies tolerate transitional measures only for a very limited time, prompting states to terminate potentially problematic policies as soon as possible. The tension between post-communist transitional justice policies and human rights standards is particularly visible under the European Convention on Human Rights (ECHR or the Convention), which was itself created in political reaction to the atrocities of World War II and the Holocaust (Ní Aoláin 2011, p. 26). As a result of this legacy, the ECtHR recognised the possibility of a derogation from certain standards of human rights protection during transition processes.

However, the accession of CEE countries to the ECHR system led to worries that the application of such derogation to transitioning post-communist democracies would lead to the erosion of the Convention's integrity (Ní Aoláin 2011, p. 33) and to the entrenchment of transitional justice precedents beyond the transition (Buyse & Hamilton 2011). The possibility of derogating human rights became a problem, particularly for those countries that had joined the CoE with the aim of locking in certain domestic practices and policies (Moravcsik 2000) and preventing backsliding to nationalist or populist authoritarianism (Sadurski 2014). This might explain why the accession of CEE countries led the ECtHR to place a stricter emphasis on the new regimes' loyalty to the Convention's rule of law. Consequently, the ECtHR allowed the derogation and limits on human rights protection only very early after the transition, typically justified by the concept of 'militant democracy'.[5]

The ECtHR developed several approaches towards CEE transitional justice policies (see Table 1). It leaves some areas, like rehabilitation processes for the unjustly prosecuted, fully at the discretion of the state (no obligation). In others, the ECtHR requires member states to either refrain from implementing certain policies (negative obligations) or, on the contrary, to do something (positive obligations).

[5]The concept of 'militant democracy' was developed in the interwar period by Karl Loewenstein, who argued for constitutional democracy authorised to protect civil and political freedom by pre-emptively restricting the exercise of such freedoms (Macklem 2006, p. 488).

TABLE 1
OBLIGATIONS CONCERNING TRANSITIONAL JUSTICE (TJ) POLICIES SET BY ECTHR CASE LAW

	No obligation	*Negative obligation*	*Positive obligation*
Retributive TJ	X	Lustration; amnesties	Prosecutions and regime condemnation; archives of the past* (uncovering perpetrators of crimes)
Restorative TJ	Rehabilitation; restitution	X	Archives of past (rights of victims to know the truth)

Note: * We split the policy related to 'archives of the past' between restorative and retributive measures, as the opening of archives follows two different aims. Disclosing the truth about perpetrators of crimes falls under 'retributive' policies, while the right of the victims to know the truth under 'restorative'.
Source: Authors.

The ECtHR does not require transitioning states to compensate the victims of past crimes (Brems 2011). Nevertheless, once states decide to implement compensation policy, the ECtHR oversees the conditions and eligibility criteria to ensure that they are not too arbitrary, do not set manifestly unequal practices,[6] and are executed in practice.[7] Stricter conditions apply for restitution. The Czechoslovak communist regime sold some nationalised properties to private individuals, whose property rights after the regime change clashed with the rights of pre-communist era owners claiming their properties back. The Court, in principle, upholds the legitimacy of restitution laws but requires compensation for collateral damages, typically damages paid to the subsequent owners who had to return the property.[8]

By contrast, the ECtHR, as well as other international bodies, criticised lustration and the vetting of public officials for putting too many restrictions on passive electoral rights, political freedoms, and respect for private life. In the CEE countries, the post-communist lustration legislation was addressed by various international organisations and bodies, including the International Labour Organisation (ILO),[9] the CoE Parliamentary Assembly (PACE),[10] the Venice Commission,[11] and the ECtHR.[12] Most of the CoE's human rights

[6] *Wos v Poland*, ECtHR judgment of 8 June 2006.

[7] Under the doctrine of legitimate expectations, see, *Broniowski v Poland*, ECtHR judgment of 22 June 2004.

[8] *Pincová and Pinc v Czech Republic*, ECtHR judgment of 5 November 2002.

[9] International Labour Organisation, Decision of the Governing Body, Report File No. GB.252/16/19, 5 March 1992. Quoted from Přibáň (2007, p. 189).

[10] 'Measures to Dismantle the Heritage of Former Communist Totalitarian Systems', Parliamentary Assembly of the Council of Europe, Resolution 1096 (1996), 27 June 1996, available at: http://assembly.coe.int/nw/xml/XRef/Xref-XML2HTML-en.asp?fileid=16507&lang=en, accessed 26 August 2020.

[11] 'Amicus Curie on the Law on the Cleanliness of the Figure of High Functionaries of the Public Administration and Elected Persons of Albania', Venice Commission, CLD-AD(2009)044, Opinion no. 524/2009, 13 October 2009; 'Amicus Curie Brief on Determining a Criterion for Limiting the Exercise of Public Office, Access to Documents and Publishing, the Co-operation with the Bodies of the State Security', Venice Commission, CDL-AD(2012)028, Opinion no. 694/2012, 17 December 2012. The Venice Commission is a popular title for the European Commission for Democracy through Law, an advisory body of the CoE on constitutional matters, especially as regards the legal and institutional structures of states.

[12] *Turek v Slovakia*, 57986/00, ECtHR judgment of 13 September 2006.

bodies refer to PACE Resolution 1096 'On Measures to Dismantle Communist Totalitarian Systems', which did not find lustration to be completely incompatible with the Convention. The resolution stated that lustration measures 'can be compatible with a democratic state under the rule of law if several criteria are met'.[13] These criteria include individual guilt proven in each individual case, the right of defence, the presumption of innocence, the right of appeal, and, finally, constant checks on whether the lustration still fulfils the pre-set aims. PACE commented several times on the negative effect of the prolongation of lustration laws.[14] The guidelines were later confirmed by a whole set of ECtHR case law, which sees lustration as a transitional justice measure justifiable by the concept of 'militant democracy' able to take measures preventing the return of totalitarian practices. At the same time, states have to ensure that lustration does not violate human rights and does not remain in force once the need for screening public figures ceases to exist—which, in the ECtHR's narrow understanding, is almost immediately after the transition and the first round of free elections.[15] The ECtHR explicitly prohibits amnesty for perpetrators of human rights atrocities as a transitional justice measure, which is supported by a significant part of the transitional justice scholarship (Bell 2009, pp. 5–27).

Positive obligations run across both restorative and retributive policies. The ECtHR recognises the necessity to prosecute perpetrators of human rights atrocities,[16] to allow debates about the past (including historical truth under the protection of freedom of expression),[17] and to provide access to personal files kept by secret security services (Brems 2011).[18]

To sum up, ECtHR case law sets some boundaries within which CoE member states are obliged to realise their transitional justice polices. Transitioning states are generally expected to uncover the truth about human rights violations and prosecute them. They are discouraged from lustration, which represents an extraordinary measure, acceptable under strict conditions for a very short time. They can proceed with rehabilitation and restitution policies, on the condition that restorative policies do not create new injustices.

[13]'Measures to Dismantle the Heritage of Former Communist Totalitarian Systems', Parliamentary Assembly of the Council of Europe, Resolution 1096 (1996), 27 June 1996, available at: http://assembly.coe.int/nw/xml/XRef/Xref-XML2HTML-en.asp?fileid=16507&lang=en, accessed 26 August 2020.

[14]'Obligations and Commitments of the Czech Republic as a Member State', Parliamentary Assembly of the Council of Europe, Recommendation 1338 (1997), available at: http://assembly.coe.int/nw/xml/XRef/Xref-XML2HTML-en.asp?fileid=15372&lang=en, accessed 26 August 2020; 'Progress of the Assembly's Monitoring Procedures', Parliamentary Assembly of the Council of Europe, 2 April 1998, available at: http://assembly.coe.int/nw/xml/XRef/X2H-Xref-ViewHTML.asp?FileID=8494&lang=EN, accessed 26 August 2020.

[15]*Sidabras and Džiautas v. Lithuania*, Application Nos 55480/00 and 59330/00, ECtHR judgment of 27 July 2004; *Rainys and Gasparavičius v. Lithuania*, Application Nos 70665/01 and 74345/01, ECtHR judgment of 7 April 2005; *Žičkus v. Lithuania*, Application No. 26652/02, ECtHR judgment of 7 April 2009; *Ždanoka v. Latvia*, Application No. 58278/00, ECtHR judgment of 16 March 2006; *Adamsons v. Latvia*, Application No. 3669/03, ECtHR judgment of 24 June 2008; *Naidin v. Romania*, Application No. 38162/07, ECtHR judgment of 21 October 2014; *Vogt v. Germany*, Application No. 17851/91, ECtHR judgment of 26 September 1995; *Turek v. Slovakia,* Application No. 57986/00, ECtHR judgment of 13 September 2006.

[16]*Sandru and Others v. Romania*, ECtHR judgment of 8 December 2009.

[17]*Monnat v. Switzerland*, ECtHR judgment of 21 September 2006; *Karsai v Hungary*, ECtHR judgment of 1 December 2009; *Feldek v Slovakia*, ECtHR judgment of 12 July 2001.

[18]*Gaskin v. the UK*, ECtHR judgment of 7 July 1989.

Research puzzle

A large body of literature suggests that constitutional courts are essential intermediaries and allies of international bodies, helping to diffuse international norms and implement their findings domestically (Stone Sweet 2012; Gerards 2014; Kosař & Petrov 2017). Nevertheless, there is no clear indication how this relationship holds in the transitional justice arena; similarly, there is no literature systematically exploring the constitutional courts' interaction with the ECtHR's demands on post-communist transitional justice.

Following the previous remarks, we expect that constitutional courts adjust transitional justice policies. However, this adjustment is constrained by the influence of international human rights commitments, which changes over time. Transitional justice policies sometimes justify departures from the general principles of human rights protection using the concept of militant democracy or extraordinary conditions. Recourse to the transitional rule of law is, however, time-limited. Therefore, the 'transitional justice' justification of departures from human rights should eventually cease. The influence of international human rights commitments, with gradually burgeoning international case law, on constitutional courts' findings increases over time. The further a state moves from the transitional period, the more difficult it is for constitutional courts to justify the specific nature of transitional justice. We expect that, over time, constitutional courts will favour human rights protection rather than transitional justice principles. With a state's increasing embeddedness in international human rights regimes, transitional justice reasoning will fade. If courts pursue transitional rule of law reasoning, they will limit its use to addressing past injustices and shift the focus to restorative transitional justice, ultimately oriented at victim rehabilitation.

We pose the following questions: do constitutional courts prefer to keep the debate on transitional justice issues within domestic confines, either respecting the choices of domestic legislatures or confronting them by pursuing their vision of transitional justice? What is the role of international human rights law in a constitutional review of transitional justice legislation? In order to answer these questions, we analyse the case of the CCC and its transitional justice jurisprudence.

Case study: Czech transitional justice jurisprudence

On 15 October 2019, almost 30 years after the Velvet Revolution, which started the transition of then Czechoslovakia to democracy, the CCC quashed legislation introducing an indirect tax on restitutions of church property.[19] The judgment drew a lot of media attention and immediate political reactions questioning the legitimacy of the Court to rule on what was essentially a political question. Church restitution has been a highly salient issue dividing the political sphere for the past 20 years. In 2010, the CCC ruled that the Parliament had failed in its constitutional obligation to legislate on the restitution and finish the transitional justice process initiated in the early 1990s.[20] The 2010 judgment eventually pushed the Czech parliament to deal with the issue and return properties to churches. In 2019, a controversial law, proposed by the Communist Party (*Komunistická strana Čech*

[19]CCC judgment No, Pl. ÚS 5/19, 15 October 2019.
[20]CCC judgment No. Pl. ÚS 9/07, 1 July 2010.

a Moravy), introduced a tax on the compensation churches receive for seized property; however, the CCC annulled the 2019 law, claiming that it violated the principles of democratic society and the commitments following from the ECHR. The chief justice of the CCC condemned the legislation as both unconstitutional and unethical, breaking promises made by the state in order to ease the injustices of the communist regime. He stressed that the law violated the principle of legitimate expectations, a concept used by the ECtHR (Mazancová & Janáková 2019).

This fresh example demonstrates that the Czech case offers a timely and compelling opportunity to study the clashes between transitional justice and international human rights commitments. Very shortly after the 1989 Velvet Revolution, the country adopted all types of transitional justice policies typical of the CEE region. The cornerstone of retributive legislation was laid out in Act No. 198/1993 Coll., 'On the Illegality of the Communist Regime', which, in Article 2, characterised the communist regime and the Communist Party as criminal, illegitimate, and reprehensible. The lustration agenda, however, attracted the most international attention. In 1991, then Czechoslovakia was the first country in the region to implement a Lustration Act (Act No. 451/19991 Coll.), arguably the harshest among the CEE states (Schwartz 1994; Skapska 2003; Robertson 2006). Far-reaching lustration, which targeted high posts in the public administration as well as in academia and culture, polarised political actors and society.[21] The law affected not only former Communist Party officials, members of the People's Militia and secret police (StB) agents and informers, but also people listed by the StB as potential candidates for collaboration. The lustration included approximately 500,000 people. Between 1991 and 2001, the Ministry of Interior issued 420,270 lustration certificates, 3% of which were positive (Nedelsky 2004, p. 76). The law originally did not recognise the right to appeal or the access of an individual accused of collaboration to archival files listing his name. A significant number of dissenters, including President Václav Havel, soon opposed the lustration agenda from a human rights perspective and warned of an impending 'witch hunt' (Kosař 2008, p. 5).

Lustration was soon followed by the establishment of the Office for the Documentation and Investigation of the Crimes of Communism (*Úřad dokumentace a vyšetřování zločinů komunismu*), enabling access to StB files on collaborators, spies, and persons under surveillance. On the restorative front, the state initiated an intensive campaign of rehabilitation of political prisoners and restitution of state property nationalised by the Communist Party in the 1950s and early 1960s.

All the while, the idea of a 'return to Europe' motivated the process of democratisation. The CoE recommendations and the European Union's accession conditionality, in particular, shaped the decision-making of all Czech political actors.[22] Despite the rapid implementation of various legislative acts in the first three years after the Velvet Revolution of 1989,[23]

[21] The Act targeted basically all governing positions inside the state administration as well as, for example, those of deans and rectors of public universities (Kosař 2008; Nalepa 2010; David 2011). A positive lustration certificate, proving collaboration or the direct participation of an individual in the communist regime, led automatically to either ineligibility for, or the loss of, public office.

[22] The Czech Republic acceded to the CoE in 1993 and to the EU in 2004.

[23] Apart from the above mentioned Act on the Illegality of the Communist Regime, two other lustration statutes, legislation restoring to its original owners property seized by the Communist Party, and three other acts regulating judicial and extrajudicial rehabilitation and the restitution of property to individuals.

transitional justice policies in the Czech Republic remained a sensitive issue even 30 years after the regime change. In 2014, the Czech Republic adopted a politically controversial decision to restitute church property, which had a significant impact on the state's budgetary policy. As demonstrated above, the legislation has been repeatedly contested before the CCC. Also, lustration remained a recurring topic among the retributive policies. Despite European Commission criticism, lustration stayed in effect, after being debated and extended by the Parliament twice, in 1995 and 2000. After the 2013 election, with significant gains by the populist political party ANO 2011 (YES 2011), led by billionaire Andrej Babiš, who has not submitted a negative lustration certificate, the policy again made the front pages of the newspapers, subsequently leading to a renewal of the debate and significant amendment of the Lustration Act in 2017.

Consequently, the long timeframe (1989–2018), with recurring transitional justice issues, offered the CCC various opportunities to become involved in very sensitive issues. However, EU and CoE membership, in addition to the long period that had passed since the transition, led the CCC to sideline transitional justice considerations and replace them with human rights ones. Overall, this combination of factors provides an opportunity to study the variability of the solutions and policies considered by the CCC.

Finally, a few words on the composition and competences of the CCC are helpful to understand the overall setting. The CCC and its federal predecessor were endowed with strong powers and could review both legislation and individual complaints. A significant proportion of the first serving judges were dissidents and scholars who had emigrated from Czechoslovakia during the 1960s. Although the Federal Constitutional Court (Federal CC) existed only for one year,[24] the majority of its judges were reappointed to the first CCC.[25] In its first decade, the CCC, chaired by former dissident Zdeněk Kessler, addressed very important political issues and decided on topics that had a fundamental impact on the design of the Czech democratic regime. The strong dissident and anti-communist atmosphere also permeated case law. In its second decade, under the presidency of former dissident and then-politician Pavel Rychetský, the CCC shifted its attention to social policy and the quality of the legislative process (Kopeček & Petrov 2016). Since 2014, the composition of the CCC has changed significantly and the dissident ethos has evaporated.[26] This translates to a more fragmented approach towards remaining issues of transitional justice.

Quantitative overview: the Constitutional Court as a transitional justice actor

Having introduced the Czech transitional justice setting, we now move to the analysis of the CCC's transitional justice case law. First, we briefly introduce the methodology used to analyse the case law. Then, we proceed with an overview of the CCC's involvement in the transitional justice legislative development. We analyse how often the CCC used references to international human rights law in transitional justice case law and focus on what purpose

[24]The Federal CC was active only from March 1992 until the end of 1992.
[25]The CCC also included several judges who were members of the Communist Party before 1989.
[26]Interview with a former Constitutional Court official, Brno, 4 December 2018.

those references served. We show how the CCC addressed conflicts between transitional justice policies and international human rights commitments and how patterns in the frequency of references and their purposes differ according to the type of transitional policy.

Methodology

We base our research on a combination of qualitative and quantitative analysis of case law and on interviews with six former and current judges of Czech apex courts, which contribute to a contextual understanding of developments.

During the observed period (1993–2018),[27] the Czech Republic adopted 16 different statutes to address various transitional justice policies. Many of these were frequently amended. Table 2 demonstrates the importance of the CCC in this process: the Court had to address almost all adopted statutes (14 out of 16) in constitutional review proceedings. This confirms our supposition that transitional justice legislative acts touched upon sensitive issues that mobilised the parliamentary opposition, which attempted to contest the legislation through constitutional review. The CCC invalidated half (seven of 14) of the acts, or their provisions, supporting our contention that it had an important position in shaping transitional justice policies.

After identifying all Czech transitional justice legislation (see Table 2), we searched the CCC electronic database[28] for all rulings contesting these statutes in either a constitutional review of the legislation or individual complaints proceedings. A constitutional review of legislation gives the Court the power to strike down statutes or their provisions in the case of incompatibility with constitutional or human rights norms, including international commitments such as the ECHR. It can be initiated by an individual whose rights are violated, or abstractly, by members of parliament, the president and other political actors. Constitutional review is therefore a powerful tool that permits political actors to contest decisions and policies pushed through by the governing political elite. Comparatively, individual complaints might seem to have a weaker impact, as they can 'only' lead to the CCC quashing other judicial or administrative decisions. However, the CCC often actively changes the interpretation of legal norms in constitutional complaint procedures, while enjoying a lower threshold of attention in doing so compared to constitutional reviews. Leaving out individual constitutional complaints would therefore run the risk of missing important decisions.

Due to the vast amount of CCC case law (over 1,500 rulings), we decided to create a sample to allow a more in-depth analysis of the CCC's approach to the clash between transitional justice policies and human rights. From the population of all CCC rulings, we selected all constitutional review rulings contesting provisions of transitional justice laws and all rulings on individual complaints published in the CCC Collection of judgments and decisions.[29] This allowed us to include all those rulings which the CCC itself

[27]Note that some statutes were enacted by the Czechoslovak Federal Republic and succeeded to by the Czech Republic.

[28]NALUS, available at: nalus.usoud.cz, accessed 24 August 2020.

[29]A collection of judgments and decisions is published a few times a year by the CCC, available at: https://www.usoud.cz/sbirka-nalezu-a-usneseni-us, accessed 5 October 2020.

TABLE 2
Overview of Key Legal Acts in the Field of Transitional Justice and their Review by the CCC

Policy	*Coll. No.*	*Legislation title*	*Reviewed?*	*Invalidated (also in part)?*
Lustration	451/1991	Big Lustration Act ('Velký lustrační zákon')	Yes	Yes
	279/1992	Small Lustration Act ('Malý lustrační zákon')	Yes	No
Regime condemnation	480/1991	On the Period of Oppression ('O době nesvobody')	Yes	No
	198/1993	On the Illegality of the Communist Regime ('O protiprávnosti komunistického režimu a o odporu proti němu")	Yes	No
	140/1996	On Access to Files of the Former StB ('O zpřístupnění svazků vzniklých činností bývalé Státní bezpečnosti')	Yes	Yes
Archives	107/2002	Amendment of Act on Access to Files of the Former StB	Yes	No
	499/2004	Archives Law ('Zákon o archivnictví')	Yes	Yes
	181/2007	The Institute for the Study of Totalitarian Regimes ('O Ústavu pro studium totalitních režimů')	Yes	Yes
	496/1990	On the Return of the Property of KSČ to People ('O navrácení majetku KSČ lidu ČSFR')	No	Not submitted
Restitution	497/1990	On the Return of the Property of Socialist Youth ('O navrácení majetku Socialistického svazu mládeže lidu ČSFR')	Yes	No
	229/1991	Land Act ('Zákon o půdě')	Yes	Yes
	119/1990	On Judicial Rehabilitation ('O soudních rehabilitacích')	Yes	No
	87/1991	On Extrajudicial Rehabilitation ('O mimosoudních rehabilitacích')	Yes	Yes
Rehabilitation	261/2001	On the Rehabilitation of Persons in Military Camps of Forced Labour ('O odškodnění osob soustředěných do vojenských pracovních táborů')	Yes	No
	172/2002	On Compensation for Persons Abducted to the USSR ('O odškodnění osob odvlečených do SSSR')	No	Not submitted
	428/2012	On Church Restitution ('O cirkevních restitucích')	Yes	Yes

Source: Authors.

considers the most influential. The rest of the case law in the sample was selected by the systematic sampling of individual complaints. This method left us with a sample of 233 rulings.

Subsequently, we tracked references to international human rights treaties and case law in our sample and coded the impact of the reference on the result of the case. We distinguished if the reference played an important role in the outcome of the case, or if it merely had a supporting function. Accordingly, we coded references to international human rights law or case law as substantive (playing an important role in CCC's reasoning) or supporting (creating an additional, but not necessary, argument for the CCC to achieve the result). We also captured situations where the CCC explicitly refused the use of a particular international human rights treaty or case law. This allowed us to uncover what role the CCC assigned to international human rights commitments.

Finally, we complemented analysis of the CCC's use of international human rights law with six interviews with past and present judges of apex courts (specifically, the CCC and the Supreme Court), some of whom had also previously worked in other positions as important court functionaries or law clerks of the CCC. The interviews served to identify the motives behind the choices the CCC made regarding transitional justice jurisprudence. Specifically, we used insiders' views to complement the analysis of how the perception of transitional justice issues evolved within the Federal CC and the CCC.

The Czech Constitutional Court in transitional justice and its use of international law

This section introduces the results of a quantitative analysis of the CCC's transitional justice case law, which allows us to understand trends in the court's jurisprudence and more general patterns in how the Court approached the potential clash between transitional justice narratives and international human rights commitments.

Firstly, we were interested in the overall activity of the CCC in the field of transitional justice. It is worth noting that the CCC had a very strong example in its predecessor, the Federal CC, which, during its first and only year of existence, issued several important judgments concerning the character of the previous regime, such as the competence of the new Parliament to enact a binding (legal) interpretation of the communist regime (Pl.ÚS 5/92), the legitimacy of the new regime as embedded in rule of law and human rights principles (Pl.ÚS 1/92), and the procedural aspects of early attempts at lustration (I.ÚS 191/92). These judgments already encompassed several references to UN Covenants accepting their direct effect.[30] This was a huge step for the Czech judiciary, as communist legal theory and practice refused to recognise a direct applicability of international human rights treaties, stating they merely bind the administrative apparatus but not the courts.[31] In other words, it was the responsibility of the executive power to implement international human rights treaties domestically. In the case of a conflict between an individual right contained in the treaty and domestic legislation, courts still had to apply domestic legislation.

The CCC built on the example set by its federal predecessor as regards the use of international human rights law. Figure 1 depicts the overall development in the proportion of CCC judgments that refer to an international human rights treaty or international human rights case law (hereinafter only 'an international human rights reference') in the transitional justice field. It demonstrates how the CCC relied on the guidance of international human rights law and how its reference patterns developed over time. Figure 1 shows a high reliance on international human rights law in the 1990s, which, however, coincided with a very low number of transitional justice rulings; for example, there was only one such ruling in 1993. The second half of the 1990s saw relatively low rates of the use of the international human rights law by the CCC, with a subsequent drop to as little

[30]Under UN Covenants, we mean the International Covenant on Civil and Political Rights (ICCPR) and the International Covenant on Economic, Social and Cultural Rights (ICESCR).

[31]See also the decision of the Czech Supreme Court (CSC) of 31 August 1994, No. Skno 1/94, in which the SC acquitted a judge who, during the communist era, convicted two individuals for distributing anti-regime material (Charter 77). The CSC claimed that the judge was not bound by the ICCPR, despite the fact that Czechoslovakia had ratified the ICCPR in 1976.

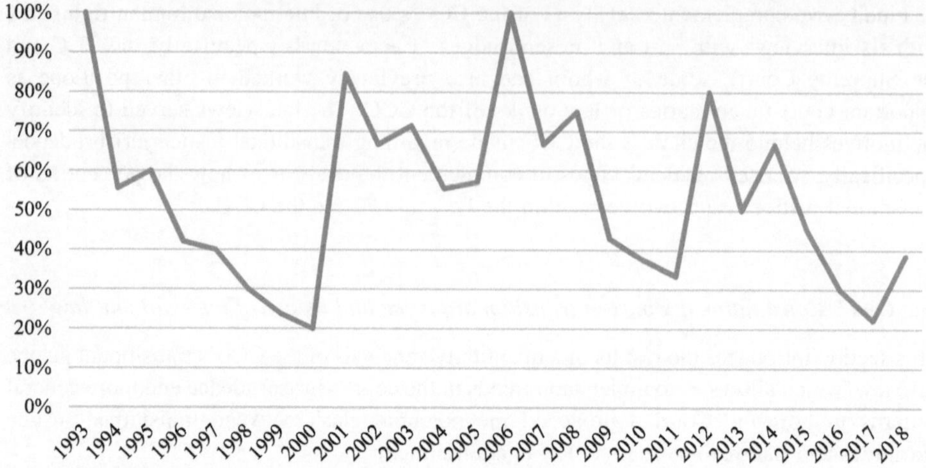

FIGURE 1. TRENDS IN THE PROPORTION OF CCC TRANSITIONAL JUSTICE RULINGS WITH INTERNATIONAL HUMAN RIGHTS LAW REFERENCES, 1993–2018 (%)
Source: Authors.

as 19% of transitional justice rulings in the year 2000. After this period, the use of international human rights law significantly increased. Overall, the CCC has used international human rights law in 54% of the relevant case law.

Czechoslovakia ratified the ECHR in March 1992 and the Czech Republic did so soon after its creation in 1993, but the CCC preferred references to the UN Covenants and a few ILO treaties throughout the 1990s. There were two reasons for this initial reluctance to use the ECHR and ECtHR case law. First, communist Czechoslovakia had ratified both UN Covenants in 1976; hence the CCC could use these commitments to condemn the practices of the previous regime without violating the principle of non-retroactivity. Second, acknowledgment and understanding of the ECHR among Czech judges developed slowly, and there were very few opportunities for CCC judges to learn about the ECHR or new ECtHR case law. Furthermore, the low number of Czech translations or commentaries on cases meant that judges with limited language skills had to rely on the experience of their colleagues (and younger clerks) who had participated in research stays abroad and learned about international human rights law (Kosař *et al.* 2020).

The low familiarity with ECtHR case law changed significantly in early 2000s. First, between 2002 and 2003, the composition of the CCC changed, with a new generation of judges coming to the bench and employing younger law clerks with a better knowledge of international human rights law. Second, in the same year, two important publications on the ECtHR and its case law were published in the Czech language (Berger 2003; Hubálková 2003), making a huge difference for judges without foreign language skills. It is worth noting that in 2003, there was still no HUDOC[32] or other online database

[32]HUDOC is the official online database of ECtHR case law, available at: https://hudoc.echr.coe.int/, accessed 5 October 2020.

allowing judges to search for ECtHR case law. Third, the rise of references to international law coincided with the constitutional amendment of 2001, which facilitated the Czech accession to the European Union. The amendment also brought about a complex revision of the relationship between domestic constitutional and international human rights law. Moreover, with the country's entry into the European Union, Czech judges participated in several training programmes aimed to foster their knowledge of both European and international law (Kosař *et al.* 2020). EU accession itself played no small role, although transitional justice measures were not a huge part of the EU accession conditionality.[33] Both the European Commission and the European Parliament criticised the extensive prolongation of the effect of lustration,[34] although the Commission admitted that the lustration enabled the establishment of an independent judiciary and public administration.[35] The EU accession raised the stakes for alignment with commitments following from the CoE (and hence, the ECtHR), as the European Commission put an emphasis on the compliance with CoE bodies' demands (Merlingen *et al.* 2000).

We might therefore argue that better accessibility and the gradual 'visibility' of the ECHR and ECtHR case law partly influenced the higher occurrence of references. In the following era, the raw number of references does not show any clear pattern. The dramatic decreases around 2010 and 2017 might have resulted from a high number of pilot, precedential domestic cases, allowing the Court to refer easily to its own previous case law instead of using international references. The final decline after 2015 happened due to a significant increase in transitional justice rulings (especially related to restitution), with very few of them containing an international human rights reference.

The use of international human rights references also differed on the basis of particular transitional justice policy. While lustration, adopted in 1991, divided society and captured a lot of attention, case law was dominated by a restorative agenda, be it restitution or rehabilitation. To a certain degree, this is understandable, as restituents' claims prompted many disputes and controversies (see the section 'Property restitution'). The scope of

[33]The lack of explicit conditions might also have been a result of a discord between the position of the European Commission and European Parliament on transitional justice. While the Parliament was rather critical of long-standing lustration and the exemption of German pre-World War II property from the restitution (the so-called Beneš decrees), the European Commission had a milder stance. While it favoured time-limited lustration, it did not impose any strict conditions on the Czech government. See 'Commission Opinion on the Czech Republic's Application for Membership of the European Union', European Commission, 15 July 1997, available at: http://eur-lex.europa.eu/legal-content/EN/TXT/PDF/?uri=CELEX:51997DC2009&qid=1480887404045&from=EN, accessed 26 August 2020; 'Agenda 2000—Commission Opinion on the Czech Republic's Application for Membership of the European Union', European Commission, 15 July 1997, available at: europa.eu/rapid/press-release_DOC-97-17_en.pdf, accessed 26 August 2020; '2000 Regular Report from the Commission on the Czech Republic's Progress Towards Accession', European Commission, 8 November 2000, available at: http://ec.europa.eu/enlargement/archives/pdf/key_documents/2000/cz_en.pdf, accessed 7 October 2020; '2002 Regular Report on Czech Republic's Progress Towards Accession', 9 October 2002, European Commission, available at: http://ec.europa.eu/enlargement/archives/pdf/key_documents/2002/cz_en.pdf, accessed 7 October 2020.

[34]'Regular Report from the Commission on Czech Republic's Progress Towards Accession', European Commission, available at: http://ec.europa.eu/enlargement/archives/pdf/key_documents/1998/czech_en.pdf, accessed 26 August 2020.

[35]'Agenda 2000—Commission Opinion on the Czech Republic's Application for Membership of the European Union', European Commission, 15 July 1997, available at: europa.eu/rapid/press-release_DOC-97-17_en.pdf, accessed 26 August 2020.

restitution on its own was long unclear. Individual complainants petitioned the CCC to return not only the property confiscated by the communist regime but also property taken during and in the aftermath of World War II. Quite a wide set of cases also resulted from the inactivity of state authorities, as the Land Registry often failed to act on its duty to offer claimants an alternative property in case the original requested property could not be restituted. Due to the Land Registry's chronic inactivity, many claimants petitioned the CCC directly. The CCC therefore actively engaged in restitution policy, allowing extensive individual restitutions, with a significant impact on state ownership. Another group of the rulings addressed immaterial damages claims; namely, violation of personal and moral rights, typically argued by political prisoners sentenced by the communist regime.

On the contrary, very few individual lustration cases reached the CCC, hence revealing an interesting paradox: although the Czech Republic adopted rather harsh lustration legislation (Sadurski 2014, pp. 344–45), it has not put it thoroughly into practice. The missing evidence and the lack of cooperation by police authorities with the Office for the Documentation and Investigation of the Crimes of Communism, as well as the unreliability of StB witnesses, led to acquittals of the majority of positive lustration holders. Only very few cases reached the top courts.[36]

The CCC used international human rights law in approximately 46% of the rulings in our sample. However, the use of international human rights law differed in individual transitional justice policies. Figure 2 captures a simple count of the three types of references (substantive, supporting, and reference where the CCC refused the application of international human rights norms) in the CCC's transitional justice case law. Although both substantive and supporting international human rights references appear in almost all transitional justice policies, the use of substantive references in rulings on rehabilitations and restitution clearly outweighs their use in rulings on archives and lustration. This coincides with the above-mentioned variance, as well as with the frequent references to the ECtHR's rulings against the Czech Republic, which are closely related to the restitution agenda. Higher coverage of the restitution agenda and more detailed rules developed by the ECtHR, often in direct response to Czech cases, made the references more pressing and also helpful for the CCC. Interestingly, petitioners frequently raised references to international human rights commitments in lustration cases, but the CCC mostly disregarded them. The CCC does not refer much and, moreover, largely denies the substantive relevance of international human rights law in rulings on archives and lustration. By contrast, however, the CCC quite often and noticeably relies on international human rights in rulings on rehabilitation and restitution, that is, in areas where rich ECtHR case law exists.

From general patterns to pivotal questions: clashes between transitional justice and human rights

As we showed in the previous section, the proceedings initiated before the CCC in the period between 1993 and 2018 addressed a very wide spectrum of topics and policies belonging to a

[36]Interview with a former CCC judge, Brno, 18 December 2018.

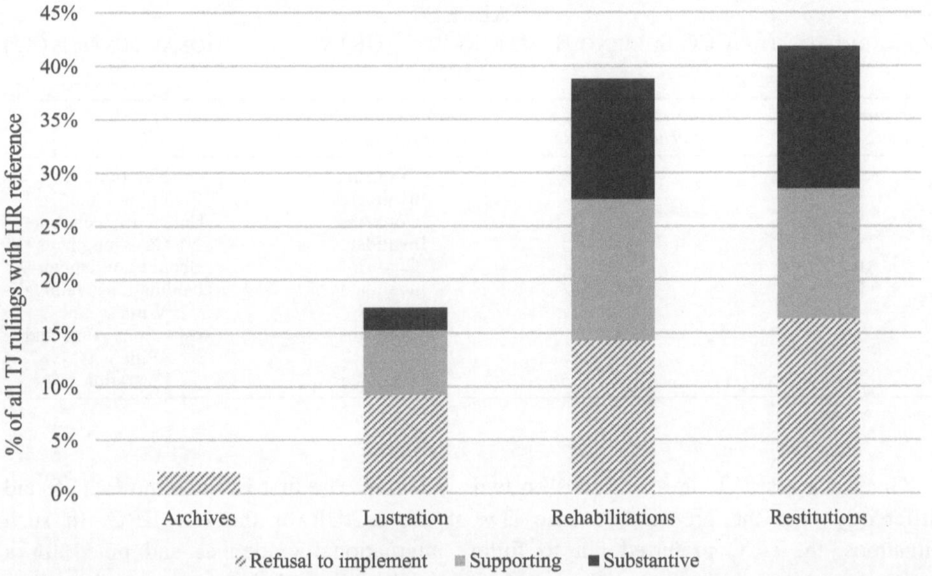

FIGURE 2. USE OF INTERNATIONAL HR LAW REFERENCES IN INDIVIDUAL TRANSITIONAL JUSTICE POLICIES IN CCC RULINGS
Source: Authors.

transitional justice framework. The CCC decided on the constitutionality of almost every single enacted transitional justice statute, invalidating and interpreting the provisions of most of them. International human rights references appear in approximately 46% of this case law, although most frequently only in the form of a supporting argument. Yet, a significant portion of the rulings incorporate references that have a substantive impact on the results of the case. We were therefore further interested in seeing how the CCC approached potential clashes between international human rights protection and transitional justice narratives in these cases. To demonstrate the dilemmas, we analysed four categories of CCC rulings that highlight the conflict between transitional justice jurisprudence and international human rights obligations. Our case selection draws on eight possible ideal scenarios of how the CCC might settle the relationship between transitional justice policy, the national charter of fundamental rights, and international human rights commitments (see Table 3). We identified which scenarios existed in CCC case law and picked those that contained a clear conflict between transitional justice policy on one hand and domestic or international human rights on the other. Conflicts with international human rights law are of special interest for us, because the CCC appears indeed to be placed between a rock—sensitive national transitional justice legislation—and a hard place, namely a disagreement with international human rights law. While discrepancies might also occur on a domestic level, constitutional courts in general primarily act as guardians of domestic constitutions, including domestic fundamental rights charters. Yet, their role is different when it comes to international treaties, as they enjoy less freedom when interpreting them. It is primarily the international human rights bodies that are entrusted with the interpretation of international human rights treaties.

TABLE 3
SCENARIOS OF THE CCC SOLVING HUMAN RIGHTS (HR) V. TRANSITIONAL JUSTICE (TJ) DILEMMA

TJ in breach of domestic HR?	*TJ in breach of international HR?*	*Response of CCC to domestic TJ policy?*	*CCC case*
No	No	Confirms	No conflict
No	No	Invalidates	Should not happen
Yes	No	Confirms	University lecturers
Yes	No	Invalidates	No CCC judgment
No	Yes	Confirms	Should not happen
No	Yes	Invalidates	Rehabilitations (Jehovah Witnesses)
Yes	Yes	Confirms	Restitutions (Pinc and Pincova)
Yes	Yes	Invalidates	Lustration I

Source: Authors.

Given our research aim, we focus on two situations. The first is when the CCC found differently than the pre-existing case law of the ECtHR or the UN HRC. In such situations, the CCC preferred not to follow international guidelines and opted for a national transitional justice solution, which typically followed the government's policy. Second, we were interested in scenarios wherein the CCC found domestic transitional justice practice to be unconstitutional. We searched for instances when the CCC had utilised pre-existing international case law, therefore favouring an international human rights solution to transitional justice dilemmas over a domestic one. Following this logic, we analysed CCC's case law in four areas, one representing each of these categories: a legislative review of the Lustration Act; the premature termination of university lecturers' contracts; the restitution of property nationalised under the communist regime; and the rehabilitation of political prisoners. We complemented the analysis with elite interviews to shed light on the motives behind CCC choices.

Lustration rulings

The petition to review the Big Lustration Act[37] reached the CC twice.[38] The first constitutional review in 1992 began with the jurisprudence of the Federal CC. The judgment Pl. ÚS 1/92 presented a value-based definition of the new democratic regime, which became a cornerstone for almost all future transition period case law. The Federal CC stressed that there was no value continuity between the new and the old regime, which had violated human rights, misused state power, and led to the loss of hundreds of thousands of lives and citizen freedoms. The Federal CC, conscious of a possible conflict

[37]'Velký lustrační zákon', 451/1991 Sb., kterým se stanoví některé další předpoklady pro výkon některých funkcí ve státních orgánech a organizacích České a Slovenské Federativní Republiky, České republiky a Slovenské republiky.

[38]The Small Lustration Act ('Malý lustrační zákon', 279/1992 Sb., o některých dalších předpokladech pro výkon některých funkcí obsazovaných ustanovením nebo jmenováním příslušníků Policie České republiky a příslušníků Sboru nápravné výchovy České republiky) was similarly challenged before the CCC. Compared to the Big Lustration Act, it only regulated the vetting of prison guards and members of the police.

of lustration with human rights and international commitments,[39] used the doctrine of militant democracy to allow these individual rights restrictions. Lustration, therefore, was not characterised as a discriminatory measure but as a justifiable condition placed on the execution of particular professions. The Federal CC was not in an easy position: Czechoslovakia was the first CEE country to introduce a lustration mechanism in practice and hence was monitored by international organisations. The CoE, and the Venice Commission in particular, followed developments closely, warning Czechoslovakia that the implementation of lustration violated the principles of the rule of law underlying the ECHR.[40] The Federal CC, however, was unified in its intention to support lustration as a necessary element of Czech transitional justice and de-communisation. It therefore recognised a potential conflict with the ICCPR, which commits the state to secure equal rights for individuals and forbids any discrimination, and ICESCR, which only allows limits on economic and social rights that promote the general welfare of a democratic society. Nevertheless, drawing inspiration from rulings of the German Federal CC[41] on the possibility of forbidding the employment of former active communists, it concluded that even these international human rights treaties allowed limitations on the freedom of occupation in public service based on past loyalty. In other words, the CCC rejected the understanding of lustration as a retributive transitional justice measure and stressed its preventive character: that every state with a totalitarian past and experience of human rights abuses has the right to implement the principle of militant democracy to prevent subversion.

The Federal CC rejected the motion to quash the Lustration Act as a whole, but it still annulled several provisions regarding the lack of guarantees for a fair trial before the Investigation Committee and the unreliability of secret police archives when it comes to those accused of collaboration.[42] The Federal CC used UN Covenants as reference criteria for the compatibility of the general principles of the Lustration Act, pointing out that vetting is not unknown in other democratic countries. The reasoning leading to the annulment of these provisions, however, rested primarily on the value-oriented interpretation of domestic constitutional norms, which would reflect the legacy of totalitarianism and coming to terms with the past. Moreover, judges of the Federal CC shared an understanding regarding their role in transitional justice, securing the goals and endpoints of the transition, just as the first CCC was to do later.[43] Preventing old cadres from assuming high positions in the newly democratic system was an essential part of the transition. This view of the Federal CC reflected public sentiments. A 1991 poll showed that 50% of respondents considered lustration to have a beneficial effect on the state administration, while 42% considered it to have a beneficial effect on democracy (CVVM 2009). Part of the Federal CC reasoning upholding the lustration legislation in 1992

[39] Interview with a former CCC judge, Brno, 5 December 2018.

[40] Interview with a former CCC judge, Brno, 18 December 2018.

[41] Interview with a former CCC judge, Brno, 5 December 2018. Generally, the German CC serves as a frequent source of inspiration for the CCC (Smekal & Vyhnánek 2016, p. 148).

[42] It was a widespread practice that some people were included on lists of collaborators without their knowledge or any active participation, either because StB planned to approach them in future or was trying to tarnish their reputations (interview with a former CCC judge, Brno, 18 December 2018).

[43] Interview with a former CCC judge, Brno, 5 December 2018.

rested on the fact that the vetting of public officers was only a transitional measure, not a permanent feature of the political system. The side effect of limiting the access of citizens to some positions in public administration was, therefore, seen only as a temporary issue, as the lustration mechanism was expected to cease its effect by the end of 1996. Nevertheless, the policy persisted. Parliament repeatedly extended the Act. In September 1995, the Chamber of Deputies prolonged its effectiveness until 31 December 2000.[44] President Havel rejected the amendment; the Chamber of Deputies however overruled his veto. In 2001, after the second prolongation, the Czech Social and Democratic Party (*Česká sociálně-demokratická strana*—ČSSD) then in power attempted to overturn the lustration law for good, claiming it had lost its social and historical function as the process of democratisation had already been completed. The CCC, however, dismissed the petition, stating that it was not up to the judiciary to evaluate whether democratisation had already reached a level where democracy no longer needed to defend itself.[45]

The CCC found itself in a much more difficult position regarding the potential conflict of lustration with international human rights commitments than its federal predecessor, the Federal CC. Apart from direct recommendations from the Venice Commission to cease applying the Lustration Act, it also had to deal with the evolving anti-lustration case law of the ECtHR and the pressure from the EU institutions to terminate the effect of lustration. Although some CCC judges were very conscious of this conflict, the rhetoric of militant democracy persisted.[46] The CCC highlighted that even the ECtHR recognised militant democracy as a legitimate derogatory principle (*Vogt v Germany*, *Glasenapp v Germany*), and that protecting equal access to civil services was never the intention of ECHR drafters. The CCC also stressed that many countries across Europe had even longer standing lustration. Hence, the twofold argument, that lustration was not a retributive measure and was used also by other democratic regimes, persisted.

Compared to the first ruling, the judges were not united in their views on the constitutionality of lustration statutes.[47] An understanding of the conflict between the lustration mechanism and human rights remains strongly present in the wording of the second ruling. Still, while formally executing judicial self-restraint, stating that it did not have the competence to review the level of Czech democratisation, the CCC decided to support a certain policy line. In fact, some CCC judges shared a belief that Czech lustration had not accomplished its aim; furthermore, that it was not fully effective because of inadequate investigations and because the testimony of former secret agents allowed lustration rulings to be overturned on the basis that the archives contained false and fabricated documentation. Some CCC judges, therefore, did not perceive lustration as an effective punitive mechanism.[48] CCC's views again reflected social sentiments: a public poll in 2000 reported increasing disillusion with the policy of lustration (CVVM 2009; Choi & David 2012).

[44]Act No. 254/1995 Coll.
[45]Pl.ÚS 9/01, CCC judgment of 5 December 2001.
[46]Interview with a CCC judge, Brno, 11 December 2018.
[47]Interview with a former CCC judge, Brno, 5 December 2018.
[48]Interviews with former and sitting CCC judges, Brno, 14 December 2018, 14 December 2018, 18 December 2018.

The Lustration Act, therefore, stayed in effect and kept emerging as an important political tool until very recently, when it almost prevented Andrej Babiš from taking a ministerial position (2013) and later the premiership (2017) after the 2013 and 2017 elections (Pl.ÚS 21/14). The example of lustration shows that the CCC saw the need to address the past crimes and rebuild social trust as justifying a certain derogation of human rights. This narrative, fuelled by constitutional judges' feelings that lustration was not being properly implemented, lost its power only very recently.

University lecturers

Lustration was a straightforward way to prevent communists and communist collaborators from holding important positions in the aspiring liberal democracy. However, the Czech legislature also used subtler means to achieve the same aim, specifically targeting university lecturers.[49] The 1993 amendment to the 1990 Law on Universities stated that the permanent contracts of university lecturers and researchers would be automatically changed to fixed-term contracts. The official purpose of the amendment was to enable researchers' mobility. The real reason was to get rid of university lecturers appointed under the communist regime. Becoming an associate professor or professor before 1989 was a political process: an academic had to prove both expertise and ideological loyalty, and was appointed by the Minister of Education or the president. A group of parliamentarians lodged a constitutional review complaint, but the CCC dismissed it and supported the legislature's transitional justice considerations instead.[50]

The CCC based its conclusions on a specific characteristic of the profession of university lecturer. Lecturers are responsible for transmitting non-ideological expertise to young generations. Such objectivity could not have been guaranteed with lecturers approved by the communist regime. Even after the 1989 Velvet Revolution, the positions of associate professors and professors (that is, those with permanent contracts) remained largely filled by the previous regime's appointees. Given the limited number of positions in academia, the legislature considered it fair to abolish permanent contracts and open the competition so that posts could be filled by people who wanted to work in academia but had not been able to do so under the communist regime. The legislature therefore justifiably sought to remove the residue of the past. The CCC emphasised that it was necessary to equalise the starting line and create equal opportunities.[51]

The Court applied Art. 6 of the ICESCR to argue that the past regime had severely violated the right of everyone to earn a living in work that they had chosen freely, and that the consequences of this violation had persisted even after the 1989 change of regime. The 1993 amendment thus merely eliminated the unjust privileges of the past.

[49]The explanatory memorandum to the Act No. 216/1993 Coll. amending the Act No. 172/1990 Coll., On Universities (Důvodová zpráva k vládnímu návrhu zákona, kterým se mění a doplňuje zákonj č. 172/1990 Sb., o vysokých školách, 24 February 1993, available at: http://www.psp.cz/eknih/1993ps/tisky/t0191_00.htm, accessed 13 October 2020) singles out university lecturers because their job requires also a very high moral character. By changing contracts from an indefinite to a fixed period, the amendment enables the replacement of old cadres by new academics who meet these requirements.

[50]Pl.ÚS 36/93, CCC judgment of 17 May 1994.

[51]Pl.ÚS 36/93, CCC judgment of 17 May 1994, part VI.

Moreover, opined the Court, without the 1993 amendment, the constitutional right of students to (high-quality) education and the development of new expertise to improve the quality of research and education could not have been guaranteed. The CCC's use of international human rights law, therefore, gave precedence to transitional justice considerations over the principle of legal certainty for academics on permanent contracts. The CCC ruling combined elements of both retributive and restorative justice. Abolishing permanent contracts had a retributory element, while restorative features included opening up academic positions so that those excluded under the communist regime had a chance to apply.

Property restitution

The aim of returning property to previous owners, who lost it during the communist regime, has led to many unforeseen consequences. Both the people whose properties were confiscated and the people who had acquired them under the communist regime and were now expected to return them to the previous owners brought their cases before the Czech courts. Some of the problems were solved in the 1990s by the CCC, which wanted to help the victims of communism and restore historical justice, returning or at least compensating for properties seized by the communists.[52] Nevertheless, many remaining problems resulted in adverse rulings by the ECtHR and the UN HRC,[53] which found numerous violations of the right to property.

Law no. 87/1991, On Extrajudicial Rehabilitation, set two crucial conditions for the restitution of properties lost due to injustice during the communist regime: citizenship of the Czech and Slovak Federal Republic and permanent residence in the territory of the Federation. After the split of the Federation, a group of Czech MPs challenged the permanent residency requirement and the newly established CCC agreed to rescind it. However, when individual applicants petitioned that the citizenship requirement be struck down as well, the CCC disagreed and upheld it. The UN HRC concluded that both the citizenship and the permanent residence conditions violated the principle of equality. The CCC refused to comply with these findings and confirmed citizenship as a condition for restitution, also pointing to ECtHR case law, which did not go as far as the UN HRC (Kosař & Petrov 2018, pp. 408–11).

Yet, in a series of cases, the ECtHR raised another concern that arose as a consequence of the Czech restitution. The ECtHR accepted that the member states had a certain leeway in dealing with the past; however, when trying to pursue justice for victims of communist injustices, its guiding principle was that the state should not create disproportionate new wrongs. One group of successful complainants before the ECtHR in restitution cases against the Czech Republic were people who had acquired properties from the communist state, arguably not knowing that the state had confiscated the property for political reasons before they bought it. The complainants were ordered to return the property to

[52]Interview with a CCC judge, Brno, 5 December 2018. The CCC perceived the seizure of property as a violation of the right to property by an illegal regime; only restitution compensated for this violation.

[53]The UN HRC monitors implementation of the ICCPR.

the previous owners because original restitution of property has generally been the preferred solution. In return, in accordance with the law, the state compensated the complainants with the price they had paid when they had bought the properties from the state, for example, back in the 1960s. However, prices had increased over the three decades, and the sums paid in the 1960s were approximately one-fiftieth of prices in late 1990s. In *Pincová and Pinc*, the ECtHR posited that the legislation should take into consideration particular circumstances and not put the burden of responsibility on persons who had acquired their possessions in good faith. Such responsibility should lie with the state. A fair balance should be maintained between the demands of the general interest and protection of the right to the peaceful enjoyment of possessions.[54]

The *Pincová and Pinc* judgment did not enjoy a warm reception in Czech elite legal circles. Interviewees generally complained that, unlike earlier cases against Germany, the ECtHR had not paid enough attention to the specific transitional context.[55] Some even urged the government to request a referral to the ECtHR Grand Chamber,[56] but the government refused to do so.

The CCC struggled with the *Pincová and Pinc* judgment when it neither quashed the provision setting the low compensation price, which placed a disproportionate burden on the current owners of the property to be restituted, nor openly defied the ECtHR. Instead, the CCC proceeded in a piecemeal fashion by complying with the ECtHR judgment in individual cases and not dealing with the situation systemically. The CCC declared that derogation of a legal provision is the last option in situations when there is no constitutionally conforming interpretation available.[57] In the meantime, in judicial practice the defective legal provision was ignored, and thus the CCC did not find a need to quash it.

The Constitutional Court deferred to the legislature in other cases as well, such as in upholding the above-mentioned requirement of citizenship for restitution, or in limiting the period to cover only the injustices of the communist regime and not extending it earlier than 1948, the year when the communists took control, to the immediate post-war period. Restitution was understood as the duty of the state to revive the original legal state of affairs and annul illegal property transfers (Pl.ÚS 16/93). While Czech transitional justice measures were aimed at previous owners harmed by the political actions of the communist regime, the ECtHR brought into play the need to also take into account the interests of the subsequent owners, who arguably acted in good faith when they bought confiscated properties from the state. The restitution saga presents a peculiar case because the CCC did not formally quash the transitional justice policy as such but settled only individual cases. It followed the ECtHR interpretation and supported the practice of Czech courts, which has since changed to reflect huge increases in property prices, making the statutory provision outdated. The whole sensitive issue of restitution is, from the CCC perspective, an uneasy exercise in deference to the national transitional justice solution alongside simultaneous attempts to deal with boundaries set by the

[54]*Pincová and Pinc v. the Czech Republic*, ECtHR judgment of 5 November 2002, paras. 58 and 64.
[55]Interviews with: a former CCC high official, Brno, 4 December 2018; a current CCC judge, Brno, 5 December 2018 and 11 January 2019; a former CCC judge, Brno, 5 December 2018.
[56]Interview with a former CCC judge, Brno, 18 December 2018.
[57]Pl.ÚS 33/10 #1, CCC judgment of 23 April 2013, part V.

ECtHR. The CCC managed to reconcile the two by pointing to newer judicial practice that already conforms to the ECtHR case law without clearly contradictory national legislation having been overturned.

Overall, the CCC focused on redressing past injustice. It was only after interventions by international human rights bodies that the CCC started considering the human rights consequences of its case law to be unfavourable.

Rehabilitation of political prisoners

A relatively large number of cases in which the domestic courts struggled with awarding financial compensation for moral (immaterial, non-financial) damages centred around the rehabilitation of political prisoners of the 1950s,[58] the most repressive era of Czechoslovak communism. Many political prisoners had refused obligatory military service because of their religious beliefs. The criminal convictions of these prisoners of conscience were invalidated by Czech military courts at the beginning of the 1990s, first, by only changing the decisions so that no punishment was decreed, then later, around 2007, invalidating the convictions themselves.[59] Nevertheless, the rehabilitation act did not cover compensation for inferred immaterial damages. The problem spurred the so-called 'judicial wars' between the CCC and the Czech Supreme Court (CSC).

The core of the dispute turned out to be the temporal application of the ECHR, which the CCC used to justify higher compensation for political prisoners against the Parliament's will.[60] The CCC thus backed a more pro-transitional justice solution. The CSC claimed that the damages as such occurred in the 1950s, therefore they could not justify the application of the Convention, which was binding on the Czech Republic only from 18 March 1992.[61] The CCC, on the contrary, advocated an interpretation that damages emerged only upon their recognition in the 1990s, essentially pushing through a retroactive use of the Convention's principles.

The dispute between the courts took several years. The CCC quashed dozens of SC decisions as 'poorly written' and 'failing to recognise which legal norms should be applied', or 'surrendering its role to find justice and unify the decision-making practice of the Czech courts'.[62] Interestingly, the quarrel with the CCC challenged the traditionally conservative CSC judges to engage in more nuanced work with ECtHR case law. The CCC directly bound the CSC with its opinion that the ECHR (Art. 5, para. 5) should be directly applied to compensate political prisoners for the immaterial damage caused by the unjust decisions of the communist era. Hoping for a resolution, the CSC attempted to settle the case by awarding the claimants only moral compensation in the form of recognition of the violation. This only further irked the CCC's judges, who adamantly and very actively pursued a change in the application of compensatory politics, arguing for the right of the victims of communism to justice.

[58] Act No. 119/1990 Coll., On Judicial Rehabilitation.
[59] Pl.ÚS-st 39/14, CCC judgment of 25 November 2014.
[60] Pl.ÚS-st 39/14, CCC judgment of 25 November 2014.
[61] See, for example, CSC, 30 Cdo 1614/2009, judgment of 8 September 2010.
[62] I.ÚS 3438/11, CCC judgment of 23 May 2012.

The argument of the CSC, that such an overarching interpretation and application of the Convention[63] to situations taking place before its ratification actually goes against the ECHR,[64] remained unheard. Although the CCC did not use any traditional transitional justice arguments justifying the derogation from standard principles, the motives of transition and coming to terms with the past were strongly present in the judges' considerations.[65] The CCC was very conscious of the fact that the exclusion of immaterial damages from the compensatory scheme was a political choice by the democratically elected legislature. Still, it attempted to bring about the change *via* an expansive interpretation of international human rights commitments.

The CCC eventually changed its line of reasoning and backtracked on the retroactive use of the Convention against the will of the Parliament.[66] However, financial compensation to political prisoners was preserved. The CCC judges used human rights language and international commitments to push through their vision of transitional restorative justice.

Discussion and conclusion

The clash between human rights and transitional justice presents young democracies with a thorny dilemma. On one hand, they seek to address the crimes of the past and distance themselves from the previous regime with a set of very specific policies, while, on the other hand, they strive to re-establish their position in international society by, amongst other things, showing serious commitment to international human rights standards (Smekal *et al.* 2016). The 'return to Europe' (Havel 1990) consisted of value reorientation towards the Western triad of liberal democracy, human rights, and the rule of law, coupled with the 'Washington Consensus' economic template. Visions for the future were set clearly but, at the same time, the CEE countries had to deal with sensitive and pressing legacies of the past.

Our essay sheds light on the role of constitutional courts in transitional justice, focusing on their role in mitigating the inherent conflicts between the concept of transitional justice and international human rights law when confronting legislative and executive transitional justice policies. We argue that constitutional courts significantly adjust transitional justice policies. However, they are constrained by respective international human rights commitments, which are supposed to eventually prevail over the transitional rule of law. In that sense, we expected the constitutional courts to gradually cease departing from general human rights principles justified by the transitional rhetoric and harmonise transitional justice policies with international human rights. Nevertheless, the study of the CCC did not confirm this expectation.

The analysis of the transitional justice jurisprudence of the CCC demonstrates that international human rights regimes work both as a constraint and a tool. The CCC has

[63] 30 Cdo 2916/2012, CSC judgment of 29 May 2013.
[64] 30 Cdo 1770/2012, CSC judgment of 24 April 2013; 30 Cdo 1663/2012, CSC judgment of 12 June 2013.
[65] Interview with a CCC judge, Brno, 18 December 2018.
[66] The Plenum even admitted that by an overreaching interpretation of the Convention, it had created an unjust dual-track justice system that could establish legitimate expectations by petitioners. Pl. ÚS-st. 39/14, CC judgment of 25 November 2014.

addressed the transitional justice issues for almost 30 years, which has allowed it to tackle all types of policies and problems. It has reviewed 14 out of 16 transitional justice statutes and their amendments and invalidated provisions in half of them, confirming its position as an important transitional justice actor, able and willing to challenge political compromises.

Our analysis of how the CCC reconciled the conflict between human rights and transitional justice principles establishes that the CCC acted as an independent player with its own conception of transitional justice. This demonstrates that the existing omission of constitutional courts by transitional justice literature has serious consequences for its findings.

Most of the case law regarding the retributive dimension of transitional justice (lustrations, condemnation of the communist regime) eschews references to international human rights law. The rulings identifying the values and democratic principles of new regimes are very normative, yet parsimonious in references. Interestingly, references (or elaborated interpretations and evaluations of compatibility) are also lacking in cases when petitioners raised the incompatibility between transitional justice measures and international obligations. If the CCC managed to find sufficient reasoning in the domestic Constitution, it did not feel the need to shield itself with international human rights arguments. That being said, we also found evidence that CCC judges were aware of the human rights clashes inherently present in 1990s transitional justice considerations. Yet, the transitional narratives prevailed, fuelled by the feeling that the core retributive measure, lustration, was not sufficiently implemented, especially in the first decade after the Velvet Revolution.

By contrast, restorative measures, including rehabilitation and the restitution of property, are full of references to international human rights law, especially the ECHR and ECtHR case law. International human rights law played a tremendous role and helped the CCC to push for more transitional justice for victims of communist crimes, often directly against the will of the legislator or the rest of the judiciary. The CCC therefore displayed a tendency to reference international human rights case law in restorative policies when it generally supported its views, while tending to withhold references to international human rights in retributive policies where ECtHR case law has not been always in line with the CCC's preferences.

Three factors explain the CCC's behaviour. First, shortly after the 1989 revolution, the CCC, composed mostly of former dissidents and enjoying a high level of social legitimacy, attempted to establish the new domestic Charter of Fundamental Rights in practice and develop the interpretation of Czech constitutional order as embedded in rule of law principles. The need to diffuse international norms came only as a second-order interest. Second, the constitutional judges only gradually gained in-depth knowledge of international human rights law. The language barrier and lack of electronic databases or literature at the beginning of the 1990s significantly constrained the judges' knowledge of international human rights law. The situation changed around 2000, when the CCC delivered most of its restorative transitional justice case law, which frequently used international human rights law. Third, the first CCC felt particularly strongly about its role in transitional justice and shared a common understanding of how the transition, at least in the most important political aspects, should evolve.

As public polls demonstrate, the CCC enjoyed high social legitimacy with its transitional justice case law shortly after 1989. The Federal and first Czech CC, composed largely of former dissidents and judges with first-hand experience of the repression of the totalitarian regime, shared public sentiments on restoring justice and punishing wrongdoers. Moreover, the few judges from the communist era who joined the CCC pursued transitional justice issues even more vehemently.[67] This supports the suggestion that pro-justice behaviour of courts in transition follows from judges seeking atonement for their service under the previous regime (Huneeus 2010).

International human rights law, especially if supported by existing case law, left the CCC less room for manoeuvring and constrained its vision of transitional justice. It was rare, therefore, for the CCC to openly oppose the content of international human rights commitment; rather, it 'cherry-picked' those aspects that conformed to its vision of transitional rule of law. On some occasions, the CCC even shifted the interpretation of some international human rights law provisions in order to gain more leverage to promote certain views. This practice has been very visible, especially in the field of restorative transitional justice, where the CCC frequently stood in for the non-active legislature. The CCC used international human rights commitments to justify new schemes for rehabilitation of victims.

To a large extent, the CCC overstepped constraints of transitional justice legislation. While formally it had clear lines of transitional justice set by domestic legislation and constrained by the ECtHR, it did not keep within those boundaries. The CCC contested and struck down provisions of most of the Czech transitional justice statutes, thus significantly reshaping their form. Moreover, we also saw a tendency to broaden the scope of transitional justice by including transitional justice rationales in policies not originally seen by the government as transitional—the case of university lecturers being one example. The CCC pushed forward its own idea of transitional justice, which it advertised as a response to widespread public demand.

The judges were disappointed with the implementation of transitional justice policies, both in their retributive (ineffective lustration) and restorative (narrow compensation) forms. When it comes to the boundaries created by the ECtHR, the CCC acted casuistically (see *Pincová and Pinc* case or the case related to prisoners of conscience described above), although showing more willingness to comply with restorative transitional justice policies. So far as international human rights law demanded more compensation to individuals, the CCC was happy to use it to support its findings. To a degree, its approach to restorative and retributive mechanisms differed. While the CCC tamed the most apparent injustices of retributive legislation, it pushed for more active restorative policies. Contrary to our expectations, the CCC did not automatically put more emphasis on 'collateral damage' and victims of transitional justice. It therefore follows that the CCC did not mitigate conflicts between human rights and transitional justice shortly after the transition. Human rights concerns prevailed over transitional justice justifications only partly and only over some time. International human rights commitments constrained the CCC only in situations when a direct ruling against the Czech Republic existed. Otherwise, the CCC merely used international human rights law where it suited its reasoning. In this sense, transitional justice reasoning still survives.

[67]Interview with a former CCC judge, Brno, 11 December 2018.

The example of the CCC carries an important lesson for transitional justice scholarship. It shows that by omitting constitutional courts, we miss a significant piece in the search for factors prompting a particular set of transitional justice policies. While largely overlooked by political science scholarship, constitutional judges, especially in the transitional setting, often have their own vision of transitional justice, prompted by their first-hand experience, and have their own, considerable, means of influencing it. The reluctance of the CCC to follow some of the ECtHR's views on transitional justice demonstrates that constitutional courts need to be understood and studied as distinctive actors, not as mere implementers of norms.

References

Bell, C. (2009) 'Transitional Justice, Interdisciplinarity and the State of the "Field" or "Non-Field"', *International Journal of Transitional Justice*, 3, 1.

Berger, V. (2003) *Judikatura Evropského soudu pro lidská práva* (Prague, IFEC).

Brems, E. (2011) 'Transitional Justice in the Case Law of the European Court of Human Rights', *International Journal of Transitional Justice*, 5, 2.

Buyse, A. & Hamilton, M. (eds) (2011) *Transitional Jurisprudence and the ECtHR. Justice, Politics and Rights* (Cambridge, Cambridge University Press).

Choi, S. Y. O. & David, R. (2012) 'Lustration Systems and Trust: Evidence from Survey Experiments in the Czech Republic, Hungary, and Poland', *American Journal of Sociology*, 117, 4.

Crocker, D. A. (1998) 'Transitional Justice and International Civil Society: Toward a Normative Framework', *Constellations*, 5, 492.

CVVM (2009) *Postoje veřejnosti k vyrovnání se s minulostí*, Centrum pro výzkum veřejného mínění, available at: https://cvvm.soc.cas.cz/media/com_form2content/documents/c2/a646/f9/100962s_po91103.pdf, accessed 24 August 2020.

Czarnota, A. (2009) 'Lustration, Decommunisation and the Rule of Law', *Hague Journal on the Rule of Law*, 1, 2.

Czarnota, A., Krygier, M. & Sadurski, W. (eds) (2005) *Rethinking the Rule of Law After Communism* (Budapest, CEU Press).

David, R. (2011) *Lustration and Transitional Justice. Personnel Systems in the Czech Republic, Hungary, and Poland* (Philadelphia, PA, University of Pennsylvania Press).

Ferreres Comella, V. (2004) 'The Consequences of Centralizing Constitutional Review in a Special Court. Some Thoughts on Judicial Activism', *Texas Law Review*, 82, 7.

Gerards, J. (2014) 'The European Court of Human Rights and the National Courts: Giving Shape to the Notion of "Shared Responsibility"', in Gerards, J. & Fleuren, J. (eds) *Implementation of the European Convention on Human Rights and of the Judgments of the ECtHR in National Case Law* (Cambridge, Intersentia).

Ginsburg, T. (2003) *Judicial Review in New Democracies: Constitutional Courts in Asian Constitutionalism* (Cambridge, Cambridge University Press).
Ginsburg, T. (2012) 'Courts and New Democracies: Recent Works', *Law & Social Inquiry*, 37, 3.
Grudzińska-Gross, I. (1994) *Constitutionalism in East Central Europe* (Prague, Czecho–Slovak Committee of the European Cultural Foundation).
Havel, V. (1990) *Speech in a Joint Session of the U.S. Congress*, Washington, DC, 21 February 1990, available at: https://www.vhlf.org/havel-quotes/speech-to-the-u-s-congress/, accessed 5 October 2020.
Hilbink, L. (2007) *Judges Beyond Politics in Democracy and Dictatorship: Lessons From Chile* (Cambridge, Cambridge University Press).
Hirschl, R. (2004) *Towards Juristocracy* (Harvard, MA, Harvard University Press).
Horne, C. (2015) '"Silent Lustration". Public Disclosures as Informal Lustration Mehcanism in Bulgaria and Romania', *Problems of Post-Communism*, 62, 131.
Hubálková, E. (2003) *Evropská úmluva o lidských právech a Česká republika: judikatura a řízení před Evropským soudem pro lidská práva* (Prague, Linde).
Huneeus, A. (2010) 'Judging from a Guilty Conscience: The Chilean Judiciary's Human Rights Turn', *Law & Social Inquiry*, 35, 1.
Huntington, S. (1991) *The Third Wave* (Oklahoma, OK, University of Oklahoma Press).
Kopeček, L. & Petrov, J. (2016) 'From Parliament to Courtroom: Judicial Review of Legislation as a Political Tool in the Czech Republic', *East European Politics and Societies and Cultures*, 30, 1.
Kornai, J. & Rose-Ackerman, A. (2004) *Building a Trustworthy State in Post-Socialist Societies* (New York, NY, Palgrave).
Kosař, D. (2008) 'Lustration and Lapse of Time: Dealing with the Past in the Czech Republic', *European Constitutional Law Review*, 4, 3.
Kosař, D. & Petrov, J. (2017) 'The Architecture of the Strasbourg System of Human Rights: The Crucial Role of the Domestic Level and the Constitutional Courts in Particular', *Heidelberg Journal of International Law*, 77, 1.
Kosař, D. & Petrov, J. (2018) 'Determinants of Compliance Difficulties among "Good Compliers": Implementation of International Human Rights Rulings in the Czech Republic', *European Journal of International Law*, 29, 2.
Kosař, D., Petrov, J., Šipulová, K., Smekal, H., Vyhnánek, L. & Janovský, J. (2020) *Domestic Judicial Treatment of European Court of Human Rights Case Law: Beyond Compliance* (Abingdon, Routledge).
Kritz, N. (1995) *Transitional Justice* (Washington, DC, US Institute of Peace Press).
Lambourne, W. (2009) 'Transitional Justice and Peacebuilding After Mass Violence', *The International Journal of Transitional Justice*, 3, 1.
Macklem, P. (2006) 'Militant Democracy, Legal Pluralism, and the Paradox of Self-Determination', *International Journal of Constitutional Law*, 4, 3.
Mazancová, H. & Janáková, B. (2019) 'Hrad bere i smrt osobností jako politiku. Doufám, že jen netrucuje, říká Rychetský', *Deník N*, 17 October, available at: https://denikn.cz/215262/hrad-bere-smrt-osobnosti-jako-politiku-doufam-ze-netrucuje-rika-rychetsky/, accessed 17 October 2019.
Merlingen, M., Mudde, C. & Sedelmeier, U. (2000) *Constitutional Politics and the 'Embedded Acquis Communautaire': The Case of the EU Fourteen Against the Austrian Government*, Constitutionalism Web-Papers 4/2000 (Bath, University of Bath), available at: https://www.wiso.uni-hamburg.de/fachbereich-sowi/professuren/wiener/dokumente/conwebpaperspdfs/2000/conweb-4-2000.pdf, accessed 24 August 2020.
Moran, J. (1994) 'The Communist Torturers of Eastern Europe', *Communist and Post-Communist Studies*, 27, 1.
Moravcsik, A. (2000) 'The Origins of Human Rights Regimes: Democratic Delegation in Postwar Europe', *International Organization*, 54, 5.
Nalepa, M. (2010) *Skeletons in the Closet* (Cambridge, Cambridge University Press).
Nedelsky, N. (2004) 'Divergent Responses to a Common Past: Transitional Justice in the Czech Republic and Slovakia', *Theory and Society*, 33, 1.
Ní Aoláin, F. (2011) 'Transitional Emergency Jurisprudence: Derogation and Transition', in Buyse, A. & Hamilton, M. (eds).
Ocantos, E. G. (2018) 'Persuade Them or Oust Them: Crafting Judicial Change and Transitional Justice in Argentina', *Comparative Politics*, 46, 4.
Pithart, P. (1993) 'Intellectuals in Politics: Double Dissent in the Past, Double Disappointment Today', *Social Research*, 60, 4.
Přibáň, J. (2007) *Legal Symbolism: On the Law, Time, and European Identity* (Aldershot, Ashgate).

Robertson, D. (2006) 'A Problem of Their Own, Solutions of Their Own: CEE Jurisdictions and the Problems of Lustration and Retroactivity', in Sadurski, W., Czarnota, A. & Krygier, M. (eds) *Spreading Democracy and the Rule of Law? The Impact of EU Enlargement on the Rule of Law, Democracy and Constitutionalism in Post-Communist Legal Orders* (Dordrecht, Springer).

Sadurski, W. (2008) 'Legitimacy, Political Equality, and Majority Rule', *Ratio Juris*, 21, 1.

Sadurski, W. (2014) *Rights Before Courts. A Study of Constitutional Courts in Postcommunist States of Central and Eastern Europe* (2nd edn) (Dordrecht, Springer).

Schwartz, H. (1994) 'Lustration in Eastern Europe', *Parker School Journal of East European Law*, 1, 2.

Sikkink, K. (2011) *The Justice Cascade. How Human Rights Prosecutions are Changing World Politics* (New York, NY, W.W. Norton & Co).

Šipulová, K., Smekal, H. & Janovský, J. (2016) 'Mezinárodní Lidskoprávní Závazky České Republiky a Slovenska', in Pospíšil, I. & Týč, V. (eds) *Mezinárodní lidskoprávní závazky postkomunistických zemí* (Prague, Leges).

Skapska, G. (2003) 'Moral Definitions of Constitutionalism in East Central Europe: Facing Past Human Rights Violations', *International Sociology*, 18, 1.

Smekal, H., Šipulová, K., Pospíšil, I., Janovský, J. & Kilian, P. (2016) *Making Sense of Human Rights Commitments: A Study of Two Emerging European Democracies* (Brno, MUNI Press).

Smekal, H. & Vyhnánek, L. (2016) 'Equal Voting Power Under Scrutiny: Czech Constitutional Court on the 5% Threshold in the 2014 European Parliament Elections', *European Constitutional Law Review*, 12, 1.

Sólyom, L. (2003) 'The Role of Constitutional Courts in the Transition to Democracy: with Special Reference to Hungary', *International Sociology*, 18, 1.

Stan, L. (2009) *Transitional Justice in Eastern Europe and the Former Soviet Union* (London, Routledge).

Stan, L. & Nedelsky, N. (2015) *Encyclopedia of Transitional Justice, Vol. I.* (Cambridge, Cambridge University Press).

Stone Sweet, A. (2012) 'A Cosmopolitan Legal Order: Constitutional Pluralism and Rights Adjudication in Europe', *Global Constitutionalism*, 1, 1.

Teitel, R. (2000) *Transitional Justice* (Oxford, Oxford University Press).

Teitel, R. (2009) 'Transitional Jurisprudence: The Role of Law in Political Transformation', *Yale Law Journal*, 106.

Uitz, R. (2009) 'The Rule of Law in Post-Communist Constitutional Jurisprudence. Concerned Notes on a Fancy Decoration', in Palombella, G. & Walker, N. (eds) *Relocating the Rule of Law* (Oxford, Hart Publishing).

Welsh, H. (1996) 'Dealing with the Communist Past: Central and East European Experiences After 1990', *Europe-Asia Studies*, 48, 3.

Whitehead, L. (2009) 'Europe's Democratization. Three "Clusters" Compared', *Taiwan Journal of Democracy*, 5, 2.

Becoming a Judge in Russia: An Analysis of Judicial Biographies

ARYNA DZMITRYIEVA

Abstract

Studies of the Russian legal system underscored the discrepancy between formal legal order and the informal practices used to maintain control over the judiciary. This essay argues that, despite laws introducing meritocratic principles of judicial selection at the beginning of the 1990s, the patronage of court presidents continues to significantly outweigh all other candidate characteristics, such as education and professional experience. By analysing 957 protocols issued by the judicial qualification boards (JQBs), I show that the influence of court presidents on the JQBs' decision-making in the selection process undermines judicial independence and accountability.

THE SELECTION OF JUDGES IS A MATTER OF CONCERN IN ANY COUNTRY. To build trust and legitimacy, the judiciary should employ judges who demonstrate a balance of legal skills, accountability and independence (Burbank & Friedman 2002; Geyh 2008; Seibert-Fohr 2012). The selection procedure has wider social implications because it improves public confidence in the court system by ensuring that carefully selected judges will make grounded and balanced decisions. It is particularly relevant for present-day Russia, as recent years have cast a shadow over the independence of Russian judges and the quality of court decisions.

Typically, the Russian judicial system is viewed as ineffective and corrupt. We can observe many ways in which the system may be manipulated, including not only high-profile political cases but also criminal cases initiated against business figures by their rivals or civil cases where the government is one of the parties. Since the beginning of the 2000s, Russian society has observed the rise of politically motivated justice. The situation worsened after the Bolotnaya Square cases in 2012 and the Crimea annexation in 2014. The most recent wave of political prosecutions came after the Moscow protests in August 2019, when the police opened an investigation into more than 20 cases of involvement in mass protests. The system worked very fast in this instance; some people were accused and convicted within months with illogical reasoning cited in court decisions, while others waited for months in pre-trial detention centres for the resolutions of their cases.[1]

[1]The most updated data on political prisoners in Russia can be found on the Memorial website, available at: https://memohrc.org/ru/pzk-list, accessed 8 November 2020.

While the number of politically restrictive laws designed to repress dissent in Russia has been growing, courts have experienced increased pressure to penalise regime opponents. Nevertheless, it is not only political pressure that shapes the behaviour of Russian judges. Quite often, their decision-making depends on the context; the law may be obeyed and disregarded in the same courtroom. The majority of cases are not political, and courts process them normally. The courts are flawed, not by reason of politicisation but, rather, by excessive legal positivism (Hendley 2017; Kurkchiyan & Kubal 2018). However, judges experience more pressure in atypical cases, for instance when deciding cases where one of the parties has administrative resources. Popova (2018) finds that, in defamation cases, regional and federal officials as well as members of law enforcement agencies win more often and receive larger compensation than ordinary citizens, and Kubal (2018) demonstrates that, in immigration cases, judges make decisions on the basis of formal evidence produced by law enforcement bodies but not on the examination of both parties of the trial. Russian judges easily switch between law-abiding and extra-legal behaviour; this proposition indicates the duality of the Russian legal system, where courts do not have a single institutional identity and operate in a tension between the administrative state (where ideology dominates) and the constitutional state, in which the law matters (Sakwa 2010; Hendley 2017).

The judicial selection system is an example of this inconsistency. In the late 1980s, reforms of the judicial selection process aimed to professionalise the judicial corps and diminish its vulnerability to political influence. With the rise to power of Vladimir Putin, the country saw the reverse of democratisation and the rise of a 'new authoritarianism'. The system that developed as a result represents the mixture of formal institutions that are supposed to promote openness and meritocracy in judicial selection and informal practices that favour discipline and subordination, a combination that does not support independence and deliberation.

This study aims to understand the mechanics of judicial selection in Russia. It harnesses judicial biographies to understand which professional and other characteristics influence a candidate's chances of being recommended for appointment by the judicial qualification board. Designed to assess the background of the candidates for judicial vacancies, the judicial qualification board (JQB) is a committee within the bodies of judicial self-governance.[2] Socio-economic background and education, previous occupation and other characteristics may influence both personal and professional values and attitudes (Shapiro 2008). Earlier findings from Russia suggest that judges socialised within the judicial system have a more legalistic and bureaucratic orientation and a lower propensity towards transparency compared to colleagues who originate from other groups of lawyers (Volkov & Dzmitryieva 2015). Studies of other elite professional groups demonstrate that sources of recruitment influence group cohesion and legitimacy (Tev 2017). The similarity of socio-professional profiles among the recruited is a prerequisite for professional cohesion.

[2] They include: All-Russian Congress of Judges, regional Congresses of Judges, Council of Judges of the Russian Federation, regional Councils of Judges, Supreme Judicial Qualification Board, regional Judicial Qualification boards, Supreme and regional Examination boards.

Legitimacy, in turn, is related to the presence of representatives of people with various socio-professional characteristics in an elite professional group (Hunter 2015).

By studying 957 judicial biographies of candidates who applied to judicial vacancies at the justice of the peace, district, and regional courts in 2014–2015, I aim to uncover the mechanisms of judicial selection in the Russian Federation. To help contextualise the findings from JQB protocols—records of candidate assessment produced by JQBs—I also used transcripts of interviews, focus groups and field notes collected by colleagues and myself. Since 2011, we have conducted more than 60 interviews and five focus groups with acting or recently retired judges. Among our interviewees there were also members of JQBs whom we specifically asked about judicial selection. The basic multilevel model of judicial selection includes two major types of covariates to check two basic hypotheses of judicial selection and a number of control variables. The first hypothesis suggests that the selection of judges should be based on meritocratic principles, namely, that it should favour the most skilled and qualified professionals regardless of gender. As a proxy for meritocratic selection, I use demographic and professional experience covariates.

I also analyse the interference of court presidents—personnel who chair court of first instances and regional courts—with the selection process. In the Russian judicial system, the power of the court president goes well beyond being the most authoritative person of the court (Muller 2012; Solomon 2012; Volkov *et al.* 2016). Court presidents control the distribution of the cases and can adjust the workload of a particular judge. They decide who will receive higher bonuses and non-monetary rewards. The second hypothesis states that, in some cases, the judicial corpus is built on the 'trust up close' principle and patronage, which I call the crony selection hypothesis. Crony selection may result in incompetence and the exclusion of some groups from the recruitment process. Although the formal power to select judges belongs to the JQBs, my analysis reveals the strong influence of court presidents on the selection of judges. The court presidents' preferences result in the diminishing diversity of the pool of candidates because only people who belong to the president's network of allies can be selected to the post. These are primarily those from the court apparatus,[3] prosecutors and state bureaucrats; candidates without government experience have little chance of being selected for a judicial post.

The essay proceeds as follows. First, I discuss the evolution of judicial selection in post-Soviet Russia. The second section provides background information on the selection process. The third section introduces the data and methods. The fourth section describes the data analysis and provides empirical evidence to support my hypotheses on factors influencing the selection of judges. The final section discusses the findings and their implications.

[3]The court apparatus is made up of the judges' staff (court secretary and judicial assistant) and other clerks who serve in the court. Since 2006, any court staff position in Russia requires a law diploma (*Prikaz Sudebnogo Departamenta pri Verkhovnom Sude*, N69, 27 July 2006). According to a court president (interviewed in St Petersburg on 20 December 2019) and a former court clerk (interviewed in Vladimir, 15 October 2019), by 2011–2012 the majority of court staff had a law degree, mainly by correspondence.

Transformation of the judicial selection process

In the late 1980s and early 1990s, empowering the judiciary was considered an important step away from the totalitarian past and towards the development of democracy in post-socialist countries. The ideology of the Soviet judiciary was to involve 'working citizens in the delivery of justice' (Serov 2013) and membership in the Communist Party was one of the most important criteria for judicial selection. Judges were elected to the People's Court (court of first instance) for five years. The last election before the collapse of the Soviet Union occurred in 1982, when 10,303 judges were appointed. A total of 93% of judges were members of the Communist Party, 65% were male and 98% had completed higher legal education (Pashin 2003). One of the goals of early reformers was to create conditions for the formation of independent and highly professional judicial corps. The Russian 'Concept of Judicial Reform in the RSFSR', published in 1991, was quixotic:

> It is no less important to formulate a particular kind of self-awareness among judges, one different from the civil-servant mentality of the composition of flattering documents and pleasing one's superiors. The service of justice should not become routine service for judges in a judicial department. In other words, it is not only a question of the formation of a sufficient judicial corpus, but also one of cultivating its corporate ethics. (Zolotukhin *et al.* 1994)

In order to increase the judges' immunity against pressure of authorities, the reformers promoted changes in the system of judicial appointment. As early as 1989, the Law 'On the Status of Judges in the USSR' established the bodies of judicial self-governance. The first congresses of the judges were held on national and regional levels. The judges participating in these congresses elected members to higher and regional JQBs. In the regions, the judicial congresses decided the procedure for electing JQB members and their heads, either by voting for a single candidate or a list of candidates.[4] By December 1993, Russia had introduced many democratically oriented institutions and procedures in its court system (Solomon 2008).

However, the implementation of formal institutions did not result in the immediate development of an effective and independent judiciary. Despite these early reforms, in the 1990s, business and the wider public accused the judges of ineffectiveness, violation of rule of law principles and widespread corruption (Blass 2007; Ledeneva 2013). At the beginning of the 2000s, President Vladimir Putin initiated reforms aimed at strengthening central power. Judicial reform was a personal priority (Solomon 2004). The reforms included the establishment of justice of the peace (magistrate) courts, a twofold increase in budget expenditures for the judicial system (Volkov *et al.* 2016, p. 34), the adoption of new criminal, civil and commercial (*arbitrazh*) codes, and the introduction of anti-corruption laws. These steps indicated the transition from the 'Soviet model' of authoritarian courts to a model in which courts were formally independent and empowered, while informal practices ensured that judges did not rule against powerful persons (Solomon 2015).

[4]Interview 60, former head of the JQB and court president, St Petersburg, 20 December 2019.

Over the 2000s, Russia developed a type of authoritarianism that is simultaneously stable and dysfunctional, open and non-ideological (Krastev 2011). Its key feature is the coexistence of a formal constitutional framework and informal political practices (Sakwa 2010). For the courts, this duality means that, their autonomy and power notwithstanding, informal practices ensure that judges do not rule against regime interests (Solomon 2015). At the same time, while judges do experience pressure in politically motivated cases, these are relatively rare. Approximately 30,000 Russian judges hear about 16 million cases annually (Volkov *et al.* 2016): the average judge is therefore likely to deal exclusively with mundane cases and will never hear a politicised case. In their everyday work, judges operate in the framework of Russian legal culture that cannot and should not be measured by Western standards (Holmes 2015; Hendley 2017; Kurkchiyan & Kubal 2018). One of the distinctive features of Russian legal culture is legal formalism. On the one hand, judges rely extensively on the law as written and discretion can be seen as a sign of corruption (Hendley 2017; Kurkchiyan 2018). On the other, it is common to encounter judges who 'follow the law to the letter or openly disregard it, depending on the context' (Hendley 2017, p. 4). Another feature is the lack of uniformity of legal practice and clearly defined institutional borders between courts and executive power: this feature often results in the breach of judicial autonomy by administrative system. Biased decision-making occurs not as a result of bribery but out of the asymmetry of power distribution where administrative power almost always outweighs judicial. People who face routine problems are confident in approaching Russian courts and do not expect that extra-legal pressure will be applied to judges. However, they tend to avoid initiating suits that involve state or well-connected individuals, whether these connections are financial or political (Hendley 2017).

While Russian citizens gradually developed competence in using the judicial system, the central government aimed at strengthening control over society. For Putin, the restoration of the power vertical was primarily associated with work with cadres, which included the re-introduction of the Soviet approach to the selection of people and the building of power networks (Ledeneva 2013). Where Putin could not establish personal relationships, as in the case of judicial selection and appointment, it was important for him to control the final decision-making institution. In 1999, this intention resulted in the introduction of law enforcers (prosecutors, police and federal security officers) as well as members of the Presidential Administration into the Presidential Commission, the organ that gives final approval to federal judges' appointments and promotions. Since then, the power of law enforcers (*pravookhraniteli*), including people with a background of serving in the Federal Security Services, has increased (Dzmitryieva & Volkov 2019). The criteria by which the Presidential Commission rejects candidates are kept secret from the public and the judicial community. About 20–25% of candidates do not pass the last stage and are not appointed to a judicial post (Kondratieva 2018b). Discussing similar situations in other countries, Moustafa concludes that, for authoritarian rulers, it is not necessary to assault judicial autonomy directly in order to obtain judicial compliance (Moustafa 2014). Judges may comply only because they anticipate sanctions from executives, or because they are aware of the impact of their ruling on sensitive political issues. The system of appointment and promotion can also serve to discipline judges and shape their rulings. Although formally independent, the selection system in Russia faces different forms of internal and external political control.

The institutions of judicial selection in Russia represent the legacy of incomplete, failed or reversed democratisation (Solomon 2008), or, as one of my respondents characterised it, 'a democratic whirl' in the system of judicial selection.[5] Although many of the propositions included in the 'Concept of Judicial Reform in the RSFSR' were implemented in the judicial selection system in 1991–2010, it was not enough to develop a strong legal culture in which the rule of law is upheld. In the section that follows, I explain the formal and informal procedures that are currently part of the judicial selection process in Russia.

Judicial recruitment procedure in Russia

Formal selection procedure

On the formal side of judicial selection there are eligibility requirements written in the Constitution and other legal acts, and ethical requirements specified in the Code of Judicial Ethics.[6] The 1993 Constitution of the Russian Federation includes a range of provisions aimed at the meritocratic selection of judges. It states that any person who is over 25 years old and who has a university degree in law and a minimum of five years' experience in legal practice can be appointed to a judicial position.[7] The details of the appointment procedure are regulated by two federal laws: 'On the Judicial System'[8] and 'On the Status of Judges in the Russian Federation'.[9]

Before applying for a judicial position, the candidate needs to first pass a judicial exam. Until the beginning of the 2010s, each regional examination commission had developed its own set of examination questions and tasks in accordance with the requirements of the Supreme Court Examination Board. Since 2015, the examination questions and tasks have been standardised for the whole country and the exams are available for download from the Supreme Court web page.[10] The exam consists of two parts. In the theoretical part candidates are asked to demonstrate knowledge of the theory of law as well as substantive law—criminal, civil, commercial and administrative. In the practical part the candidate needs to solve two factual problems and write a sample procedural document.

Furthermore, the candidate has to present a health certificate and certificates of income and personal assets for themselves, and their spouses, parents and adult children, in accordance with anti-corruption requirements. The list of anti-corruption checks is not specified under federal law. It was only in 2017 that the Supreme Court developed anti-

[5] Interview 60, former head of the JQB and court president, St Petersburg, 20 December 2019.

[6] Code of Judicial Ethics, adopted by the 8th All-Russia Congress of Judges on 19 December 2012. As amended by the Ruling of the 9th All-Russia Congress of Judges on 8 December 2016, available at: http://www.supcourt.ru/en/judicial_system/code_judical_ethics/, accessed 20 September 2018.

[7] Art. 119 of the Constitution of the Russian Federation, available at: http://www.constitution.ru/10003000/10003000-9.htm, accessed 10 November 2020.

[8] Federal Constitutional Law No 1-FKZ ot 31 dekabrya 1996g 'O sudebnoi sisteme Rossiiskoi Federatsii', available at: http://pravo.gov.ru/proxy/ips/?docbody=&nd=102045098, accessed 10 November 2020.

[9] Federal Law No 3132-1-FZ ot 26 iyunya 1992g 'O statuse sudei v Rossiiskoi Federatsii', available at: http://pravo.gov.ru/proxy/ips/?docbody=&nd=102017065, accessed 10 November 2020.

[10] 'Voprosy dlya podgotovki k sdache kvalifikatsionnogo ekzamena na dolzhnost' sud'i suda obshchei yurisdiktsii', available at: http://vekrf.ru/publication/1714/, accessed 24 March 2018.

corruption guidelines,[11] which provide more detailed requirements for regional JQBs in their decision-making. The JQBs also request a police background check on the candidate and their family members. Finally, the candidate must provide a detailed *curriculum vitae*. With all these documents to hand, the candidate can apply for a vacant position.

The application and supplementary documents are then considered by the JQBs, who gather monthly to consider candidates for open vacancies. Normally, a candidate will be invited for interview, although this is not a formal requirement. If the candidate lives in a remote place their application will be considered *in absentia*.

The informal selection process

A study of qualitative data allows us to outline the informal part of judicial selection. First, our interviews revealed the widespread practice of selecting candidates from a so-called 'reserve list' (*kadrovyi reserv*). The 'reserve' is usually made up of young judicial assistants but is not limited to them. Members of the prosecution office and lawyers of state government offices, such as the tax office, the Federal Migration Service (before it was abolished and joined with police) and other regulatory agencies (if they had represented their offices in court hearings), could be selected for the 'reserve'. Second, interviewees indicated the importance of court presidents at all stages of the process: from the selection of candidates to the 'reserve' to participation in JQB meetings. Additionally, according to the interviewees, the Supreme Court and the Presidential Commission do not communicate their appointment decision to regional courts, which creates pressure on JQBs and makes the whole system dependent upon changing administrative policies.

The tradition of creating a reserve of candidates for a judicial post goes back to Soviet times when judges were elected and regional branches of the CPSU controlled judicial appointments. As one former judge noted:

> At that time there was a reserve list made of court clerks and bailiffs. All [the candidates] needed was to be 25, to have a higher education and to be party member. So, here I was, just 30 years ago, on this path. I entered the court as a secretary and learnt all types of work in the court. Then, I graduated from the institute [college]; I studied in the evening and worked in court. And then I joined the [Communist] Party in my final year of study. Then a vacancy opened, elections were scheduled [and I was appointed].[12]

Although less formal these days, the practice of creating a reserve of candidates remains. Interviewees from all regions mentioned 'a reserve list' or, as one remarked, 'a queue' for a judicial post.[13] Another current judge told us:

> It may happen that someone from the prosecution may approach me directly and ask: 'Elena Petrovna [name changed] do you already have someone in mind? I would like to work in your

[11]'Metodicheskie rekomendatsii po realizatsii kvalifikatsionnymi kollegiyami sudei norm zakonodatel'stva Rossiiskoi Federatsii o protivodeistvii koruptsii', utverzhdennye resheniem VKKS RF ot 26 yanvarya 2017 g (red. ot 21 sentyabrya 2018 g), available at: http://www.vkks.ru/publication/42259/, accessed 10 November 2020.

[12]Interview 18, former court president, St Petersburg, 24 April 2011.

[13]Interview 43, former court president, Moscow, 28 October 2015.

> court'. It may happen that an intelligent person, even someone who comes from the street, comes to me and become a part of the 'personnel reserve'.[14]

The practice of hiring people from the reserve is justified by the necessity of having reliable people who are accustomed with the court's organisational culture. According to another judge, 'we try to hire people who have been vetted. Those who we can rely on and do not worry that they will … to put it mildly … they will make a hash of things'.[15]

However, the range of attitudes towards the selection of judges from a 'personnel reserve' is very broad. One court president said 'a person who did not work in the court from the very bottom of the career ladder [as a court secretary], should not become a judge', and adds 'unfortunately we cannot shield ourselves from candidates from prosecution or police'.[16] Others are more open-minded and believe that people with a different professional background may become good judges providing they have clerkship experience. Some judges also suggest that the practice of hiring exclusively from the 'reserve' results in people with very limited experience of practical work outside the court and narrow understandings of real-life cases.

Presidents of the courts not only form the 'reserve' but also provide their opinions on the candidate to the JQBs. Here a member of a JQB explains that the president's opinion is one of the most decisive factors in selecting a candidate:

> A: At the JQB's monthly meeting the chairman reports who is applying and whether there is competition. Once we even had six applicants for one post. After that, JQB members may ask anyone questions. Then they hear the applicants, [then] the opinion of the court president, whether he/she supports one of these applicants. In the end, JQB members decide by open vote.
>
> Q: What do you pay most attention to?
>
> A: Well … there are so many things. Each member of the JQB has full information about an applicant. Everything related to their previous work, to their characteristics … motivation … and then … the president of the court means a lot. If he makes a recommendation, then, in principle, this should also be taken into account.[17]

Interviewees also touched on the problem of communication with the Supreme Court and the Presidential Commission on issues of judicial selection. These bodies do not inform JQBs about the reasons why a candidate was rejected. The lack of information bewilders judges in the regions bewildered and increases their concern about the preservation of their own posts.

> After JQBs have made a decision, the application goes to the Presidential Commission … . And you know … they are sending these documents back and forth. The procedure is hidden. And when an application returns with a rejection, nobody understands what was wrong.[18]

[14]Interview 17, former court president, St Petersburg, 6 November 2011.
[15]Interview 12, court president, Irkutsk, 17 November 2010.
[16]Group interview 2, court president and a judge, St Petersburg, 14 February 2011.
[17]Interview 3, court vice-president, Irkutsk, 17 November 2010.
[18]Group interview 7, four judges, St Petersburg, 3 February 2012.

To sum up, interviews suggest that informal relationships between the candidate and court president and between the court president and JQB are essential to the whole selection process. For a potential judge it is important to be a part of a network. The extended network also includes prosecutors and lawyers from regulatory agencies who regularly participate in court hearings. Court presidents consider the qualification exam as confirmation that the informally selected candidate possesses the necessary knowledge to occupy a judicial post, but this criterion never plays a decisive role in the selection process. A JQB pays close attention to the anti-corruption and 'credibility checks' provided by the tax office and police, and also takes the opinion of the court presidents into account.

It can be concluded that, in most cases, selection begins well before a vacancy is advertised and starts with the formation of the 'reserve list'. The formal stage of the selection process includes various participating institutions and multiple checks on the candidate. The JQB collects all the information and makes a decision about each candidate. In the next section, I analyse JQB decisions and model the outcome depending on different factors.

Research data and methods

For the quantitative part of this research, I built a novel dataset collected from the protocols of JQBs in Russia. The publication of these data aims at increasing 'publicity and transparency of court activity' (Timoshin 2013) and is regulated by federal law.[19] The idea behind the publication of JQB decisions was 'to saturate the information environment around courts with objective facts' (Timoshin 2013) in order to increase the appearance of judicial independence.

The protocols are published on the webpages of regional JQBs. However, not all regional JQBs had published their protocols at the time of my research. I downloaded the protocols from 32 out of the 85 regions of the Russian Federation for 2014–2015. After excluding regions with missing data, I was left with protocols from 27 regions where the number of protocols was either higher than or very close to the number of judges appointed. Since I only worked with available protocols, I performed a number of representativeness checks. There are no systematic differences in the patterns of published protocols correlating to a region's level of economic development as measured by the Independent Institute for Social Policy, in 2010 (see Appendix Table A1) or geographical distribution (see Appendix Figure A1). Finally, the distribution of the outcome variable in the dataset corresponds to the national distribution of JQB-recommended candidates out of all candidates in Russia (see Appendix Table A2). The whole dataset consists of 2,200 protocols regarding the selection of new judges and the promotion of acting judges. This study focuses exclusively on the selection of new judges and so uses a subset of 957 protocols.

[19]Federal Law No 262-FZ ot 22 dekabrya 2008g. 'Ob obespechenii dostupa k informatsii o deyatel'nosti sudov v Rossiiskoi Federatsii', available at: http://pravo.gov.ru/proxy/ips/?docbody=&nd=102126522&intelsearch=262-%D4%C7, accessed 10 November 2020.

Given significant variation in the structure and content of the protocols, I resorted to manual coding. The coders were instructed to extract relevant text parts from protocols and input them into the coding form.

Despite the regional variation in the approaches to writing protocols, in most cases it was possible to obtain information on four types of variables. The first type were basic variables: the year of appointment, region, level of the court (justice of the peace, district, regional, *arbitrazh*) and the position for which the candidate applied. The second type were biographical variables: birth year, birthplace, university, year of graduation. The third were occupation variables: location, position and period of work in each prior post. The last variable was the outcome of application: whether the person was recommended, reasons (if available), results of the JQB vote and background checks on candidates' sources of income and prior penalties.

There were a number of challenges in data collection, coding and pre-processing. First, the data are limited to two years of observation, meaning that the data cannot be used for tracking changes in the selection process over time. Second, the regional variability of data presentation imposed additional pressure on coders, who needed to work with the different structure of documents from each region. Finally, the initial data were written in natural language, which required intensive coding work in order to prepare the data for statistical analysis. I used OpenRefine, which proved to be a powerful tool for data cleaning and recoding.

Factors influencing the selection of candidates for appointment

This section discusses different factors that could potentially influence the selection of judges and sets out my hypotheses about meritocratic selection and what I term 'crony selection'.

In the narrowest sense, 'merit selection' uses observed criteria, such as educational credentials and tested competencies and abilities (Daniels 1978, p. 206; Hanson 1993). A broader definition also includes professional achievements (Armytage 1996). Meritocratic appointment also implies that the selection of professionals is unbiased in terms of gender (Abel 1985; Rhode 1996). Narrow and broad definitions of meritocratic appointment provide insight into approaches for measuring the meritocratic component of the judicial selection process. For this study, I use educational attainment, demographic data and professional experience as explanatory variables to build models of meritocratic selection. The next sections will discuss these variables in more detail.

Meritocratic selection: training and qualification

Appointment on merit implies that the best specialist is selected from the pool of available candidates. Education and the results of the entrance exam are taken into consideration by JQBs. In Soviet times, the loyalty of the judges was always put ahead of expertise (Solomon 2008). The reforms of the 1990s sanctioned the requirement of higher legal education and passing the judicial examination with the aim of improving the quality of justice in Russia. The underlying assumption was that proper technical competence, gained through high-quality legal education, would secure the quality of analysis and develop powers of legal analysis. One point of view values legal education as a vehicle to develop critical thinking skills, enhance personal freedom, increase professional confidence and promote empathetic judgement (Nussbaum 1997). Ginsburg, taking a more cynical approach, considers legal training as a means of professional indoctrination and the promulgation of an ideology that secures loyalty to a supreme power (Ginsburg 2008). Students of courts in authoritarian regimes find that legal positivism is quite compatible with authoritarian rule (Hilbink 2007). Both these dimensions—importance of technical competences and authoritarian indoctrination—can be found in the Russian judiciary.

The level of professional training of lawyers in Russia in general (Maleshin 2017), and judges in particular (Voskobitova 2017), is widely criticised. In 1989, the number of law graduates was 16,200 (Goskomstat 1989): by 2012 it had reached 160,000. A majority (70%) of students admitted to law departments in the 2000–2010s received their education by means of distance learning (Moiseeva 2015). There are questions about the capability of higher education institutions with no prior legal specialism to provide a legal education of sufficient quality (Maleshin 2017; Hendley 2019).

Law schools do not have the freedom to design their own curricula but are obliged to teach in accordance with federal educational standards developed by the Ministry of Education and Science.[20] The Russian system of legal education inherited a very formalistic and dogmatic approach to law, which was typical for all post-socialist countries (Kühn 2012). The post-socialist development of legal academia in Russia has not produced any internationally competitive legal scholarship (Guba & Ilchenko 2018). Therefore, young lawyers who start their judicial careers after graduation and without any other professional experience have no opportunity to learn other approaches to legal reasoning besides formalism and textualism.

The poor quality of education results in overall low performance at the judicial qualification exam. According to reports published by regional JQBs, about 40% of candidates who took the examination failed their first sitting of the exam (Plotnikova 2014). Unfortunately, in my dataset detailed information about exam results is missing for half of the candidates and therefore strong conclusions could not be drawn from this variable. Exam grades, which are available in my dataset, show that 33% of candidates passed the qualification exam with a grade of 'excellent', while 54% were graded 'good' and 13% 'satisfactory' for their knowledge of substantive and procedural law.

Human capital theory suggests that employers do not have complete information about candidates and that their abilities and competencies are instead signalled by the quality of their education (Spence 1973). Since much of the data on grades from the judicial qualification exams are missing, I cannot use this information to assess the level of legal knowledge of candidates. Instead, I resort to a proxy variable of quality of education. Graduates of full-time law diploma programmes taught at established state universities

[20]Prikaz ministerstva obrazovaniya i nauki RF ot 4 maya 2010 g N 464 'Ob utverzhdenii i vvedenie v deistvie federal'nogo gosudarstvennogo obrazovatel'nogo standarta vysshego professionalnogo obrazovaniya po napravleniyu podgotovki 030900 'Yurisprudentsiya' (kvalifikatsiya (stepen) 'bakalavr'), available at: https://rulaws.ru/acts/Prikaz-Minobrnauki-RF-ot-04.05.2010-N-464/, accessed 10 November 2020.

received the code 'good education'. Both the general public and the expert community recognise this type of education as high quality and prestigious (Bocharov & Moiseeva 2016).

Graduation from a more prestigious law school could also serve as a signal of unobserved candidate characteristics, such as diligence, intelligence and a wider range of technical skills. These considerations allow the formulation of the following hypothesis regarding the relationship between education and the outcome of an application: (H1) candidates who graduate from a prestigious law school have a higher probability of being recommended for a judicial post.

Meritocratic selection: professional experience

In addition to the years of legal experience required by the Constitution, two dimensions can be added to the concept of professional experience. The first is socialisation in a particular legal profession; the second is diversity of professional experience. The eligibility criteria stipulated in federal laws do not specify the type of professional experience in legal practice necessary for a judicial post. Any post-law school professional experience is eligible, including working as legal counsel, prosecutor, defence attorney, law clerk, law professor, police officer or notary.

Socialisation in a particular legal profession plays an important role in shaping normative structure, patterns of thoughts and ethical commitments (Remus 2016). Primary professional socialisation working in a prosecutor's office is different from that gained working as a defence lawyer or in the private sector. Different paths taken into the legal profession could also influence the decision to enter the judicial profession. One professional trajectory may more likely lead to a judicial post than another. According to the data provided by the Supreme Court, in 2010–2011, out of 65,843 attorney lawyers (*advokaty*), only 144 (0.2%) applied for a judicial position, and 40 were selected to the bench; 573 (1.2%) of 45,865 prosecution attorneys applied for judicial posts, and 65% of them were selected (Ermoshin 2016). These numbers contrast with the pattern of selecting judges in countries where a professional model with a strong and independent bar dominates. In the United States and the United Kingdom, lawyers who have appeared regularly in courts and who have already acquired practical skills and familiarity with court routine are most likely to be recruited to the judiciary (Gee 2012). In Russia, where the bar is weak (Bocharov & Moiseeva 2016), candidates with law-clerking professional experience are more successful than commercial lawyers in obtaining judicial positions.

Table 1 accounts for the distribution of candidates' professional experience. Initially, the professional experience of candidates was coded into 26 positions, which were later grouped into six types of primary professional experience. In this context, primary experience indicates either a candidate's longest experience in one position or their most recent experience before applying for a judicial position if the number of years of experience in the two positions was equal.

In 1997, the majority of judges were from prosecution and non-governmental bodies and about 11% of judges were from the court apparatus (Solomon & Foglesong 2000). Among those who were appointed in the 2000s, the proportion of former clerks had risen to 30% (Volkov & Dzmitryieva 2015). The present study shows that the primary experience of

TABLE 1
PROFESSIONAL EXPERIENCE OF THE CANDIDATES

Primary experience	Position	Share (%)
Only court apparatus experience	Judicial assistant, court clerk	48.5
Primary experience in apparatus	Judicial assistant, court clerk	17.0
Prosecution	Prosecutor, investigator or clerk at prosecutor's office	12.4
Police	Police investigator, policeman, police detective, police administrator, police operative agent, bailiff	4.8
State lawyer	Legal counsel/advisor of state body	6.3
Non-state lawyer	Advocate, corporate lawyer, lecturer/professor, legal counsel in an NGO, notary	11.0

over two-thirds of candidates is that of clerking. In our previous research, we found that court presidents make a tacit contract with their staff, forming the 'reserve list' from court clerks who understood that, after a period of hard and low-paid work,[21] their efforts would be rewarded with promotion to a judicial position (Volkov & Dzmitryieva 2015). As a result, we observe the aforementioned two-thirds of candidates with clerkship experience who become judges.

In many international jurisdictions, court clerking is considered a very effective way to gain legal experience. This is not the case in Russia. The work of the court secretary is mainly bureaucratic: preparing protocols, filing documents and contacting the parties to a dispute. Although judicial assistants perform more advanced legal work, including legal research and assistance to parties, reviewing changes in legislation, and organising the documents and the evidence related to the case, the job is low paid and not considered prestigious.

Another variable of interest is the variety of professional experience. By variety I mean the transition between different legal professions. For instance, transferring from the post of state lawyer to that of corporate lawyer is considered a new professional experience, since it implies a significant change of professional duties and accommodation to a new organisational culture; promotion from being a clerk at the prosecutor's office to a prosecutor does not. The scope of professional experience could influence the decision of JQBs in two opposite directions. On the one hand, the experience of working in multiple spheres extends a candidate's professional knowledge, develops their ability to work in different circumstances and within different organisational cultures, and offers the opportunity to experience all sides of legal work. On the other hand, staying at one workplace may signal loyalty and dedication to work, especially governmental work, indicating a commitment to state values. These values may be preferred by JQBs.

Table 1 suggests that, for almost half the candidates, their only prior experience was of court clerkship. The reputation and professional characteristics of a candidate who started

[21]According to job portal *Headhunter.ru* (available at: hh.ru, accessed 10 July 2019), the salary of court clerks and judicial assistants was R15,000–26,000 in 2018, while the average salary in Russia amounted to R43,724 (Rosstat 2020), and the salary of a newly appointed judge started at R70,000 (Borzenkova 2019).

their professional career in court and never left are favourably regarded by the JQB. However, the legal community recognises that the professional and life experience of such candidates are framed by their background and, therefore, tend to be formalistic and narrow (Morschakova 2014; Bevzenko 2016).

With respect to professional experience, I put forward the following hypotheses: (H2a) in a meritocratic selection process, the probability of obtaining a recommendation from the JQB is positively associated with the number of years of professional experience in legal practice and negatively associated with more varied professional experience; and (H2b) the experience of work in the court apparatus is positively associated with the probability of getting a recommendation for a post.

Demographic characteristics

Merit-based appointment should not allow for gender-based discrimination. Despite the rising recognition of gender inequality within the legal profession, gender remains one of the most influential discriminating factors worldwide (Schultz & Shaw 2003). The prestige of a particular profession is often found to correlate highly with the proportion of men and women working in these professions, with more prestigious professions having a greater share of men (Bose & Rossi 1983).

At the last Soviet election of People's Court judges in 1982, men accounted for 63.5% of all judges (Pashin 2003). However, in 1994 the gender proportion had already changed and the share of women among newly appointed judges reached 58% and remained constant at about 60% (Ilchenko 2017). The increase of female judges in the 1990s was explained by the rapid decrease in the salaries of public sector workers due to the inability of the government to collect taxes and pay its employees (Solomon & Foglesong 2000). This coincided with the rapid increase of a market for qualified lawyers in the corporate world. The opportunity to have a better paid although less secure job resulted in competent male lawyers leaving the judiciary. At the beginning of the 2000s, the state managed to bring budget flows under control. As a result, courts saw an increase in their operational budgets. However, pouring money into the judicial system did not affect the prestige of the profession when measured as a proportion of women.

The observed increase of female judges reflects the process of self-selection under the pressure of structural conditions. In the dataset, women amount to 73% of candidates, while among appointed judges in the same period the share of women was 67% (Ilchenko 2017). These numbers reflect the overall trend of the feminisation of the judicial profession. Female court secretaries and judges' assistants are not only more strategic candidates capable of waiting a long time before they will become judges, but they are also more prepared for the conditions of work, and therefore may be given preference. On the other hand, significant under-representation of men in the pool of candidates might force the JQBs to give preference to male candidates in order to achieve gender equality on the bench. Thus, the hypothesis regarding the influence of gender on the outcome of the selection can be formulated as follows: (H3) in meritocratic selection there will be no difference between male and female candidates in getting a recommendation from JQBs.

Crony selection

Meritocratic selection implies the promotion of the candidate who has proven their professional competence and achieved excellence in their job. Its antithesis is crony selection, which implies the promotion of people from the same social network. Cronyism can be found in all societies and in all spheres of activities, including business, academia, government and non-profit institutions. Such networks evolve because they improve communication, mitigate the agency problem and may increase employee commitment and loyalty (Hudson & Claasen 2017). Nevertheless, the negative sides of crony networks outweigh their benefits. They develop norms of conformity and limit innovation. The selection of people from a limited pool harms the efficient operation of an organisation, especially in a complex and changing environment (Hudson & Claasen 2017). Unequal access to the controlling agent within the crony network creates tension between members and is associated with job insecurity and dissatisfaction (Khatri & Tsang 2003). Cronyism is often based on superior–subordinate relationships and is associated with a mutual commitment in the form of patronage working downwards and personal loyalty upwards (Khatri & Tsang 2003). Recruitment to the network does not exclude high requirements of professionalism and competence by the prospective members; however, shared values are fundamental. However, crony selection creates benefits for a connected person at the expense of people outside the network and ties members of a network by reciprocal obligations. Having defined cronyism, I will now move on to discuss how it functions in the judicial selection process.

The participation of the court president in judicial selection takes several different forms. Formally, the role of the court president is limited to the announcement of the vacant position. In practice, there is no open job market for judicial posts. Although vacancies are announced in local newspapers and on websites, as required by law, generally a post is offered to a person from the 'reserve list' rather than decided on the basis of direct applications. On some occasions, a person from the reserve list who does not have relevant clerkship experience and wishes to work at a particular court will start to work there as a judge's assistant. If the court president does choose to support a candidate, he may provide the candidate with a reference letter, referred to as *khodataistvo*, which can be literally translated as 'solicitation' or 'patronage'.

Having the court president's patronage is not obligatory, but it is widespread and is often mentioned in JQB protocols. In the sample, 54% of the protocols contained an indication of the president's patronage.

My research unveiled a series of different scenarios in relation to *khodataistvo*. First, there is one candidate for one vacant position and the support of the president of the court is explicitly mentioned for this candidate (23%). Second, there is more than one candidate for a vacancy and the president's support is explicitly mentioned only with respect to one of these candidates (28.6%). Third, there is a contradiction in the opinions of the district court president and the president of the regional court (1.3%) when the former recommends the candidate, and the latter does not. Fourth, there is strong opposition from the court president to the candidate (0.4%). Finally, no opinion is provided (46%).

The exclusive responsibility of recommending a candidate for a vacant position rests with the JQB. In a scenario of meritocratic selection, the candidate's professional qualities will be decisive in a JQB's decision to recommend the candidate. If the outcome is decided by *khodataistvo*, crony selection is indicated thus: (H4) if there is no tendency to crony judicial selection, the patronage of the court president will not significantly influence the probability of JQB recommendation.

However, it is possible to assume that the court president's encouragement in the selection process is based on an accurate assessment of the candidate's professional qualities. Ledeneva remarks that, in Russia, criteria of professionalism and qualification might be as important for the recruitment into a network as values of loyalty and obedience (Ledeneva 2013, p. 94). The data allow examination of this hypothesis and the building of additional models in which the dependent variable is the patronage of the president. In cases where the court president's decision is based solely on professional qualities, meritocratic criteria (education, professional experience and gender neutrality) will be significant. This leads to the following hypothesis: (H5) if court presidents support only the most qualified candidates, meritocratic proxies will be statistically significant.

The court presidents may also try to think strategically and patronise politically desirable candidates. My qualitative data suggest that the criteria of political desirability of the central judicial and presidential power are not transparent to the regional judiciary. Yet, Hendley (2019) finds that Russian law graduates who intend to work for the state develop different values to those who want to work in the private sector. Both groups of law graduates show considerably more trust in the power of written law and courts than the average Russian citizen; however, those who intend to work for the state are more confident that Russian judges are impartial and not corrupt, and also more likely to accept the verdicts in politicised cases circulated in the mass media, which demonstrates their pre-programmed willingness to accept accusatorial bias (Hendley 2019). Thus, court presidents may prefer candidates who demonstrate loyalty, willingness to comply with court routines, and legal formalism.

Modelling the outcome of judicial selection

Dependent and independent variables

The dependent variable of interest is recommendation of the JQB, which is coded '1' if the candidate received a recommendation and '0' if the application was rejected.

Meritocratic selection proxies comprise three types of variables: sex, education and professional qualifications. Professional qualifications are measured by three variables. The first is primary professional experience, a factor variable with six levels. When a candidate does not have any work experience outside the court system, the variable is coded 'only court apparatus experience'; when the candidate has other experience outside the court but has spent most of their career in positions in the court apparatus, the variable is coded as 'primary experience in apparatus'. The other categories include primary experience in prosecution, as a police officer, government lawyer or corporate lawyer. The second variable is the length of professional experience in legal practice, measured by years working in any legal profession after graduation from law school.

Third is the scope of professional experience, measured as the number of transfers between different legal positions, where '0' means that the person did not change positions.

The variable 'president of the court patronage' is a proxy to measure the crony element in the judicial selection process. It is coded '1' if the protocol of the commission contains mention of the court president's support and '0' otherwise, including missing data. These dependent and independent variables are reported in Table 2.

I also include two control variables to identify any institutional influence on the selection process. The first variable is the level of the court. On the regional level, the Russian judicial hierarchy includes justices of the peace, district courts and a regional court, which serves as the appellate court for courts of lower jurisdictions and also considers criminal cases of severe gravity and some civil cases. There is also a separate branch of *arbitrazh*, courts which specialise in commercial cases. JQBs are responsible for selecting judges for all these types of courts. It can be assumed that the selection committee imposes stricter requirements on candidates applying for positions at the regional or *arbitrazh* court since serving on these courts is associated with higher prestige and complexity of work. The level of the court is a factor variable with four levels: 'justice of the peace', 'district court', 'regional court' and '*arbitrazh* court'.

The second variable is the type of location where a vacancy is open. The chances of being recommended by a JQB might differ for those who apply for a judicial post in the regional capital and those who want to work in smaller, more isolated cities. The location of the court may influence the results in two different directions. On the one hand, a candidate may consider court positions located in the regional capital to be a more desirable position

TABLE 2
SUMMARY STATISTICS FOR THE STUDY VARIABLES

Variables	(1) *N*	(2) Mean	(3) Codes or min/max
Dependent variable			
Recommendation of qualification board	957	0.590	0/1
Meritocratic selection proxies			
Male	957	0.260	0/1
Good education (1 = yes)	957	0.321	0/1
Years of experience in legal practice	950	9.629	5:29
Scope of professional experience (number of jobs)	957	1.496	1:7
Primary experience			
Only court apparatus	957	0.487	0/1
Primary experience in apparatus	957	0.168	0/1
Prosecution	957	0.124	0/1
Police	957	0.0481	0/1
State lawyer	957	0.0627	0/1
Business lawyer	957	0.110	0/1
Crony selection proxy			
Court president's patronage	957	0.380	0/1
Controls			
Regional capital (1 = yes)	957	0.419	0/1
Justice of the peace	957	0.475	0/1
District court	957	0.382	0/1
Regional court	957	0.00313	0/1
Arbitrazh court	957	0.139	0/1

Note: Statistics on non-missing values are included.

since it provides access to all benefits available in big cities. On the other hand, there are more jobs that provide a comparative level of income and prestige as a judicial post for a competent lawyer in regional capitals and thus fewer people will compete for a judicial vacancy. In small cities the competition for a judicial position could be stronger as it is one of the most highly paid jobs available in these cities. The variable 'is region capital' was coded as '1' if the court to which a candidate applies is located in the capital city of the region.

Results

The models below evaluate the outcome of the selection procedure. The variables of interest are gender, professional and educational background as the elements of meritocratic selection and the patronage of the court president as an element of cronyism.

I first evaluate the hypothesis of meritocratic selection (Model 1), and then add the crony proxy into the model (Model 2). The third model includes institutional characteristics as control variables. This approach helps to identify the factors associated with the selection of judges.

Table 3 reports the estimated logistic regression models where the dependent variable takes 1 if the JQB recommends candidates and 0 otherwise. The results are reported as model coefficients (ß) and average marginal effects ($\partial y/\partial x$).

The models in Table 3 uncover three main tendencies of the judicial selection process in Russia.

First, there are elements of meritocratic selection. The candidates' gender has no significance in the model, which allows me to exclude the hypothesis that in search of diversity, male candidates are given preference in response to the significant over-representation of female candidates. The hypothesis that the chances of receiving a recommendation are higher for the candidates who have better education is supported. However, the effect is very small.

Second, certain professional sub-groups—lawyers with experience in corporate legal practice, defence attorneys and other lawyers with non-state experience—are considered undesirable for judicial posts. Candidates with a professional background from any state body, including the Public Prosecutor's office, police, governmental or court apparatus have a significantly greater chance of being recommended than candidates with experience in the private sector. A person with a non-governmental background has a 9.7% lower probability of receiving a JQB recommendation.

Third, Model 2 indicates that the effect of the court president's patronage is overwhelming. The power of the court president, as discussed in the literature and in my interviews with judges, is strongly empirically supported. Patronage of the court president increases the probability of a favourable decision by 53.2%.

The inclusion of the patronage variable also increased the goodness of fit measured by pseudo R-square and the Bayesian Information Criterion (BIC). The share of JQB decisions correctly predicted by Model 2 is 85.1%, showing improvement compared to the 70.89% accuracy of Model 1 where only meritocratic variables are included.

The inclusion of institutional controls in Model 3 does not shift the major findings in Models 1 and 2 but adds some new possible explanations. It appears to be easier to

TABLE 3
LOGISTIC REGRESSION ESTIMATES OF RECOMMENDATION FOR JUDICIAL POST

	Model 1		Model 2		Model 3	
	β	Average marginal effect (∂y/∂x)	β	Average marginal effect (∂y/∂x)	β	Average marginal effect (∂y/∂x)
Male	0.366	0.069	0.102	0.011	0.144	0.015
	(0.191)	(0.036)	(0.246)	(0.027)	(0.248)	(0.026)
Good education	0.630***	0.119***	0.653**	0.071**	0.604*	0.065*
	(0.191)	(0.035)	(0.249)	(0.027)	(0.253)	(0.027)
Years of experience in legal practice	−0.014	−0.003	−0.032	−0.004	−0.030	−0.003
	(0.025)	(0.005)	(0.036)	(0.004)	(0.036)	(0.004)
Variety of professional experience	−0.164	−0.031	−0.239	−0.026	−0.193	−0.021
	(0.134)	(0.025)	(0.173)	(0.019)	(0.175)	(0.019)
Primary experience: baseline = only court apparatus						
Primary experience in apparatus	0.247	0.046	0.272	0.030	0.362	0.039
	(0.261)	(0.049)	(0.337)	(0.037)	(0.345)	(0.037)
Prosecution	−0.157	−0.030	0.167	0.018	−0.112	−0.012
	(0.286)	(0.054)	(0.394)	(0.043)	(0.406)	(0.043)
Police	−0.464	−0.087	−0.549	−0.060	−0.516	−0.055
	(0.373)	(0.070)	(0.478)	(0.052)	(0.489)	(0.052)
State lawyer	−0.562	−0.106	−0.210	−0.023	−0.127	−0.014
	(0.368)	(0.069)	(0.466)	(0.051)	(0.461)	(0.049)
Business lawyer	−1.012**	−0.191**	−0.932**	−0.102**	−0.960**	−0.103**
	(0.317)	(0.059)	(0.353)	(0.038)	(0.353)	(0.037)
Patronage (directly expressed)			4.869***	0.531***	4.931***	0.527***
			(0.412)	(0.026)	(0.421)	(0.025)
Regional capital					0.522*	0.056*
					(0.259)	(0.027)
Court level: baseline = justice of the peace						
District court					0.294	0.031
					(0.222)	(0.024)
Regional court					0	0
					(.)	(.)
Arbitrazh court					−0.834*	−0.089*
					(0.381)	(0.040)
Region FE	yes	yes	yes	yes	yes	yes
Observations	916	916	916	916	913	913
Model diagnostic						
Pseudo R^2	0.185		0.488		0.497	
BIC	1213.9	.	843.7	.	850.1	.
chi2	178.2		269.3		275.4	
% correctly classified	70.85%		85.04%		85.43%	

Note: Robust standard errors in parentheses * $p<0.05$, ** $p<0.01$, *** $p<0.001$.

obtain a recommendation from the JQB if the vacancy is located in the regional capital rather than in a non-urban or rural area. This might signify that either the competition for vacant positions is higher in remote courts than in regional capitals or that the quality of candidates who apply for a position in small remote cities is lower and JQBs have to reject more candidates. It is also slightly more difficult to receive a recommendation when a candidate applies for a position in the more prestigious *arbitrazh* court than in a court of general jurisdiction.

The next set of models examines the alternative hypothesis that court presidents give their *khodataistvo* to candidates with the best professional qualities. The dependent variable in the following two models is the patronage of the court's president; it receives '1' in cases where the president provided *khodataistvo* to the candidate and '0' otherwise. Table 4 reports the estimated logistic regression model.

Models 4 and 5 show that in general the court presidents' preferences correspond with patterns of JQB decision-making. However, there are also differences. While I did not find any gender preferences in JQB decisions (see Table 3), court presidents expressed a preference for male candidates. Given that the majority of applicants are female, this

TABLE 4

LOGISTIC REGRESSION ESTIMATES OF THE COURT PRESIDENT'S PATRONAGE

	Model 4		Model 5	
	β	Average marginal effect ($\partial y/\partial x$)	β	Average marginal effect ($\partial y/\partial x$)
Male	0.495*	0.0791*	0.484*	0.0771*
	(0.207)	(0.0322)	(0.210)	(0.0327)
Good education	0.453*	0.0724*	0.436*	0.0695*
	(0.211)	(0.0335)	(0.214)	(0.0339)
Years of experience in legal practice	0.00893	0.00143	0.00812	0.00129
	(0.0259)	(0.00414)	(0.0257)	(0.00409)
Variety of professional experience	−0.0149	−0.00238	0.00398	0.000634
	(0.169)	(0.0270)	(0.169)	(0.0269)
Primary experience: baseline = only court apparatus				
Primary experience in apparatus	0.0835	0.0133	0.0654	0.0104
	(0.296)	(0.0472)	(0.296)	(0.0471)
Prosecution	−0.435	−0.0695	−0.523	−0.0833
	(0.298)	(0.0471)	(0.306)	(0.0483)
Police	−0.222	−0.0355	−0.191	−0.0304
	(0.460)	(0.0733)	(0.462)	(0.0736)
State lawyer	−0.733	−0.117	−0.751	−0.120
	(0.444)	(0.0703)	(0.449)	(0.0709)
Business lawyer	−0.874*	−0.140*	−0.884*	−0.141*
	(0.359)	(0.0567)	(0.364)	(0.0572)
Regional capital (1=yes)			0.0593	0.00945
			(0.212)	(0.0337)
Court level: baseline = justice of the peace				
District court			0.236	0.0376
			(0.190)	(0.0302)
Regional court			0.742	0.118
			(1.083)	(0.173)
Arbitrazh court			0.00522	0.000832
			(0.322)	(0.0514)
Region FE	yes	yes	yes	yes
Observations	899	899	899	899
Pseudo R^2	0.279		0.281	
BIC	1053.1	.	1078.5	.
chi2	180.1		181.9	
% correctly classified	77.75%		77.98%	

Note: Robust standard errors in parentheses * $p<0.05$, ** $p<0.01$, *** $p<0.001$.

finding might hint that presidents are looking to increase gender diversity in their courts or that they have widespread gender bias. A 'glass escalator' hypothesis provides an alternative explanation for such preferences: in female-dominated professions, male candidates receive preferences both at the hiring and promotion stages of their careers (Williams 2012).

Surprisingly, the hypotheses that court clerks receive more support from the presidents of the court is not supported. This may be explained by the fact that court clerks already constitute 75% of the pool of candidates. In the case of competition for the judicial post, their chances are equal to those of candidates from other governmental bodies and diverge from the chances of candidates whose primary experience is in business. Court presidents demonstrate a clear preference for candidates able to work in a bureaucratic environment and who are familiar with the hierarchy of state bodies.

Discussion and conclusion

The purpose of this essay was to uncover the mechanisms of judicial selection in Russia. The essay began by asking which factors influence the decision of a JQB to support a particular candidate for a judicial post. This question was driven by the normative statement that the quality of the judicial system and its level of independence is determined by the quality of the judicial corpus and the ability and willingness of judges to make independent decisions. The transparency of the process of judicial selection and recruitment is considered to be a basic prerequisite for judicial independence and professionalism. Over the last ten years, the Russian judicial system has implemented a range of reforms to increase the transparency of this process. As a result, it was possible to create a dataset which provided an exceptional opportunity to compare the characteristics of both successful and unsuccessful candidates to the judicial post and apply multilevel modelling to examine those who were selected for judicial positions and those who were rejected.

The demographic data of the pool of candidates suggest that it is unbalanced and that there are patterns of strong self-selection into the profession. Previous research found the gradual feminisation of the judiciary and prevalence of court clerks among appointed judges (Solomon & Foglesong 2000; Volkov & Dzmitryieva 2015). This study supports previous findings. There is a considerably higher number of female candidates for the bench (73.9%) as compared to the proportion of female and male lawyers in general. Data from the RLMS survey show that number of law graduates in 2016 was more gender balanced with 58.5% female and 41.5% male graduates (Bocharov & Dzmitryieva forthcoming). However, this research proposes that there is a slight inclination to discriminate in favour of male judges. Although the 'reserve list' is made up of court clerks who are mainly female, court presidents demonstrate stable preference for male candidates. Their preferences might indicate either gender bias or intentions to diversify the judiciary. By contrast, the JQBs remain gender neutral and this variable remains statistically insignificant through all models unless the candidate is not supported by the court president.

Another source of imbalance is the candidates' professional background. In 1997, about one-third of judges had a background in the private sector; about 20% came from prosecution and only 11% had a background in clerkship (Solomon & Foglesong 2000).

According to a 2013 survey, the composition of judges with different experience was more balanced, where the breakdown of judges with clerkship experience was 30%, prosecutors 20%, private lawyer 16% and public lawyers 10% (Volkov & Dzmitryieva 2015). This study establishes the increasing tendency to choose judges from candidates who have worked in the court apparatus, who constitute two-thirds of the candidate pool and also two-thirds of the selected candidates. This may mean that lawyers with experience outside the court apparatus hesitate to apply to these posts because they do not expect to succeed. As a result, the diversity of the judicial corps in terms of professional experience is decreasing. Socialisation inside the court results in the development of a professional culture characterised by conformism and formal bureaucratic orientation.

Previous studies and qualitative data suggest that the role of court presidents goes well above the formal requirements of the law. The results of the multilevel models provide strong support for the crony selection hypothesis. Whereas the strong influence of court presidents in the selection, promotion and evaluation of judges has been discussed elsewhere (ICJ 2010), the models in this essay show the magnitude of their influence. I found a robust relationship between the patronage of the court president and the chances of success for an application to a judicial position. The influence of the court president's patronage on the application outcome is many times higher than any other demographic and professional factors. It means that the real selection has shifted from JQBs to the presidents of the courts. It seems that empirical evidence on how institutions of judicial self-governance work in many countries often contradicts the theory (Garoupa & Ginsburg 2009; Bobek & Kosař 2013; Ortiz & Jose 2017). The present study provides further evidence that the introduction of the JQB in itself does not always help to protect judicial independence by encouraging meritocratic selection of judges but, rather, plays a symbolic role in approving decisions made at earlier stages. The court presidents are determined to reduce the risks that new judges will not conform to the culture of the workplace. Knowing the new judges personally helps to ensure this. In turn, the JQBs tend to place more emphasis on the oversight of judicial work rather than on recruitment. Thus, they happily pass the right to select new judges to the court presidents. This supports previous observations about the vulnerability of institutional borders in the Russian legal system (Kurkchiyan 2018).

The second major finding of the essay is the systematic disinclination to select lawyers with a non-government background. The initial hypothesis was that candidates with experience in the court apparatus would have an advantage in the selection process as compared to candidates from other segments of the legal profession. In contrast, it appeared that the dividing line lies between all those who have worked in state bodies and those who have worked in the private sector, as *advokaty*, corporate lawyers or legal counsel. This result is robust for evaluation of candidates by JQBs and by court presidents. This finding is in concordance with a recent study by Hendley (2019), who finds that Russian law graduates who want to work for the state demonstrate higher political and legal compliance. This consideration adds to the previous finding that ability to work in a highly bureaucratised and hierarchical environment makes candidates with state experience more attractive. Candidates from state bodies are selected not only on the basis of their institutional belonging but also on the basis of shared values, which are rooted in the process of professional socialisation.

To sum up, these findings raise the following question: are there any institutional arrangements that would effectively protect judicial candidates from such influence and move the process back to meritocratic selection?

Reformers expected that the greater independence of the judicial councils would change the type of candidates who are selected. Nonetheless, we observe the opposite trend. The pool of potential candidates is shrinking (Kondratieva 2018a) and, in recent years, more candidates fail to pass through all of the filters to take up judicial posts (Kondratieva 2018b). Apparently, potential candidates observe that only candidates with particular characteristics and professional backgrounds are appointed to the judicial bench and decline to apply for vacant positions if they do not have those qualifications. The influence of court presidents in the judicial selection process is disproportionally significant considering their role laid down by law. The informal practice of recommendation by the president of the court demonstrates the existence of invisible obstacles to the judicial bench and emphasises the institutionalisation of cronyism in the judiciary.

References

Abel, R. L. (1985) 'Comparative Sociology of Legal Professions: An Exploratory Essay', *American Bar Foundation Research Journal*, 10, 1.

Armytage, L. (1996) *Educating Judges. Towards a New Model of Continuing Judicial Learning* (The Hague, Kluwer Law International).

Bevzenko, R. (2016) 'Pomoschniki sud'i: Kakaya eto stupen'ka v yuridicheskoi kar'ere?', *Zakon.ru*, available at: https://zakon.ru/blog/2016/12/1/pomoschnik_sudi_kakaya_eto_stupenka_v_yuridicheskoj_karere, accessed 1 February 2019.

Blass, T. (2007) 'Combating Corruption and Political Influence in Russia's Court System', in Rodriguez, D. & Ehrichs, L. (eds) *Global Corruption Report 2007. Corruption in Judicial Systems* (Cambridge, Cambridge University Press).

Bobek, M. & Kosař, D. (2013) *Global Solutions, Local Damages: A Critical Study in Judicial Councils in Central and Eastern Europe*, Research Paper in Law, 07/2013 (Bruges, College of Europe).

Bocharov, T. & Dzmitryieva, A. (forthcoming) *Legal Education in Russia: Between University, Profession, State and Market* (St Petersburg, European University in St Petersburg Press).

Bocharov, T. & Moiseeva, E. (2016) *Byt' advokatom v Rossii* (St Petersburg, European University in St Petersburg Press).

Bocharov, T., Volkov, V., Voskobitova, L. A., Dzmitryieva, A., Smola, A., Titaev, K. & Tsvetkov, I. (2018). *Predlozheniya po sovershenstvovaniyu sudebnoi sistemy Rossiiskoi Federatsii* (Moscow, Tsentr strategicheskikh razrabotok).

Borzenkova, E. (2019) 'Tsena sud'i: skolko poluchayut rossiiskie sud'i', *Pravo.ru*, 1 March, available at: https://pravo.ru/story/209079/, accessed 10 November 2020.

Bose, C. E. & Rossi, P. H. (1983) 'Gender and Jobs: Prestige Standings of Occupation Affected by Gender', *American Sociological Review*, 48, 3.

Burbank, S. B. & Friedman, B. (2002) 'Reconsidering Judicial Independence', in Burbank, S. B. & Friedman, B. (eds) *Judicial Independence at the Crossroad* (New York, NY, Sage).

Daniels, N. (1978) 'Merit and Meritocracy', *Philosophy and Public Affairs*, 7, 3.

Dzmitryieva, A. & Volkov, V. (2019) 'Kak sistema otbora sudei delaet ikh zavisimymi ot silovikov', *Vedomosti*, 3 October, available at: https://www.vedomosti.ru/opinion/articles/2019/10/03/812707-sistema-otbora-sudei, accessed 10 November 2020.

ENCJ (2009) 'Judicial Ethics Report 2008–2009', European Network of Councils for the Judiciary, available at: https://www.encj.eu/images/stories/pdf/ethics/encjreportjudicialethics20082009.pdf, accessed 10 November 2020.

Ermoshin, G. T. (2016) *Status sud'i v Rossiiskoi Federatsii* (Moscow, Rossiiskii Gosudarstvennyi Institut Pravosudiya), available at: https://rgup.ru/rimg/files/_ДИССЕРТАЦИЯ_Г.Т._ЕРМОШИН.pdf, accessed 20 November 2020.

Garoupa, N. & Ginsburg, T. (2009) 'Guarding the Guardians: Judicial Councils and Judicial Independence', *The American Journal of Comparative Law*, 57, 1.

Gee, G. (2012) 'The Persistent Politics of Judicial Selection: A Comparative Analysis', in Seibert-Fohr, A. (ed.).

Geyh, C. G. (2008) 'The Endless Judicial Selection Debate and Its Implications for the Future of an Independent Judiciary', *The Georgetown Journal of Legal Ethics*, 21.

Gibbs, H. (1987) 'The Appointment and Removal of Judges', *Federal Law Review*, 17.

Ginsburg, T. (2008) 'Administrative Law and the Judicial Control of Agents in Authoritarian Regimes', in Ginsburg, T. & Moustafa, T. (eds) *Rule by Law: The Politics of Courts in Authoritarian Regimes* (Cambridge, Cambridge University Press).

Goskomstat (1989) *Narodnoe obrazovanie i kultura v SSSR (Statisticheskii sbornik)* (Moscow, Finansy i statistika).

Grigoriev, L. M., Zubarevich, N. V. & Khasaev, G. R. (2011) *Rossiiskie regiony: ekonomicheskii krizis i problemy modernizatsii* (Moscow, TEIS).

Guba, K. & Ilchenko, N. (2018) *Otsenka effektivnosti otraslevykh yuridicheskikh vuzov* (St Petersburg, Institute for the Rule of Law).

Hanson, A. F. (1993) *Testing, Testing: Social Consequences of the Examined Life* (Berkley, CA, University of California Press).

Hendley, K. (2017) *Everyday Law in Russia* (Ithaca, NY, Cornell University Press).

Hendley, K. (2019) 'Nature Versus Nurture: A Comparison of Russian Law Graduates Destined for State Service and for Private Practice', *Law & Policy*, 41, 2.

Hilbink, L. (2007) *Judges Beyond Politics in Democracy and Dictatorship: Lessons from Chile, Cities* (Cambridge, Cambridge University Press).

Holmes, S. (2015) 'Imitating Democracy, Feigning Capacity', in Przeworski, A. (ed.) *Democracy in a Russian Mirror* (Cambridge, Cambridge University Press).

Hudson, S. & Claasen, C. (2017) 'Nepotism and Cronyism as a Cultural Phenomenon?', in Aßländer, M. S. & Hudson, S. (eds) *The Handbook of Business and Corruption* (Bingley, Emerald Publishing).

Hunter, R. (2015) 'More than just a Different Face? Judicial Diversity and Decision-making', *Current Legal Problems*, 68, 1.

ICJ (2010) *The State of the Judiciary in Russia. Report of the ICJ Research Mission or Judicial Reform to the Russian Federation* (Geneva, International Commission of Jurists).

Ilchenko, N. (2017) 'Empiricheskoe issledovanie kar'ernykh traektorii rossiiskikh sudei arbitrazhnykh sudov i sudov obshchei yurisdiktsii v 1994–2016', unpublished manuscript.

Khatri, N. & Tsang, E. W. K. (2003) 'Antecedents and Consequences of Cronyism in Organizations', *Journal of Business Ethics*, 43, 4.

Kondratieva, I. (2018a) 'Glava VKKS: zhelayushchikh stat' sud'ey stanovitsya men'she', *Pravo.ru*, 19 July, available at: https://pravo.ru/news/204126/, accessed 1 March 2019.

Kondratieva, I. (2018b) 'Otfil'trovali: pochemu kandidaty v sud'i ne prokhodyat prezidentskuyu komissiyu', *Pravo.ru*, 20 July, available at: https://pravo.ru/story/204155/, accessed 1 March 2019.

Krastev, I. (2011) 'Paradoxes of the New Authoritarianism', *Journal of Democracy*, 22, 2.

Kubal, A. (2018) 'In Search of Justice: Migrants' Experience of Appeal in the Moscow City Court', in Kurkchiyan, M. & Kubal, A. (eds).

Kühn, Z. (2012) 'Judicial Administration Reforms in Central-Eastern Europe: Lessons to be Learned', in Fohr, A. S. (ed.) *Judicial Independence in Transition* (Heidelberg, Springer).

Kurkchiyan, M. (2018) 'The Professionalization of Law in the Context of the Russian Legal Tradition', in Kurkchiyan, M. & Kubal, A. (eds).

Kurkchiyan, M. & Kubal, A. (eds) (2018) *A Sociology of Justice in Russia* (Cambridge, Cambridge University Press).

Ledeneva, A. V. (2013) *Can Russia Modernize?* (Cambridge, Cambridge University Press).

Maleshin, D. (2017) 'The Crisis of Russian Legal Education in Comparative Perspective', *Journal of Legal Education*, 66, 2.

Moiseeva, E. (2015) *Legal Education in Russia* (St Petersburg, Institute for the Rule of Law).

Morschakova, T. (2014) *Tamara Georgievna Morshchakova o sudebnoi sisteme Rossii. (Golitsino, iyul 2014)*, available at: https://zakon.ru/blog/2014/8/25/tamara_georgievna_morshhakova_o_sudebnoj_sisteme_rossii_golicyno_iyul_2014_goda_tekst, accessed 1 February 2019.

Moustafa, T. (2014) 'Law and Courts in Authoritarian Regimes', *Annual Review of Law and Social Science*, 10.

Muller, L. F. (2012) 'Judicial Administration in Transitional Eastern Countries', in Seibert-Fohr, A. (ed.).

Nussbaum, M. C. (1997) *Poetic Justice: The Literary Imagination and Public Life* (Boston, MA, Beacon Press).

Ortiz, C. & Jose, P. (2017) 'Councils of the Judiciary and Judges' Perceptions of Respect to Their Independence in Europe', *Hague Journal on the Rule of Law*, 9.

Pashin, S. A. (2003) 'Kratkii ocherk sudebnykh reform i revolyutsii v Rossii', *Otechestvennye zapiski*, 2.

Plotnikova, I. (2014) 'EGE dlya sudei: kodeksy mozhno, mobilniki net', *Vechernyaya Kazan'*, 22 July, available at: http://www.evening-kazan.ru/articles/ege-dlya-sudey-kodeksy-mozhno-mobilniki-net.html, accessed 14 November 2020.

Popova, M. (2018) 'Journalists, Judges and State Officials: How Russian Courts Adjudicate Defamation Lawsuits Against the Media', in Kurkchiyan, M. & Kubal, A. (eds).

Remus, D. A. (2016) 'Reconstructing Professionalism', *Georgia Law Review*, 51.

Rhode, D. L. (1996) 'Myths of Meritocracy', *Fordham Law Review*, 65.

Rosstat (2020) 'Rynok truda, zanyatost' i zarabotnaya plata', available at: https://rosstat.gov.ru/labor_market_employment_salaries, accessed 16 November 2020.

Sakwa, R. (2010) 'The Dual State in Russia', *Post-Soviet Affairs*, 26, 3.

Schultz, U. & Shaw, G. (eds) (2003) *Women in the World's Legal Profession* (Oxford, Hart Publishing).

Seibert-Fohr, A. (ed.) (2012) *Judicial Independence in Transition* (Heidelberg, Springer).

Serov, D. (2013) 'Rossiiskie sud'i i vysshee yuridicheskoe obrazovanie', *Vysshee obrazovanie v Rossii*, 10.

Shapiro, M. (2008) 'Courts in Authoritarian Regimes', in Ginsburg, T. & Moustafa, T. (eds) *Rule by Law: The Politics of Courts in Authoritarian Regimes* (Cambridge, Cambridge University Press).

Solomon, P. H. (2004) 'Judicial Power in Russia: Through the Prism of Administrative Justice', *Law & Society Review*, 38, 3.

Solomon, P. H. (2008) 'Judicial Power in Authoritarian States: The Russian Experience', in Ginsburg, T. & Moustafa, T. (eds) *Rule By Law: The Politics of Courts in Authoritarian Regimes* (Cambridge, Cambridge University Press).

Solomon, P. H. (2012) 'The Accountability of Judges in Post Communist States: From Bureaucratic to Professional Accountability', in Seibert-Fohr, A. (ed.).

Solomon, P. H. (2015) 'Law and Courts in Authoritarian States', in Wright, J. D. (ed.) *International Encyclopedia of the Social and Behavioral Sciences* (2nd edn) (London & New York, NY, Elsevier).

Solomon, P. H. & Foglesong, T. (2000) *Courts and Transition in Russia. The Challenge of Judicial Reform* (Boulder, CO, Westview Press).

Spence, M. (1973) 'Job Market Signalling', *The Quarterly Journal of Economics*, 87, 3.

Tev, D. B. (2017) 'Deputaty Gosudarstvennoi Dumy VI sozyva: sotsialno-professionalnye istochniki rekrutirovaniya', *Economicheskaya Sotsiologia*, 18, 5.

Timoshin, N. V. (2013) *Udovletvoryat' potrebnosti sudebnoi sistemy. Doklad Predsedatelya Vysshei kvalifikatsionnoi kollegii sudei Rossiiskoi Federatsii*, available at: http://www.vkks.ru/publication/14889/, accessed 20 February 2018.

Volkov, V. & Dzmitryieva, A. (2015) 'Recruitment Patterns, Gender, and Professional Subcultures of the Judiciary in Russia', *The International Journal of the Legal Profession*, 22, 2.

Volkov, V., Dzmitryieva, A., Pozdnyakov, M. & Titaev, K. (2016) *Rossiiskie sud'i: sotsiologicheskoe issledovanie professii* (Moscow, Norma).

Voskobitova, L. A. (2017) *Teoreticheskie osnovy sudebnoi vlasti* (Moscow, Norma, INFRA-M).

Williams, C. L. (2012) 'The Glass Escalator: Hidden Advantages for Men in the "Female" Professions', *Social Problems*, 39, 3.

Zolotukhin, B. A. A., Vitsin, S. M., Larin, A. M., Mikhailovskaya, I. B., Morshchakova, T. G., Nazarov, R. V., Pashin, S. A., Petrukhin, I. L. & Stetsovskii, Iu. I. (1994) 'The Conception of Judicial Reform in the RSFSR', *Statutes and Decisions*, 30, 2.

Appendix

TABLE A1

Portion of Regions Present in the Sample According to the Level of Regional Development

Level of economic development	Absent in dataset	Present in dataset
Highly developed	66.7	33.3
Developed	70.6	29.4
Semi-depressed	55.1	44.9
Low developed	72.7	27.3
Total number of regions (*N*)	51	32

Source: Data on economic development are taken from Grigoriev *et al.* (2011).

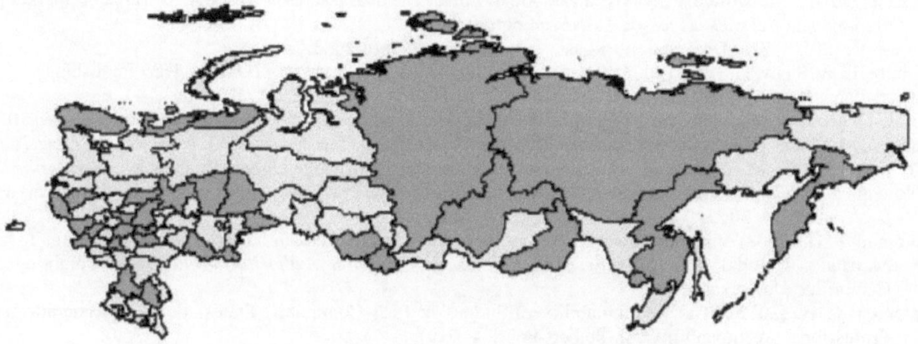

FIGURE A1. Regional Data Availability
Note: White areas depict regions with available data.
Source: Created by the author.

TABLE A2

Representativeness Check

Year	% of candidates recommended by JQBs in the dataset	% of candidates recommended by JQBs out of all applicants in Russia
2014	79	73
2015	75	74

Source: Country-level data provided by the Presidential Human Resource Commission (Bocharov *et al.* 2018).

Building Socialist Legality: Political Order and Institutional Development in the Soviet and Chinese Procuracies

MARGARET HANSON & MICHAEL THOMPSON-BRUSSTAR

Abstract

Why do some attempts to use legal institutions to exert central state control fail, while others succeed? Through a controlled comparison of the Soviet Union (USSR) and the People's Republic of China (PRC), we analyse the institutionalisation of the procuracy, an agency charged with enforcing central legal directives. We show that institutional design, competition, and political support during critical junctures created a positive feedback for the institutionalisation of the procuracy in the USSR but left it weak in China. These findings contribute to our understanding of institutional development, state-building, and authoritarian legal control.

WHAT EXPLAINS WHY LEGAL INSTITUTIONS TRIUMPH as tools for political control in some authoritarian regimes but fail to do so in others? Huntington characterised both the USSR and China as 'effective' political systems (2006, p. 1), but that compliance with central mandates did not emerge overnight: in the chaotic wake of revolution and civil war, enforcing its laws and mandates was a pressing concern for Communist Party leaders in both countries. Local officials' interests often diverged sharply from those of the central government, and consequently, they resisted implementing orders imposed from above. Thus, though central authorities possessed the power to make decisions, they often lacked the power to enforce them. To better police 'political order', the Soviet Union and China introduced a procuracy (*prokuratura* in Russian, *jiancha yuan* in Chinese) with powers of 'general supervision', that is, a mandate to monitor local officials for compliance with central laws and regulations, at similar points in their histories. In the Soviet Union, the procuracy became a highly institutionalised, integral component of the party's efforts to use law to bring local state officials to heel, a role it continues to play in contemporary Russia (Solomon 1997; Vakhitova 2003; Pomeranz 2019); in China, despite the 'borrowing' of the Soviet institutional template of the procuracy (and advice from Soviet experts), the procuracy failed to develop similarly deep roots. Today its order-enforcing functions have mostly been absorbed by other institutions. What explains these divergent outcomes?

This work was supported by the University of Michigan Rackham Graduate School Research Grant and by the Institute for Humane Studies Fellowship.

We argue that in China, political suspicion towards bureaucracy and friction between top-down (professionalised) and bottom-up (mass campaign) approaches to enforcing legal compliance rendered general supervision obsolete even before its Mao-era abolition. In contrast, in the Soviet Union, workers' and peasants' groups proved ineffective at supervising state officials' response to central mandates comparatively early in the Bolsheviks' rule. That perceived failure, coupled with disagreements among party leaders as to what shape such control should take, informed Lenin's concerted push for a procuracy with vast legal authority answerable only to the party leadership. That design later proved useful to Stalin, who adopted the procuracy as a tool in his push for agricultural collectivisation and as a part of the infamous *troikas* during the purges. Following Stalin's death, the procuracy was recalibrated to focus on its original, Leninist mandate, and it became a powerful tool for top-down control over the vast Soviet bureaucracy.

By comparing the development of the procuracy in the Soviet Union to its development in the People's Republic of China, this essay makes two contributions. First, it identifies crucial structural conditions for the successful use of authoritarian legality to enforce central political control: clear functional hierarchy and the use of 'blueprints', that is, existing models of institutional design. Second, by tracing the evolution of the procuracy across critical junctures in the state-building periods of both regimes, we show that differences in how party leaders adopted and understood these blueprints depended on their experience with alternative institutional approaches and the political context. In addition, this essay demonstrates the fruitfulness of expanding the study of authoritarian legality beyond courts. By focusing on the understudied procuracy, we show how examining legal institutions outside of courts can shed light on authoritarian state-building and institutional development.

Theory and implications

Both China and the Soviet Union emerged from revolution and civil war facing a similar challenge: the need to combat local officials' non-compliance and rampant abuses of power. Both states adopted a procuracy with powers of general supervision in an attempt to get local officials to more closely abide by central mandates. This power refers to supervising the 'exact and full execution of all laws by administrative organs, enterprises, social organisations, officials, and citizens', as well as determining whether local laws comply with existing federal or central legislation and policy; in both regimes those investigations could also be triggered by citizen complaints, meaning that the institution also served an 'ombudsman' function (Smith 1978, p. 3; Wu 2000). Although the Soviet and Chinese procuracies' closest institutional 'relative' in Western legal systems is the office of the prosecutor, the power of general supervision is one way in which these countries extended the authority of the procuracy well beyond criminal cases and, at least on paper, made it an extraordinarily powerful institution for enforcing legality.[1] In the

[1]While the words 'general supervision' do not appear in the PRC state constitution, the expansive language of the procuratorial mandate in the constitution and the Organic Law of the People's Republic of China were interpreted as granting the procuracy the power of general supervision by experts of the period (Duan 2018).

Soviet Union, that mandate was fulfilled: the procuracy grew to become a powerful agency with extensive influence over law in form and practice (Smith 1978).

In contrast, despite similar starting conditions, a shared institutional template, and the same mandate, the Chinese procuracy only weakly institutionalised, and never played a key role in centralised political control. Instead, the PRC procuracy ended up being secondary to party organs and mass campaigns in supervising local policymaking and enforcing Mao's will across China (Li 2016).[2] Thus, while both the Soviet and Chinese procuracies were established with extensive formal authority over legality in their respective states—and the latter adopted the institutional design of the Soviet procuracy, with the help of Soviet advisers (Xie 2008)—the Chinese procuracy never developed the institutional strength of its Soviet counterpart. What explains this, and what implications does it have for our understanding of law and institutional development in new authoritarian regimes?

We argue that these divergent paths can be attributed to three mechanisms: increasing returns, competition, and changing political contexts. First, a subtle but critical divergence in institutional design led to increasing returns in the Soviet case. Increasing returns is the process whereby political processes can become increasingly preferable to their alternatives by generating path dependence (Pierson 2011). An initial difference in its placement in the state's institutional hierarchy made the Soviet procuracy a more attractive tool for projecting central authority than its Chinese counterpart: while the Chinese procuracy was 'dually subordinate' to superior procuratorates and to regional authorities in China, the procuracy enjoyed formal independence from the latter in the USSR. This direct link to party leadership imbued the Soviet procuracy with a heightened authority *vis-à-vis* other state institutions that, in turn, facilitated the central government's increasing reliance on it. As that dependence grew, the procuracy became ever-more entrenched as a key tool for enforcing legality and with it, the party leadership's political control.

Second, competition between the procuracy and other institutions at critical junctures, especially following the successful personalisation of power and the death of the previous leaders, affected the dynamics of institutional choice: continued investment in administrative legality for political control (USSR), or a reversion to bottom-up campaigns for generating compliance (PRC). In short, we find that the initial distinction in design became magnified by differences in sequencing at critical junctures, contributing to institutionalisation in the Soviet case and the lack thereof in China.

Finally, changes in political context contributed to subsequent levels of investment in the procuracy in each case and thus, its institutionalisation. This competition was compounded and complicated by two kinds of changes in the international political context: changes in Sino–Soviet relations and changes in top party leadership. Falleti and Lynch argue that 'causal effects depend on the interaction of specific mechanisms with aspects of the context within which these mechanisms operate' (Falleti & Lynch 2009, p. 1144). We

[2]This was true in China even before the Cultural Revolution forced almost all legal organs to suspend normal operation.

argue that which of the two supervision approaches attracted increasing returns depended heavily on these contextual changes.

The first contextual change was in the political relationship between the USSR and the PRC, which began to deteriorate after de-Stalinisation. We show that, after the early 1950s, the political capital of the Soviet model of the procuracy waned due to increased friction between the two countries (Walder 2015). This made it a soft target for the ensuing political campaign by associating it with revisionism and 'rightist' thinking. Costly and time-consuming investment in studying the Soviet procuracy, obtaining training from Soviet legal experts, and practising legal supervision as specified by law thus became a political liability due to a change in the political context. This undermined the potential for entrenching any independent supervision authority in the PRC.

In contrast, because the Soviet procuracy drew on domestic historical rather than contemporary blueprints, the trajectory of its institutionalisation depended on internal political processes. Specifically, the development of the procuracy hinged on the role of key personalities—namely, Lenin and Stalin. Lenin's insertion of personal authority and influence at the key critical juncture of the procuracy's creation decisively shaped its design. In turn, that design proved useful in Stalin's subsequent centralisation and personalisation of power and, in doing so, helped the institution endure this period of relative de-institutionalisation. Moreover, the death of Stalin in 1953 constituted a critical juncture and external 'shock' that led the party leadership to recalibrate goals and 'rediscover' Leninist principles from the early 1920s. In particular, the party reduced its reliance on the highly weaponised use of legal institutions for repression and renewed its emphasis on general supervision to ensure local compliance with central directives.[3]

It is important to note that the procuracy was not the sole means by which either the Soviet or Chinese regimes attempted to develop centralised political control. Other institutions, most notably the internal security apparatus—the People's Commissariat of Internal Affairs (*Narodnyi komissariat vnutrennikh del*—NKVD) in the USSR and the police (*gong an xitong*) and Ministry of State Security (*guo an xitong*) in China—obviously constituted key components of the party's 'toolkit' for state-building as well. Rather, our focus is on the institutionalisation or the abandonment of one legal institution explicitly introduced to improve control over the state apparatus through 'legal' means. Moreover, that institution is one that, in the post-Soviet era, has successfully defended its mandate against reform efforts (Huskey 1997) and continues to be widely used to hold state officials accountable (Pomeranz 2019).

Methodology

Our case selection leverages what comparative historical analysts call a controlled comparison. Slater and Ziblatt (2013) argue that a successful controlled comparison has three crucial components: the selection of cases that capture 'representative variation' on

[3]This is not to argue that repression ceased, but that the party reduced the scope and arbitrariness of the use of legal institutions for repression. With the exception of the KGB and the highest levels of party and central administration, the procuracy enjoyed broad authority to investigate and bring local and ministry officials and policies in line with central mandates.

the dependent variable; the use of mechanisms and variables that can travel to other cases; and the selection of cases that help eliminate alternative explanations. The successful combination of these components allows comparative historical researchers not only to develop internally valid but also (potentially) externally valid inferences.

Comparing Maoist China and the Soviet Union allows us to control for the influences of party system, ideology, revolutionary experience, type and scope of civil conflict, and immediate post-conflict conditions, including similarly profound economic restructuring. The two countries shared a Leninist party-state system that sought to impose socialism on large, predominantly rural populations with overall low levels of education. They also faced manpower shortages, as the number of loyal, well-trained or well-educated cadres was insufficient to staff the state bureaucracy. These challenges were further complicated by their vast territories and post-conflict status. Finally, economic collapse threatened party control over the state in both cases and with it, the development of socialism. Core similarities between the countries give a rich set of factors that can be held constant as explanations for why the procuracy became a powerful force for Soviet legality while its counterpart in China languished.

Most crucially, our cases share a problem with local enforcement of central directives. Even after they had established military control over Russian territory, the Bolsheviks' orders continued to be subject to widespread resistance from regional and local state officials. Moreover, the local soviets initially posed strong resistance to the central government's attempts to curb their autonomy and centralise state control in the party leadership (Rees 1987). Indeed, Lenin sharply decried *mestichnost'*, or local influence, as a pressing threat to Soviet efforts to build the new socialist state, referring to it as 'one of the greatest, if not the greatest, opponents of the establishment of law and culture' (Lenin 1922, pp. 197–201). Given the magnitude of political and economic challenges facing the nascent regime at that time, this characterisation is remarkable.

Chinese leaders similarly struggled to bring local officials in compliance with central directives after conflict had subsided. Even as the Chinese Communist Party (CCP) implemented land reform and eliminated local elites, it struggled to keep grassroots cadres engaged in political activism while following party directives without creating local peasant backlash or localised abuse by newly appointed leaders. Notwithstanding the CCP's victory in the civil war, the acquisition of new territory and the extension of the state beyond any previous regime meant that it encountered real resistance to the policies it implemented, including local rebellions (Walder 2015, pp. 50–3). Resistance persisted, albeit unevenly, throughout the Maoist period.

The Soviet Union and the PRC therefore faced similar governance challenges at the same kind of post-conflict juncture: they needed to strengthen the accountability of local agents to the party leadership. The vast size of their territories, the lack of loyal, qualified party cadres to replace existing state officials, and a shared institutional design meant that the procuracy was introduced under similar conditions in both countries.

Institutionalisation: the Soviet procuracy

First created by a 1722 edict the tsarist procuracy expanded and largely replaced the supervisory functions of the fiscal, itself a short-lived attempt to improve central control over imperial finances that lasted from 1711 until Peter's death in 1725 (Kazantsev 1993, p. 25). The procuracy was given the initial mandate of supervising the Senate; its intent was to protect citizens from officials impinging on their rights and to improve the prosecution of illegal actions (Gredinger 1914, p. 200, cited in Smith 1978, p. 4). Its authority was expanded under Catherine II to include the power of prosecution on behalf of the state and control over prisons. The power of general supervision was added under Paul I, when the procuracy became responsible for overseeing the implementation of law by not only the Senate and ministries but also provincial authorities throughout the Empire (Kazantsev 1997). However, the Soviet procuracy did not constitute a simple continuation of this far-reaching legal authority. Following the Judicial Reform of 1864, the procuracy lost its powers of general supervision and its mandate was severely circumscribed, to include only criminal prosecution and investigation. This remained the *status quo* until the Bolsheviks' seizure of power more than half a century later (Kazantsev 1997). The incarnation of the procuracy in place in the half-century leading up to the revolution therefore bore little resemblance to the version introduced in 1922.

When the Bolsheviks came to power in 1917, they almost immediately dissolved tsarist legal institutions. A decree by the Council of the People's Commissars on 17 November 1917 replaced courts with elected judges,[4] eliminated the procuracy and court investigators entirely, and charged the local soviets with selecting commissars to fulfil those duties in their stead. Marxist ideals translated into the belief that 'the socialisation of the means of production would eliminate social and economic bases for crime', making legal bodies obsolete; informal conflict-resolution mechanisms would suffice instead (Smith 1978, p. 5). A 1918 resolution of the All-Russian Extraordinary Congress of Workers' and Peasants' Deputies' Councils urged active involvement of the working classes in ensuring the new regime's laws were carefully observed and sought their involvement in bringing to light those officials who failed to do so.[5] Similarly, Lenin's earlier writings called for individuals' vigilance in observing and enforcing law. In a 1919 letter he exhorted, 'the slightest confusion, the slightest violation of the laws of Soviet power, the slightest carelessness or negligence serve immediately to strengthen the landowners and capitalists, and contribute to their victories' (Lenin 1919, pp. 155–56). He emphasised founding a new 'people's justice' without a need for anything resembling the previous tsarist courts, which had been 'an apparatus of bourgeois exploitation' (Lenin 1918, p. 197). This primarily took the form of a revolutionary tribunal and workers' control councils in factories.

However, this approach proved unable to either prevent or punish widespread illegal actions and abuses of power by state officials, particularly at the local level (Smith 1978). In response, the Bolsheviks imposed a top-down order over the state bureaucracy by charging a successor organisation to workers' control councils, the Commissariat for Workers' and Peasants' Inspection (*Rabkrin*, *Raboche-krest'yanskaya inspektsiya,* also referred to as RKI), with general supervision in 1920. But *Rabkrin*'s inability to adequately fulfil that mandate likely contributed to a consensus among Soviet leadership

[4] *Dekret Soveta Narodnykh Komissarov RSFSR ot 24 noyabrya 1917 g.* (SU RSFSR, 1917, No. 4, st. 50).
[5] *O Tochnom Soblyudenii Zakonov. Postanovlenie Vserossiiskogo Chrezvychainogo S"ezda Sovetov Rabochikh i Krest'yanskikh Deputatov ot 8 noyabrya 1918 g.* (SU RSFSR, 1918, 90, st. 908).

that the procuracy should be reintroduced (Zvyagintsev 2012). While the *Rabkrin* and the procuracy are rarely treated conjointly by scholars, the two institutions evolved during the same period of early state-building by Party leadership, and—we argue—in competition with one another at that critical juncture.

This juncture began in the early 1920s, when the party increasingly abandoned its utopian vision of bottom-up control over the state bureaucracy in favour of a more centralised approach. Earlier decrees that sought to enforce laws through worker and peasant participation and incorporation gave way to new edicts designed to strengthen top-down control. One such decree equated 'Soviet construction throughout the entire territory of the RSFSR [Russian Soviet Federative Socialist Republic]' with 'the enforcement of revolutionary legality'.[6] The party leadership gave *Rabkrin* the mandate to carry out this enforcement and appointed Stalin as its head. *Rabkrin* combined the functions of the former workers' inspectorates (initially created, bottom-up, at the factory level but overseen by powerful trade unions) with the recently-reformed, imperial-era state auditory agency, known as *Goskon* (*Gosudarstvennyi Kontrol*, State Control). The resulting hybrid agency led efforts to combat bureaucracy and red tape in Soviet institutions, strengthen top-down control through regular audits, monitor the decrees and decisions adopted by Soviet authorities, and check the activities of all organs of state power from the perspective of their results.[7] In other words, it was responsible for ensuring compliance with central directives—for general supervision. In accordance with this mandate, party leaders gave *Rabkrin* wide latitude in obtaining documents or evidence in pursuit of these goals.

Shortly after its creation, however, Lenin wrote a letter sharply criticising Stalin's approach to these tasks, pointing out that *Rabkrin*'s main role should consist not so much in 'catching' and 'exposing' (*lovit*' and *izoblichat*'), as in knowing how 'to put things right in good time' (*umet' popravit' … vovremya*) (Perrins 1980, p. 232).[8] At the same time, Boim (1966, p. 55) describes these efforts as ineffectual: misuse or outright theft of state property continued to increase, and bureaucratic inefficiency and malfeasance remained major problems. Consequently, Lenin chose to abandon *Rabkrin* as a purely state-run entity and merge it with the Party Central Control Commission (*Tsentral'naya Kontrol'naya Komissiya*). Scholars have attributed much of *Rabkrin*'s inability to curb corruption and abuses of power during its existence to the low educational and technical qualifications of its inspectors (Perrins 1980). Confusion over the exact nature of its role and place in the state hierarchy further undermined the institution's effectiveness; Perrins (1980, p. 231) writes that 'many local inspectorates had become in effect departments of the local soviets', a situation that severely undermined their ability to serve any control function for the central state or party leadership. Rees (1987, p. 30) cites an account from a member of the *Rabkrin* collegium who, by 1921, declared that the institution had 'failed

[6]*Ob Usilenii Deyatel'nosti Mestnykh Organov Yustitsii. Dekret Vserossiiskogo Tsentral'nogo Ispolnitel'nogo Komiteta ot 25 avgusta 1921 g.* (SU RSFSR, 1921, No. 63, st. 456).

[7]*O Raboche-Krest'yanskoi Inspektsii. Dekret Vserossiiskogo Tsentral'nogo Ispolnitel'nogo Komiteta ot 8 fevralya 1920 g. No 94. Sobranie uzakonenii i rasporyazhenii pravitel'stva za 1920 g.* (Upravlenie delami Sovnarkoma SSSR M, 1943, str. 123–25).

[8]See also Rees (1987, p. 33).

both as an agency of mass control and rationalisation. It lacked authority, its proposals were ignored or obstructed, and, even in Moscow, its functionaries were unceremoniously kicked out of the institutions they were investigating'. In short, it lacked the ability to impose centralised political order.

As the civil war reached its end in 1922 and non-compliance by local state officials became an ever-more pressing concern, party leaders recognised the need for additional mechanisms of top-down control. The decision to introduce the procuracy clearly reflected growing concern over the regime's inability to control local officials' disregard for new laws. In contrast to Lenin's earlier calls for bottom-up law enforcement, his 1922 letter on the procuracy—coming at the tail-end of the civil war, when a Bolshevik victory was imminent—dramatically referred to the 'sea of illegality' that characterised the Soviet state as a whole, and argued that 'local influence is one of the highest, if not the highest, forces opposing the establishment of law and culture' (Lenin 1922, p. 199). In the words of a late-Soviet introduction to a document collection, at that time 'it was necessary to found a special organ, which acted on behalf of the highest central power, which would carry out the implementation of a single legality throughout the entire territory of the country' (Pavlischev & Shishkov 1981, p. 3). The creation of the procuracy reflected a major shift in Lenin's approach to legal institutions, from one that emphasised bottom-up (and then hybrid) methods to one focused on top-down enforcement.

Information on the exact circumstances surrounding the decision to reintroduce the procuracy is unfortunately scant. According to Zvyagintsev (2012, p. 22), the XI All-Russian Conference of the Communist Party 'recognised the necessity of adopting and introducing in all spheres of life strict revolutionary law'. Founding an agency that could 'guarantee supervision of the observation of laws' therefore became a 'hot topic' (*ostrui vopros*), and as the Department of Justice 'clearly could not cope with this task', Lenin suggested that the agency could be the procuracy (Zvyagintsev 2012). Lenin drew on the imperial procuracy as a readily available blueprint for an institution that could help in ensuring adherence to law and decrees issued by the central party leadership (Kazantsev 1993, p. 1). This motion apparently attracted little initial disagreement among members of the Politburo, and the task of developing the procuracy fell to a committee of the Collegium of the People's Commissar of Justice (Salmina 2008).

In contrast to the relative ease with which the idea of recreating a procuracy was accepted, discussions about the form it was to take involved substantial controversy. Members of the Collegium disagreed on nearly everything, even its name (Salmina 2008, p. 21). The sharpest point of contention was the procuracy's place in the institutional hierarchy of the state. There were two opposing camps: one argued that the procuracy should become part of the Ministry of Justice, while the other insisted on linking it directly to the central government. In January 1922, the first edition of the journal *Weekly Soviet Justice* (*Ezhenedel'nik sovetskoi yustitsii*) published a plan for its proposed organisational structure; it reflected the former viewpoint.[9] According to this design, the procurators would be embedded in and chosen by local departments of justice; they would be

[9]'K 4-mu Vserossiiskomu s'ezdu deyatelei sovetskoi yustitsii: Otdel yustitsii, prokuratura i prochie gubernskie organy yustitsii', *Ezhenedel'nik sovetskoi yustitsii*, 1 January 1922.

subordinate to both the Central Committee and to the regional and local governments. Lenin disagreed vehemently with this approach, convinced that it would fail to curb regional waywardness. He repudiated calls for the procuracy's 'dual subordination' to both local administrative organs and the Soviet, arguing that, it was 'not only fundamentally wrong, not only hinders the basis of our goal of introducing consistent legality, but it also manifests the interests and prejudices of the local bureaucracy and local influences' (Lenin 1922, p. 201). Lenin felt so strongly that the procuracy would be ineffectual were the proposal to be accepted that he asked that the Politburo consider the design of the procuracy directly, and while ill, dictated the above-quoted letter to Stalin to be read at the 24 May 1922 meeting. His criticism was, as Salmina notes (2008, p. 20), not groundless; if the plan for 'dual subordination' had been approved by the Central Committee, the procurator would have needed to request permission to submit protests about unlawful decisions of the regional executive committee to the very same regional executive committee (which controlled the local branch of the Department of Justice).

Following that hearing by the Politburo, Lenin's proposal was accepted, and the Central Committee created the procuracy by decree in May 1922, subordinate directly (and only) to the Central Committee. The new institution's first listed mandate was that of general supervision, which was defined as 'the function of supervision in the name of the state of the legal activities of all of the organs of power, economic institutions, social and private organisations and individuals by prosecuting the perpetrators and protesting the decisions that violate the law'.[10] Subsequent laws on the procuracy retained general supervision as the first and primary duty of the procuracy, and the structure of the agency remained stable throughout Soviet rule. Its institutional form thus remained fixed following this initial, and contentious, critical juncture. Moreover, the procuracy was, unlike courts, funded directly from the central budget.[11] Procurators were also armed and not subject to arrest by other organs of power without the approval of the General Procurator.[12] These stipulations, coupled with the procuracy's direct link to and supervision by the Central Committee of the Communist Party, provided the procuracy with substantial resources and authority from its inception.

Shortly after the creation of the procuracy, in 1923, *Rabkrin* was reorganised, reduced in size, and merged with the Communist Party control organ to form the People's Commissariat of Workers' and Peasants' Inspection (*Narodnyi komissariat Raboche-krest'yanskoi inspektsii*—NKRKI). The new agency was to focus on the scientific study of state administration and, contrary to a controversial proposal by (a now-severely ill) Lenin, 'placed in *de facto* subordination to the Central Committee' (Rees 1987, p. 61). However, it retained its powers of general supervision. A subsequent circular from the People's Commissar of Justice clarifying the interrelationship between the NKRKI and the

[10] *Postanovlenie o Prokurorskom Nadzore. Postanovlenie 3i sessii Vserossiiskogo Tsentral'nogo Ispolnitel'nogo Komiteta 9 sozyva ot maya 1922g.* (SU RSFSR, 1922, No. 36, st. 424).

[11] *Polozhenie o Verkhovnom Sude Soyuza Sovetskikh Sotsialisticheskikh Respublik. Uverzhdeno Postanovleniem Tsentral'nogo Ispolnitel'nogo o Komiteta SSR* (Vestnik CIK, SNK i STO Soyuza SSSR, 1923, No. 10, st. 311).

[12] *O Poryadke Aresta Prokurorov, ikh Pomoshchnikov, Predsedetalei i Chlenov Revolyutsyonnykh Tribunalov i Sovetov Narodnykh Sudei, Narodnykh Sudei i Sledovatelei. Dekret Vserossiiskogo Tsentral'nogo Ispolnitel'nogo Komiteta ot 16 noyabrya 1922 g.* (SU RSFSR, 1922, No. 77, st. 960).

Procuracy and judicial organs suggests that the overlap between the two institutions' powers —specifically, their ability to supervise other state organs—may have been a point of contestation in the wake of *Rabkrin*'s reform. Directed to procurators and members of the judicial branch, it confirms the authority of the NKRKI inspectors to observe court hearings and receive materials necessary to its investigations; this included the right to conduct investigations of their own regarding the court (and its conduct).[13] The head of the NKRKI also urged greater cooperation between the organisation and the procuracy, but 'these demands were successfully resisted by the legal organs' (Rees 1987, p. 93). This apparent contestation subsided as the NKRKI, under the leadership of Grigory Ordzhonikidze, a close associate of Stalin, was transformed into 'a skeleton planning and operational administration within the government' focused on industrial policymaking (Shearer 1996, p. 77); there is no further mention or clarification of the two agencies' mandates *vis-à-vis* one another.

Archival and primary source information on the procuracy during the mid-1920s to the 1930s is scarce. For example, records in the central archives on the activities of the procuracy from its creation through 1925 are limited to a single 25-page report and offer only a broad overview of its activities.[14] Interestingly, however, this early report reflects Morgan's (1959, p. 148) argument that the party leadership 'revived' the procuracy's role in general supervision due to a renewed emphasis on 'revolutionary legality', or strict observance of law developed by Communist Party elites; the party leadership drew on the procuracy to 'help stamp out various illegalities' at the local level.

Beginning in 1930, law was emphasised as 'a system of rules expressing the will of the state' (Smith 1978, p. 6), and the function of the procuracy was shifted from ensuring legal compliance to enforcing individuals' compliance with forced collectivisation and industrialisation (Morgan 1959). In this changing context, the procuracy's clear top-down, hierarchical structure, direct link to party leadership, and dependence on the centre made it a tool easily adapted to collectivisation efforts. This intensified the repression of peasants who had resorted to violence to contest the forced collectivisation campaign (Zvyagintsev 2012, p. 111).

The procuracy's ability to adapt to this changing focus in state construction marked increasing returns of investment in the agency for the central leadership. By continuing to prove its utility despite a changed policy emphasis, the procuracy entered into a positive feedback loop (Pierson 2000) that helped transform it into an equilibrium institution. This 'loop' was possible because—thanks to a combination of the initial failures of *Rabkrin* and Lenin's insertion of specific preferences in institutional design—the initial impetus to improve central control over local administrations took a specific organisational form ready to suit a markedly different political environment from the post-civil war and the New Economic Policy (NEP) period in which it was introduced. The procuracy's activities in this period became subsumed by the concerted top-down focus on economic centralisation throughout the country. However, its direct link to the Central Committee,

[13] *O Vzaimootnosheniyakh mezhdu Organami RKI i Organami Sovetskoi Yustitsii i Prokuratury. Tsirkular Nardonogo Kommissariata yustitsii ot 12 iyunya 1924 g. No 87* (*Ezhenedel'nik sovetskoi yustitsii*, 1924, No. 25, s. 594).

[14] Tsentral'nyi Gosudarstvennyi Arkhiv, f. 55, r. 8131, op. No. 1, ed. hp. No 5.

top-down institutional structure, and the fact it was already in existence (thus eliminating 'startup' costs associated with creating an entirely new agency) contributed to its continued utility and thus, to further institutionalisation, despite the changing political and economic context.

This overarching process cannot be divorced from the repressiveness of the larger political environment in the Soviet Union during this period: Stalin's increasing centralisation of the economy, his own personal power in the office of the General Secretary, and purges of the party and state in the late 1930s. The procuracy again proved to be an easily adaptable tool, becoming co-opted as an instrument of repression dressed as legality: a procurator formed one-third of the infamous *troikas* that carried out Stalinist-era show trials (with a member of the NKVD, or internal security forces, and the local communist party secretary comprising the remaining two-thirds). Here, as in later years, the procuracy worked in a complementary capacity to the security forces. In this way, procurators were 'drawn into the politics of the "Great Terror", the massive political repression that occurred under Stalin from 1937–1939, [and] which continued with differing levels of cruelty and intensity through 1952' (Vakhitova 2003, p. 17).

Stalin's death instigated rapid change in the openly and highly coercive use of law to bolster state power. In addition to reform in Soviet criminal and civil legislation, there was renewed attention by party leadership to the need for a new approach to legality. This in turn sparked 'a revival of interest in general supervision and the rights of the individual against state administration' (Smith 1978, p. 7). This shift was reflected in legislation 'On Procuratorial Supervision in the USSR' enacted in May 1955, which emphasised strengthening 'Leninist principles of organisation and activities of the procuracy, defined as the task of procuratorial supervision in all spheres of state and social life'.[15] While, as Frolov (2011) notes, there has been very little dedicated analysis of the development of the procuracy in the immediate postwar years, this renewed emphasis on the procuracy's mandate for general supervision and upholding a Soviet vision of legality is evident in the types of protests lodged by the procuracy in this period. Procuratorial actions published in the postwar era show that these concentrated on the enactments of local government organs; by far the largest proportion of protests concern labour cases, particularly the hiring and dismissal of workers (Morgan 1966, pp. 104, 115).

The labour cases reflected a renewed attention to the procuracy's responsibility for citizen complaints. Under Stalin's rule, such complaints were more frequently used as justification in purges; in the post-Stalinist era, party leadership turned to the procuracy as a mechanism for citizen redress against administrative organs. Article 55 of the aforementioned Statute on the Procuracy obligates procurators to respond to citizen complaints; of all 99,045 complaints received by local procuracies in 1972, 44.4% were 'satisfactorily resolved'—that is, substantiated and addressed in favour of the complainant; over half of these complaints concerned labour violations (Smith 1978, p. 65). Morgan (1966) finds that this ombudsman function became one of the primary means by which the procuracy learned

[15] *Polozhenie o Prokurorskom Nadzore v SSSR. Utverzhdeno Ukazom Prezidiuma Verkhovnogo Soveta SSSR* (Vedomosti Verkhovnogo Soveta SSSR, 1955, No. 9, st. 222).

about regional and local officials' illegal directives, a feature common to authoritarian regimes (Dimitrov 2014). Protests issued by local procuracies in response to citizen complaints were sometimes challenged by local officials, but those appeals—at least in those cases made publicly available—were always upheld by higher-level procurators, and the offending legislation or directive rescinded. By offering an outlet for some aggrieved citizens, the procuracy continued the positive feedback loop for party leadership established during the early years of state formation. By the mid-1960s this institutionalisation was sufficiently well-established that Mironenko wrote, 'there is every reason to say that the *prokuratura* is now the principal instrument of the Party Central Committee for supervising the activities of all organisations, institutions, and enterprises in the USSR' (Mironenko 1964, p. 40).

This institutionalisation proved durable not only throughout the Soviet period, but also in post-Soviet Russia. The procuracy continually used its powers of general supervision to deflect challenges to the scope and strength of its institutional authority, even as the Soviet regime that had created it crumbled. As Smith writes, 'with the collapse of the USSR, … the major coercive bureaucracies of the former Soviet state were disarmed or destroyed—all except the procuracy' (Smith 1997, p. 348). This was all the more remarkable given the identification of the procuracy and specifically, its powers of general supervision, as 'a key obstacle to the development of Russian courts' (Solomon 1997, p. 5). In sum, through the influence of context and agency at critical junctures combined with a positive feedback loop initiated by crucial features of its design, the Soviet (and subsequently, Russian) procuracy came to exemplify Huntington's (1996, p. 12) criteria for institutionalisation: adaptability, autonomy, complexity, and coherence in an organisation.

Dissipation: the Chinese procuracy

The legacies and uneven state-building efforts of the Republican government under Chiang Kai-shek, Japanese proxy-rule in the northeast of China (1932–1935), institutional variation in CCP liberated areas, and Soviet advice provided a diverse set of institutional models and legacies for early PRC state-building (Mattingly 2017). Despite this variety, early PRC policymakers had settled on the Soviet-inspired procuratorate as the home of legal supervision by 1949.[16] The design and adoption of the procuracy was based on the Soviet experience; however, unlike in the USSR, the Chinese procuracy did not evolve into a powerful weapon for ensuring local compliance with centrally-imposed laws, nor developed deep institutional roots. Instead, the PRC leadership gradually transformed a vision of institutionalised legal monitoring into a vehicle for popular supervision, then later eliminated the institution entirely as the CCP moved campaign mobilisation directly to 'the masses'.

The history of the criminal law aspect of the Chinese procuracy began as the Qing dynasty (1636–1911) undertook governance reforms (Mühlhahn 2009, pp. 41–57), but the

[16]See especially 'Zhonggong zhongyang guanyu zhongyang renmin jianchashu si xiang guiding de tongbao' (January 1950), and 'Zhonggong zhongyang guanyu jianli jiancha jigou wenti de zhishi' (September 1950), in *Jiancha Zhidu Cankao Ziliao (Xin Zhongguo Bufen)* (Beijing, Supreme People's Procuratorate Research Office, 1959).

procuracy first gained powers of general supervision in the Communist base areas during the civil war against the Nationalists and the war with Japan (Lin 2001), a feature attributed by one study to the availability of Soviet advising (Ye & Huang 2003, p. 20). It is in these base areas—spread across China but most famously on the border of Hunan and Jiangxi (the Jiangxi Soviet) and later, in Western Shanxi (the Yan'an Liberated Area)—that many of the party's state-building strategies were initially developed (Heilmann & Perry 2011). This meant that the Chinese procuracy that later emerged from the base areas possessed a mandate that, like its Soviet counterpart, bridged criminal prosecution and legal supervision of state and society. However, prior to the civil war's end in 1949, the procuracy's supervisory and criminal justice functions were split between the Chinese equivalent of the *Rabkrin* (Worker Peasant Supervisory Councils, *gong nong jiancha wei*) and procurators. Worker Peasant Supervisory Councils possessed a mandate for supervision but were unconnected to procuracies. Like their Soviet counterpart the *Rabkrin*, these councils relied on political control by worker-peasant correspondents; rather than supervise the implementation of legal mandates, however, they oversaw the implementation of policies and campaigns (Lin 2001, pp. 69–71, 124–37).[17] These organs would eventually be spun by the party centre into the state institution of the Ministry of Supervision (*jiancha bu*), and into the party organisation of Monitoring and Inspection Committees (*jiancha weiyuanhui*) (Li 2016, p. 452). The procurators, who had no supervision mandate until 1949, were organisationally located within the courts during the 1930s and 1940s (Zeng & Zheng 1992, pp. 299–301; Ye & Huang 2003, p. 19). Consequently, the procuracy of this time was an 'unstable, incomplete, and ununified' system (Zeng & Zheng 1992, p. 275).

Echoing the disagreement of early Soviet policymakers over the optimal design of the procuracy for strengthening uniform legality and central control, there was extensive debate in the pages of legal journals and state-run newspapers about the appropriate leadership structure of the procuracy in various base areas during the civil war period: on the one hand, central policymakers advocated the 'vertical' supervision structure, where procuratorates would be responsible only to superior procuratorates in a chain up to the centre; others opposed the change in leadership structure (and, in early debates, even the necessity of a procuracy's existence at all), instead advocating for variations of 'dual' subordination that added the oversight of the local party committee or the courts at each level (Zeng & Zheng 1992, p. 279). Soviet legal advisers, part of the nearly 10,000 experts in many fields sent to China after 1953, were almost exclusively in favour of increasing 'vertical' leadership of procuracies. Initially, the procuracy followed this blueprint: a 'vertical' structure of procuracies overseeing other procuracies from centre to locality was set by temporary regulation in 1949 (Ginsburgs & Stahnke 1964). However, this design was quickly eclipsed by new regulations introduced in 1950, which temporarily transformed local branches of the procuracy into extensions of the Public Security Bureau (*gong an bu*), which housed it and shared leadership with it under a new regulation, the 'Circular Concerning Four Regulations of the Central People's Procuracy'

[17] 'Zhonghua Suwei'ai Gongheguo Gongnong jianchabu de zuzhi taioli' (1931, esp. section 6), reprinted in Min *et al.* (2011).

(Min & Xue 2009, p. 5). In addition, in 1950 the whole procuracy was allotted just 1,000 cadres for a country with more than 2,500 counties (Min & Xue 2009, p. 40). Understaffing and organisational confusion eroded the procuracy's independent establishment in much of the country for the next year.

The procuracy's initial influence was limited by both institutional design and scope. In 1951, vertical supervision was replaced with 'dual' leadership of the procuracy, meaning organisational subordination to superior procuracies and the local party committee, nominally due to insufficient legal capacity to staff and run the procuracy on its own (Min & Xue 2009, p. 45). This marks a critical departure from the Soviet blueprint during the early development of the Chinese procuracy: as noted above, Lenin opposed this structure explicitly arguing that the value of a general supervision power is critically undermined when horizontal authorities supervise a local procuracy.

Throughout this early period, the CCP's resources were spread thinly between competing priorities to mobilise society and bureaucrats and to institutionalise its governance across a broad territory. This meant that campaign-based mobilisation (both of society and of bureaucrats *via* party campaigns) was in tension with attempts to institutionalise the procuracy and other legal institutions as the dominant strategy for achieving policy compliance in the localities. At the heart of this competition were ongoing campaigns to suppress counterrevolutionaries, fight corruption, and to counter 'rightist' thinking. The procuracy (along with the rest of the bureaucracy) played a role in channelling these campaigns, especially in the prosecution of counterrevolutionary 'criminals' and the 'Three Anti' and 'Five Anti' mass campaigns against malpractice, waste, and corruption in 1951, but campaigns were a bottom-up rather than a top-down strategy for the party-state centre to ensure local compliance and did little to empower formal institutions outside of the party. In contrast to the Soviet case, it was this party-led mobilisational technique that attracted 'increasing returns' in China, as it proved to be a more flexible mode of enforcing political compliance than legal supervision during the drastic and sudden changes that characterised the Maoist period.

The difficulties of procuratorial capacity continued during attempts to establish institutionalised legality in the process of 'regularisation' (*zhenggui hua*) from 1951 to 1954. A shortage of trained cadres was compounded by the elimination of holdover bureaucrats from the Nationalist period in the court and policing systems, which increased the workload of procurators. For example, in 1952, of approximately 28,000 cadres associated with the court system, more than 6,000 were leftovers from the previous regime. Only one-third of those cadres remained after efforts to eliminate 'old legal thinking' removed and punished thousands of judicial officials in that year (Min & Xue 2009, pp. 65–6).

Although the work of the procuracy and the work of the Public Security Bureau, China's policing institution, were not separable for most of this period, new procedures for criminal law enforcement were gradually expanded and put into practice.[18] Legal state-building proceeded slowly—by 1953, only 69% of prefectural level jurisdictions and 29% of

[18]Anonymous interviewee, The Stanley Lubman Hong Kong Interview Collection (2018, p. 142). On file with authors.

county level jurisdictions had even established a separate procurator's office (Ye & Huang 2003, p. 25), to say nothing of having begun the work of general supervision.

This began to change after 1954, a landmark year that saw the passage of numerous laws and the first PRC Constitution. It also began a period of rapid expansion of capacity for the procuracy, which increasingly shouldered responsibilities previously allocated to the Public Security Bureau and the People's Courts. Despite the relative chaos in the localities at this time (or perhaps because of it), the procuracy was switched back to vertical supervision with the passage of the 1954 Organic Law of the Procuracy. Under this law, the procuracy grew: it consolidated the establishment of grassroots procuratorates, and staffing increased substantially. This also expanded the exercise of general supervision in some jurisdictions (Ginsburgs & Stahnke 1964). For their part, Soviet advisers met the enshrinement of the more independent (vertical) functioning of the Chinese People's Procuracy in the 1954 Organic Law with relief, believing as they did that it was only under the conditions of institutional independence that 'the procuratorate is able to safeguard uniform revolutionary legality' when, in particular, 'even today individual employees of the state apparatus are infected by "localism"' (Ginsburgs & Stahnke 1968, p. 92).

In early 1955, the party centre approved plans for expansion of the procuracy staffing, increasing the allotment to 19,400 (Li 1988, p. 579). It was not before this time that many procuratorates, even at high levels, began exercising general supervision, although the exercise expanded significantly both in supervision of other legal organs and over other bureaucratic organs, at least in coastal areas (Zhang 1998, p. 257). The emphasis on and support for the power of general supervision was evident in party media, where it was discussed as one of the key differentiating characteristics between socialist legality and its degenerate capitalist counterpart (Shao 1955).

At the same time, however, the procuracy came under fire from the political-legal wing of the Communist Party, which argued that the procuracy's mission and strategy were out of touch with the masses (*qunzhong*). Competing modes of supervision, especially 'mass' supervision, were increasingly emphasised by the central leadership instead (Andreas & Dong 2017, p. 210).

To compensate, the procuracy expanded its reliance on 'correspondents' during this time, especially in 1956, evidence of borrowing from other more 'mass-oriented' state organs (Zhang 1985). These correspondents were often party activists who brought information about violations to the procuracy and spread information to the masses about the most recent developments in the legal system. This was intended to help connect the procuratorates to the mass line as well as to aid them in performing general supervision. In early 1956, there were almost 4,000 correspondents employed by the procuracy in Guangxi (Ou 1996, pp. 149–50); there were more than 94,000 across the country by September of that year.[19]

In other words, during this period, the procuracy grew in size (bureaucratic allocation), expertise, and importance in the administration of justice and the legal supervision of the state. The procuracy drew increased support after the 8th National Congress of the CCP

[19]'Quanguo jiancha tongxunyuan da jiuwan siqian duo ming, tong weifa fanzui fenzi zuo douzheng qi le henda zuoyong', *The People's Daily*, 5 September 1956.

in 1956, which repeatedly emphasised the importance of legal compliance in the state apparatus (Ye & Huang 2003, p. 28). These changes included the expanded practice of general supervision at increasingly lower levels of government in addition to increased independence in the administration and prosecution of cases (Ginsburgs & Stahnke 1968, p. 116). Tensions remained about the procuracy's precise function, however; directives from the Supreme People's Procuracy, including plans for institutional construction and reform, moved rapidly back and forth between emphasising the leadership of party committees in determining if general supervision was necessary, and encouraging its development, especially in supervising the actions of county-level jurisdictions.[20]

As the rules for supervision oscillated, the political context changed, and central initiatives were increasingly implemented either directly by mass mobilisation in campaigns or by using such campaigns to create compliance in the bureaucracy (Strauss 2006). This was driven partially by Mao's particular brand of Stalinist fundamentalism, which put him at odds with the Soviet model, especially after the secret speech in 1956, in which Khrushchev criticised Stalin to the 20th Congress of the Communist Party of the Soviet Union. Mao's critiques of Soviet models as 'revisionism' of appropriate socialist practice in the late 1950s[21] made the political credentials of Soviet-trained legal cadres suspect and caused any commitment to institutionalised legality among party elites to evaporate. In this way, Khrushchev's de-Stalinisation compounded the procuracy's legitimacy deficit in China by changing the political context in which the procuracy was viewed by Chinese elites.

Mao's disillusionment and its consequences were exacerbated during China's failed attempt at rectification during the 'Hundred Flowers' movement in 1956 and 1957, in which a thaw allowing for criticism of the party created a torrent of calls for reform. The movement was brutally suppressed and a mass campaign to rectify 'rightist errors' followed, with victims publicly criticised and sent to labour camps. This purge devastated the bureaucracy, intelligentsia, and legal institutions (Walder 2015, ch. 7). As elite and mass politics became increasingly charged, the Supreme People's Procuratorate issued a directive in September of 1957 to localities instructing them to 'hang up the weapon' of general supervision and closing general supervision offices within the procuracy, sometimes after less than a year of full-time functioning (Zhang 1998, p. 259).

By 1958, the tide of mass and elite politics had turned completely against institutionalisation and with it, general supervision: the anti-Rightist campaign, launched in the wake of the reversal after the Hundred Flowers Movement, found a soft target in the procuracy. An article in a 1958 issue of *Political Legal Research* (*Zhengfa yanjiu*), China's leading legal journal, criticised procurators who 'swallow Soviet experience without chewing', in the process neglecting the party, and a connection to mass politics

[20]See, 'Zuigao renmin jinachayuan dangzu guanyu jiancha yewu gongzuo huiyi qingkuang he jinhou zongzuo yijian xiang zhongyang de baogao' (January 1955), and '1956 nian zhi 1957 nian jiancha gongzuo guihua' (1957), compiled in *Zhongguo Jiancha Zhidu Ziliao Xuanbian* (Beijing, Supreme People's Procuratorate Research Office, 1987).

[21]For example, critiques of the 'legal supervision' and general supervision in 'Jiancha jiguan fanyoupai douzheng dahuo shengli: Liu Huizhi, Wang Lizhong cuangai jianchayuan zhuanzheng zhineng de yinmou fencui', *Guangming Daily*, 20 December 1957; 'Zuigao renmin jianchayuan chedi jiefa youpai fenzi, buxu Li Huizhi Wang Lizhong diandao zhuanzheng de maotou', *People's Daily*, 20 December 1957.

(T'an 1958, quoted in Cohen 1968). At this same time, the party's Monitoring and Inspection Committees, reintroduced in 1955, began to play an increasingly large role in disciplining local cadres and in the implementation of campaigns (Li 2016, p. 452). As part of the Great Leap Forward downsizing and consolidating of the state apparatus, political and legal organs across the country were centralised under one roof and their functional specialisations eroded. The creation of 'Political Legal Bureaus' (*zheng fa bu*) swept the country, with procuracies, public security bureaus, and courts combined into a single organ. In Guizhou, for example, only 12 out of more than four dozen procuracies were left unincorporated by the end of 1958 (Yuan 1996, p. 3). Pressures to make 'great leaps' created movements like the 'one leader replaces three leaders' (*yi zhang dai san zhang*), in which the heads of the procuracy, police, and people's courts were made bureaucratically interchangeable for the purposes of cutting red tape. The purge of 'rightists' went to the top: 22 senior cadres from the Supreme People's Procuratorate (SPP) were denounced as 'rightists' and sent to labour camps, including party committee member Li Huizhi, whose alleged rightist crimes were centred precisely around his advocacy for the supervisory role of the procuracy.

An article by Wang Guiwu, one of Li's colleagues at the SPP, shows how political context and campaign mobilisation turned against legal system elites who advocated for the power of general supervision. In the official newspaper of the Chinese Communist Party's Central Committee, the *People's Daily*, Wang argued that Li's emphasis on the power of general supervision was 'ridiculous' and that to turn the power of general supervision away from egregious violations towards 'routine errors' was actually turning the weapon of socialist legality 'against the people' (Wang 1958). Similarly, a revisionist report from the August 1958 National Procuratorial Work Conference argued that rightist-leaning procurators' previous support for general supervision was the result of an incorrect understanding of the character of the procuracy,[22] highlighting the extent to which general supervision was no longer politically tenable. Wang proposed that general supervision was a weapon for use against enemies of the regime, while errors in bureaucratic implementation and deviations in policymaking should be addressed through party campaigns aiming to increase discipline and improve cadres' understanding of rules (Sun 2018). This type of criticism shows the fracture between a 'people's' legality focused on the masses and party process, and a formalistic legality based on bureaucratic expertise and institutionalised checks; this turn marked the end of general supervision to enforce central mandates, and a move toward a more bottom-up approach.

Within the procuracy, attacks like this demonstrated that the weapon of general supervision was more dangerous to those who wielded it than to those who might otherwise fear it. The weak institutionalisation of general supervision across different localities and the increasing use of mass mobilisation campaigns undermined the procuracy even before the Great Leap Forward drastically reduced staffing and ended most remaining supervision work in 1958. The Great Leap Forward's consolidation of government institutions and creation of an inescapable 'campaign' atmosphere accelerated

[22]'Guanyu zhaokai disi quanguo jiancha gongzuo huiyi xiang zhongyang de baogao', reprinted in *Jiancha zhidu cankao ziliao (Xin Zhogngua Bufen)* (Beijing, Supreme People's Procuratorate Research Office, 1980).

what previous party rectification campaigns had already begun. That process continued with the Cultural Revolution, when Mao further emphasised mass-based campaigns to enforce ideological and political 'control' (Thornton 2007, pp. 130–34). As a consequence of this trend, procuracies across the country were forced to close; most would not reopen until after Mao's death. General supervision as practised in the 1950s would not reappear as such in China.

Unlike Stalin's, Mao's death had little effect on the viability of legal supervision. The procuracy was eventually reinstated, but its supervisory role was confined solely to the implementation of criminal justice, and even this has remained weakly exercised (Mou 2017). In the domain of government oversight, the procuracy remains overshadowed by the Chinese Communist Party's Discipline Inspection Commissions in the institutionalised monitoring of local cadre policymaking and performance, despite being formally charged with the investigation and prosecution of illegal conduct by state employees (Ma 2008). In sum, in contrast to its Soviet counterpart and early model, the Chinese procuracy experienced a rocky, up-and-down developmental trajectory rather than steady growth in scope, autonomy, complexity, and coherence. Its authority gradually dissipated as a result.

Conclusions

Notwithstanding popular perceptions that 'law' does not matter under authoritarian regimes, we find that, in specific settings, legal institutions can be powerful instruments of 'infrastructural power', extending and regularising the government's reach across territories and into the lives of its citizens (Slater 2003, p. 82). This study sheds important light on the introduction, development, and strengthening or dissipation of legal institutions under authoritarianism: even strong regimes emerging from the trials of revolution and civil war may not successfully develop legal institutions to enforce political order, as the negative case of Maoist China documents. Despite introducing a procuracy explicitly for this purpose, its functions were eventually absorbed by party discipline commissions.

Instead, we find that a political structure favouring 'high modern' technocratic management (Scott 1998), successful competition against 'bottom up' supervision alternatives, and institutional alignment with rapidly changing political contexts may support the construction of authoritarian legal control. Notwithstanding initial competition from bottom-up institutional alternatives, in the Soviet Union, the procuracy's direct connection to central authority created increasing returns to 'investing' in the procuracy and in general supervision in the Soviet Union. This effect was compounded by opportunities for the top party leadership to use the procuracy as an institution beyond its supervision powers, as it became a weapon of repression during Stalin's rule.

While certainly involved in state repression, the Chinese procuracy was initially subordinated to local authorities, which stunted the availability of general supervision as a tool for enforcing central directives. Further, a critical juncture caused by de-Stalinisation and the subsequent critique of Mao prevented the accrual of positive feedback that helped strengthen the Soviet procuracy. This largely confirms findings about the friction between a popular, mass-based role for law and a professionalised 'external' law in China (Li 1970;

Altehenger 2018). Beyond this confirmation, however, we document the consequences of competition between formalised and informal legal supervision and enrich previous accounts by comparison with the positive case of the Soviet Union, where the procuracy was able to outcompete its popular legal rivals to play a crucial role in governance.

Our work builds the foundation for future work on legality, supervision, and authoritarian durability, both within the former Soviet bloc, where procuratorial institutions remain powerful, and across 'rule-by-law' regimes where authoritarian states have invested in legal institutions. The addition of more cases could help elucidate the relationship between successfully institutionalised supervision and decisions to implement political reform. Recent work on the conditions under which regimes democratise 'from strength' (Slater & Wong 2013) suggests that centralised and powerful institutions of supervision could potentially make autocrats feel secure enough to grant political concessions in a crisis and thus unintentionally exacerbate it by raising expectations.

Our research also raises questions about connections between different modes of central political control and regime durability. Further use of the fruitful comparison between the USSR and PRC can contribute to still growing literatures on the sources of authoritarian institutional change (Slater 2009), the origins of revolutionary regime stability (Levitsky & Way 2013), and the trade-off between powerful but 'rigid' Leninist structures and chaotic but 'flexible' policy implementation (Heilmann & Perry 2011).

Finally, recent work has repeatedly demonstrated the value of studying legal dynamics and actors in non-democracies (Helmke 2002; Hilbink 2007; Shen-Bayh 2018). Unfortunately, these approaches remain largely confined to the courts themselves. We study the conditions for successful institutionalised control *via* the procuracy, providing insight into how legal institutions outside the courts matter for political outcomes under authoritarianism. Our focus on general supervision also builds on the argument that a core function of authoritarian institutions is to extend regime power; by showing how the introduction of a legal institution increases infrastructural power in one case but fails in another, we contribute to the ongoing renaissance in the literature on legality's contested functions under authoritarianism.

References

Altehenger, J. (2018) *Legal Lessons: Popularizing Laws in the People's Republic of China 1949–1989* (Cambridge, MA, Harvard University Press).

Andreas, J. & Dong, Y. (2017) '"Mass Supervision" and the Bureaucratization of Governance in China', in Shue, V. & Thornton, P. M. (eds) *To Govern China: Evolving Practices of Power* (Cambridge, Cambridge University Press).

Boim, L. (1966) 'Party-State Control in the Soviet Union', in Boim, L., Morgan, G. & Rudzinksi, A. (eds) *Legal Controls in the Soviet Union* (Leiden, A.W. Sijthoff-Leyden).

Cohen, J. A. (1968) *The Criminal Process in the People's Republic of China, 1949–1963: An Introduction* (Cambridge, MA, Harvard University Press).

Dimitrov, M. K. (2014) 'What the Party Wanted to Know: Citizen Complaints as a "Barometer of Public Opinion" in Communist Bulgaria', *East European Politics and Societies: and Cultures*, 28, 2.

Duan, R. (2018) 'Renmin jiancha zhidu chuangshe chuqi "yiban jiandu" zhiquan kaocha (1949–1954)', *Xiandai Fazhi Yanjiu*, 10, 4.

Falleti, T. G. & Lynch, J. F. (2009) 'Context and Causal Mechanisms in Political Analysis', *Comparative Political Studies*, 42, 9.

Frolov, V. V. (2011) 'Organy sovetskoi prokuratury v pervye poslevoennye gody (1945–1955): sovremennaya istoriografiya problemy', *Voprosy teorii i praktiki*, 4, chast' 3.

Ginsburgs, G. & Stahnke, A. (1964) 'The Genesis of the People's Procuratorate in Communist China 1949–1951', *The China Quarterly*, 20.

Ginsburgs, G. & Stahnke, A. (1968) 'The People's Procuratorate in Communist China: The Institution Ascendant, 1954–1957', *The China Quarterly*, 34.

Heilmann, S. & Perry, E. (2011) 'Embracing Uncertainty: Guerrilla Policy Style and Adaptive Governance in China', in Perry, E. & Heilmann, S. (eds) *Mao's Invisible Hand: The Political Foundations of Adaptive Governance in China* (Cambridge, MA, Harvard University Press).

Helmke, G. (2002) 'The Logic of Strategic Defection: Court–Executive Relations in Argentina Under Dictatorship and Democracy', *American Political Science Review*, 96, 2.

Hilbink, L. (2007) *Judges Beyond Politics in Democracy and Dictatorship: Lessons from Chile* (New York, NY, Cambridge University Press).

Huntington, S. P. (1996) *The Clash of Civilizations and the Remaking of World Order* (New York, NY, Simon and Schuster).

Huntington, S. P. (2006) *Political Order in Changing Societies* (New Haven, CT, Yale University Press).

Huskey, E. (1997) 'Russian Judicial Reform After Communism', in Solomon Jr, P. H. (ed.) *Reforming Justice in Russia, 1864–1996* (New York, NY, Sharpe).

Kazantsev, S. M. (1993) *Istoriya tsarskoi prokuratury* (St Petersburg, Sankt-Peterburgskogo Universiteta).

Kazantsev, S. (1997) 'The Judicial Reform of 1864 and the Procuracy in Russia', in Solomon Jr, P. H. (ed.) *Reforming Justice in Russia, 1864–1996* (New York, NY, Sharpe).

Lenin, V. I. (1918) 'Ocherednye Zadachi Sovetskoi Vlasti', in *Polnoe sobranie Sochenenii, 5-e izdanie, 1967–1981g.*, vol. 36 (Moscow, Izdatel'stvo Politicheskoi Literatury).

Lenin, V. I. (1919) 'Pis'mo k Rabochim i Krest'yanam po Povodu Pobedy nad Kolchakom', in *Polnoe sobranie Sochenenii, 5-e izdanie, 1967–1981g.*, vol. 39 (Moscow, Izdatel'stvo Politicheskoi Literatury).

Lenin, V. I. (1922) 'O 'dvoinom' podchinenii i zakonnosti', in *Polnoe sobranie Sochenenii, 5-e izdanie, 1967–1981g.*, vol. 45 (Moscow, Izdatel'stvo Politicheskoi Literatury).

Levitsky, S. & Way, L. (2013) 'The Durability of Revolutionary Regimes', *Journal of Democracy*, 24, 3.

Li, V. H. (1970) 'The Role of Law in Communist China', *The China Quarterly*, 44.

Li, S. (ed.) (1988) *Dangdai zhongguo de jiancha zhidu* (Beijing, China Social Sciences Press).

Li, L. (2016) 'The Rise of the Discipline and Inspection Commission, 1927–2012: Anticorruption Investigation and Decision-Making in the Chinese Communist Party', *Modern China*, 42, 5.

Lin, H. (ed.) (2001) *Zhongyang suqu jiancha shi* (Beijing, China Procuracy Press).

Ma, S. K. (2008) 'The Dual Nature of Anti-Corruption Agencies in China', *Crime, Law and Social Change*, 49, 2.

Mattingly, D. C. (2017) 'Colonial Legacies and State Institutions in China: Evidence from a Natural Experiment', *Comparative Political Studies*, 50, 4.

Min, S., Xie, R. & Xue, W. (eds) (2011) *Zhongguo Jiancha Zhidu Faling Guifan Jiedu* (Beijing, China People's Procuracy Press).

Min, S. & Xue, W. (eds) (2009) *Gongheguo jiancha lishi pianduan* (Beijing, China Procuratorate Press).

Mironenko, Y. (1964) *Bulletin of the Institute for the Study of the USSR*, XI, 8, August.

Morgan, G. (1959) 'The Soviet Procuracy's General Supervision Function', *Soviet Studies*, 11, 2.

Morgan, G. (1966) 'The Protests and Representations Lodged by the Soviet Procuracy Against the Legality of Government Enactments, 1937–1964', in Boim, L., Morgan, G. & Rudzinski, A. (eds) *Legal Controls in the Soviet Union* (Leiden, A.W. Sijthoff-Leyden).

Mou, Y. (2017) 'Overseeing Criminal Justice: The Supervisory Role of the Public Prosecution Service in China', *Journal of Law and Society*, 44.

Mühlhahn, K. (2009) *Criminal Justice in China: A History* (Cambridge, MA, Harvard University Press).

Ou, W. (ed.) (1996) *Guangxi tongzhi: jiancha zhi* (Guangxi, Guangxi People's Press).

Pavlischev, K. S. & Shishkov, I. N. (1981) 'Predislovie', in Sireyaev, I. N. & Metelkina, G. A. (eds) *Sovetskaya Prokuratura: Sbornik Dokumentov* (Moscow, Yuridicheskaya Literatura).

Perrins, M. (1980) 'Rabkrin and Workers' Control in Russia 1917–34', *European Studies Review*, 10, 2.
Pierson, P. (2000) 'Increasing Returns, Path Dependence, and the Study of Politics', *American Political Science Review*, 94, 2.
Pierson, P. (2011) *Politics in Time: History, Institutions, and Social Analysis* (Princeton, NJ, Princeton University Press).
Pomeranz, W. E. (2019) 'Russia's Resilient Legal Powerhouse: The Procuracy Enters the 21st Century', Kennan Cable No. 42, available at: https://www.wilsoncenter.org/publication/kennan-cable-no-42-russias-resilient-legal-powerhouse-the-procuracy-enters-the-21st#_edn2, accessed 11 December 2020.
Rees, E. A. (1987) *State Control in Soviet Russia: The Rise and Fall of the Workers' and Peasants' Inspectorate, 1920–34* (London, Macmillan).
Salmina, S. J. (2008) 'Polemika o putyakh sozdaniya sovetskoi prokuratury.' *Vestnik Yuzhno-Ural'skogo gosudarstvennogo universiteta.* 28, 128 (Chelyabinsk, Russian Federation, Seriya: Pravo).
Scott, J. (1998) *Seeing like a State* (New Haven, CT, Yale University Press).
Shao, M. (1955) 'Duiyu renmin jianchayuan de yiban jiandu gongzuo de renshi', *Guangming ribao*, 30 March.
Shearer, D. R. (1996) *Industry, State, and Society in Stalin's Russia, 1926–1934* (Ithaca, NY, Cornell University Press).
Shen-Bayh, F. (2018) 'Strategies of Repression: Judicial and Extrajudicial Methods of Autocratic Survival', *World Politics*, 70, 3.
Slater, D. (2003) 'Iron Cage in an Iron Fist: Authoritarian Institutions and the Personalization of Power in Malaysia', *Comparative Politics*, 36, 1.
Slater, D. (2009) 'Altering Authoritarianism: Institutional Complexity and Autocratic Agency in Indonesia', in Mahoney, J. & Thelen, K. (eds) *Explaining Institutional Change: Ambiguity, Agency, and Power* (New York, NY, Cambridge University Press).
Slater, D. & Wong, J. (2013) 'The Strength to Concede: Ruling Parties and Democratization in Developmental Asia', *Perspectives on Politics*, 11, 3.
Slater, D. & Ziblatt, D. (2013) 'The Enduring Indispensability of the Controlled Comparison', *Comparative Political Studies*, 46, 10.
Smith, G. (1978) *The Soviet Procuracy and the Supervision of Administration* (Alphen aan den Rijn, Sijthoff & Noordhoff).
Smith, G. (1997) 'The Struggle Over the Procuracy', in Solomon Jr, P. H. (ed.) *Reforming Justice in Russia, 1864–1996* (New York, NY, Sharpe).
Solomon Jr, P. H. (1997) 'Court Reform in Russian History', in Solomon Jr, P. H. (ed.) *Reforming Justice in Russia, 1864–1996* (New York, NY, Sharpe).
Strauss, J. (2006) 'Morality, Coercion and State Building by Campaign in the Early PRC: Regime Consolidation and After, 1949–1956', *The China Quarterly*, 188.
Sun, J. (2018) 'Wang Guiwu tongzhi de shengping yeji he zhuyao gongxian', *Procurator Daily*, 17 October.
Thornton, P. M. (2007) *Disciplining the State: Virtue, Violence, and State-Making in Modern China* (Cambridge, MA, Harvard University Asia Center).
Vakhitova, R. R. (2003) *Prokuratura v mekhanizme gosudarstva (istoriko-pravovoe issledovanie) Avtoreferat*, PhD thesis (Kazan, Bashkirskii Gosudarstvennyi Universitet).
Walder, A. (2015) *China Under Mao: A Revolution Derailed* (Cambridge, MA, Harvard University Press).
Wang, G. (1958) 'Bo Li Huizhi de "Zuigao jiandu lun"', *People's Daily*, 7 January.
Wu, X. (2000) 'Woguo jianchajiguan "yiban jiandu" he "chuizhi lingdao" qian lishi bianqian jiqi fansi', *Journal of Ningde Normal University*, 4.
Xie, P. (2008) 'Qian sulian jiancha zhidu gei women liuxia le shenme?', *Procuracy Daily*, 15 May, available at: http://www.spp.gov.cn/zdgz/200805/t20080515_27875.shtml, accessed 27 May 2019.
Ye, Q. & Huang, Y. (eds) (2003) *Zhongguo jiancha zhidu yanjiu* (Shanghai, Shanghai Academy of Social Science Press).
Yuan, H. (ed.) (1996) *Guizhou sheng zhi: jiancha zhi* (Guiyang, Guizhou People's Press).
Zhang, C. (1985) 'Wo sheng wushi niandai jiancha tongxunyuan lüekao', *Hebei Faxue*, 23–26.
Zhang, F. (ed.) (1998) *Shandong sheng zhi: sifa zhi* (Jinan, Shandong People's Press).
Zeng, X. & Zheng, Q. (1992) *Jiancha Zhidu Shilue* (Beijing, China Procuracy Press).
Zvyagintsev, A. G. (2012) *Istoriya Rossiskoi Prokuratury, 1722–2012* (Moscow, Olma Media Group).

The Limits of Authoritarian Modernisation: Zero Tolerance Policing in Kazakhstan

GAVIN SLADE, ALEXEI TROCHEV & MALIKA TALGATOVA

Abstract

We study police inertia and the depth of public mistrust in, and apathy towards, zero tolerance policing (ZTP) in Kazakhstan. Using survey, social media and official data we show how ZTP failed: politicians did not summon any political will for the policy, the police subverted any attempted reforms, while citizens ignored them. The failure of ZTP delineates the limits of authoritarian modernisation. We argue that modernisers require assistance from citizens in reforming police yet cannot mobilise such assistance due to public distrust which itself is created by authoritarian modernisers' preference for police loyalty over police good behaviour. The consequence is a decoupling of the rhetoric from the reality of police reform.

FROM EDUCATION AND HEALTH TO TAX POLICIES, THE SUCCESS OF reform projects varies considerably in conditions of authoritarian modernisation (Gel'man 2017). Police reform is an area where success is especially difficult to achieve, revealing a limit to authoritarian modernisers' ambitions. This essay aims to demonstrate this claim through a case study of police reform from a non-democratic context, Kazakhstan. Zero tolerance policing (ZTP) is an internationally renowned policing slogan and strategy originally developed in the United States. We will demonstrate empirically that the adoption of ZTP in Kazakhstan has had minimal impact on policing practices or citizen behaviour. Instead, we find significant evidence of what Meyer and Rowan (1977) call 'decoupling', understood as the gap between the legitimating, institutionalised myths of an organisation and the everyday practice of its parts. Government, police and civil society perform their ceremonial roles around police reform but otherwise simulate, subvert or ignore it (Wilson 2005; Heathershaw 2014; Paneyakh 2014).

Why does decoupling occur? For the government, it is a consequence of the 'politician's dilemma', as described by Geddes (1994), in which a politician faces two undesirable choices: to reform and face the resistance and possible disloyalty of police

The authors would like to thank the anonymous reviewers for very helpful suggestions. All these contributions have improved the final piece. In particular, one anonymous reviewer suggested utilising Meyer and Rowan's (1977) work which we found very useful for theoretically thinking through our findings. All remaining errors are our own.

structures, or to not reform and allow high degrees of police discretion, which can lower societal trust. In non-democratic contexts, where losing police loyalty can lead to regime change, politicians often lean towards the latter choice up to and including allowing abusive behaviour and corruption. However, they cannot reveal this preference publicly; instead, they employ the rhetoric of reform. For the police, aware of the 'politician's dilemma', the aim is to strike a balance: sustain the benefits of rent-seeking and corruption that discretion allows but not so egregiously as to shift the political calculus too far in favour of real reform (Sykes 1985; Savage 2003; Skogan 2008). Citizens, aware of this symbiotic relationship between police and the political elite, have minimal incentive to assist the police (Beck & Chistyakova 2002, 2004; Goldsmith 2005; Pino & Wiatrowski 2016) but still search for ways to express displeasure in the hope of improving the politician's calculus in their favour.

We aim to demonstrate in this essay that ZTP failed in Kazakhstan, as well as how it failed, and what this tells us about the limits of authoritarian rulers' ambitions to modernise their states. The essay is structured as follows: we provide background on the emergence of the ZTP slogan in the former Soviet Union and review the literature on the reasons for the implementation of ZTP. We then analyse the three official narratives for ZTP in Kazakhstan. We focus on how the narrative shifted and contradicted itself in the face of police inertia and changing circumstances. Following this, we assess the effects of ZTP on attitudes as well as the behaviour of the public. We then look at police responses to the policy. We find that for politicians, ZTP has been a rhetorical virtue-signalling device rather than a genuine reform goal, subverted by the police and ignored by society. This leads us to a final discussion of what this result means more broadly. We suggest that the failure of police reform points to wider stagnation in political and social processes and provides an insight into the capacity of an authoritarian regime, in this case Kazakhstan, to bring about change and renewal.

Zero tolerance policing in the former Soviet Union

Zero tolerance policing as a strategy was first adopted in New York City in the 1990s (Greene 1999). According to Willie Bratton, the head of the New York Police Department and one of the main authors of the policy in the city, major crimes emerge from minor crimes and neglect in communities. This central premise underpinned the 'broken windows theory' of crime developed by academics in the 1980s (Wilson & Kelling 1982). Police, going by this argument, should target minor crimes vigorously, thus creating an inhospitable environment for criminal and anti-social behaviour (Bratton 1997; Greene 1999). In the New York case, ZTP involved policy innovations concerning police powers to stop and search people and technological advancements in mapping crime and directing police resources to crime hot spots. In the years following the policy's launch, serious crime in New York dipped. However, the relationship between ZTP and this decrease in crime is not clear: regardless of the adoption of ZTP, cities across the United States experienced a decline in serious crime at the same time as New York. Moreover, the policy was associated with a number of negative consequences, most seriously the police's targeting of disadvantaged and minority populations through the stop-and-search policy.[1]

Regardless of the dubious evidence for any ZTP effect on crime rates, the policy was transferred outside US borders in no small part thanks to its promotion by former New York mayor Rudy Giuliani. 'Zero tolerance' has become a frequently used term around the world for 'get tough' policies (Bowling 1999; Bowling & Sheptycki 2012). The policy was adopted in different guises in the United Kingdom, Mexico and the Philippines, *inter alia*. All of these countries, like the United States, have high levels of wealth inequality as well as high levels of public anxiety about crime. Former Soviet countries, likewise, became increasingly unequal through the 1990s and 2000s while crime rates and public anxieties about order also went up. There were many elective affinities in this part of the world for zero tolerance policing policies to take on a new lease of life.

ZTP initially emerged in the former Soviet Union in Georgia in 2005. President Mikheil Saakashvili, who had been a law student in New York at the time of the original ZTP, declared a policy of 'zero tolerance' of crime and corruption. Georgian ZTP went beyond reforms to the institution of the police and involved significant changes across the criminal justice system (Slade 2012; Strakes 2013; Light 2014; Kupatadze 2016). Mandatory custodial sentencing, increased expenditures on professionalising prosecutors and expanded police powers led to a marked increase in the prison population (Slade 2017; Marat 2018). Georgia's version of ZTP mirrored the US example in several ways: the increase of police powers, the use of force when interacting with citizens and increasing punitiveness in the court system.

In contrast, Ukraine's application of ZTP, emerging in 2014, resembled a hybrid reform. Ukraine's reformers incorporated elements of the Georgian project with aspects of community policing, a broad term for a strategy aimed less at order maintenance and more at increasing civic participation in security provision and deepening trust between citizens and police. In Ukraine, as in Georgia, a new policing division was created called the 'Patrol Police' (*patrul'na politsiia*) following the Euromaidan protests of 2014. Many recruits to this new body were drawn from civil society activists and protestors who had taken part in this uprising (Marat 2018). A number of Georgian reformers were involved in drawing up the new policing strategy, focusing on enhancing police–citizen interactions. Due to the development of alternative sentencing, the Ukrainian version of ZTP did not affect prison rates and the overall prison population declined dramatically after 2014.[2]

Existing studies of ZTP in the former Soviet Union focus either on why the policy was adopted or on the results of the policy. In terms of the latter question, studies of Georgia's ZTP recognise some of the terrible abuses of power the strategy entailed while tending to count ZTP as a success on its own terms: crime went down, corruption decreased and trust in some sections of the police went up (Slade 2012; Light 2014; Kupatadze 2016; Nasuti 2016). It has been recognised, though, that these successes did not involve wider

[1]For a review of ZTP critiques, see Davis (2017).
[2]*Database on Worldwide Prison Rates*, World Prison Brief, 2019, available at: https://www.prisonstudies.org/world-prison-brief-data, accessed 29 January 2020.

changes in overall attitudes to the police or greater cooperation with them (Slade & Kupatadze 2017; Marat 2018). In terms of Ukrainian police reform since Maidan, Friesendorf (2019) claims that an institutional 'bricolage' consisting of recent innovations combined with inertial legacies in police organisation structure and culture have prevented deep change from occurring. Path dependencies produced police resistance to attempts to reduce the levels of discretion with which they were familiar and comfortable (Friesendorf 2019).

Friesendorf's findings for Ukraine follow studies that show how well-entrenched organisations can impede reform (Sykes 1985; Savage 2003; Taylor 2014). In his case study of Russian police reform, Taylor (2014) shows how Russia's hybrid regime type narrows the policymaking process into a small circle focused on the presidential administration. Due to this, Russian police reforms were more responsive to the needs of the powerful Ministry of Interior than to those of the Russian people. In such cases, reform can often have little impact in improving societal views of the police. Yet, public attitudes to police are seen as important drivers for police reform, particularly in democracies (Tyler 2007; Tyler & Fagan 2008). In the former Soviet Union, studies show how attitudes to police are connected specifically to the fortunes of reform projects (Beck & Chistyakova 2004; Goldsmith 2005; Pino & Wiatrowski 2016). Specifically, these studies show the irony of how low trust and low engagement with the police in the first place make reform towards more democratic forms of policing less likely.

We present data that demonstrate how engagement with ZTP in Kazakhstan was simulated by politicians, subverted by the police and largely ignored by the public. Simulation, subversion and ignorance are all manifestations of decoupling between the legitimating myths of how government, police and civil society should conduct and engage with police reform relative to what they actually do, given the incentives and opportunities available to them. The next section traces the emergence of zero tolerance in the discourse of Kazakhstan's political elite. We show that the official discourse treats ZTP as a catch-all term and ranges between three broad but separate policy goals that shift continuously, responding shallowly to changing circumstances. At first, ZTP emerged discursively as zero tolerance to corruption and the need to control wayward police actors. Later the discourse changed to zero tolerance to petty crime. Finally, ZTP problematised the lack of civic vigilance against anti-social behaviour. None of the narratives were fully developed into concrete action plans or long-lasting programmes of change.

Three aims of ZTP, Kazakhstani-style

Marat (2018, 2019) argues that, in Kazakhstan, ZTP extended the reach of the police as a response to two issues. First, growing discontent with the ruling regime made protest more likely. The events in Zhanaozen where, in 2011, striking oil workers were shot by police, had to be regarded as an act of 'transformative violence', catalysing attempts to strengthen police control, particularly in rural regions. Second, as cities such as Nur-Sultan, Almaty and Shymkent grow while the economy continues to stutter, there is an increasing need to govern marginalised urban groups such as the poor and recently arrived rural migrants.

Marat's convincing take on the reasons for ZTP are very far from the official narratives. The ZTP strategy adopted in Kazakhstan moved away from the US model and was not initially tied only to the tasks of policing. Instead, the term 'zero tolerance' was tightly connected to anti-corruption and bureaucratic discipline. President Nursultan Nazarbayev decreed on 22 April 2009 a set of measures to guarantee the 'imminence of the state's response to any legal violations' and the legal liability of all offenders.[3] In a commentary to this decree entitled 'The Policy of Zero Tolerance to Crime and Corruption', Constitutional Council Chairman Igor Rogov (2009) explained that these measures aimed at creating the 'atmosphere of intolerance towards corruption in society' by obligating government officials to report corruption, by imposing penalties on them for failure to report, and by obligating the state to make payments to citizens who report corruption. Rogov (2009) cited the success of ZTP in the United States yet provided no details on how to carry out this policy, except for listing proposals that are not usually associated with ZTP: imposing harsher punishments for crimes against minors, crimes committed by groups of offenders and organised crime. A further 340-page book entitled 'Combating Corruption in the Judicial System' (Mami 2009) repeatedly mentioned the 'imminence' of responsibility and punishment for legal violations but only with regard to corruption-related offences by government officials and judges. It mentioned the term 'zero tolerance to corruption' in the context of the experience of Seoul.

In August 2011, police and municipal authorities in Petropavl city, the administrative centre of the North Kazakhstan province, introduced the concept of a 'neighbourhood watch' with no ZTP label attached. Having studied Estonia's neighbourhood watch model, police chiefs in this province set up a special office consisting of a 24-hour telephone hotline manned by civilians to respond to citizen complaints and anonymous tip offs. To support their work, the provincial authorities spent 15 million tenge that year to set up billboards and play television and radio ads encouraging citizens to report wrongdoing or anything suspicious to the police: 'the safety of your home, your family and friends is in your hands'. By the end of 2012, this hotline had received 3,245 calls and in 2013, 2,797 calls. The police chiefs viewed this as a success.[4] In 2013, the North Kazakhstan province police chief was transferred to lead the police department of the Almaty province and he launched the neighbourhood watch programme there by linking it explicitly to ZTP.[5] Some attempts to introduce the neighbourhood watch programme have been made in the cities of Taraz (2016), Aqtau (2017) and Qyzylorda (2020) but they produced little success and have been largely ignored in other parts of the country.

In April 2012, the zero tolerance discourse shifted fully towards the problem of petty crime. Using New York's ZTP as an example, President Nazarbayev proposed to punish

[3] 'Ukaz Presidenta Respubliki Kazakhstan "O dopolnitel'nykh merakh po usileniyu bor'by s prestupnost'yu i korruptsiei i dal'neishemu sovershenstvovaniyu pravookhranitel'noi deyatel'nosti v Respublike Kazakhstan"', no. 793, 22 April 2009, available at: http://adilet.zan.kz/rus/docs/U090000793_, accessed 29 January 2020.

[4] 'Glazok v pomoshch", *Kazakhstanskaya Pravda*, 19 June 2019, available at: https://www.kazpravda.kz/articles/view/glazok-v-pomoshch, accessed 16 October 2020.

[5] 'V Almatinskoi oblasti po programme "Sosedskii prismotr" za god postupilo bolee 7 tys. zvonkov', *Kazinform*, 7 June 2015, available at: https://www.inform.kz/ru/v-almatinskoy-oblasti-po-programme-sosedskiy-prismotr-za-god-postupilo-bolee-7-tys-zvonkov_a2784069, accessed 16 October 2020.

chewing-gum litterers by a three-day jail sentence and insisted that police had to start doing their job: 'to catch all petty offenders and to let everyone know that every offender will be punished. Then there will be order and no serious crime'.[6] Immediately following his criticism, traffic police in Kazakhstan's capital city reported that, in a two-day campaign, it had punished 295 drivers for littering the city streets. In June 2012, Rogov, the head of the Constitutional Council, defended ZTP and heavier punishments for offenders at a scholarly conference, citing his own travels in Georgia and the success of Saakashvili's government in combating street-level crime in Tbilisi.[7]

At the end of 2012, a huge victimisation survey of 219,500 households (356,000 respondents) was conducted by the State Statistics Agency at the request of the head of the Security Council. According to the survey, 3.5% of respondents reported being a victim of crime in the previous 12 months and only half of those said that they had reported the crime to the police.[8] The presidential administration chose not to release any further details from this survey to the public. Perhaps in response to the survey results, President Nazarbayev highlighted in his 2012 State of the Union address the need to tackle crime through police action as well as higher levels of civic consciousness, trust in the police and public vigilance with regard to anti-social behaviour. The president vowed to introduce a 'zero tolerance principle towards disorder'. Drawing directly on the 'broken windows' thesis, Nazarbayev stated: 'developed society starts from discipline and order everywhere: comfortable doorways, safe backyards, clean streets and friendly faces.... A feeling of disorder and permissiveness creates grounds for more serious crimes' (Nazarbayev 2012).

In a public meeting with the heads of all law-enforcement agencies (Procuracy, the Ministry of Internal Affairs, the Anti-Corruption Agency and the Service of Economic Investigations) at the end of January 2013, Nazarbayev ordered the Ministry of Internal Affairs (MVD), the ruling *Nur Otan* party, the Justice Ministry and the Ministry of Culture to 'create zero tolerance of legal violations in society'.[9] Within a week, the MVD and *Nur Otan* leaders announced a Soviet-style campaign aimed at 'the participation of citizens in preventing crimes, the transparency of the MVD's work and the mobilisation of efforts of non-governmental organisations in maintaining law and order'.[10] MVD chiefs went to the regions to inform police about this campaign. Deputy Minister Amantai Kurenbekov told police in the Aqtobe province that they should promptly register all

[6]'Nazarbayev predlagaet sazhat' na troe sutok za broshennuyu na ulitse zhevatel'nuyu rezinku', *Tengrinews.kz*, 11 April 2012, available at: https://tengrinews.kz/kazakhstan_news/nazarbaev-predlagaet-sajat-troe-sutok-broshennuyu-ulitse-211964/, accessed 16 October 2020.

[7]'V strane gryadet liberalizatsiya ugolovnogo zakonodatel'stva', *Ekspress-K*, 8 June 2012, available at: https://online.zakon.kz/Document/?doc_id=31203788, accessed 16 October 2020.

[8]'Gosudarstvennaya programma dal'neishei modernizatsii provookhranitel'noi sistemy', General'naya Prokuratura Respubliki Kazakhstan, 31 December 2013, available at: http://prokuror.gov.kz/rus/gosudarstvo/o-merah-po-dalneyshemu-razvitiyu-pravoohranitelnoy-sistemy/gosudarstvennaya-programma, accessed 29 January 2020.

[9]'Segodnya Glava gosudarstva Nursultan Nazarbayev provel soveshchanie s rukovodyashchim sostavom pravookhranitel'nykh organov', *Akorda.kz*, 30 January 2013, available at: https://www.akorda.kz/ru/events/akorda_news/meetings_and_sittings/segodnya-glava-gosudarstva-nursultan-nazarbaev-provel-soveshchanie-s-rukovodyashchim-sostavom-pravoohranitelnyh-organov, accessed 16 October 2020.

[10]'V Kazakhstane startuet aktsiya po formirovaniyu nulevoi terpimosti k melkim pravonarusheniyam', *KazInform*, 5 February 2013, available at: https://online.zakon.kz/Document/?doc_id=31327655, accessed 16 October 2020.

complaints about crimes and impose 'the maximum punishment for the slightest violation of law. Police should not be indifferent to the population; a polite and attentive attitude to citizens is one of the main tasks of policing'.[11] Throughout the country police promptly started to raid street corners and public places to penalise petty hooligans: smokers, drunks and litterers as well as noise-makers and those who walked dogs without muzzles. The MVD ordered its provincial branches to hold Soviet-style 'zero tolerance' campaigns several times a year, which usually lasted between two and four days and were supposed to detect and catch high numbers of petty offenders.[12]

As part of these campaigns, the police held meetings in communities, most of which were poorly attended and had a 'window-dressing nature' (Kollektiv avtorov 2018, p. 55); they also distributed brochures about law-abiding behaviour, installed posters about traffic lights in school buildings, and mounted billboards in cities such as Almaty discouraging jaywalking and drunk driving. Photographs of the local beat officers were displayed in shops and apartment blocks with messages encouraging citizens to get in touch if they witnessed anti-social behaviour. Citizens' policing brigades, which existed in the Soviet period as *dobrovol'nye narodnye druzhiny* (LaPierre 2012), were resurrected in 2013, having been abandoned twice, in the early 1990s and in 2003. One rationale for resurrecting them was that these brigades would walk the streets together with police patrols and shame the patrols if they were less than diligent in their duties. However, public opinion surveys showed citizens were reluctant to take part in these brigades because citizens did not wish to become both witnesses in legal proceedings and targets of revenge by offenders and their relatives, a reflection of lack of confidence in the police (Simakova 2015).

In September 2013, Nazarbayev told Parliament that 'nobody should have doubts about the inevitability and fairness of punishment for any offences and violations of the law'.[13] In January 2014, he signed the Legal Policy Concept and the Concept of Kazakhstan's joining the top 30 developed countries by 2050,[14] both of which prioritised societal zero tolerance of legal violations. The MVD responded by designing two ZTP action plans, one for 2014–2016 and another for 2017–2019: both plans used the Soviet-era indicators of registering and solving crimes as the key measures of the crime rate (Kollektiv avtorov 2018, p. 32). The first plan aimed at a decline of the crime rate from 190 per 10,000 of the population in 2015 to 187 in 2016. This plan also envisaged a 10% decline in crimes committed by government officials in 2015 and a 20% decline in

[11]'V DVD Aktyubinskoi oblasti rasskazali o nedostatkakh v rabote politseiskikh v 2012 g.', *KazInform*, 5 February 2013, available at: https://www.inform.kz/ru/v-dvd-aktyubinskoy-oblasti-rasskazali-o-nedostatkah-v-rabote-policeyskih-v-2012-g_a2532279, accessed 16 October 2020.

[12]'V Karagande studenty patruliruyut ulitsy vmeste s politseiskimi', *KazInform*, 23 April 2013, available at: https://www.inform.kz/ru/v-karagande-studenty-patruliruyut-ulicy-vmeste-s-policeyskimi_a2552968, accessed 16 October 2020.

[13]'Prezident Kazakhstana poruchil sformirovat' v obshchestve nulevuyu terpimost' k pravonarusheniyam', *TengriNews.kz*, 2 September 2013, available at: https://tengrinews.kz/kazakhstan_news/prezident-kazahstana-poruchil-sformirovat-obschestve-240855/, accessed 16 October 2020.

[14]Decree No. 732, 'O Kontseptsii po vkhozhdeniyu Kazakhstana v chislo 30-ti samykh razvitykh gosudarstv mira', *Akorda.Kz*, 27 January 2014, available at: http://www.akorda.kz/ru/legal_acts/decrees/o-koncepcii-po-vhozhdeniyu-kazahstana-v-chislo-30-ti-samyh-razvityh-gosudarstv-mira, accessed 16 October 2020.

2016. There was no additional funding and no accountability for failure to reach these targets, and no new indicators for preventing crimes or building public confidence in police were established. Moreover, no other government agencies, such as the ministries of Education and Labour and the Anti-Corruption Agency, included societal zero tolerance of legal violations in their multi-year plans and concepts (Amirov 2017; Kollektiv avtorov 2018).

In May 2015, as a part of his '100 concrete steps' programme, Nazarbayev authorised the creation of a local police service (Step 30). The local police service, led by the deputy chief of the province's department of the MVD, would be responsible for ZTP 'in close cooperation with the local community'.[15] The provincial departments of the MVD transferred the following broad responsibilities to the local police service: local beat policing, juvenile delinquency, preventing violence against women, road patrolling, environmental protection and non-pre-trial detention facilities. The Soviet-era dual subordination system, whereby local police were accountable both to the provincial government and the provincial police chief, was revived. The local police service was set up in January 2016 and staffed and led by existing MVD officers, with no new recruits for the local police force (Amirov 2017).[16] The local police service quickly began duplicating the functions of provincial police departments and used Soviet-era statistical indicators of policing instead of implementing closer cooperation with local citizens. According to one official from Nazarbayev's administration, who had visited local police services in several provinces, neither rank-and-file officers nor their chiefs understood the essence of ZTP and the need for close cooperation with local residents (Biekenov 2017). For example, in March 2017, the head of the local police service of the Pavlodar province could not tell journalists whether any cases launched as a result of tip offs from citizens had actually reached the courts.[17]

Meanwhile, the chiefs of the local police service were dismissed for general incompetence in Kazakhstan's South Kazakhstan province on 29 March 2017,[18] in Aktobe province on 19 June 2017[19] and in the former capital city of Almaty on 3 August 2018.[20] In Taraz (on 15

[15]'President Nazarbayev Unveils 100 Concrete Steps to Implement Five Institutional Reforms', *Kazinform*, 2 June 2015, available at: http://www.inform.kz/en/president-nazarbayev-unveils-100-concrete-steps-toimplement-five-institutional-reforms_a2782614, accessed 16 October 2020.

[16]'Vo vsekh regionakh Kazakhstana naznacheny nachal'niki mestnoi politsii', *Today.kz*, 12 January 2016, available at: http://today.kz/news/kazahstan/2016-01-12/707103-vo-vseh-regionah-kazahstana-naznachenyi-nachalniki-mestnoj-politsii/, accessed 16 October 2020.

[17]'Nachal'nik MPS ni ustno, ni pis'menno ne smog otvetit' na ryad voprosov, zadannykh na ego brifinge', *GorodPavlodar.kz*, 13 March 2017, available at: http://www.gorodpavlodar.kz/News_49799_2.html, accessed 16 October 2020.

[18]'V YuKO smenili oskandalivshegosya nachal'nika MPS', *Tengrinews.kz*, 30 March 2017, available at: https://tengrinews.kz/kazakhstan_news/v-yuko-smenili-oskandalivshegosya-nachalnika-mps-315061/, accessed 16 October 2020.

[19]'V Aktobe smenilsya rukovoditel' mestnoi politseiskoi sluzhby', *MoiGorod.kz*, 22 June 2017, available at: https://mgorod.kz/nitem/v-aktobe-smenilsya-rukovoditel-mestnoj-policejskoj-sluzhby/, accessed 16 October 2020.

[20]'Nachal'nik mestnoi politseiskoi sluzhby Almaty ushel s posta', *Zakon.kz*, 3 August 2018, available at: https://online.zakon.kz/Document/?doc_id=32475329, accessed 16 October 2020.

February 2018)[21] and in Uralsk (on 22 February 2018), local police chiefs were dismissed for bribery.[22] Nazarbayev abolished the local police service in July 2018 and transferred its responsibilities back to the MVD provincial departments.[23]

In the wake of police incompetence following the murder of Denis Ten, a famous Olympic figure skater killed in central Almaty in August 2018, Nazarbayev publicly asked: 'A police officer abroad is a friend but who is our police officer?' He threatened to purge the whole Kazakhstani police force at once and hire civilians—young law school graduates for police jobs with much higher salaries—using Georgia's model.[24] However, in mid-September 2018, the Interior Minister, Kalmukhanbet Kassymov, promptly disavowed Nazarbayev's criticism of the police, declaring that police reform would instead start with the design of a new police uniform. He announced publicly that a Georgian-style wholesale purge of police was not going to happen, and that Kazakhstan had nothing more to learn from Georgia's police reform, though it was not clear at this point that Kazakhstan had learned anything at all from Georgia other than the ZTP slogan.[25] To improve ZTP he proposed, in December 2018, to encourage citizens to report minor offences by paying them 40% of the amount of the fine.[26] The next month the Ministry backtracked on the implementation of this proposal.[27] In September 2019, Nazarbayev blamed *Nur Otan* for failing to unite society on the basis of zero tolerance of corruption.[28] A year later, in September 2020, Nazarbayev's successor, Kassym-Zhomart Tokayev, announced in his Address to the Nation the transition to the 'service police model' with the local police to be based on the principle of the 'police close at hand' (*politsiya v shagovoi dostupnosti*).[29] According to one senior MVD official, this model

[21] 'Nachal'nika mestnoi politsii Taraza zaderzhali za poluchenie vzyatok s podchinennykh', *Zakon.kz*, 15 February 2018, available at: https://www.zakon.kz/4903976-nachalnika-mestnoy-politsii-taraza.html, accessed 16 October 2020.

[22] 'V Ural'ske trekh sotrudnikov politsii rukovodyashchego zvena otstranili ot dolzhnosti iz-za vzyatki podchinennykh', *Time.kz*, 28 February 2018, available at: https://time.kz/news/politics/2018/02/28/v-uralske-treh-sotrudnikov-policii-rukovodjashego-zvena-otstranili-ot-dolzhnosti-iz-za-vzjatki-podchinennih, accessed 18 October 2020.

[23] 'Prezident RK utverdil popravki, ob"edinyayushchie DVD i MPS v departamenty politsii', *Informburo.kz*, 20 July 2018, available at: https://informburo.kz/novosti/prezident-rk-utverdil-popravki-obedinyayushchie-dvd-i-mps-v-departamenty-policii.html, accessed 18 October 2020.

[24] 'Nursultan Nazarbaev zadumyvaetsya o reforme politsii po gruzinskomu tipu: "uvolit' politseiskikh, nanyat' yuristov"', *Factum.kz*, 24 August 2018, available at: https://factum.kz/2018/71941, accessed 18 October 2020.

[25] 'Reformy politsii "po-gruzinski" v Kazakhstane ne budet', *Forbes.kz*, 14 September 2018, available at: https://forbes.kz/process/reformyi_politsii_po-gruzinski_v_kazahstane_ne_budet, accessed 18 October 2020.

[26] 'Kazakhstantsam budut platit' za video pravonarushenii', *TengriNews.kz*, 7 December 2018, available at: https://tengrinews.kz/kazakhstan_news/kazahstantsam-budut-platit-za-video-pravonarusheniy-359162, accessed 18 October 2020.

[27] 'Vyplaty za foto i video narushenii: v MVD vyskazalis' o WhatsApp-rassylke', *TengriNews.kz*, 18 January 2019, available at: https://tengrinews.kz/kazakhstan_news/vyiplatyi-foto-video-narusheniy-mvd-vyiskazalis-WhatsApp-361563, accessed 18 October 2020.

[28] 'K nulevoi terpimosti', *Kazakhstanskaya Pravda*, 13 September 2019, available at: https://www.kazpravda.kz/fresh/view/k-nulevoi-terpimosti1, accessed 18 October 2020.

[29] 'President of Kazakhstan Kassym-Jomart Tokayev's State of the Nation Address', *Akorda.kz*, 1 September 2020, available at: https://www.akorda.kz/en/addresses/addresses_of_president/president-of-kazakhstan-kassym-jomart-tokayevs-state-of-the-nation-address-september-1-2020, accessed 16 October 2020.

envisions having police precincts within walking distance of local communities and beat cops as authoritative and resourceful managers mobilising communities in solving their local problems.[30] It tries to emulate community safety partnerships, which had been implemented in the UK in the late 1990s under Tony Blair (Johnston 2003) who had been Nazarbayev's consultant in the 2010s (Lillis 2018). While very few within the police understood what a 'service police model' meant in practice, the MVD has already reported to President Tokayev about refurbishing dilapidated police precincts and the building of new ones.[31]

Anti-corruption, the control of petty crime and engaging the public were the three official reasons for the adoption of ZTP. Yet all three appeared to be empty buzzwords with no clear implementation strategy, and to be emerging in response to changing law-and-order crises. What were the effects of ZTP on its own terms, as articulated above by the political elite? In the next section we show that ZTP failed to bring about a change in police behaviour or public engagement in Kazakhstan, drawing on survey, social media and official data sources that cover public attitudes to helping the police, the reporting and recording of crime, police–citizen interactions online and the implementation of punishment.

Zero tolerance, zero effect?

This section partly relies on three surveys ($n = 1,600$) assessing public knowledge of ZTP, legal consciousness and willingness to work with the police. These surveys were produced by the Almaty-based Public Foundation 'Center for Social and Political Research "Strategy"' (Obshchestvennyi fond 'Tsentr sotsial'nykh i politicheskikh issledovanii "Strategiya"') (Ileuova 2014; Ileuova & Simakova 2014; Simakova 2015) on behalf of the Kazakhstani government in December 2013, November 2014 and October 2015. We also include results from a fourth survey in October 2018, carried out by the Nur-Sultan-based NAC Analytica, which assessed general public opinion ($n = 3,024$).[32] We included 11 extra questions in this fourth survey, some of which reproduced items from Strategy's earlier surveys. The goal was to assess whether there were any changes to public opinion about ZTP in the five years that ZTP had been in action. All surveys were nationally representative and included all *oblasti* and regions of Kazakhstan through stratified random sampling. Aside from the national level, to capture police–citizen interactions as part of ZTP at the local level we scraped, coded and analysed data from two police-operated forums on the social media platform Telegram and from an app called Zero Tolerance used in Pavlodar province as part of ZTP innovations (further details below). In addition, we analysed official statistics for minor crimes and the prosecution of police officers.

[30]'"Servisnaya model" kazakhstanskoi politsii: videnie i perspektivy', *Polisia.kz*, 18 September 2020, available at: https://polisia.kz/ru/servisnaya-model-kazahstanskoj-politsii-videnie-i-perspektivy/, accessed 16 October 2020.

[31]'Kak budet rabotat' "politsiya v shagovoi dostupnosti" v Kazakhstane, dolozhili Tokaevu', *Kazakhstanskaia Pravda*, 7 September 2020, available at: https://kazpravda.kz/news/prezident2/kak-budet-rabotat-politsiya-v-shagovoi-dostupnosti-v-kazahstane-dolozhili-tokaevu, accessed 16 October 2020.

[32]*Attitudes to Criminal Justice in Kazakhstan*, Corporate Fund NAC Analytica (Astana, NAC, 2018). On file with authors.

Public attitudes to ZTP in Kazakhstan: survey evidence

Overall, the survey data show some improvements in public attitudes to intervening in and reporting crime to police. In 2014 only 20% of respondents said they would definitely intervene if they witnessed anti-social behaviour; this figure had increased to 34% in 2018. When asked if they would aid the police in fighting petty crime, in 2014 52% reported 'definitely' or 'probably' yes compared to 39% who reported 'probably' or 'definitely' no. The corresponding figures were 57% and 33% in 2015 and 68% and 32% in 2018. Of those who said they would assist, there was an increase in the percentage of people willing to come forward as a witness in 2018, 38% up from 26% in 2014 and up from 30% in 2015. Willingness to join voluntary organisations and societal bodies tasked with maintaining order, such as citizen policing brigades, had also increased from 7% to 12% across the time period. Basic statistical tests show that these are all statistically significant differences ($p<0.05$). Figure 1 illustrates these changes and includes a further comparison across years. During the time that this shift in attitudes took place, knowledge of ZTP had declined. In 2014, only 18% of respondents reported knowing the policy 'well'. In 2015, 15% answered the same. By 2018, this statistic had dropped lower, to only 14%. A further 19% had 'heard something' about it. In cities, the figure stood at a miserly 12%. These survey findings are summarised in Figure 1.

The above attitudinal changes occurred while other attitudes, including trust in the police, remained constant. Thus, both in 2014 and 2018 respondents reported that they were moved more by a willingness to report crime for personal security rather than any desire to help the police. In both 2014 and 2018, the top three main obstacles to assisting the police remained the same: the time–cost of providing testimony; fear of criminals taking revenge; and distrust of the police. There was also cultural disapproval of those who become 'police informants'.

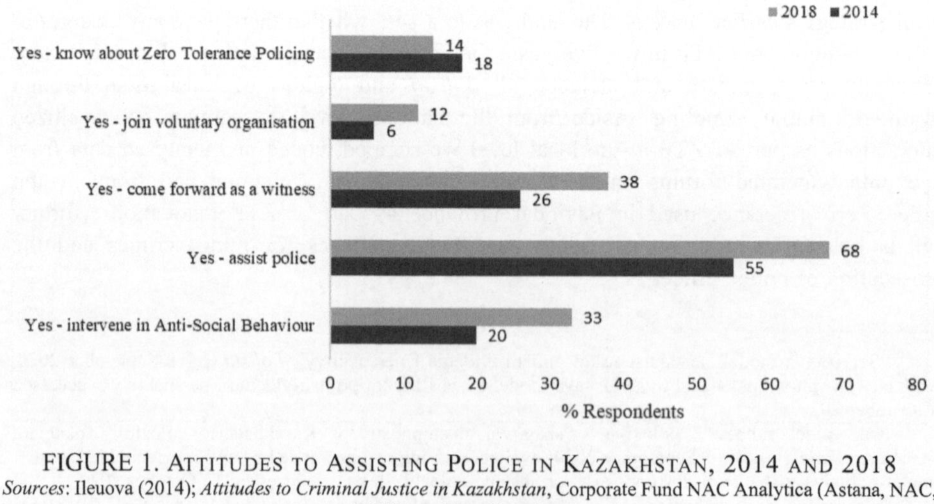

FIGURE 1. ATTITUDES TO ASSISTING POLICE IN KAZAKHSTAN, 2014 AND 2018
Sources: Ileuova (2014); *Attitudes to Criminal Justice in Kazakhstan*, Corporate Fund NAC Analytica (Astana, NAC, 2018), on file with authors.

In 2014, almost one quarter of Kazakhstanis stated that being labelled a *stukach'* (snitch) was an obstacle to cooperating with the police; there had been no statistically significant change to this by 2018. In the 2018 survey, 30% of respondents reported that where they lived people disapproved of helping the police. In a separate survey of 700 Nur-Sultan residents, conducted by an independent academic, fewer than 15% of respondents were prepared to inform the police about crime (Amirov 2017). A 2013 UNICEF-sponsored survey of 1,358 schoolchildren in four regions of Kazakhstan confirmed that snitching was severely stigmatised, and that snitches were ostracised and physically abused in schools across the country (Haarr 2013).

The attitudinal improvements in public vigilance were not matched by behavioural indicators either. In 2018 the first International Crime and Victimisation Survey (ICVS) ever conducted in Kazakhstan revealed extremely low levels of reporting crime to the police (van Dijk *et al.* 2018). Only one in five crimes were reported to the police in Kazakhstan, down from the 46% reporting rate recorded in the government-conducted 2012 survey.[33] For many crime types, including sexual crimes, theft of personal property and assault, reporting is lower in Kazakhstan than in other former Soviet countries such as Kyrgyzstan and Georgia, where the ICVS has also been carried out in recent years (GORBI 2011, 2015). Of those who did report crime in Kazakhstan, 44% were 'completely dissatisfied' and 21% 'rather dissatisfied' with their treatment by the police. The presidential administration itself had concluded in 2012 that a lack of politeness and civility towards citizens was the main obstacle to public assistance to the police.[34] In 2018, for victims of crime, this analysis of the problem still rang true.

Although few people had heard of ZTP, is it possible that they had been unconsciously affected by the policy to the point that the improvements in vigilant attitudes were caused by the policy? It seems unlikely. If ZTP were driving changes in attitudes towards vigilance and cooperation with police, then we would expect other indicators, such as attitudes to snitching and trust in the police, to also change. Here, the large gap between attitudes to involvement with the police and actual behaviour towards the police moreover suggests that respondents might be responding to cues about what answers are expected of them when surveyed; strong social desirability bias in survey responses has been shown to be a particular problem in Kazakhstan (Javeline 1999). In this case, while attitudes in the abstract change, actual behaviour remains the same: Kazakhstanis avoid contact with the police even when they are themselves the victim of a crime.

Citizen–police interactions: evidence from the ZTP apps

To investigate behaviour towards the police further, we analysed citizen engagement and police responses to this on social media forums and apps developed as part of ZTP policy

[33]'Gosudarstvennaya programma dal'neishei modernizatsii provookhranitel'noi sistemy', *General'naya Prokuratura Respubliki Kazakhstan*, 31 December 2013, available at: http://prokuror.gov.kz/rus/gosudarstvo/o-merah-po-dalneyshemu-razvitiyu-pravoohranitelnoy-sistemy/gosudarstvennaya-programma, accessed 29 January 2020.

[34]'Prikaz Ministra vnutrennikh del Respubliki Kazakhstan ot 29 dekabrya 2014 goda No. 957', available at: https://online.zakon.kz/Document/?doc_id=33055672, accessed 29 January 2020.

in a few Kazakhstani regions. We scraped data from a bespoke app called 'Zero Tolerance Pavlodar' launched by the local procurators and used in the city of Pavlodar and neighbouring Ekibastuz, Kachirskii and Aktogaskii districts within the Pavlodar province.[35] We also scraped data from two forums created on Telegram by the Prosecutor's Office for the Saryarka district in Kazakhstan's capital city and the town of Satpayev in the Karagandy province entitled 'Legal Order Saryarka/Satpayev' (*Pravoporyadok Saryarka/Satpayev*). In both the Telegram forums and the app, we analysed the data in terms of content: what people were asking for help with; how people were asking for help (text, photos, audio/visual recordings); from whom they were asking for help; and the state's response. We were primarily interested in police response. We also looked to see what, if anything, determined response time.[36]

Results show that citizens very rarely engaged with these apps or forums to report crime or administrative violations. Overwhelmingly, citizens utilised these mediums for complaining about municipal services and, in many cases, the police either did not respond or responded slowly. Nouns used by users of the ZT app in Pavlodar and surroundings were correlated and grouped by how frequently they occurred together. Five of the word groupings are given in Table 1.

The word groupings give a sense of the type of complaints received by authorities through the ZT app. They mainly concerned municipal services such as roads, children's play areas, street lighting, rubbish and water. Thus, in Pavlodar city, of 1,901 requests, only 513 or 30% were actually directed to the police.[37] In 39 of these requests to the police, the request was then redirected to other bodies. The police responded in 90% of cases, but the average response time within the app itself was 84 hours (see Table 2). We found no relationship between the number of comments from other app users about requests and the speed of the response; it remained slow regardless. Moreover, there was no relationship between the speed of the response and the end of quarterly police reporting periods when, we assumed, police might be more proactive or fearful of prosecutorial inquiries. Similar results in terms of response times, length of response and to whom the request was addressed held for Ekibastuz and the other Pavlodar regions, though the number of requests was much smaller.

[35] For users, the app offers a lot of advantages over the forums—posts are anonymous and complaints can be directed to a variety of public bodies. The app was thought up by the Prosecutor's Office, directed by the local government (*Akimat*), developed by a private firm and rolled out in spring 2017. 'Zapushcheno mobil'noe prilozhenie "Zero Tolerance"', *Pavlodartv.kz*, 19 May 2017, available at: https://pavlodartv.kz/ru/news/society/zapushcheno-mobilnoe-prilozhenie-zero-tolerance, accessed 16 October 2020. According to the developer, the app had been advertised using posters and billboards and there had been 20,000 downloads by October 2018 (personal communication with the authors, 23 October 2018).

[36] By 20 February 2019, there were 1,971 specific complaints on the ZT app for the four locations in Pavlodar *Oblast'*. The forums were harder to analyse. There were, for example, 17,417 messages on the Saryarka Telegram forum, yet many of these were not specific complaints but instead comments on other posts, general chat and so on. We did not attempt to categorise all of the content but focused on cases where there was a police response, to ascertain what the response was to and how quick it was.

[37] A total of 513 complaints were directed to the police; however, 39 of these were redirected to other non-policing bodies and seven were redirected to the police from those other bodies. This leaves a total of 481 complaints to police or 25% of the total.

TABLE 1
MOST FREQUENT GROUPINGS OF WORDS IN COMPLAINTS SENT TO THE 'ZERO TOLERANCE' APP IN PAVLODAR, APRIL 2018–FEBRUARY 2019

Group 1	*Group 2*	*Group 3*	*Group 4*	*Group 5*
Lighting	Yard	Violation	Water	Asphalt
Road	Area	Child	Sign	Crossing
House	House	Car	Well	Car
Lamp	Condition	Hole	Waters	Part
Action	Action	Number	Action	Lomov Street
Yard	Rubbish	Parking	Pavement	Road
Street	Year	Rule	Case	Action
Complaint	Terrace	Sign	Driver	Work
Area	Snow	Pavement	Car	Hour
Work	Region	Yard	Estate	Order

Source: Authors' own calculations.

TABLE 2
USAGE OF THE 'ZERO TOLERANCE' APP IN PAVLODAR, APRIL 2018–FEBRUARY 2019

Complaint directed to ...	*Number of complaints*	*Percentage*	*Average response time (hours)*	*Average length of response (words)*
Department for Housing and Communal Services, Public Transport and Roads of Pavlodar City	588	35	370	25
Department of Internal Affairs (Police)	513	30	84	48
Department for Housing Inspection of Pavlodar City	181	11	77	25
Pavlodar Heating Network (company)	66	4	142	69
Anti-Corruption Bureau, Pavlodar Oblast'	22	1	48	9
Other	318	19	111	69

Source: Authors' own calculations.

Police response times on the officially sanctioned Telegram forum for the Saryarka District in Nur-Sultan were much quicker; overall levels of engagement by police representatives were variable. A total of 17,417 messages had been sent in from the 617 members of the forum by 20 February 2019. Of these messages, 2,323 were interventions by police. Of those interventions, 794 were by a bot, and 1,529 by a police representative. This means one message from a police representative was posted for every ten messages sent in by citizens. On average it took a police representative 50 minutes to respond to a message when they did respond, using on average seven words. It took the bot seven hours, using 16 words.

Citizen engagement with the ZT app and ZT forums on Telegram indicated continued apathy towards support to the police in terms of citizens' actual behaviour, despite the reported attitudes concerning willingness in the abstract to assist the police. The app data suggest that citizens simply wanted better basic provision of public goods and used these online innovations to express their discontent with municipal authorities. They were rarely, if ever, willing to report crime or snitch on a neighbour, even in the anonymous Pavlodar ZTP app. Secondly, the data from the app and forums on response counts, response times and length of response indicated police mimicking of genuine attempts to produce security in close cooperation with citizens. Even officially, prosecutors across the country have criticised the local police and government officials for not carrying out ZTP action plans, instead falsifying statistics and failing to cultivate contacts with citizens.[38] By the end of February 2019, the ZTP Pavlodar app had stopped being used yet the procurators had made no public announcement about its discontinuation.

ZTP in Kazakhstan through the lens of official crime statistics

Perhaps the most salient indicator of the failure of police engagement with the public are the MVD's own reports showing that ordinary citizens helped police to catch on average between 2% and 4% of offenders with no change before and during ZTP. While the MVD boasted about 30,000 volunteers helping it to combat crimes and minor offences under the 2004 law 'On Participation of Citizens in the Maintenance of the Law and Order', prosecutors discovered that many of these volunteers existed on paper only (Amirov 2017). Indeed, municipalities provided much lower numbers of volunteers. For example, in September 2015, Astana police had 840 registered volunteers, and awarded the total of nine million tenge to over 700 of them (US$64 per volunteer) for 'active assistance in maintaining law and order' since the beginning of that year.[39] In 2016, the mayor of Shymkent, the third largest city in the country, had only 100 volunteers and was ordered to raise that number to 1,000. The mayor negotiated with the city employment office and police so that unemployed males could be given temporary (six-month) jobs in this role rather than volunteer. Recent university graduates would receive a monthly salary of

[38] 'Prokurory raskritikovali realizatsiyu proekta "Nulevaya terpimost'" v Mangistau', *Zakon.kz*, 28 September 2014, available at: https://www.zakon.kz/4656247-4656247-prokurory-raskritikovali-realizaciju.html, accessed 16 October 2020; 'Prokurory obvinyayut mestnye vlasti v simulyatsii raboty po aktsii "Nulevaya terpimost'"', *RIKA-TV*, 28 May 2015, available at: http://rikatv.kz/news/prokurory-obvinyayut-mestnye-vlasti-v-simulyatsii-raboty-po-aktsii-nulevaya-terpimost.html, accessed 16 October 2020; 'Prokuratura goroda raskritikovala rabotu temirtauskikh politseiskikh', *Etemirtau.kz*, 10 August 2015, available at: http://etemirtau.kz/news/city/3205-prokuratura-goroda-raskritikovala-rabotu-temirtauskih-policeyskih.html, accessed 16 October 2020; 'Prokurory raskritikovali rabotu politseiskoi sluzhby v Pavlodare', *Informburo.kz*, 5 March 2017, available at: https://informburo.kz/novosti/prokurory-raskritikovali-rabotu-policeyskoy-sluzhby-v-pavlodare.html, accessed 16 October 2020; 'Prokuror YuKO predlozhil uprazdnit mestnuyu politseiskuyu sluzhbu', *Informburo.kz*, 17 April 2017, available at: https://informburo.kz/novosti/prokuror-yuko-predlozhil-uprazdnit-mestnuyu-policeyskuyu-sluzhbu.html, accessed 16 October 2020.

[39] 'Obshchestvennykh pomoshchnikov politsii pooshchrili v Astane', *DailyNews.kz*, 28 September 2015, available at: http://dailynews.kz/society/obschestvennyh_pomoschnikov_politsii_pooschrili_v_astane, accessed 18 October 2020.

56,000 tenge, while those with a high school diploma would receive 40,000 tenge. Even with the incentive of payment, this policy only raised the numbers of 'volunteers' to just 218, out of a planned 1,358 volunteers needed.[40] As procurators later discovered, however, most provincial authorities had transferred the award amounts to the police chiefs instead of municipalities, who, then, awarded these amounts to their cronies, not to citizen-activists who had actually reported crimes (Kollektiv avtorov 2018, pp. 85–9).

Police also failed to engage with ZTP in other ways. For example, in 2014 and 2015 procurators reported that officials in the Mangystau province had failed to produce mandated videos and booklets about law-abiding behaviour.[41] In 2018, police chiefs in that province blamed residents for still tolerating minor offences as petty hooliganism, drinking and smoking in public places grew steadily year on year. In 2019, they announced that they had allocated 2.6 million tenge to make 103 awards of 25,250 tenge (US$66) to volunteers who had helped solve crimes and administrative offences that calendar year.[42]

A likely reason that police attempts to enact ZTP remained at a surface level is the fear that the policy would enable civilian oversight of police work and thus erode the discretion and impunity enjoyed by police. In Kostanai province the police chief publicised an example of a traffic police patrol caught for bribery through a tip off from drivers, and advertised the hotline for reporting police abuses.[43] Similarly, police in the Zhambyl province reported a rise in traffic violations by police officers and threatened to publish information about the punishment of each offending officer and their superior in the media, with a view to creating 'zero tolerance in society'.[44] Two police officers in Almaty city (September 2016) and in the West Kazakhstan province (February 2017) were fired after photos and

[40]'Kogo voz'mut v pomoshchniki Mestnoi politseiskoi sluzhbe Shymkenta', *Otyrar.kz*, 3 February 2017, available at: https://otyrar.kz/2017/02/kogo-vozmut-v-pomoshhniki-mestnoj-policejskoj-sluzhbe-shymkenta/, accessed 18 October 2020.

[41]'Prokuratura Aktau: "Akimat i politseiskie ispolnyayut plan po 'Nulevoi terpimosti' formal'no"', *Tumba.kz*, 30 August 2014, available at: https://online.zakon.kz/Document/?doc_id=31596137, accessed 18 October 2020; 'Prokurory raskritikovali realizatsiyu proekta "Nulevaya terpimost'" v Mangistau', *Zakon.kz*, 28 September 2014, available at: https://www.zakon.kz/4656247-4656247-prokurory-raskritikovali-realizaciju.html, accessed 16 October 2020; 'Itogi raboty po printsipu "nulevoi terpimosti" obsudili v akimate Aktau', *Lada.kz*, 7 August 2015, available at: https://www.lada.kz/aktau_news/society/30427-itogi-raboty-po-principu-nulevoy-terpimosti-obsudili-v-akimate-aktau.html, accessed 18 October 2020; 'Rabota pushchena na samotek … ', *Ogni Mangystau*, 30 September 2015, available at: http://nomad.su/?a=13-201509300003, accessed 18 October 2020.

[42]'Politsiya Mangistau: Grazhdane budut voznagrazhdat'sya za sodeistvie pravookhranitel'nym organam', *Lada.kz*, 26 February 2019, available at: https://www.lada.kz/aktau_news/society/68372-policiya-mangistau-grazhdane-budut-voznagrazhdatsya-za-sodeystvie-pravoohranitelnym-organam.html, accessed 18 October 2020.

[43]'Printsip "nulevoi terpimosti" otnosisya i k deyatel'nosti sotrudnikov politsii—DVD Kostanaiskoi oblasti', *Zakon.kz*, 27 February 2013, available at: http://online.zakon.kz/Document/?doc_id=31338230, accessed 18 October 2020.

[44]'V Zhambylskoi oblasti rastet kolichestvo DTP, sovershaemykh samimi politseiskimi', *Zakon.kz*, 15 April 2013, available at: https://www.zakon.kz/4551909-v-zhambylskojj-oblasti-rastet.html, accessed 18 October 2020.

videos of them urinating in public had gone viral on social media.[45] Yet these cases were exceptions that proved the rule. Many police officers objected to this citizen-initiated policing of the police, especially with the use of filming on smartphones, while the top MVD officials disagreed on the legality of citizens' videotaping police actions. Facing numerous viral videos about drunk, sleeping, rude and violent police officers, the MVD finally announced in 2017 that only drivers had the right to video traffic police while nobody had the right to record police investigative activities.[46]

The extent of the pushback against the possibility of greater civilian control and oversight through ZTP is revealed in the number of police officials charged with corruption. Official statistics show an upward trend in law-enforcement officials charged with breaking the law during ZTP, but the overall change is minimal. In 2015, the figure stood at 528; it increased to 637 by 2018 and dropped to 524 in 2019. Breaking this down to corruption charges within the police only, the figures stood at 203 in 2014, increased to 307 in 2017 and dropped to 165 in 2019.[47] These campaign-style zigzagging trends are still miniscule considering the scale of police bribe-taking in Kazakhstan. The ICVS reports that in a one-year period (June 2017–May 2018), 5.2% of Kazakhstanis were victims of official bribe-seeking and in almost half of these cases the bribe-seeker was a police officer (van Dijk *et al.* 2018). Taking only the adult population of Kazakhstan into account, the ICVS police bribery figures suggest around 400,000 incidents of police bribery every year in Kazakhstan. These calculations are most likely very conservative in that they only capture when a bribe has been solicited and exclude instances of citizen-initiated bribery. Certainly, there are other ways of dealing with wayward officers other than criminal prosecution, such as discrete dismissal or requesting resignation. However, dismissals have not increased. By the end of 2018, Kazakhstan's MVD was as large as ever, counting 160,000 staff, including a police force of 87,000 officers, a figure larger than that of Kazakhstan's army. The MVD has one officer for every 212 citizens; more police proportionately than during the Soviet period.[48]

A further police incentive to resist ZTP is that, if the public became more active in reporting crime, it would create more work for the police. As part of ZTP, police were required to alter the procedure of registering crime. Any violations reported to the police had to be recorded, regardless of whether the case was pursued or not. Police resistance

[45] '"Pisayushchii politseiskii" uvolen', *Matritca.kz*, 29 September 2016, available at: http://www.matritca.kz/news/36293-pisayuschiy-policeyskiy-uvolen.html, accessed 18 October 2020; 'Pisayushchii politseiskii v ZKO: strazha poryadka snyali na video v otklyuchke', *Informburo.kz*, 3 February 2017, available at: https://informburo.kz/novosti/pisayushchiy-policeyskiy-v-zko-strazha-poryadka-snyali-na-video-v-otklyuchke.html, accessed 18 October 2020.

[46] 'Zakonno li snimat' na video sotrudnikov dorozhnoi politsii', *KazInform*, 14 June 2017, available at: https://www.inform.kz/ru/zakonno-li-snimat-na-video-sotrudnikov-dorozhnoy-policii_a3036019, accessed 18 October 2020.

[47] Official crime statistics are taken from the website of the Legal Statistics Committee of the General Procuracy of the Republic of Kazakhstan, available at: https://qamqor.gov.kz/portal/page/portal/POPageGroup/Services/Pravstat, accessed 18 October 2020.

[48] 'V 2019 godu dolzhna nachat'sya samaya masshtabnaya reforma MVD za 20 let. Chto khotyat izmenit'?', *Informburo.kz*, 3 January 2019, available at: https://informburo.kz/stati/v-2019-godu-dolzhna-nachatsya-samaya-masshtabnaya-reforma-mvd-za-20-let-chto-hotyat-izmenit.html, accessed 18 October 2020.

to these changes created the rationale behind hiring civilian non-police dispatchers to the 'neighbourhood watch' (*sosedskii prismotr*) programme in the North Kazakhstan province on the grounds that civilians had no incentive to ignore or hide information.[49] Moreover, reforms were made to the Code of Administrative Transgressions to simplify punishments for administrative violations worthy of a fine only. From now on, police had the power to impose fines for over 100 kinds of violations without taking the offender to court.[50] With this simplification, police have less leeway to hide the number of violations in their jurisdictions and are more frequently tasked with pursuing fines rather than criminal prosecutions (Tukiev & Parmankulova 2015). The subsequent increase in the number of recorded violations is shown in Table 3.

Looking at the statistics in more depth, however, suggests that, while the registering of violations has increased dramatically, it does not necessarily follow that the police are more vigorously pursuing the culprits. The data for 2016 reveal that fines are the most frequent form of punishment for administrative violations. While hundreds of thousands of fines are imposed, only a small percentage of them are actually paid and there is significant regional variation.[51] Table 4 provides 2016 data across selected regions and the national averages. Table 4 shows that fines were the most common form of punishment for administrative violations, yet those same fines have low collection rates. These data, once again, reveal a disconnection between the official ZTP rhetoric, the façade of increased police action and the reality. A group of experts from the Nur-Sultan-based Law Enforcement Academy who studied the impact of ZTP using official statistics between 2014 and 2017 also confirmed that the rise in registration and punishment of minor crimes was 'a consequence of the launch of just another campaign' and was not the result of higher societal intolerance towards minor crimes (Kollektiv avtorov 2018, pp. 40–3).

All the above data point to the fact that ZTP has not brought about any significant changes in how policing is conducted in Kazakhstan. Police have engaged in limited outreach activities and half-heartedly supported innovations aimed at greater engagement with citizens. They have made attempts to bring corrupt colleagues to justice, but these efforts are dwarfed by overall levels of corruption. They have become more active in pursuing petty crime, but changes remain largely on paper. Meanwhile, the public, while apparently responding to cues about what constitutes a good citizen, in their actual behaviour still manifest an extreme scepticism towards the police. The main aims of ZTP as outlined in the official discourse—anti-corruption, reduction of petty crime and enhancing citizen vigilance—have all been obviated by politicians who prefer a slogan to a programme, a policing apparatus that enjoys high degrees of discretion and a citizenry that engages as little as possible.

[49]'Pravookhranitel'nye organy SKO vnedryayut programmu "Sosedskii prismotr"', *KazInform*, 12 July 2011, available at: https://www.inform.kz/ru/pravoohranitel-nye-organy-sko-vnedryayut-programmu-sosedskiy-prismotr_a2392805, accessed 18 October 2020.

[50]'Novshestva administrativnogo zakonodatel'stva', *Zakon.kz*, 20 May 2015, available at: https://online.zakon.kz/Document/?doc_id=35914668, accessed 18 October 2020.

[51]Official administrative fine statistics are taken from the website of the Legal Statistics Committee of the General Procuracy of the Republic of Kazakhstan, available at: https://qamqor.gov.kz/portal/page/portal/POPageGroup/Services/Pravstat, accessed 16 October 2020.

TABLE 3
REGISTERED MINOR OFFENCES IN KAZAKHSTAN, 2012–2017

	Year			
Offence	*2012*	*2013*	*2014*	*2017*
Petty hooliganism	36,002	65,232	68,289	60,000
Smoking in public	31,872	71,846	94,006	112,700
Street selling	270	ND	26,300	ND
Noise-making	33,000	ND	48,900	37,700
Public consumption of alcohol	137,800	ND	187,400	182,100
Littering	73,600	ND	114,700	124,200

Note: ND = no data.
Source: Committee of Legal Statistics of the General Procuracy of the Republic of Kazakhstan, available at: https://qamqor.gov.kz/portal/page/portal/POPageGroup/Services/Pravstat, accessed 29 January 2020.

TABLE 4
TYPE OF PUNISHMENT FOR ADMINISTRATIVE VIOLATIONS AND PERCENTAGE OF FINES COLLECTED IN KAZAKHSTAN, 2016

Type of punishment for administrative violation (%)				*Fines collected (selected regions; %)*			
Fine	*Warning*	*Arrest*	*Other*	*Astana*	*Almaty*	*Zhambyl Oblast'*	*Kazakhstan*
77	17	2	4	45	51	39	55

Source: Committee of Legal Statistics of the General Procuracy of the Republic of Kazakhstan, available at: https://qamqor.gov.kz/portal/page/portal/POPageGroup/Services/Pravstat, accessed 29 January 2020.

Conclusion

This essay has demonstrated that ZTP has had little effect in Kazakhstan and failed on its own terms. The function of government to carry out reform and improve public services is a highly institutionalised accepted understanding or 'myth' (Meyer & Rowan 1977). Yet, in Kazakhstan, the government's declarations of reform are decoupled from the reality of the compromises on modernisation goals imposed by the consequences of potential police disloyalty, vested bureaucratic interests in the ministries and organisational inertia within local police forces. There is also an accepted understanding of the purpose of having a police force: to control crime efficiently. Yet, everyday tasks for the police in Kazakhstan are conducted by low-salaried officers working within an inertial and reactionary organisational culture burdened by Soviet operational legacies, with few incentives to work more, make changes or overcome sunk costs in the *status quo* (Trochev & Slade 2019). In Meyer and Rowan's (1977) terms, the police formally maintain legitimating myths and ceremonial rules; they pay lip service to the concept of reform while upholding a gap between outward expression and internal operations. Finally, citizens understand that civic participation and assistance in the creation of social order is something they should do. Citizens outwardly acknowledge a willingness to assist police in the creation of social order in the abstract; this is, however, decoupled from their actual everyday experiences and behaviours.

The decoupling demonstrated in this essay, we argue, can be explained logically by the perverse incentives that begin with the resolution of 'the politician's dilemma'—that is, reform and face police disloyalty, or do not reform and accept police abuses—in favour of the latter: police loyalty in return for police discretion. This resolution to the dilemma is much more likely in authoritarian regimes, where police loyalty is a necessary condition for their survival. Without the pressure valve of elections with genuine political alternatives, authoritarian rulers are reliant on police loyalty to suppress challenges to their rule. This dependency means authoritarian rulers allow little civilian oversight of the police and have few reliable feedback mechanisms for monitoring the latter's performance. However, all successful police reformers require public engagement to change the police, and this in turn depends upon a civic culture that authoritarianism diminishes. These contradictory realities produced the failure of police reform in Kazakhstan. Authoritarian modernisation has its limits. These links are identifiable by the extent of the decoupling of institutionalised myths about organisations' roles and functions from the realities of organisations' everyday incentives and practices. Police reform, as we have tried to show in this essay, provides an opportunity to study how this decoupling works and thus sketch where these limits are.

References

Amirov, A. (2017) 'Realizatsiya printsipa "nulevoi terpimosti" k besporyadku i pravonarusheniyam v Respublike Kazakhstan: problemy i puti resheniya', *Molodoi uchenyi*, 21, 282, available at: https://moluch.ru/archive/155/43819/, accessed 29 January 2020.

Beck, A. & Chistyakova, Y. (2002) 'Crime and Policing in Post-Soviet Societies: Bridging the Police/Public Divide', *Policing and Society*, 12, 2.

Beck, A. & Chistyakova, Y. (2004) 'Closing the Gap Between the Police and the Public in Post-Soviet Ukraine: A Bridge Too Far?', *Police Practice and Research*, 5, 1.

Biekenov, N. (2017) 'Some Conceptual Issues of Organization and Activities of Local Police Service in the Republic of Kazakhstan', *Munitsipal'naya sluzhba. Pravovye voprosy*, 2, available at: https://elibrary.ru/item.asp?id=28914507, accessed 16 October 2020.

Bowling, B. (1999) 'The Rise and Fall of New York Murder: Zero Tolerance or Crack's Decline?', *British Journal of Criminology*, 39, 4.

Bowling, B. & Sheptycki, J. (2012) *Global Policing* (New York, NY, Russell Sage).

Bradford, B., Huq, A., Jackson, J. & Roberts, B. (2014) 'What Price Fairness When Security is at Stake? Police Legitimacy in South Africa', *Regulation & Governance*, 8, 2.

Bratton, W. J. (1997) 'Crime is Down in New York City: Blame the Police', in Dennis, N. (ed.) *Zero Tolerance: Policing the Free Society* (London, IEA Health and Welfare Unit).

Davis, H. E. (2017) 'Broken and Disordered: Selected Critical Readings on Broken Windows Policing', *Legal Reference Services Quarterly*, 36, 3–4.

Friesendorf, C. (2019) 'Police Reform in Ukraine as Institutional Bricolage', *Problems of Post-Communism*, 66, 2.

Geddes, B. (1994) *Politician's Dilemma: Building State Capacity in Latin America* (Berkeley, CA, University of California Press).

Gel'man, V. (ed.) (2017) *Authoritarian Modernization in Russia: Dilemmas, Challenges and Constraints* (Oxford, Routledge).

Goldsmith, A. (2005) 'Police Reform and the Problem of Trust', *Theoretical Criminology*, 9, 4.

GORBI (2011) *International Crime and Victimization Survey: Georgia* (Tbilisi, Georgian Opinion Research Business International).

GORBI (2015) *International Crime and Victimization Survey: Kyrgyzstan*, Georgian Opinion Research Business International (Bishkek, Civic Union).

Greene, J. A. (1999) 'Zero Tolerance: A Case Study of Police Policies and Practices in New York City', *Crime & Delinquency*, 45, 2.

Haarr, R. (2013) *Assessment of Violence Against Children in Schools in Kazakhstan* (Astana, UNICEF), available at: https://www.unicef.org/kazakhstan/en/reports/assessment-violence-against-children-schools, accessed 29 January 2020.

Heathershaw, J. (2014) 'The Global Performance State: A Reconsideration of the Central Asian "Weak State"', in Reeves, M., Rasanayagam, J. & Beyer, J. (eds) *Ethnographies of the State in Central Asia: Performing Politics* (Bloomington, IN, Indiana University Press).

Ileuova, G. (2014) *Formirovanie novoi obshchestvennoi kul'tury, osnovannoi na printsipe 'nulevoi terpimosti' k besporyadku* (Almaty, OF 'TsSPI 'Strategiya').

Ileuova, G. & Simakova, O. (2014) 'Formation of a New Social Culture Based on the Principle of Disorder "Zero Tolerance"', *Aleumettanu-Sociology*, 2, 52, available at: http://iph.kz/doc/kz/226.pdf, accessed 29 January 2020.

Javeline, D. (1999) 'Response Effects in Polite Cultures: A Test of Acquiescence in Kazakhstan', *Public Opinion Quarterly*, 63, 1.

Johnston, L. (2003) 'From "Pluralisation" to "the Police Extended Family": Discourses on the Governance of Community Policing in Britain', *International Journal of the Sociology of Law*, 31, 3.

Kollektiv avtorov (2018) *Problemy formirovaniya nulevoi terpimosti k pravonarusheniyam v obshchestve: Nauchno-prakticheskoe posobie* (Astana, Akademiya Pravookhranitel'nykh Organov).

Kupatadze, A. (2016) 'Georgia's Break with the Past', *Journal of Democracy*, 27, 1.

LaPierre, B. (2012) *Hooligans in Khrushchev's Russia: Defining, Policing, and Producing Deviance During the Thaw* (Madison, WI, University of Wisconsin Press).

Light, M. (2014) 'Police Reforms in the Republic of Georgia: The Convergence of Domestic and Foreign Policy in an Anti-Corruption Drive', *Policing and Society*, 24, 3.

Lillis, J. (2018) *Dark Shadows: Inside the Secret World of Kazakhstan* (London, Bloomsbury).

Mami, K. (ed.) (2009) *Protivodeistvie korruptsii v sudebnoi sisteme* (Astana, Supreme Court of the Republic of Kazakhstan).

Marat, E. (2018) *The Politics of Police Reform: Society Against the State in Post-Soviet Countries* (Oxford, Oxford University Press).

Marat, E. (2019) 'Mimicking "Broken Windows" Policing in Post-Soviet Cities: Expanding Social Control in Uncertain Times', *Policing and Society*, 29, 9.

Meyer, J. W. & Rowan, B. (1977) 'Institutionalized Organizations: Formal Structure as Myth and Ceremony', *American Journal of Sociology*, 83, 2.

Nasuti, P. (2016) 'Administrative Cohesion and Anti-Corruption Reforms in Georgia and Ukraine', *Europe-Asia Studies*, 68, 5.

Nazarbayev, N. (2012) 'Strategy Kazakhstan 2050: New Political Course of the Established State', Speech delivered in Astana on 14 December, available at: https://strategy2050.kz/en/page/multilanguage/, accessed 29 January 2020.

Paneyakh, E. (2014) 'Faking Performance Together: Systems of Performance Evaluation in Russian Enforcement Agencies and Production of Bias and Privilege', *Post-Soviet Affairs*, 30, 2–3.

Pino, N. W. & Wiatrowski, M. D. (eds) (2016) *Democratic Policing in Transitional and Developing Countries* (Oxford, Routledge).

Rogov, I. (2009) 'Politika nulevoi tolerantnosti k prestupnosti i korruptsii: kommentarii k ukazu ot 22.04.2009g.', *Kazakhstanskaya Pravda*, 24 April.

Savage, S. (2003) 'Tackling Tradition: Reform and Modernization of the British Police', *Contemporary Politics*, 9, 2.

Simakova, O. (2015) 'The Investigation of Formation of a New Social Culture Based on the Principle of "Zero" Tolerance Culture for Offense', *Aleumettanu-Sociology*, 2, 86.

Skogan, W. G. (2008) 'Why Reforms Fail', *Policing and Society*, 18, 1.

Slade, G. (2012) 'Georgia's War on Crime: Creating Security in a Post-Revolutionary Context', *European Security*, 21, 1.

Slade, G. (2017) 'Punishment and State-building in Post-Soviet Georgia', in Heathershaw, J. & Schatz, E. (eds) *The Paradox of Power: The Logics of State Weakness in Eurasia* (Pittsburgh, PA, University of Pittsburgh Press).

Slade, G. & Kupatadze, A. (2017) 'Popular Punitiveness? Punishment and Attitudes to Law in Post-Soviet Georgia', *Europe-Asia Studies*, 69, 6.

Strakes, J. E. (2013) 'Political Opposition, External Threats, and Elite Responses: Analyzing Domestic Security Policy in Post-Rose Revolution Georgia', *Defense & Security Analysis*, 29, 4.

Sykes, G. W. (1985) 'The Functional Nature of Police Reform: The "Myth" of Controlling the Police', *Justice Quarterly*, 2, 1.

Taylor, B. D. (2014) 'Police Reform in Russia: The Policy Process in a Hybrid Regime', *Post-Soviet Affairs*, 30, 2–3.

Trochev, A. & Slade, G. (2019) 'Trials and Tribulations: Kazakhstan's Criminal Justice Reforms', in Caron, J. F. (ed.) *Kazakhstan and the Soviet Legacy: Between Continuity and Rupture* (Singapore, Palgrave).

Tukiev, A. S. & Parmankulova, B. A. (2015) 'O perspektivakh reformirovaniya administrativnogo zakonodatel'stva po itogam obobshcheniya praktiki primeneniya novogo Kodeksa Respubliki Kazakhstan ob administrativnykh pravonarusheniyakh', *Vestnik Instituta zakonodatel'stva i pravovoi informatsii Respubliki Kazakhstan*, 5, 41, available at: https://cyberleninka.ru/article/n/o-perspektivah-reformirovaniya-administrativnogo-zakonodatelstva-po-itogam-obobscheniya-praktiki-primeneniya-novogo-kodeksa, accessed 16 October 2020.

Tyler, T. R. (ed.) (2007) *Legitimacy and Criminal Justice: An International Perspective* (New York, NY, Russell Sage).

Tyler, T. R. & Fagan, J. (2008) 'Legitimacy and Cooperation: Why do People Help the Police Fight Crime in their Communities', *Ohio State Journal of Criminal Law*, 6, 1.

Van Dijk, J., van Kesteren, J., Slade, G. & Trochev, A. (2018) *Issledovanie 'Otsenka urovnya bezopasnosti naseleniya i doveriya k pravookhranitel'nym organam'* (Astana, Delegation of European Union in Kazakhstan), available at: https://www.researchgate.net/publication/340004372_criminal_victimization_in_Kazakhstan, accessed 16 October 2020.

Wilson, J. Q. & Kelling, G. L. (1982) 'Broken Windows', *Atlantic Monthly*, 249, 3.

Wilson, A. (2005) *Virtual Politics: Faking Democracy in the Post-Soviet World* (New Haven, CT, Yale University Press).

Propaganda and the Police: The Softer Side of State Control in China

SUZANNE E. SCOGGINS

Abstract

Confronting a rising tide of police–society conflict, China's Ministry of Public Security (MPS) is stepping up its propaganda campaigns. From television specials to social media accounts, this essay identifies the MPS's public outreach efforts and tracks their prevalence and development. Using data from content analysis of policy documents and interviews with ministry officials, I argue that public relations campaigns have grown alongside the agency's sometimes violent efforts to enforce law and order. Together with stability maintenance and the appearance of crime control, these tactics are part of a sophisticated and multipronged strategy to underpin regime legitimacy that extends far beyond brute force coercion.

IN APRIL 2016, *JINGCHA TEXUN YING* (POLICE TRAINING CAMP) joined the ranks of reality television shows streaming on screens around China. The first episode featured dramatic shots from atop the iconic CCTV building in Beijing, high speed car chases, and panoramic views of a police training campus nestled somewhere in the hills of Beijing on a perfect blue-sky day. Good-natured hosts introduced six police officers—five males and one female of various ages and experience levels from around the country—and began the reality television convention of putting the contestants through a series of increasingly difficult challenges. The camera followed the officers' ups and downs as they tried to turn police cars around in small glass enclosures or drive motorcycles around mannequins and through narrow passageways in a quest to catch a fake terrorist holding a child at knifepoint. The description of the episode on CCTV's website notes that the programme will 'restore the image of the People's Police' by showing them in real combat.[1]

The show, in and of itself, would be unremarkable were it not part of a coordinated effort by the Ministry of Public Security (MPS) to showcase the strength and humanity of its frontline officers. In fact, *Police Training Camp* is the crown jewel in the MPS's new public outreach strategy. It joins other television specials produced by CCTV, MPS, and provincial stations that focus on the world of frontline policing, aiming to present a more

Research for some of the interviews in the article was conducted when the author was a doctoral candidate at UC Berkeley.

[1]*Police Training Camp*, 2016, available at: http://tv.cctv.com/2016/05/01/VIDEO1LPJDiDMoPbpuBviaSp160501.shtml, accessed 31 January 2019.

sympathetic view of police officers by highlighting the cases they solve and the people they help. Taken together with recent improvements to the organisation's social media presence, these efforts constitute a sleek new campaign designed to reveal a more positive, reform-oriented image of the police.

This strategy is not out of character for an organisation that has long espoused communist-era rhetoric about listening to the masses and adhering to the 'mass line' (Du 1997). The recent push, however, raises a broader question: why should police in an authoritarian regime care about their image? Even in the most democratic of regimes, policing is about exercising power over people in ways that often involve coercion and force. In this respect, China is no exception. Ruled by a single party regime intent on prioritising 'stability maintenance', the MPS is under orders to keep protests in check and crime low. It would seem that the Chinese police have neither the time nor the inclination to concern themselves with public opinion. Why then, are they pouring resources into public relations at a time when police funding remains uneven (Greitens 2017) and scarce (Xie 2013)?

My research finds that, rather than eschewing attention to public opinion, the ministry's public relations campaigns have grown in recent years due to the proliferation of new media opportunities and the organisation's larger commitment to reinforcing regime stability in new and innovative ways. This finding fleshes out the MPS's multipronged strategy to underscore regime legitimacy, which also depends on stability maintenance and the appearance of crime control (Xu 2017). Other facets of this strategy may be more familiar to readers. The Communist Party's prioritisation of stability maintenance is well documented (Xie 2012; Trevaskes 2013; Yang 2017), and the police and the People's Armed Police (PAP) are arguably the most active agents in efforts to pursue regime stability through tactics such as quickly stamping out protests and preventing the spread of dissent.[2] However, analysis of policy statements reveals that public outreach is another, softer side of the ministry's strategy to promote regime legitimacy. To this end, we see the police bureaucracy engaging in efforts to win the hearts and minds of the public, perhaps hoping to offset the negative effects that are a necessary by-product of stability-maintenance activities and coercive policing more generally. While these efforts are not as vital to regime stability as sustained economic growth, they nevertheless demonstrate that the police bureaucracy is engaged in efforts to undergird the regime that take advantage of new media opportunities and are far more refined than brute force coercion.

To assess the ministry's intent to use public outreach as a strategy to strengthen regime legitimacy, this essay draws upon policy statements, relevant policing journal articles, and interviews with ministry officials. Its findings are based on content analysis of 141 reform-related press releases and documents released by the ministry between 1993 and 2018. This information is supplemented with analysis of related articles published in *Policing Studies* (*Gongan yanjiu*), the official journal of the Chinese Police Studies Association, and triangulated with interviews conducted between 2011 and 2019 with

[2]An article published by *The Legal Daily* in 2012 reported that over 75% of mass incidents in China end after one day or less. '2012 nian qunti xing shijian yanjiu baodao', *Legal Daily*, 27 December 2012, available at: http://www.legaldaily.com.cn/index_article/content/2013-01/05/content_4109610.htm?node=5954, accessed 31 January 2019. For a discussion of recent crackdowns on dissent, see Tang *et al.* (2015).

ministry officials at the provincial and central levels. Gaining access to populations of this nature is difficult but not impossible (Scoggins 2014). To preserve the anonymity of respondents, footnotes reveal minimal information about informants and the year in which the interview was conducted.

This essay proceeds in five parts to make the case that recent public relations campaigns are part of a broader strategy to pursue regime legitimacy. The first section details the history of the police bureaucracy's public outreach strategies and community involvement. The second section outlines the need for these campaigns by reviewing recent evidence of state–society conflict. In the third section, I present evidence of the current campaign push and analyse documents from the ministry and other government sources to draw a link between current outreach efforts and calls for the institution to improve its public image. The fourth section assesses these public relations campaigns in the context of the ministry's grander strategy to strengthen regime legitimacy, and the conclusion provides preliminary insight into how the strategy has been received by the public.

History of the Chinese police and public outreach

Policing in China is governed from the top down, although control over the frontlines is largely decentralised due to the ministry's limited resources. The National People's Congress establishes the policy agenda and the Ministry of Public Security formulates rules and regulations that are transmitted to the provincial public security bureaus that oversee municipal or county departments and stations. Local governments also exercise a considerable degree of control over local police activities since they provide the funding for the day-to-day operations of stations. Because much of policing in China is a local endeavour rooted in the relationship between the police stations and the community, most of the everyday interactions between the police and the public occur on the streets. These interactions allow for some local variation as different stations—and different officers—adopt various techniques for dealing with the public. Nevertheless, the grander strategies of public engagement are officially dictated by the Ministry of Public Security in Beijing and its public relations department. This essay looks at the policies of the latter, since local stations and officers are often too busy toiling under poor working conditions to do much innovating in the area of public relations (Scoggins & O'Brien 2016).

Although it may seem odd for police in an authoritarian regime to care about public opinion, China's public security apparatus has a long history of reaching out to the masses. In the 1950s, the 'mass line' (*qunzhong luxian*) was a defining feature of police work and was interpreted by MPS to mean that officers should pay special attention to the public or 'masses' by working with them and keeping their interests in mind (Du 1997; Wong 2001; Dutton 2005). In many ways, the mass line was an attempt to ease the inevitable tension between policing and communism, since police by their very nature are agents of state enforcement, charged with using a variety of coercive means over the masses. In emphasising that police departments must listen to and maintain contact with the masses through formalised associations, including neighbourhood public security committees (*zhibaohui*), the Communist Party was able to narrow the gap between the police and the public while simultaneously providing benefits to an understaffed force that needed more eyes and ears on the ground. Incorporating the masses into the mission of the police thus expanded the reach of the public security bureaucracy at a time when it faced formidable criminal and political threats (Dutton 2000, 2005).

The local neighbourhood public security committees that emerged from police leaders' adherence to the mass line during the Mao era were established across the country. These committees were made up of local cadres and members of the community—often retirees—who worked together with the police on a number of fronts. Aiming to root out local crime, the committee acted as a bridge between the police and the masses, thus serving as an extension of the police (Dai & Huang 1993; Chen 2002). In many areas, they also worked with neighbourhood people's mediation committees (*renmin tiaojie weiyuanhui*) to settle local disputes and domestic conflicts. Together, these groups served as supplemental forces of social control (Zhang *et al.* 1996) that fulfilled the party's imperative to incorporate the ideas and opinions of the masses into public security work.

Rather than fading away as cultural artefacts of the Mao era, these institutions and ideas about connecting with the masses have persisted into the reform era (1978–present). Ministry press releases periodically draw on some version of mass line language, and police training institutes typically stress the role of the police as servants of the people who must listen to and accept the supervision of the masses (Bracey 1989, p. 132).[3] Moreover, Chinese policing journals[4] continue to publish articles about incorporating elements of the mass line into criminal investigations (Li & Beckley 2018). In terms of institutions, research shows that public security committees proliferated between 1986 and 1997 (Chen 2002). Committee members—who often stand on street corners or at the entrance of residential blocks and are easily identified by red armbands—provide more than just surveillance. Continuing their role as a bridge between the police and the masses, they also distribute legal materials, educate residents about laws and rights, and visit offenders and their families.

Since the early 1980s, police in China have also adopted new measures of community outreach and engagement. The implementation of team policing strategies and resident input efforts through the public security committees has led a number of scholars to draw parallels between policing in China and community policing in the West (Jiao 1995, 2001; Wang & Wong 2012). The government has also introduced new reporting mechanisms that demonstrate an effort to understand and gauge public perceptions of experiences with local police. The 1995 Police Law allowed residents to file official complaints with police departments or the people's procuratorate, and the 1989 Administrative Litigation Law gave residents the right to sue government agencies, including the police (Ma 1997, pp. 128–30). In the early 2000s, the ministry established hotlines for city and rural residents who wish to complain about the local police. Since 2013, those lines have been consolidated into the 12389 hotline, which connects directly to the Ministry of Public Security Reporting Centre (*Gonganbu Jubao Zhongxin*).

[3]For example, in late 2014, MPS head Guo Shengkun issued a statement on the importance of linking police reform to public opinion. In the speech, Guo stressed the need for police across levels to address social concerns and focus on meeting the expectations of the public. 'Guo Shengkun: jianchi wenti daoxiang minyi yinling quanmian shenhua gongan gaige', *CPC News*, 17 October 2017, available at: http://cpc.people.com.cn/n/2014/1017/c87228-25857762.html, accessed 31 January 2019.

[4]In addition to national level journals, each public security college and university in China publishes at least one law or police academic journal.

Some of these strategies serve multiple purposes. Public security committees help understaffed departments work around some of their manpower issues, and reporting mechanisms provide the ministry with details about local police misconduct and public dissatisfaction with how laws are implemented. In one interview,[5] a ministry official praised the hotlines: 'supervision of the lower levels remains a problem, but the hotlines are very helpful .... In the past, our main way of getting information from the local level was to send a team there or read the news'.[6] Such practical applications aside, these strategies and programmes demonstrate the desire of the party and the police leadership to connect with residents in ways that we would not expect from a heavy-handed coercive apparatus. Policing strategies in China thus extend well beyond basic crime control or political repression and take a more nuanced approach to public relations that aims to counterbalance public dissatisfaction with the police.

The need for public outreach

To an international audience, it is no secret that police efforts to secure what the Chinese government terms a 'harmonious society' and enforce stability maintenance are anything but harmonious. Strategies of stability maintenance (*weiwen*) have received much attention since the term entered wide use in the early 2000s, and the phrase itself is now nearly synonymous with police violence and coercion. China watchers are familiar with photos depicting heavily armed police forces putting down protesters in the name of stability maintenance, and the reports coming out of western Xinjiang suggest an unprecedented militarisation of policing that is marked by heavy investments in coercive capacity (Zenz & Leibold 2017). While these activities have captured international attention, their domestic impact is less certain. Images and stories about *weiwen* activities are often erased—or 'harmonised' (*bei hexie*) in the words of netizens on WeChat and Weibo—and we know that government leaders move quickly to censor articles about mass incidents, especially with regard to sensitive topics.[7]

Perhaps of greater detriment to police–society relations outside of sensitive areas are the widely discussed scandals that highlight police corruption and brutality. Stories of everyday police encounters that end in violence or death are known to strike a chord with the Chinese public, much as they do elsewhere, and the biggest such scandal in recent years is the Lei Yang case. Lei was a young environmental researcher and new father who died in May 2016 while in the custody of Beijing city police. Lei was reportedly on his way to the airport to pick up relatives who were coming into town to see his new baby when he had a run-in with local police outside a brothel. Family members say police unfairly entrapped Lei and later lied about the circumstances

[5]Due to political sensitivities surrounding the research and in order to protect the anonymity of all human subjects, only the year and general title of interviewees are given here and in subsequent footnotes.

[6]Interview with MPS official, Beijing, 2012. Although the media in China is state controlled, stories about local official and police misconduct are often reported in the news. In some cases, this coverage is later censored.

[7]See for example censorship directives obtained by *China Digital Times* that instructed journalists and editors not to spread articles, photos, or videos of events leading up to a riot in Tangshan, Xinjiang (Wade 2017).

surrounding his death. The incident went viral on Chinese social media, where netizens railed against the official account and what many saw as the unchecked authority of local police. Lei's status as an ordinary person who was believed to have been in the wrong place at the wrong time caused some commentators to ask whether they themselves could become the next Lei Yang.[8] The case garnered so much attention that even President Xi Jinping weighed in on the matter by releasing a statement that admonished local police to adhere to the law.[9] Although the officers involved were ultimately not found guilty of misconduct, the ministry takes such incidents seriously. Fu Hualing has argued that police reform in China is often driven by scandal, citing a series of brutal incidents in the early 2000s that gave former Minister of Public Security Zhou Yongkang enough momentum to implement key reforms such as the Five Prohibitions Campaign (Fu 2005).

Aside from well-publicised scandals, perceptions of the police are also coloured by reports of brutality against civilians that emerge in local news reports or on video-sharing sites such as iQIYI or Tencent Video. Evidence of police–society conflict is often short on details, but because local news clips or user videos are more difficult to search and slightly less likely to be 'harmonised' by censors, such reports tend to remain in the public realm for a longer period of time. Since the subject of police–society conflict is not universally forbidden, local news outlets periodically publish stories of police brutality. In one such incident in 2016, multiple news outlets reported that local police in Gansu province severely beat two students who were caught filming police officers. Several of these accounts included pixelated photos of the students' backs.[10] Individuals also upload videos that show police–society clashes, such as a fight that broke out between workers and police in Henan province in 2012 or an incident in which officers in Hebei province brutally beat four individuals said to be local gang members in 2016.[11] Sometimes such conflicts result in serious injury, as in the case of police officers in Shandong province in 2016 who were injured after intervening in a fight.[12] At other times, they may result in the death of civilians or officers, as did one altercation between police and residents in Heilongjiang province in 2008.[13] Incidents of everyday conflict do not always make the national news or result in viral videos, yet their availability to the public may further necessitate damage control by the state.

[8]For a selection of social media reactions to the Lei Yang incident, see Koetse (2016).

[9]'Commentary: Don't Exploit Powers in the Name of Law Enforcement. Did you hear what Xi said, Police?', *People's Daily Online*, 21 May 2016, available at: http://en.people.cn/n3/2016/0521/c90000-9061035.html, accessed 31 January 2019.

[10]'Jingfang huiying "daxuesheng pigu bei jingcha dakai hua": wang chuang shushi', *Xinhua News*, 18 May 2016, available at: http://china.huanqiu.com/article/2016-05/8943938_2.html, accessed 31 January 2019.

[11]The videos and articles referenced are no longer available online at their original links. For additional details, please contact the author directly.

[12]'Shandong minjing bei qun ou darenzhe xi bendi qiye laoban bei xing ju', *Sina*, 15 April 2016, available at: http://finance.sina.com.cn/sf/news/2016-04-15/113127355.html, accessed 17 August 2020.

[13]'Harbin yiming daxuesheng bei minjing huohuo dasi', *Radio Free Asia*, 13 October 2008, available at: https://www.rfa.org/cantonese/news/police_killer-10132008112040.html, accessed 31 January 2019.

The new public relations and the police

From high-profile stability-maintenance activities and scandals to more mundane, everyday conflict with the masses, China's Ministry of Public Security has cause to concern itself with the organisation's public image. During the Mao and early reform eras, the MPS faced different challenges on this front. From 1949 to 1978, China operated under a Soviet-style propaganda state model in which political information was produced solely by the party and distributed hierarchically by the Central Propaganda Department and outlets such as the *People's Daily* and *Xinhua* (Esarey & Xiao 2011). Because the state controlled information flows, news of scandals, police misconduct, and even large protests were mostly contained. Now police leaders face a much thornier problem of information control where news of incidents in one locale can spread quickly across the web and social media. Although government censors work constantly to quell the online dissemination of rumours and other negative information, complete sanitisation of the internet remains impossible. In response, the ministry has updated its outreach efforts and is now waging a sophisticated public relations campaign that promotes the image of a competent, approachable, reform-oriented police organisation serving the needs of the people. These efforts are further aided by the proliferation of new media platforms, which the ministry is harnessing for the purpose of reaching the broadest possible audience.

Public outreach strategies—the softer side of policing

Media-savvy efforts to manage the public image of the police date back to the early 2000s when public security officials at all levels began routinely engaging the public through three platforms: television, social media, and promotional materials and signage that use cartoon characters to convey public security messages. Whether it was a Weibo post reminding drivers to slow down in foggy conditions or a sign adorned with a smiling cartoon police officer urging people to keep an eye on their personal belongings, these efforts represented a new push to engage the public by utilising the most popular and publicly accessible means of communication and entertainment. They also presented a friendlier, more approachable version of the police at a time when crime was steadily rising,[14] embodying the ministry's push to take active control of its image across the country.

Among these three categories of public relations efforts, the television productions are perhaps the most elaborate. The ministry's 'Grassroots Police Culture Group' (*Gongan wenhua jiceng xing*) was formed in 2006 and is known for over-the-top entertainment specials. These events typically follow in the tradition of other government productions, by utilising a variety show format filmed in front of a live audience, including catchy songs, dancing, skits, and audience pans of clapping spectators in uniform. Designed to tout the achievements of local police and to honour officers for their service to the country, the group's performances are geared towards local police officers, and members of the group frequently travel around the country to put on performances for

[14] According to national data from the *Law Yearbook of China*, the *per capita* number of criminal cases has been rising fairly steadily since 1950. In 2000 the average was 287.3 cases per 100,000 people. By 2016, that number was 642.7. For a complete chart of the changes over time, see Scoggins (2018, p. 87).

local or provincial departments.[15] Their specials also frequently run on the widely broadcast CCTV channels and thus disseminate positive images of the police to a national audience. Similar groups, known as *jingcha yishu tuan* (police officer art troupes), have been formed at the provincial and municipal levels and frequently put on performances in their area and beyond. In early January 2019, for example, the Deyang Municipal People's Government established a Deyang Economic Development Zone Police Art Troup to 'promote police culture' through art performances.[16]

As the previous description of the *Police Training Camp* reality show suggests, the ministry is also creating programmes that are more exclusively geared towards engaging the general population. In these specials, producers trade consolidated television show tropes for public outreach programming that features a more realistic version of local police activities. Shifting the venue from auditoria to actual police stations and field sites, this new programming uses footage of real officers in the field solving problems and helping residents, albeit through carefully edited or staged clips. For example, one CCTV special from 2017 focused on five local police officers from around the country who had saved lives or solved important cases. The programme honoured the officers with the designation of 'Role Model Police' (*Gongan kaimo*), telling their stories by interspersing real case footage with re-enactment shots that focused on the skills, dangers, and hardships of their jobs.[17] Although the abovementioned Grassroots Police Culture Group and the local and provincial police officer art troupes are still active, this grittier version of public relations programming is becoming more popular across the country, and many provincial bureaus now work with their local stations to mimic the style of CCTV programming.[18]

The ministry and police departments across the country also engage the public directly through social media platforms. As early as 2010, many police bureaus and stations opened Weibo accounts to communicate directly with the public about daily news, police activities, and other issues of interest, in addition to collecting potentially helpful information about cases (Ma 2013). At the time of writing, Weibo's popular Peaceful Beijing (*Pingan Beijing*) account had more than 12 million followers and over 55,000 posts. In March 2013, Peaceful Beijing also opened a WeChat account (a feature-rich social media platform similar to Facebook and WhatsApp) to catch the wave of users migrating to the newer, more popular platform as well as to provide more specific services to users.[19] Although most social media accounts do not have as many users as the relatively popular Peaceful Beijing, these social media platforms on WeChat and Weibo remain a popular way to reach

[15]On 20 July 2018, the group celebrated its 454th production on *Weibo*. See *Gongan wenhua jiceng hang*, 2019, available at: https://www.weibo.com/gawhjcx?is_all=1#_loginLayer_1548354364647, accessed 31 January 2019. For a history of the group, see '2013 nian "gongan wenhua jiceng hang" huodong Beijing jieshao', 31 October 2013, available at: http://www.mps.gov.cn/n2255079/n2255988/c4197422/content.html, accessed 31 January 2018.

[16]'Deyang jing kai qu jingcha yishutuan chengli', Denan City Government website, 14 January 2019, available at: http://www.deyang.gov.cn/xwdt/bmdt/908461.htm, accessed 17 August 2020.

[17]'Zhijing gongan kaimo', CCTV, 18 January 2017, available at: http://tv.cntv.cn/video/VSET100325286772/8be67540ab4340de8a88bd1de09dc753, accessed 17 August 2020.

[18]In 2018, for example, Shanghai Police helped produce and release a documentary called *Shanghai Police, Real Stories* (*Xunluo xianchang shilu*).

[19]'Shi gonganju kai weixin haijiao "Pingan Beijing"', *People's Daily*, 12 March 2013, available at: http://politics.people.com.cn/n/2013/0312/c70731-20754015.html, accessed 31 January 2019.

TABLE 1
POLICE WEIBO ACCOUNTS FOR CHINA'S TEN MOST POPULOUS CITIES AND THE EIGHT LARGEST CITIES IN HENAN PROVINCE

City	Account name*	Number of followers†	Number of posts†	City population (in millions)‡
Shanghai	People's Police Express Train	4,555,695	41,761	22.7
Beijing	Peaceful Beijing	12,531,681	59,827	20.4
Guangzhou	Guangzhou Public Security	5,737,239	67,876	18.8
Shenzhen	Shenzhen Public Security	3,689,562	58,077	12.2
Tianjin	Peaceful Tianjin	3,239,049	32,709	11.3
Chengdu	Peaceful Chengdu	943,422	10,567	10.7
Dongguan	Peaceful Dongguan	508,443	8,363	8.3
Wuhan	Peaceful Wuhan	1,910,999	75,967	7.6
Hangzhou	Hangzhou Public Security	479,831	17,623	7.6
Chongqing	Peaceful Chongqing	428,018	13,536	7.4
Zhengzhou, Henan	Peaceful Zhengzhou	2,330,441	29,885	3.68
Luoyang, Henan	Peaceful Luoyang	4,003,025	57,206	1.58
Xinxiang, Henan	Xinxiang Police Online	361,345	38,889	0.92
Anyang, Henan	Peaceful Anyang	294,962	29,153	0.91
Nanyang, Henan	Peaceful Anyang	307,486	21,884	0.90
Kaifeng, Henan	Peaceful Kaifeng	288,989	20,873	0.89
Pingdingshan, Henan	Peaceful Pingdingshan	995,809	21,576	0.86
Jiaozuo, Henan	Peaceful Jiaozuo	199,840	28,565	0.70

Notes: * Account information for the police-managed Weibo account with the most users for each city. Most cities have multiple departments and districts with additional Weibo accounts. † Follower and post counts collected on 15 January 2019. ‡ Population estimates for the first ten cities provided by China's National Bureau of Statistics. Population data for the eight major cities in Henan provided by 2010 census data ('2010 Population Census', National Bureau of Statistics of China, available at: http://www.stats.gov.cn/english/Statisticaldata/CensusData/, accessed 9 November 2020).

the public more directly and are used widely, if not uniformly, throughout China (Ma 2013). To better demonstrate the popularity and reach of the social media accounts, Table 1 shows user information for a sampling of Weibo accounts from China's ten largest cities as well as eight major cities in the randomly selected province of Hunan.[20]

As one might expect, the content on social media sites is mostly positive, running the gamut from stories of police officers helping the elderly to news of recent arrests. Following the conventions of Chinese social media, Peaceful Suzhou's Weibo account even posts messages that wish followers a good morning or evening, complete with pictures of pandas, sunflowers, or puppies.[21] Like the television programmes, social media accounts also post and repost stories that portray the police in a sympathetic light or discuss recent attacks against officers. These posts typically focus on the difficulty of the job the officers do, their loyalty to the country and their devotion to their work, and the suffering of their families when officers are injured or even killed in the line of duty.

[20]Data for Weibo are used rather than WeChat because of differences in how the platforms operate. Follower information for WeChat is not publicly accessible, and user counts for the WeChat followers may be higher, particularly in large cities.

[21]*Pingan Suzhou*, 2019, available at: https://www.weibo.com/suzhoujingfang, accessed 31 January 2019.

FIGURE 1. Cardboard Cartoon Police Officer at a Restaurant in Xian
Source: Author's photo, 2012.

In one example, law enforcement Weibo accounts from various localities posted details about Yang Xuefeng, a Chongqing municipal police officer who was murdered while working on traffic patrol during Chinese New Year in 2018.[22] After Yang stopped a resident for illegally allowing two people to ride on the back of his motorcycle, the angry motorist went home and returned with a knife, stabbing Yang repeatedly in the neck and back. News accounts highlight Yang's continued bravery during the attack. Yang eventually died of his injuries in a local hospital later that day. The story of Yang's death spread quickly on Weibo and was picked up by official accounts from the Ministry of Public Security Traffic Safety Department, local police stations, and even local courts, in addition to local and national news stations.

The police also rely on cartoon characters to present a friendlier image of the state. Perhaps inspired by similar outreach efforts in Japan, the Chinese police began using cartoon-style police officers on signage and promotional materials in the early 2000s.[23]

[22]'Minjing jiuzheng jiaotong weifa bei jiashiyuan cisi gonganbu fa yandian aidao', *China Police Net*, 19 February 2018, available at: http://www.ce.cn/xwzx/gnsz/gdxw/201802/19/t20180219_28202221.shtml, accessed 31 January 2019.

[23]In 1987, the Tokyo Metropolitan Police Department introduced Pipo-kun, a fuzzy, orange, mouse-like mascot for the department. All 47 prefectural police departments in Japan now have their own mascots. Sabine Fruhstuck explains that these mascots are designed to make 'an organization that is, at least in certain cases, charged with exercising state violence look unthreatening, warm, and fuzzy' (Todd 2017).

The city of Beijing was the first to place a cartoon officer on signs around the city and even in elementary and middle school textbooks. Other provinces and cities soon followed suit, and now it is difficult to travel in China without seeing one of these friendly faces staring back at you from a street sign or a notice in restaurants, hotels, public squares, or subway cars. The original press release for the Beijing character (see Figure 1) presents the rationale behind the image: 'the language [which includes reminders like "close the window", "lock the door", "be wary of strangers"] is like that of a police officer who is very familiar with the neighbours and aunties. It's as though the police are standing next to you, lessening the distance between the police and the people'.[24]

Not all reminders are so friendly. The original cartoon characters, like the one pictured above, also inspired the creation of 'internet police' Jingjing and Chacha. Created by the Shenzhen Public Security Bureau's Internet Security and Surveillance Division in 2006, Jingjing and Chacha were designed to be more serious in their demeanour as they popped up on users' computer screens on websites and forums in Shenzhen. Although users can click on the cartoon icons to get information about laws and legal regulations, the division director told a reporter that the purpose of Jingjing and Chacha is 'to intimidate, not to answer questions' and 'to let all internet users know that the internet is not a place beyond the law' (Xiao 2006).

Together, these public outreach efforts on television and social media and *via* promotional materials are an effort by various arms of the police bureaucracy to engage the public through user-friendly formats that allow these agencies to showcase what Chinese police do for the public. Moreover, these efforts have been implemented nationally, even in restless areas such as Xinjiang and Tibet. For example, the public security bureaus of Lhasa (Tibet) and Urumqi (Xinjiang) produce similar content to police Weibo accounts in other areas, despite having different policing needs and demands due to social unrest in these areas. Moreover, the Xinjiang provincial bureau maintains a police and rule of law art troupe. When viewed together, these efforts are part of a much larger strategy to promote a carefully curated image of the police in society. Evidence of that strategy is available not just in the form of television shows or signs on street corners, but also through reform-related documents created by the ministry and published online. These materials provide a clearer picture of what the ministry wants to accomplish through public relations campaigns.

Image control as a strategy

Although many empirical details about policing in China are difficult for researchers to access (Dai 2008; Scoggins 2014), a surprising amount of information about reforms at the ministerial level is available online and through domestic policing journals. To understand how the ministry's strategy of image control developed, I conducted a content analysis of ministry press releases, public meeting minutes, *Xinhua* press releases, and other state media reports about MPS activities, a total of 141 documents. All documents

[24] 'Beijing katong jingcha jiang shanggang', *People's Daily*, 20 August 2002, available at: http://www.people.com.cn/GB/shehui/43/20020820/803444.html, accessed 31 January 2019.

are or were made available through the ministry's website and range in year from 1993 to 2018. Although additional documents were available, the analysis presented here is limited to these 141, since their placement on the ministry's website implies their significance to the public face of the organisation. There are limitations to this type of data collection. For some years, there is only one document, whereas for other years there are many. A Table showing the distribution of documents per year is available in Appendix 1. Moreover, these are state documents that aim to present the very best image of the ministry and policing in China more generally. As such, they are characterised by flowery language praising state leaders and touting the police bureaucracy's accomplishments in achieving its goals of state security and legal enforcement and development. Few of the documents openly acknowledge the challenges the ministry faces in reforming its bureaucracy.

The documents nevertheless reveal the key reform priorities of the organisation across time and, in some cases, lay out detailed plans for specific areas of interest. For example, mentions of a comprehensive management strategy and information technology/big data solutions for crime control and stability maintenance appear uniformly across the years 2015–2018, reflecting the MPS's commitment to using new technologies in this time period. Other issues are also addressed by the documents, such as the reform of the auxiliary police (*xiejing*), a group of contract workers who are hired to do police work by stations in many areas. Mentions of auxiliary police reform appear only in a single year, indicating that reports of the ministry's progress in developing significant changes to that issue were limited to a matter of months.[25] The documents also track larger political developments. For example, the language mentioning loyalty (*zhongcheng*) or loyalty to the party (*duidang zhongcheng*) does not appear in the documents until 2017, shortly before President Xi Jinping announced a constitutional amendment to abolish term limits. By late January 2018—just weeks before the announcement—we see mention of the party's 'absolute leadership over public security work' and reminders that police must support the 'core' (Xi Jinping).[26] Such documents show the range of information available online to analysts and others interested in understanding the priorities of the ministry or key policy details.

With regard to public opinion work, 66 of the 141 documents refer to the importance of appealing to and working for the people, the public, or the masses. These sentiments are expressed in calls for officers and others in the public security bureaucracy to pay attention to public opinion, to protect the public, and to accept the supervision of the masses. Table 2 shows a frequency count of the most commonly used terms related to the importance of the public. These mentions occur in nearly every year covered by the documents, illustrating both the duration and depth of the ministry's commitment to making public statements about the importance of serving the people or the public

[25]Because the analysis is limited to publicly available documents, tracing actual changes to the operating procedures can be difficult. In the case of auxiliary police, the relatively short-lived attention may mean that sufficient progress was made on the issue, but it could also indicate a stalling of progress or need to turn attention to other matters. It is also possible that reporting on the matter became too sensitive.

[26]'Gonganbu jiji sheying xin shidai fenli kaichuang gonan gongzuo xin jumian', *Xinhua News*, 25 January 2018, available at: http://www.gov.cn/xinwen/2018-01/25/content_5260683.htm, accessed 31 January 2019.

TABLE 2
FREQUENCY COUNT OF APPEALS TO THE PUBLIC

Issue	Number of mentions
Public opinion	16
Protect the people	30
Improve service	60
Accept public supervision	16
Propaganda	60

interest in policy formation and implementation. The counts also indicate the ministry's preferred forms of expression and references to 'propaganda' (*xuanchuan*) for public education purposes.

Distribution also matters. Changes in language over time indicate new organisational policies and preferences, and Table 3 shows frequency counts of commonly used terms that accompany calls for public outreach. There is, for example, a tendency to appeal to Mao-era language of 'the masses' and, to some extent, the 'mass line' across time. These calls increase in frequency beginning in 2015. Similarly, mentions in the documents of propaganda and public opinion both increase in frequency around the same time. There are also subtle shifts in language over the years. Between 2014 and early 2016, reform documents largely emphasised the need for police reforms to foster social fairness, respect people's rights, and serve the public. Reform documents in this period also occasionally included general calls to pay attention to public opinion. By 2016, the emphasis on public opinion had become centred on building positive opinions of public security reform. Documents in 2017 and 2018 contained language urging the police to enhance the public's 'sense of security' and 'sense of access' to understanding the benefits of police reforms.[27] Other documents encouraged increasing the public's understanding of police reform to give them a 'real sense of gain'.[28] Two documents in 2016 and 2017 even refer to reform as a gift or 'red envelope' (*hongbao*) for the people.[29]

Alongside the trends captured by frequency counts is more specific evidence pointing to the campaigns taking place. In 2016, the ministry began publishing detailed reform documents that commanded public security organs to increase the publicity and promotion efforts and 'intensify the public opinion propaganda work'.[30] As of 2018, the

[27] 'Guo Shengzhao zai gonganbu quanmian shenhua gaige lingdao xiao zu disanci (kuoda) huiyi shang qiangdiao qieshi zengqiang zhua luoshi de zenren dandang quebao gongan gaige jingzhun luodi qude shixiao', 20 March 2017, available at: http://www.mps.gov.cn/n2255079/n4876594/n4974590/n4974598/c5660566/content.html, accessed 31 January 2019.

[28] 'Guo Shengzhao zai gonganbu quanmian shenhua gaige lingdao xiao zu disanci (kuoda) huiyi shang qiangdiao qieshi zengqiang zhua luoshi de zenren dandang quebao gongan gaige jingzhun luodi qude shixiao', 1 April 2017, available at: http://www.mps.gov.cn/n2255079/n4876594/n4974590/n4974598/c5675199/content.html, accessed 31 January 2019.

[29] In traditional Chinese culture, red envelopes filled with money are given as gifts to children and young people during Chinese New Year or for weddings, births, and other special occasions.

[30] 'Quanguo gonganjiguan gaige ban zhu ren zuotnhui zhaokai shenru xuexi guanche Xi Jinping zongshuji xilie zhongyao jianghua jingshen yi youli cuoshi he guoying zuofeng hen zhua gongan gaige tuijin luoshi', 25 April 2017, available at: http://www.mps.gov.cn/n2255079/n4876594/n4974590/n4974598/c5688242/content.html, accessed 31 January 2019.

TABLE 3

FREQUENCY COUNTS OF COMMONLY USED LANGUAGE ACCOMPANYING CALLS FOR PUBLIC OUTREACH

Year	Mass line *(qunzhong luxian)*	The masses *(qunzhong)*	Red envelope *(hongbao)*	Public opinion *(yulun,minyi)*	Propaganda *(xuanchuan)*	Fairness *(gongpin, gongzheng)*	Service *(fuwu)*	Rights of the people *(quanli, renquan)*
1993	–	–	–	–	–	–	–	–
1994	–	–	–	–	1	–	–	–
1995	–	2	–	–	–	–	–	1
1996	–	–	–	–	–	–	–	–
1997	–	–	–	–	–	–	–	1
1998	–	–	–	–	1	–	–	2
1999	–	3	–	1	–	1	–	–
2000	–	2	–	–	–	1	2	–
2001	–	–	–	–	7	2	2	–
2002	–	–	–	–	–	–	–	–
2003	1	1	–	–	–	2	2	–
2004	–	–	–	–	–	1	–	–
2005	–	–	–	–	–	1	–	–
2006	–	–	–	–	2	–	–	–
2007	–	–	–	–	–	–	–	–
2008	–	–	–	–	–	1	–	–
2009	–	–	–	–	–	–	–	–
2010	–	1	–	–	–	–	–	–
2011	–	–	–	–	12	–	2	1
2012	–	–	–	–	4	5	–	6
2013	–	–	–	–	–	1	–	–
2014	–	–	–	3	4	3	16	3
2015	–	19	–	2	11	11	14	14
2016	1	45	2	5	2	9	8	1
2017	1	21	1	3	5	1	8	–
2018	–	10	–	2	7	1	8	1
Total	**3**	**104**	**3**	**16**	**56**	**40**	**62**	**30**

ministry's website linked to 47 media reports from state-run sources in the same time period that represented at least some of the fruits of these efforts. These calls occurred around the same time when the new style of television programming emerged. Notably, this dataset does not reveal additional information about the other campaigns that used social media or promotional materials. In fact, the one reference about using Weibo to transmit information to the public appears in 2018, nearly eight years after the first accounts were set up, and there are no discernible changes to language around the time social media or promotional materials emerged and increased in popularity. This is perhaps due to the distribution of available documents in the dataset, which were more numerous in 2015–2018 (see the Appendix). It is also possible that such calls were made internally but not publicised by the ministry. Evidence from policing journal articles suggests that these were indeed topics of debate at the time (Liao 2011; Zhang & Liu 2011).

Finally, interviews shed light on waves of prioritising public opinion. One official at the provincial level explained that, while the ministry had long included language about improving relations with the public in official documents, recent efforts represented a new push to improve the image of police in society, particularly in the wake of the Lei Yang scandal.[31] The official also pointed to the new television programming on CCTV as a key example of how the ministry was reaching out to the public in new, more engaging ways. When considered in conjunction with the ministry's own press releases and other documents, these sources present evidence of a concerted effort to improve public relations and curate an image of the police that emphasises public service, efficiency, and reform-oriented policies that improve the lives of ordinary people.

Image control and state legitimacy

While the current public relations efforts are perhaps a continuation of Mao-era rhetoric about serving the needs of the people, the emergence of new terminology, the recent increase in calls to pay attention to public opinion, and the human and financial resources currently devoted by the ministry to reaching out to the public in new, more accessible ways are all signs of a larger strategy. When we further consider that the ministry is facing scandals like the Lei Yang incident, cases of everyday conflict with the public, and potential backlash against stability-maintenance activities, it is clear that the push to show police in a sympathetic light and as highly competent arises from a broader perception that the regime ultimately depends on public approval and that old-fashioned coercion needs to be balanced by winning hearts and minds. These efforts are all the more relevant when we view them in the context of building the legitimacy of the police and the regime more broadly.

In the absence of free and fair elections or other routinised methods of public participation, the Chinese government has a vested interest in pursuing alternative avenues of regime legitimacy to promote stability and prolong its longevity. Since the beginning of reforms, a common perception is that the basis of regime legitimacy in China is economic development and the spread of affluence. However, as recent

[31]Interview with provincial ministry official, 2017.

economic downturns reminded us, China's impressive record of growth cannot be sustained forever. China's leaders are thus wise to diversify their efforts, and new scholarship points to evidence that the party is reaching out to the public in unconventional ways. For example, Han (2018) shows that the Chinese party-state has recently upgraded its propaganda apparatus to co-opt the content of internet novels, a specific genre of online literature, to be more regime-friendly, while according to Fang (2018) the regime is even hiring or creating anime and pop idols to produce patriotic social media content that seeks to generate support for government policies. Such efforts go well beyond traditional notions of state censorship by creating and shaping the content of widely used forms of entertainment, particularly among young people.

The Ministry of Public Security's current public relations efforts fall within this new tradition of reaching out to the public in unexpected ways. It is also a deviation from the more traditional ways in which MPS undergirds the regime. Scholars know well the importance of coercive capacity for regime survival (Skocpol 1979), and the ministry's efforts to maintain stability indicate that police and central government leaders believe that their ability to control protests and dissidents is essential to the preservation of the state. In taking on the task of stability maintenance, the Chinese police bureaucracy supports the interests of the regime by forcibly subduing challenges to its authority that—if unchecked—might undermine the party-state's legitimacy in the eyes of the public.

However, recent research on the police bureaucracy has uncovered more sophisticated efforts to underscore the legitimacy of the organisation and the regime. Notably, Xu Jianhua's work examines the manufacturing of official crime statistics and shows how the 'great crime decline' does not reflect an actual decrease in crime but is instead a myth propagated by systematic statistical manipulation (Xu 2017). Xu outlines the benefits that police stations and station leaders incur for underreporting crime as well as the overall advantages for the ministry and the regime for allowing local police to record inaccurate data, ultimately arguing that the legitimacy of the regime depends on the appearance of crime control.

When viewed in conjunction with stability-maintenance efforts and the facade of crime control, the public relations campaigns reveal a third facet of the ministry's strategy to promote its legitimacy and that of the regime. Both the language of reform documents and timing of the three public outreach campaigns demonstrate that public security organs have promoted a positive image of the police. However, the new television campaigns and the recent emphasis on public opinion and helping the public understand the benefits of reform demonstrate a more active effort to win the support of the people and counteract some of the negatively perceived actions of the police. Collectively, these efforts provide solid evidence that the ministry is investing in more diversified strategies to promote the organisation's legitimacy in ways that are ultimately supportive of the regime. These efforts also serve a dual purpose of persuading both the agents of the government and the general public that the public security organs are legitimate, further solidifying state power (Weber 2004).

Finally, these public relations developments can be viewed in the light of China's recent efforts to forge its own, unique political and economic path. In 2007, Liqun Cao wrote that rising crime rates and levels of individual anomie in China's reform era mirrored similar developments in Western countries and represented a significant departure from the relatively low levels of the Mao era. At the time of Cao's writing, it looked as though one effect of the economic reform period's maturation was China's return to 'normal' social development, of which crime and anomie are an inextricable part (Durkheim 2014). Under the Xi Jinping administration, a new, more authoritarian approach is changing once more the political and social landscapes again. We know that new surveillance tactics are specifically designed to root out political opposition in ways that are reminiscent of—yet also surpass—the Mao era. Similarly, the new public relations tools are a digitally enhanced version of old propaganda campaigns and are designed to block undesirable social developments in addition to promoting state legitimacy. In the realm of public security, we are thus witnessing the modernisation of past practices in ways that seek to advance the goals of current government leaders.

Further implications

Among authoritarian states, China is unique in its engagement of carefully orchestrated efforts to promote a positive image of the police in society. While police in many countries use various social media strategies to engage the public or increase transparency (Meijer & Thaens 2013), the Ministry of Public Security is unmatched in its high-level, concerted strategy to define how people in China see the police. These efforts show a new side to the state from an unlikely angle. We would expect that the coercive arm of an authoritarian state that is bent on survival and willing to spend as much as it can in the name of stability maintenance would be completely uninterested in promoting public relations, and yet that is simply not the case. The details presented here provide incontrovertible evidence that the MPS is doing far more than paying lip service to concern for the masses. This move has been driven by the emergence of new media opportunities from 2010 onwards, but as the reform documents show, the push is also part of a larger campaign to bolster public opinion that has grown and developed over the last ten years. Ultimately, these efforts are meant to be supportive of regime legitimacy and assuage any negative feelings towards the internal security branches that are engendered by public scandals and other stability-maintenance activities such as protest or dissident control.

One question remains: are these public outreach campaigns working? Scholars are understandably interested in the related issue of public trust and the police. Unsurprisingly, mainland publications report high levels of trust in the police, though some studies outside of China have also reached similar conclusions.[32] One comparative study even found that the public's confidence in the police ranked eighth out of 49 countries, putting China roughly on a par with Switzerland (Jang *et al.* 2015). However, there is, as yet, no conclusive work on public perceptions. An earlier comparative study found that public confidence in the police was lower in China than in the United States (Cao & Hou 2001). Finer grained analyses have also provided a better understanding of the potential dynamics at play behind positive assessments of the police in China. For

[32]Wu and Sun (2009) found nearly 75% of respondents trusted police. A later study by Sun, Hu, and Wu also found urban residents 'exhibited a highly favourable opinion of the police', with the caveat that the respondents may be reluctant to acknowledge or simply be ignoring problems with police (Sun *et al.* 2012, p. 100).

example, a study of college students found that, while the students indicated overall satisfaction with the police, the majority of respondents had 'substantially less positive views of police fairness, effectiveness, and integrity … [and] did not consider their local police as honest, upright, or ethical' (Wu & Sun 2010, p. 106). Other studies have found potentially valuable variation, such as lower degrees of trust in police held by urban residents (Wu *et al.* 2016). We must be cautious with studies surrounding public perceptions, however, since potential indicators, such as fear of crime, are deeply rooted in social, cultural, economic, psychological, and geographic considerations, and are not a mere reflection of the ability of police to manage crime and public security in a given locale.[33]

In-depth interviews or focus groups might be helpful in shedding light on contradictions in the survey-based literature and parsing out reactions to the public relations campaigns. Because ratings information for shows like *Police Training Camp* are not publicly available, there are few other ways to gauge the public's response to the ministry's efforts. Similarly, it would be helpful to compare the ministry's public relations efforts with those in other bureaucracies to get a better sense of how the government is shaping its public image more broadly. While few bureaucracies face the same image challenges as the public security bureaucracy, recent high-profile scandals related to food safety or environmental protection have put other Chinese public bodies in the spotlight. Understanding how these organisations respond to those scandals and seek to rehabilitate their image would provide additional insight into the public relations campaigns that the Ministry of Public Security is currently pursuing.

Ultimately, however, the police bureaucracy's own agents may undercut efforts to improve public relations. One ministry official, interviewed in 2019, acknowledged the potential limits of the campaigns by pointing out the confusion frontline police may feel about calls to serve the public and improve public relations:

> The issue is that the people and the police have a very different understanding of 'public service'. The people may think of it more like the service in a restaurant: how was the officer's attitude? Was he polite and helpful? That's not what public service means to the police. Their job is about reducing crime and protecting public security.

How and whether or not these tensions develop as the ministry ramps up calls for public service and attention to public opinion may ultimately influence the success of the campaigns.

[33]For an overview of the literature on fear of crime, see Pain (2000). Individual vulnerability also matters. For analysis of fear of crime and vulnerability in China, see Zhang *et al.* (2009).

References

Bracey, D. (1989) 'Policing the People's Republic', in Troyer, R., Clark, J. & Rojek, D. (eds) *Social Control in the People's Republic of China* (New York, NY, Praeger).

Cao, L. (2007) 'Returning to Normality: Anomie and Crime in China', *International Journal of Offender Therapy and Comparative Criminology*, 51, 1.

Cao, L. & Hou, C. (2001) 'A Comparison of Confidence in the Police in China and in the United States', *Journal of Criminal Justice*, 29, 2.

Chen, X. (2002) 'Community and Policing Strategies: A Chinese Approach to Crime Control', *Policing & Society*, 12, 1.

Dai, M. (2008) 'Policing in the People's Republic of China: A Review of Recent Literature', *Crime, Law and Social Change*, 50, 3.

Dai, Y. & Huang, Z. (1993) 'Organization and Functions of Public Security Agencies of the People's Republic of China', *EuroCriminology*, 5.

Du, J. (1997) 'Police–Public Relations—A Chinese View', *Australian & New Zealand Journal of Criminology*, 30, 1.

Durkheim, E. (2014) *The Division of Labor in Society* (New York, NY, Free Press).

Dutton, M. (2000) 'The End of the (Mass) Line? Chinese Policing in the Era of the Contract', *Social Justice*, 27, 2.

Dutton, M. (2005) *Policing Chinese Politics: A History* (Durham, NC, Duke University Press).

Esarey, A. & Xiao, Q. (2011) 'Digital Communication and Political Change in China', *International Journal of Communications*, 5.

Fang, K. (2018) 'Anime and Pop Idols as Ideology Propagators in China: Novel Strategies and Limitations of State Propaganda in the Social Media Era', paper presented at the Association for Asian Studies Annual Conference, Washington DC, 22–25 March.

Fu, H. (2005) 'Zhou Yongkang and the Recent Police Reform in China', *Australian & New Zealand Journal of Criminology*, 38, 2.

Greitens, S. (2017) 'Rethinking China's Coercive Capacity: An Examination of PRC Domestic Security Spending, 1992–2012', *The China Quarterly*, 232.

Han, R. (2018) 'Dancing with Shackles On: State Control over Internet Novels in China', paper presented at the Association for Asian Studies Annual Conference, Washington DC, 22–25 March.

Jang, H., Lee, J. & Gibbs, J. (2015) 'The Influence of the National Government on Confidence in the Police: A Focus on Corruption', *International Journal of Law, Crime and Justice*, 43, 4.

Jiao, A. (1995) 'Community Policing and Community Mutuality: A Comparative Analysis of American and Chinese Police Reforms', *Police Studies*, 18.

Jiao, A. (2001) 'Police and Culture: A Comparison Between China and the United States', *Police Quarterly*, 4, 2.

Koetse, M. (2016) '"We could all be the next Lei Yang"—Chinese Netizens on the Lei Yang Case', *What's on Weibo*, 18 May, available at: http://www.whatsonweibo.com/lei-yang-case/, accessed 8 March 2017.

Li, Y. & Beckley, A. (2018) 'Policing with the People in China: Implementing the Mass Line in Criminal Investigation: A Synthesis of the Literature', *Police Practice and Research*, 19, 1.

Liao, J. (2011) 'Gongan weibo de zuoyong ji xiangguan wenti yanjiu', *Journal of Chinese People's Public Security University*, 3.

Ma, L. (2013) 'The Diffusion of Government Microblogging: Evidence from Chinese Municipal Police Bureaus', *Public Management Review*, 15, 2.

Ma, Y. (1997) 'The Police Law 1995: Organization, Functions, Powers and Accountability of the Chinese Police', *Policing: An International Journal of Police Strategies & Management*, 20, 1.

Meijer, A. & Thaens, M. (2013) 'Social Media Strategies: Understanding the Differences Between North American Police Departments', *Government Information Quarterly*, 30.

Pain, R. (2000) 'Place, Social Relations and the Fear of Crime: A Review', *Progress in Human Geography*, 24, 3.

Scoggins, S. (2014) 'Navigating Fieldwork as an Outsider: Observations from Interviewing Police Officers in China', *PS: Political Science & Politics*, 47, 2.

Scoggins, S. (2018) 'Policing Modern China', *China Law and Society Review*, 3, 2.

Scoggins, S. & O'Brien, K. (2016) 'China's Unhappy Police', *Asian Survey*, 56, 2.

Skocpol, T. (1979) *States and Social Revolutions: A Comparative Analysis of France, Russia and China* (Cambridge, Cambridge University Press).

Sun, I., Hu, R. & Wu, Y. (2012) 'Social Capital, Political Participation, and Trust in the Police in Urban China', *Australian & New Zealand Journal of Criminology*, 45, 1.

Tang, N., Hand, K., Pils, E., Zhang, T. & Kellogg, T. (2015) 'China's "Rule by Law" Takes an Ugly Turn', *Foreign Policy*, 14 July, available at: http://foreignpolicy.com/2015/07/14/chinas-rule-by-law-takes-an-ugly-turn-rights-lawyers-crackdown-xi-jinping/, accessed 31 January 2019.

Todd, S. (2017) 'Pipo-kun is Basically Cuteness, Weaponized', *Quartz*, 24 December, available at: https://qz.com/1164167/tokyos-adorable-police-mascot-pipo-kun-is-basically-cuteness-weaponized/, accessed 31 January 2019.

Trevaskes, S. (2013) 'Rationalising Stability Preservation Through Mao's Not So Invisible Hand', *Journal of Current Chinese Affairs*, 42, 2.

Wade, S. (2017) 'Minitrue 2017: September—19th Congress, NK, Riots', *China Digital Times*, 26 December, available at: https://chinadigitaltimes.net/2017/12/minitrue-2017-september-party-congress-north-korea-tangshan-riot/, accessed 31 January 2019.

Wang, X. & Wong, S.W. (2012) 'Police Social Service Work in China: Community Policing with Chinese Characteristics', *Asia Pacific Journal of Police and Criminal Justice*, 9, 1.

Weber, M. (2004) *Max Weber: The Vocation Lectures* (Indianapolis, IN, Hackett Publishing Company).

Wong, K. (2001) 'The Philosophy of Community Policing in China', *Police Quarterly*, 4, 2.

Wu, Y. & Sun, I. (2009) 'Citizen Trust in Police: The Case of China', *Police Quarterly*, 12, 2.

Wu, Y. & Sun, I. (2010) 'Perceptions of Police: An Empirical Study of Chinese College Students', *Policing: An International Journal of Police Strategies & Management*, 33, 1.

Wu, Y., Sun, I. & Hu, R. (2016) 'Public Trust in the Chinese Police: The Impact of Ethnicity, Class, and Hukou', *Australian & New Zealand Journal of Criminology*, 49, 2.

Xiao, Q. (2006) 'Image of Internet Police: JingJing and ChaCha Online-Hong Yan', *China Digital Times*, 22 January, available at: https://chinadigitaltimes.net/2006/01/image-of-internet-police-jingjing-and-chacha-online-hong-yan, accessed 31 January 2019.

Xie, Y. (2012) 'The Political Logic of *Weiwen* in Contemporary China', *Issues & Studies*, 48, 3.

Xie, Y. (2013) 'Rising Central Spending on Public Security and the Dilemma Facing Grassroots Officials in China', *Journal of Current Chinese Affairs*, 42, 2.

Xu, J. (2017) 'Legitimization Imperative: The Production of Crime Statistics in Guangzhou, China', *The British Journal of Criminology*, 58, 1.

Yang, D. (2017) 'China's Troubled Quest for Order: Leadership, Organization and the Contradictions of the Stability Maintenance Regime', *Journal of Contemporary China*, 26, 103.

Zenz, A. & Leibold, J. (2017) 'Xinjiang's Rapidly Evolving Security State', *China Brief*, 17, 4, available at: https://jamestown.org/program/xinjiangs-rapidly-evolving-security-state/, accessed 31 January 2019.

Zhang, L., Messner, S., Liu, J. & Zhuo, Y. (2009) 'Guanxi and Fear of Crime in Contemporary Urban China', *The British Journal of Criminology*, 49, 4.

Zhang, L., Zhou, D., Messner, S., Liska, A., Krohn, M., Liu, J. & Lu, Z. (1996) 'Crime Prevention in a Communitarian Society: *Bang-Jiao* and *Jiao-Jie* in the People's Republic of China', *Justice Quarterly*, 13, 2.

Zhang, Y. & Liu, J. (2011) 'Weibo: gongan jiguan tuijin shehui guanli chuangxin de xin meijie', *Journal of Jiangxi Police Institute*, 3.

Appendix 1

TABLE A1
Distribution of Reform Documents in Dataset across Years

Year	Number of documents
1993	1
1994	1
1995	2
1996	2
1997	3
1998	2
1999	7
2000	6
2001	6
2002	2
2003	1
2004	4
2005	2
2006	2
2007	1
2008	10
2009	5
2010	3
2011	3
2012	9
2013	1
2014	8
2015	14
2016	16
2017	13
2018	17
Total	**141**

'Vigilante Shows' and Law Enforcement in Russia

GILLES FAVAREL-GARRIGUES

Abstract

Moral entrepreneurs who volunteer to enforce rules by themselves have spread in 2010s Russia. As 'rule enforcers' they patrol the streets to catch offenders. Some of these enforcers have conflictual relations with the police, while others operate in cooperation with it. This essay describes the development of vigilante justice in contemporary Russia. Two particularities of the Russian case are striking. First, the activities of several citizen policing initiatives are in fact recorded and posted on YouTube and VKontakte, where they reach a large audience, generating support for their activities and, in particular, for the leaders of such groups. Second, the development of these groups is not the simple outcome of a powerless state failing to maintain order or to fight crime. The essay will reveal how these new forms of policing contribute, paradoxically, to the strengthening of state authority.

LIKE ELSEWHERE IN RUSSIA ON THIS SUNNY SUNDAY, THREE friends share a picnic and some beers in a local park. This banal scene is interrupted by four young men with shaved heads, wearing tracksuits, who start taking the friends to task while filming the scene. After having reminded them that drinking alcohol is prohibited in the park, they request with exaggerated politeness that the friends empty their bottles and glasses or else the youths will call the police. The three friends protest, and the vigilantes call their comrades: now they are a group of 12, ready to fight. One of the picnicking men asks, 'but who are you guys precisely? Are you pigs [*musorskie*]? Because, honestly, the more I look at you, the more you look like troublemakers [*bespredel'shiki*]'.[1]

Moral entrepreneurs who decide to enforce rules by themselves and render justice in the name of 'civil society' have spread in Russia throughout the 2010s. These 'rule enforcers', to use Becker's terminology, differ from 'rule creators', that is, moral crusaders among the political elite or religious groups who engage in promoting norms against 'deviant'

I would like to dedicate this essay to the late Carlo Morselli (1969–2020) for providing me the opportunity to visit the International Centre for Comparative Criminology at the University of Montreal in 2016, during which I wrote a first draft of this essay, as well as my colleagues Anthony Amicelle, Matthew Light, Erica Marat, Lauren McCarthy, Peter H. Solomon, Jr., and Samuel Tanner for their support and comments on earlier versions of this essay.

[1] 'Lev Protiv ne na tekh narvalis', *YouTube*, 14 June 2017, available at: https://www.youtube.com/watch?v=ot6UW68DcZQ, accessed 12 November 2020.

behaviours (Becker 1963).[2] Rather, rule enforcers patrol the streets to catch offenders: depending on their specialty, they target, for example, badly parked cars obstructing pedestrian walkways, shops selling expired products, people smoking or drinking in public places where this is prohibited by law, illegal immigrant shelters, corrupt police officers, crooked public-transportation inspectors, drug dealers, sex workers and their customers, and paedophiles.

Similar forms of citizen contributions to policing do not correspond to police–citizen partnerships (Jobard & De Maillard 2015, pp. 242–44) such as neighbourhood watches (Bennett *et al.* 2006) or current *druzhiny* (volunteer squads) in Russian cities (Khodzhaeva 2016, 2019). Calling themselves *aktivisty* (activists), self-proclaimed rule enforcers share the same *modus operandi*: at first, they film their actions in public spaces and disseminate them through social media; later, they usually break the law to enforce rules, and often humiliate their targets during their *reidy* (raids) and *safari* (safaris), pushing them to their limits in front of the camera. Brawls often happen during these interactions, boosting the online popularity of some of these groups on social media and on YouTube.

This essay aims to test the hypothesis that the range of initiatives discussed reflects the development of vigilantism (Johnston 1996; Abrahams 1998) in contemporary Russia. While the phenomenon of vigilante justice that emerged in the mid-nineteenth century in the US context has become global (Pratten & Sen 2007), the term 'vigilantism' is rarely employed in the Russian context (Galeotti 2007).[3] However, the combination of general distrust of the police (Gerber & Mendelson 2008; Taylor 2011), still widespread in the 2010s (Semukhina & Reynolds 2014), the development of moral panics, and the sudden offer of 'cheap forms of law enforcement' (Pratten & Sen 2007, p. 3) by youth groups invite analysis of the relevance of the term, in spite of its fundamental ambiguities (Moncada 2017), in the Russian context. Such an ambition does not mean that Russian vigilantes are mere imitations of their European, American, Asian or African counterparts. On the contrary, this essay will help to identify particularities, which in turn may enrich the general understanding of contemporary vigilantism as a social phenomenon.

As the essay will show, two particularities of the Russian case are striking, at least at first glance. First, citizen policing initiatives take the form of vigilante shows. Raid videos posted on YouTube and social media aim at reaching a large audience and generating a profit. Second, although they share a critique of the performance of law-enforcement agencies, Russian vigilantes are not to be seen as a homogeneous political group. While Russian vigilantes may be sometimes connected with the ruling elite—especially with pro-government youth organisations like *Nashi* (Hemment 2012)—others are affiliated to neo-Nazi groups and therefore do not support the current political regime. A close examination of these mobilisations reveals different kinds of shifting configurations (Elias & Dunning 1994), in which the relationships of vigilante groups with law-enforcement agencies are sometimes cooperative and sometimes conflictual. Moreover, the authorities'

[2]See also, Gusfield (1963) and Lapointe (2014).

[3]Since 2018, the NGO *Obshchestvenny Verdikt* (Public Verdict) has developed *Vigilanty*, a project to monitor Russian vigilante groups, available at: http://vigilant.myverdict.org/, accessed 12 November 2020.

attitude to a given group can vary over time and space. Observation of these groups shows how the government actually controls the distribution of policing functions by allowing legitimate 'civil society' representatives to exercise sovereign prerogatives, excluding from the field any initiatives considered 'extremist', and ultimately giving credit to the idea that maintaining order is a more legitimate goal than complying with the law. Far from weakening state authority, Russian vigilantes contribute to strengthen it.

To prepare this article, I have studied a sample[4] of more than 15 Russian vigilante groups;[5] some of these groups conduct their activity in more than just one city. Organisations as diverse as *StopKham* (Stop a Douchebag—the movement against badly parked cars) or *Restrukt* (managing the project Occupy Paedophilia before it was banned) have fuelled the emergence of 'copycat movements' (Gabowitsch 2018) in dozens of Russian cities, as well as in some neighbouring countries like Ukraine,[6] especially during the peak of Russian vigilante activity in the mid-2010s. While these groups are usually short-lived (from three months to two years), *StopKham* has been patrolling the streets since 2010. Their popularity should certainly not be overestimated, yet their presence in the digital space is remarkable. Several of these groups have their own YouTube channel, uploading videos regularly and attracting hundreds of thousands of subscribers. Moreover, these groups raise interest in the media; as guests in shows on crime fighting, they have generated many a debate on the legitimacy of self-justice practices and on the boundaries of acceptable law and order maintenance.

This essay is based primarily on sources produced by the observed groups themselves in order to communicate their activity on social media. Since 2014, I have archived more than 200 videos, showing how these groups present themselves during their 'raids', how they interact with one another, how they select what can be shown or not, how they subdue their targets and how they justify their actions. This archiving has allowed me to keep videos that were later withdrawn from groups' official pages for legal or other reasons.[7] Added to this self-produced discourse are sources about these groups, in particular when they blatantly transgress the law during their 'raids', when their victims voice their complaint or when law-enforcement agencies take explicit stands on them. I have also done ethnographic observation of several raids organised in 2017 and 2018 by *Lev Protiv* (Leo Against)—a Moscow-based group funded in 2014 to fight alcohol and tobacco consumption in public places. Such observation is facilitated by the presence of a crowd

[4]While this sample remains comprehensive, there are many local groups with notoriety that does not reach beyond a city's younger population. As an example, in March 2016, when I was in the city of Tver, there were youngsters patrolling the city centre's streets to prevent people from siphoning gasoline from cars.

[5]*Antidiler* (Antidealer), *Datsik*, *Davidych na Okhote* (Davidych on Hunt), *Dvizhenie* (Movement), *Guestbusters*, *Khryushi Protiv* (Piglets Against), *Lev Protiv* (Leo Against), *Molodezhny antinarkoticheski spetsnaz—MAS* (Youth Anti-Drug Commando), *Nochnoi Patrul* (Night Patrol, in Kirov and in Samara), *Okhotniki nad Golovami* (Headhunters), *Restrukt*'s projects (Occupy Paedophilia and Occupy Narcophilia *inter alia*), *Sdai Pedofila* (Turn in a Paedophile), *Shchit Moskvy* (Shield of Moscow), *Stop Nelegal*, *StopKham* (Stop a Douchebag), *Trezvye dvory* (Sober Courtyards).

[6]See, for instance, the YouTube channel of *StopKham* in Ukraine: StopKham UA, available at: https://www.youtube.com/user/w9875/featured, accessed 12 November 2020.

[7]This does not, however, mean that these videos are no longer accessible on the web. As an example, since the liquidation of *Restrukt*, videos produced by Occupy Paedophilia have been considered extremist, but they are still easily accessible on the Runet in November 2020.

(including fans and detractors) surrounding and filming the vigilantes when they appear in a spot where young Muscovites gather to drink and party.[8]

I will first give a definition of vigilante justice, relying on the literature in this field, before showing why the development of citizen policing initiatives in Russia, as a social phenomenon, may be considered vigilantism. I will finally discuss two particularities of the Russian vigilante initiatives: their ability to connect a punitive stance with the pursuit of commercial goals, with their YouTube channels as an asset; and their propensity to present themselves as 'civil society' activists, imposing citizen oversight of police activity on the ground. Then I will present three patterns of relationship between public authorities and Russian vigilantes: explicit delegation, implicit support and rejection.

Vigilantes in Russia

The Spanish term vigilante acquired common usage in the United States in the nineteenth century to designate groups that, on the frontier, took the law into their own hands in the place of institutions that were simply absent or seemed ineffective (Brown 1975). The word, along with the concept of vigilantism, soon acquired a derogatory dimension, raising concerns and controversies. Despite shortcomings in the definition (Moncada 2017), the term then spread to other contexts (Abrahams 1998) and today raises new questions regarding its globalisation (Pratten & Sen 2007). Other scholars underscore the rise of so-called digital vigilantism, considering how the internet has changed the stakes involved in this form of policing (Trottier 2017; Favarel-Garrigues *et al.* 2020; Trottier *et al.* 2020).

In order to appreciate the relevance of the concept in the Russian context, I will limit myself to discussing the six classic features of vigilantism as listed by Johnston (1996). First, vigilantism is a premeditated form of action, excluding spontaneous collective reactions to the transgression of a norm. Second, a vigilante posse is a 'private voluntary agency' (Johnston 1996, pp. 224–26): private security agencies, death squads and law-enforcement agents involved in social cleansing operations are therefore not included in this definition. Third, vigilantes are autonomous citizens engaged in policing. They do not do it for commercial profit, and they act without the state's authority or support. Fourth, vigilantes use or threaten to use force in order to fulfil their self-proclaimed mission. Critical about the efficiency of 'due process' (Pfeifer 2004), vigilantes' rough justice is not only cheap, but also fast, accusatory and brutal. Fifth, they focus either on 'crime control' or 'social control', including 'the maintenance of communal, ethnic or sectarian order and values' (Johnston 1996, p. 228). Targeting not only delinquents external to the community but also, very often, the community's own deviants, vigilantes engage in crime fighting as much as in social control (Rosenbaum & Sederberg 1976). Finally, vigilantes act in order to offer assurances of security both to participants and to other members of a given established order. In other words, they act in the name of a community. To Johnston's definition two remarks may be added. Firstly, vigilantes seek to be known to the public either because their activities are carried out publicly, in the

[8]Personal observation at *Lev Protiv*'s raids, 2017 and 2018.

name of a reference community, or because witnesses of the more discreet punitive expeditions spread the information and feed the group's reputation. Secondly, vigilante groups exist for a period of time, long enough for their activity to become a routine, but generally have a limited lifespan (Favarel-Garrigues & Gayer 2016).

The Russian case corresponds to five features of Johnston's definition. Private voluntary persons unquestionably premeditate the 'raids' and 'safaris' they conduct. They use, or threaten to use, force. They are involved in crime control or social control issues; they claim to defend legal or moral norms. These purposes are actually intertwined in certain cases, for instance, when an offender belongs to a community that the vigilantes despise (for example, an ethnic or sexual minority). Finally, they act in the name of a community and protect an established order, based on moral values. The most problematic feature is the third, autonomous citizenship, which is not developed very much in Johnston's argument (Favarel-Garrigues & Shukan 2019). Vigilantes are citizens choosing to take the law into their own hands. This feature has two implications: vigilantes are not motivated by potential commercial gains and they are not supported by state authorities. I will show further down in the essay why these two assertions are debatable in the Russian case but at this point I would like to stress that this definition may be contested by prior research. In US history, vigilante movements have also often been connected with the local elite who, while not taking part directly in these groups' activities, offered them political or financial support; for instance, shopkeepers and landowners (Rosenbaum & Sederberg 1976). In a similar vein, contemporary 'cow vigilantes' in India have spread in a political context promoting Hindu nationalism and hate speech against Muslims (Jaffrelot 2019). Before delving deeply into the implications mentioned above, however, I proceed to illustrate the groups observed while researching this essay, with a view to paint a comprehensive picture of their agendas and *modus operandi*.

Rule enforcers

While the Soviet regime promoted the involvement of the population in policing and enforcing justice through *druzhiny*, *komsomolskie spetsotryadi* (Komsomol volunteer squads) or comrades' courts (Gorlizki 1998),[9] the post-Soviet context witnessed the development of citizen initiatives to enforce Russian law, especially regarding the use of drugs. Almost 15 years before he was elected mayor of Ekaterinburg (2013–2018), businessman Yevgeny Roizman became famous locally for launching a crusade against drugs in the late 1990s. Roizman not only opened controversial rehabilitation clinics, but also involved local gangsters from the Uralmash group in the surveillance and repression of customers and dealers (Roizman 2005). During the 2000s, far-right vigilante groups also started to contribute to flush out the *nelegaly* (illegals) in the name of the law. The Movement against Illegal Immigration (*Dvizhenie Protiv Nelegal'noi Immigratsii*—DPNI) voiced anti-migrant feelings and organised raids in markets and in workers' residences. The punitive expeditions against migrants were already part of the repertoire of Russian

[9]A comrades' court was a nonprofessional and popularly elected tribunal, ruling on minor disputes, that existed in Soviet societies.

far-right groups before the web was widely accessible in Russia (Shnirel'man 2011, pp. 412–31). From the mid-2000s, the rise of the Runet has nevertheless given more visibility to these practices. In the late 2000s, skinhead gangs competed by filming their merciless racist attacks and showing them with impunity on social media. During the next decade, in the tradition of DPNI raids, far-right groups, including The Shield of Moscow (*Shchit Moskvy*, 2012–2013)[10] and Guestbusters (2013–2014),[11] continued to enforce the fight against illegal migrants and accommodation providers. Supported by *Shchit Moskvy*, *StopNelegal*—active mostly in 2013–2015—targeted illegal migrants working as taxi drivers.[12]

The first half of the 2010s witnessed the spread of citizen initiatives in the fight against crime and deviant behaviours: these initiatives no longer encompassed exclusively anti-migrant and anti-drug raids, but supported a variety of causes, from sexual and health norms to driving rules. This evolution took place in a context that sharpened police distrust. Criticism of the police force as an institution, a feature of the late Soviet era, has continued through to the present day. Media, human right activists, businessmen and politicians have denounced its indifference, corruption and violence (Favarel-Garrigues 2011). Under Vladimir Putin, in spite of significant institutional changes (Taylor 2011), the police force has continued to suffer from a 'lack of institutional trust' (Semukhina & Reynolds 2014).[13] The Medvedev presidency witnessed the eruption of several scandals involving law-enforcement officers: in 2009, police major Denis Evsyukov engaged in a multi-casualty drunken shooting spree in a Moscow supermarket; in 2010, Alexei Dymovski publicly denounced, on YouTube, police corruption in Novorossiisk (Galeotti 2012). Many events in the late 2000s reflected tensions between the population and the police, as illustrated in the numerous riots triggered by ethnic tensions between Russians and Caucasians, including those which erupted in Moscow in 2010[14] or in Biryulyovo in 2013.[15] In 2010, after a series of assaults on police officers, the *Primorskie Partizany* (Primorye Partisans), a gang of young ultranationalists whose alleged aim was to end police corruption, were finally caught by the police in an Ussuriisk apartment. Two of them committed suicide and four others surrendered. Across the country, many people suddenly showed their support for these young anti-police rebels.[16] After a decade of criticism, institutional reorganisation and incremental changes (Taylor 2011), a major reform of the Ministry of Interior was finally introduced in 2011, in the pre-electoral

[10]See *Shchit Moskvy*'s VKontakte page, available at: https://vk.com/board_of_msk, accessed 12 November 2020.

[11]See Guestbusters VKontakte page, available at: https://vk.com/guestbusters, accessed 12 November 2020.

[12]See *Stop Nelegal*'s VKontakte page, available at: https://vk.com/stopnelegal, accessed 12 November 2020.

[13]See also Gerber and Mendelson (2008).

[14]On 11 December 2010, five days after a *Spartak* Moscow fan was killed during a clash between Russians and Caucasians, football fans and nationalist youth gathered on Manezhnaya Square in Moscow, challenging the police and behaving aggressively against ethnic minorities in the centre of Moscow. See: 'Moskva Manezhnaya', *Lenta.ru*, 12 December 2010.

[15]On 13 October 2013, in a district in southern Moscow, a crowd of locals and nationalist activists attacked properties owned by migrants in reaction to a murder allegedly committed by migrants.

[16]See for instance, Kozlov (2016).

context. The reform included incentives for citizens to cooperate with the police as well as to denounce police suspected of incompetence or venality via a special hotline (Galeotti 2012). However, the ability of the reform to purge the Ministry of Interior was quickly dismissed; in 2012 another scandal of police brutality in Kazan led to the ousting of Minister Rashid Nurgaliev (Le Huérou 2012).

In the early 2010s, the government attempted to frame the civic contribution to law enforcement, for instance with relation to the prevention of terrorist attacks.[17] The most significant example of this policy is the 2014 law on citizen participation in law enforcement,[18] which offers a new framework to the activities of *druzhiny*—volunteers, often retired police officers, patrolling a district with a police officer for remuneration or not—and also to the contribution to policing of Cossack units (Khodzhaeva 2016, 2019). Besides, such a policy offers resources to support the development of policing initiatives within 'civil society'. Three of the groups I studied situated themselves within this framework: *Lev Protiv*, *StopKham* and *Khryushi Protiv* (Piglets Against)—a group monitoring the sale of expired products. Initially connected with *Nashi*, these groups received government grants for a few years to enforce rules that government law-enforcement bodies did not have the means to deal with. As *aktivisty* and responsible citizens, they consider themselves good role models for the youth.

Health issues are at the core of vigilante activity in Russia. The government has sought to limit the consumption of alcohol and tobacco, in particular among the youth, and to promote a healthy lifestyle (*zdorovy obraz zhizni*—ZOZh).[19] The weak enforcement of these laws is invoked by certain vigilantes to justify carrying out civil policing initiatives. The willingness to promote a 'healthy lifestyle' as advocated by the government leads these groups to enforce, in particular, the legislation concerning alcohol consumption. The Moscow-based group *Lev Protiv* is the most active and popular in this field, fighting alcohol consumption in streets and parks, as well as smoking and swearing in public.[20] Following this example, several local groups, also named *Lev Protiv*, have been observed in Russian provincial cities.[21] Another group based in Chelyabinsk, *Trezvye dvory* (Sober Courtyards, founded in 2014), had national-level success with its videos.[22] Other groups, rather than patrolling parks and streets, monitor how alcohol-selling shops comply with the law, in particular, whether vendors check the age of the purchaser and refrain from

[17]'Sovet pri Prezidente RF po razvitiyu grazhdanskogo obshchestva i pravam cheloveka', *Soyuz dobrovol'tsev Rossii sformiruet grazhdanskuyu koalitsiyu dlya profilaktiki terroristicheskoi ugrozy*, 10 December 2015, available at: http://president-sovet.ru/members/blogs/post/1824/, accessed 12 November 2020.

[18]Federal'nyi zakon ot 02.04.2014 g. N 44-FZ 'ob uchastii grazhdan v okhrane obschestvennogo pravoporyadka', 2 April 2014, available at: https://rg.ru/2014/04/04/poryadok-dok.html, accessed 2 December 2020.

[19]This expression is used by the government to promote a healthy lifestyle. See for instance the page 'Zdorovyi obraz zhizni' on the government website, available at: http://government.ru/rugovclassifier/522/events/, accessed 12 November 2020.

[20]See *Lev Protiv*'s YouTube channel, available at: https://www.youtube.com/channel/UCUBoIo2p7GSRMt1YcSswDEw, accessed 12 November 2020.

[21]Several channels such as 'Lev Protiv—Volgograd Volzhsky', 'Lev Protiv—Novosibirsk', 'Lev Protiv—Saint Petersburg' or 'Lev Protiv—Samara' (all channels accessed 12 November 2020).

[22]See *Trezvye dvory*'s YouTube channel, available at: https://www.youtube.com/channel/UCGD7rj3a0lwn-lvoZZf_3ZA, accessed 12 November 2020.

selling alcohol at night.[23] At the local level, *Alkostop* in Nefteyugansk and Surgut, active mostly from 2015 to 2018, also used these tactics.[24] In the continuity of Roizman's initiative in the late 1990s, Russian vigilantes target drug trafficking and use. The Youth Anti-Drug Commando (*Molodezhny antinarkoticheski spetsnaz*—MAS), active between 2010 and 2013, remains the best known, due to its brutality, its success among Russian youth, and to the proximity of its leader to the government.[25]

Some groups develop multifaceted action to promote a healthy lifestyle, encompassing raids on shops selling alcohol, inspections of pharmacies selling restricted medications without prescription, and operations against drug dealing. As of 2020, *Antidiler*, which self-describes as a 'Russian social anti-drug movement', was the most active group in this field.[26] Founded in Krasnoyarsk in 2013 by Dmitri Nosov, a sportsman and an Olympic medallist who became a Liberal Democratic Party of Russia (*Liberal'no Demokraticheskaya Partiya Rossii*—LDPR) deputy in the State *Duma* from 2011 to 2016, *Antidiler* claims to act in most Russian regions but, according to *Obshchestvenny Verdikt* experts, exaggerates its territorial expansion.[27] The promotion of a healthy lifestyle is a competitive sector within Russian civil society, comprising both state-sponsored social projects like *Trezvaya Rossiya* (Sober Russia), founded in 2012,[28] and raids by vigilante groups. The few groups involved in consumer protection in the name of health issues, like *Khryushi Protiv*, also take part in this competition.[29]

Besides health issues, Russian vigilantes also focus on sexual issues. In the early 2010s the most reactionary political elites—deputies like Elena Mizulina and Vitalii Milonov, known for their deep-rooted attachment to values such as family or the Orthodox faith—launched moral crusades against the LGBT community. The activism of these 'rule creators' enabled the passing of the 2013 law prohibiting propaganda of 'non-traditional' sexual relations among minors.[30] In this context, defending sexual order has become one of the main objectives of moral policing by Russian vigilante groups. Paedophile hunting shows the most activity in this field, involving rule enforcers who use this cause to justify

[23]Federal'nyi zakon ot 22.11.1995 N 171-FZ 'O gosudarstvennom regulirovanii proizvodstva i oborota etilovogo spirta, alkogol'noi i spirtosoderzhashchei produktsii i ob ogranichenii protrebleniya (raspitiya) alkogol'noi produktsii', 22 November 1995, available at: http://www.kremlin.ru/acts/bank/8506, accessed 12 November 2020.

[24]See *AlkoStop*'s YouTube channel, available at: https://www.youtube.com/channel/UC0e1uzP2v1ZMbIdw3q800TQ/videos, accessed 12 November 2020.

[25]Their videos are still available on YouTube. See for instance: Molodezhny Antinarkoticheskii Spetsnaz. Reid, 6 June 2013, available at: https://www.youtube.com/watch?v=3CaaWLrZ6Qw, accessed 12 November 2020.

[26]See *Antidiler*'s VK page, available at: https://vk.com/antidiler_official, accessed 12 November 2020.

[27]See the file on *Antidiler*, available at: http://vigilant.myverdict.org/files/antidiler21, accessed 12 November 2020.

[28]See the website of Sober Russia's project, available at: http://www.trezvros.ru/, accessed 12 November 2020.

[29]See *Khryushi Protiv*'s YouTube channel, available at: https://www.youtube.com/channel/UCSdzksftzE7Tu2KAAZ4OvXQ, accessed 12 November 2020.

[30]Federal'nyi zakon ot 29.06.2013 N 135-FZ 'O vnesenii izmenenii v stat'yu 5 Federal'nogo zakona "O zashchite detei ot informatsii, prichinyayushchei vred ikh zdorov'yu i razvitiyu" i otdel'nye zakonodatel'nye akty Rossiiskoi Federatsii v tselyakh zashchity detei ot informatsii, propagandiruyushchei otritsanie traditsionnykh semeinykh tsennostei', 29 June 2013, available at: https://rg.ru/2013/06/30/deti-site-dok.html, accessed 12 November 2020.

homophobic speeches. The Headhunters (*Okhotniki Za Golovami*), led by Sergei Zhuk, were the first to post raids against presumed child sex abusers on social media starting in 2010. The Occupy Paedophilia project, led by Maksim Martsinkevich aka Tesak, started its activities in 2012 and was the most popular vigilante group before the skinhead activist was sent to jail in 2014 for incitement to ethnic hatred and *Restrukt* shut down.[31] Dozens of local paedophile-hunters organised 'safaris' under this name in their own cities. After Tesak's imprisonment, local groups, using the label Occupy Paedophilia, have continued to act, for instance, in Rostov-on-Don. Other paedophile-hunting initiatives have been promoted by activists closer to the government, in particular, Ana Levchenko's project, *Sdai pedofila* (Favarel-Garrigues 2020a). Other vigilante initiatives in the field of moral policing targeted prostitution, such Vyacheslav Datsik's raids in two St Petersburg brothels in 2016.[32] After the 2013 law prohibiting propaganda for 'non-traditional sexual relations' was passed,[33] activists such as Timur Bulatov became active in digital vigilantism, targeting LGBT activists and non-heterosexual teachers on Russian social media and shaming them (Turovskii 2014).

Along with moral crusades dealing with health and sexuality issues, enforcing traffic laws neglected by police is another important branch of vigilante activity in Russia. Combatting badly parked vehicles and careless driving in Moscow and other Russian cities, *StopKham* is the most famous in this category of groups, with its signature large stickers placed on car windows to shame bad drivers and its local chapters in many Russian cities.[34] They are no longer sponsored by the state: as of 2020, however, their YouTube channel is still functioning, making *StopKham* the most enduring vigilante group in Russia. *StopKham* has inspired other traffic policing initiatives like Stop a Jerk (*StopZhlob*, 2014–2015)[35] or Road Control (*Dorozhny Kontrol'*, active since 2013 in Voronezh),[36] which did not reach such popularity. Other unrelated vigilante groups are also involved in road-traffic policing, for instance, Movement (*Dvizhenie*) in Moscow, recording road-traffic offences since 2013 and still active as of this writing.[37] Vigilantes seek also to target drunk drivers, for example, Night Patrol (*Nochnoi Patrul'*), created in 2013 in Samara and Kirov. These local groups patrol the streets and answer emergency calls reporting

[31]Tesak was found dead in a prison cell on 16 September 2020. On Tesak, see Solopov (2020).

[32]'Natsionalist Datsik ustroil oblavu na bordeli Peterburga', *Rossiya 24*, 18 May 2016, available at: https://www.youtube.com/watch?v=XsKnNhB9sbY, accessed 12 November 2020.

[33]Federal'nyi zakon ot 29.06.2013 g. N 135-FZ g. Moskva 'O vnesenii izmenenii v stat'yu 5 Federal'nogo zakona "O zaschite detei ot informatsii, prichinyayuschei vred ikh zdorov'yu i razvitiyu" i otdel'nye zakonodatel'nye akty Rossiiskoi Federatsii v tselyakh zaschity detei ot informatsii, propagandiruyuschei otritsanie traditsionnykh semeinykh tsennostei', 29 June 2013, available at: https://rg.ru/2013/06/30/deti-site-dok.html, accessed 2 December 2020.

[34]See the Stop a Douchebag YouTube channel, available at: https://www.youtube.com/channel/UCMrKscEv_Ri1pvlRsLxsqJQ, accessed 12 November 2020.

[35]See the VKontakte page of *StopZhlob*, available at: https://vk.com/stopzlob, accessed 12 November 2020.

[36]See the VKontakte page of *Dorozhny Kontrol'* in Voronezh, available at: https://vk.com/dk36ru, accessed 12 November 2020.

[37]See *Dvizhenie*'s YouTube channel, available at: https://www.youtube.com/channel/UC5DWMy_XjL3v3VfLIZFZvpw, accessed 12 November 2020.

suspicious drivers.[38] Road vigilantes also target corrupt traffic police officers: the most popular among them was Erik Kituashvili aka Davidych, a car-blogger who, between 2013 and 2016, exposed the corruption of road-traffic policemen on social media. One of his favourite provocations was to pretend to be drunk while driving; he would film the interaction, hoping that the police officer would try to get a bribe out of him. These videos proved very popular.[39]

The texts and the videos produced by these groups, as well as those shot by their victims or observers and revealing the coercive means vigilantes use but try to hide, help us to understand the sociological profile of rule enforcers. First, all these groups are headed by a charismatic leader, whose face is associated with the project and who is sometimes popular among the youth. Despite variations concerning their level of education and their socio-professional background, these leaders are usually young urban male entrepreneurs and biographical data about them are available. It is more difficult to learn anything about the rank-and-file *aktivisty* who form the threatening posse around the leader. The video evidence shows that they are also young urban males, sometimes minors, able and ready to fight. Except for 'Piglets Against', which is comprised of mostly women, women appear in *StopKham* actions and sometimes in anti-paedophile raids. Ekaterina Zigunova used to organise 'safaris' for the St Petersburg chapter of Occupy Paedophilia (Turovskii 2020). In October 2013, Alena Gorbushkova, nicknamed 'Alena SS', a member of the Naberezhnye Chelny chapter of the group, was stabbed to death (Romanov 2013). The rhetoric of young Russian rule enforcers is, however, fundamentally macho and misogynist. For instance, Mikhail Lazutin, the leader of *Lev Protiv*, shouted the following at one of his targets, a man old enough to be his father: 'You're a girl! I'm telling you this publicly because you can't even defend yourself'.[40] The macho tone of Russian vigilantism is evidenced by their focus on a 'healthy lifestyle'. The leaders of these groups are usually athletic and often combat-sports enthusiasts, as shown in the innumerable fight scenes included in the videos. The demonstrated skill in the use of force is sometimes of a quasi-professional level, and some leaders can be considered as 'violent entrepreneurs', converting organised force into money (Volkov 2002). Older than other Russian vigilantes, the leader of the Chelyabinsk-based group *Trezvye dvory*, Alexander Volozhanin, was known as 'Yakuza' when he worked as a bodyguard in the 1990s (Fedorov 2015). As digital natives, these young activists are adept at presenting themselves on social media and publicising their activity by producing reasonably good quality videos of their 'raids', 'safaris' and other punitive expeditions. The care taken in communication (logos, signs of recognition, language, dedicated spaces on social media) indicates that all of these groups aim to gain notoriety among Russian web users.

[38]See the VKontakte page of *Nochnoi Patrul'* Samara, available at: https://vk.com/patrolsamara, accessed 12 November 2020; and also the VKontakte page of *Nochnoi Patrul'* Kirov, available at: https://vk.com/patrolkirov43, accessed 12 November 2020.

[39]The videos of 'Davidych na okhote' are available on YouTube at: https://www.youtube.com/playlist?list=PLyzrNBf9KMdqDgzWASwAiGrLQ–NAEUvj, accessed 12 November 2020.

[40]See Mikhail Strykov's video, 'Lazutin Mikhail Dzhemalovich vmeste so svoei shaikoi provotsiruiet', VKontakte, 10 October 2015, available at: https://vk.com/video184672279_171329243, accessed 12 November 2020.

Lastly, activists present themselves as active citizens doing something concrete to protect the community, beyond politics (*vne politiki*). Their initiatives take the form of goal-oriented and accountable 'social projects', aiming at defending human rights and justifying crowdfunding campaigns. The activists justify their action by referring to a larger whole, that is, from mothers walking with their kids and neighbours to 'the people' in general. Their use of the 'civil society' label results from their willingness to access public resources. Such an appropriation is partly the outcome of a governmental policy that, in the 2000s, sought to frame civil society by co-opting NGOs, prompting them to focus on socially useful projects and to remain loyal to the political authorities (Hemment 2012; Daucé 2013; Cheskin & March 2015). Even the neo-Nazi Tesak, who was involved in anti-paedophile safaris, used to present himself in a provocative manner as a 'human-rights defender' (Martsinkevich 2014). However, the unanimous claim of being 'outside of politics' should be considered cautiously; there are many strings tying these groups to politics, as I will show.

'Raids' and 'safaris'

Whether fighting illegal migrants, maintaining sexual order, promoting a healthy lifestyle or enforcing traffic laws, these groups have much in common. Working as a team entails a role division that is not completely made public: a cameraman and a posse adopting a provocative attitude assist the leader. The 'raids' and 'safaris' provide content for the videos—the tangible result of the action taken. Profit-making groups tend to upload new videos more rapidly and frequently, as proof of accountability for the use of the funds they are allocated by the government, by advertisers or through crowdfunding. The cameras serve both as a means of dissemination and self-justification for activities, as well as a means of coercion, a weapon that exposes non-consenting people (Trottier 2017). By serving to provide proof of the offences committed, the aggressiveness of offenders and the appropriateness of activists' behaviour, the use of the camera shows that the raid is conducted in strict accordance with the law. This is in fact the argument used to justify its presence, for though the law prohibits filming someone without his or her consent, it does authorise recording an offence being committed (Levo-Pravo 2020). Moreover, the camera records any aggression committed against the enforcers, hence guaranteeing the safety of all, according to vigilantes. Such discourse on recording as legal proof and as an act of transparency seems rather dubious, however; the disseminated videos are carefully edited to justify the decisions made by the vigilantes and to give credence to the idea that they resort to physical violence only in situations of self-defence. It is nevertheless important to note that rule enforcers consistently refer to the law and cite precisely the articles under which their actions are allowed: filming people, reminding them of the law, stopping an offence being committed, neutralising an offender and resorting to self-defence in the case of aggression. During the *Lev Protiv* raids that I observed in 2017 and 2018, I noticed, perhaps surprisingly, that most verbal interactions between activists and their targets dealt with legal issues.

Russian activists present policing as a spectacle. They have created a new genre, the raid video, which turns their civic involvement in law enforcement into a vigilante show. The spectacle of vigilante justice is ruled by a particular pattern of violence: pretending to act within the legal framework and resorting to coercion only in the case of aggression, the activists explore all possibilities to infuriate their targets and make them hit first. The popularity of the raid videos is indeed closely related to the level of violence in the filmed interactions. The ways in which these groups attract their target audience to their website by associating the videos with an image and a title intended to make people click and view them, is eloquent in this respect. *Lev Protiv* activists, for instance, select stills of face-to-face altercations, weapons and aggressive faces, underscored by sensationalist captions such as 'Attack on the activists' or 'They blow their smoke in children's faces'.[41] The videos give the viewers the pleasure of a transgressive spectacle, where scenes of destruction of property (cars or shops, as for MAS), brawls (*Lev Protiv*) and humiliation that borders on sadism (Occupy Paedophilia) receive the most 'likes', views and subscribers on vigilantes' channels. The appeal for youth can be summarised by the term *ekshen*, borrowed from the English 'action'. Hunting terminology is all-pervading: 'safaris' are 'hunting' scenes in which 'live bait' is sometimes used to 'catch prey' (Favarel-Garrigues 2020a). The editing of the videos takes the audience's expectations of *ekshen* into account; some of them follow a formatted script, in which the interactions, increasingly conflictive, lead to a climax of physical confrontation. The music selected for these videos is often fast and noisy, like that of a trailer for an action movie.

However, the groups cannot fully reveal their violence, which would make them liable to criminal prosecution. Some of them partially elude the violence by hiding scenes considered non-presentable while revealing their existence to the public. When the anti-paedophile vigilantes of Kurgan physically assault their 'prey', for instance, they hide the image behind the words 'Stop violence' in Russian but leave the explicit soundtrack. As paradoxical as this may seem, even Tesak, the leader of Occupy Paedophilia, whose ingeniousness in the sadistic treatment of his 'prey' on the screen seems limitless, had to pull some of his disciples in the city of Kamensk-Uralsky back in line when, in the heat of the moment, they punched the alleged paedophile and thus discredited the action (Turovskii 2013). Tesak makes constant efforts to present himself as a professional hunter and not a hooligan, following a precise set of rules (Favarel-Garrigues 2020a).

In several cases, there is a striking contrast between the level of violence by these groups and their apparent courtesy during the interactions. Taking great care to present themselves as courteous, they make a point of using polite language when addressing their target and, critically, not resorting to using abusive language (*mat*).[42] By referring to the code of administrative offences prohibiting swearing in public (art. 20.1)[43]—which is impossible for the police to implement—they impose on the interaction a language register that enables them to qualify as 'inadequate' (*neadekvatny*) any deviant behaviour or strong language, which in their eyes testifies to the 'abnormal' nature of the person they are speaking to. Combined with means of intimidation such as an aggressive use of cameras

[41]See the videos on *Lev Protiv*'s YouTube channel, available at: https://www.youtube.com/user/lionversusSmoking/videos, accessed 12 November 2020.

[42]See for instance *Trezvye dvory* raids on their YouTube page, available at: https://www.youtube.com/channel/UCGD7rj3a0lwn-lvoZZf_3ZA, accessed 12 November 2020.

[43]See art. 20.1 of the Russian code of administrative offences on *melkoe khuliganstvo* (petty hooliganism), available at: http://koapkodeksrf.ru/rzd-2/gl-20/st-20-1-koap-rf, accessed 12 November 2020.

and flashes, or the mass effect produced by a mob of athletic young men, this apparent courtesy is aimed at provoking the target. As a weapon, this polite aggression is not limited to young rule enforcers: during a famous altercation between Alexei Naval'nyi and Kuban Cossacks, which occurred in May 2016 at Anapa airport (Krasnodar *Krai*), the blogger and opposition leader, having just been sprayed with water and milk, reacted by insulting one of his attackers and then was reprimanded by the Cossacks for his use of *mat*.[44]

Their calculated use of violence demonstrates these groups' ambiguous relationship with the law. As I have already observed, the activists do not deny the law: on the contrary, they apparently display a scrupulous observance of the law; for instance, reminding a presumed offender which law they have broken and showing a conspicuously detailed knowledge of their rights. Most Russian vigilantes nevertheless consider it legitimate to break the law in order to enforce it. They thus impose, by force, their own hierarchy of standards by which fighting against paedophilia, drug dealing or prostitution warrants committing criminal offences, including damaging property, extra-judicial restraint and acts of *khuliganstvo* (hooliganism). Imposition of this hierarchy is also based on conjuring up innocent victims. The emblematic figure of the victim is that of the child, used not only by the anti-drug and anti-paedophile vigilantes, but also by those opposed to public smoking and drinking.

This being said, techniques of investigation, policing and punishment depend on the group. All of them go to great lengths to prove the guilt of their target, or to use Tesak's words, to show their evidence base (*dokazatel'naya baza*) (Favarel-Garrigues 2020a) by performing 'purchase checks', or stings (for illegal drugs, drugs sold without a prescription, sex workers), or by publishing the social-media messaging between an alleged paedophile and the victim to set a date. In such cases, activists present themselves as investigators. Once the guilt has been proven, nothing prevents the vigilantes, as far as they are concerned, from filming the rest of their operation. In the case of *Lev Protiv*, raids take the form of reminding offenders of the law and requesting them to stop their wrongdoing by emptying their bottle of alcohol or putting out their cigarette. If they do not obey, activists confiscate their bottle or put out their cigarette with a spray of water; they thus put an end to the offence. These acts of coercion are in fact debatable from a legal point of view, since the offender is deprived of the possibility of simply continuing to commit the offence and paying the corresponding fine if caught by an actual police officer. In many other cases, alleged offenders are overpowered: they can be surrounded by a band of young men until the arrival of police forces (as in *Lev Protiv*'s raids), tied to a post in the street (a method used by MAS) or trapped in their victim's home, a method used by Occupy Paedophilia and *Okhotniki za Golovami* (The Headhunters), which started to hunt paedophiles in 2010.[45]

The target's fate varies depending on the group involved. In most cases, after having overpowered an alleged offender, the groups call the police and film law-enforcement

[44]Telekanal Dozhd', 'Na vedushchego Dozhdya Artema Torchinskogo i Alekseya Naval'nogo napali v Anape', *YouTube*, 17 May 2016, available at: https://www.youtube.com/watch?v=_x7gqi1p_-Y, accessed 12 November 2020.

[45]See the interview of Sergei Zhuk, the leader of the Headhunters: 'Vsya Set' imi kishit', *Vzglyad*, 21 September 2011, available at: https://vz.ru/society/2011/9/21/524232.html, accessed 12 November 2020.

agents arriving at the crime scene, arresting the offenders and taking them to the police station. However, the offender is also frequently subjected to the particular group's homespun punishments; MAS covers some of its prey with paint and feathers, while Occupy Paedophilia activists ritually humiliate their prey. During a typical interrogation, Tesak and his followers name and shame their target: they reveal the alleged paedophile's identity for the benefit of the cameras and force him to confess his crimes. The individual is then compelled to call his family and reveal his sexual preferences. His head is forcibly shaved and 'Fuck LGBT' is written on his forehead; he may also be forced into ridiculous postures and made to drink urine: urotherapy is in fact Tesak's signature punishment (Favarel-Garrigues 2020a). As put by Tesak himself: 'Occupy Paedophilia is a show. My intention is not to have someone put in jail; my intention is to completely destroy his life'.[46] Within the framework of another project named 'Occupy Narcophilia', Tesak used to force dealers to eat the drug they sold until he was jailed in 2014. When the activist Datsik decided to cleanse St Petersburg of brothels, he forced the sex workers and their customers to go to the police station naked and filmed them.[47] Not all the observed mobilisations are so punitive, but they are all based on the belief that it is legitimate for a private individual to judge that a crime has been committed and deal out punishment on the spot. Being at the same time 'auspices'[48] and 'providers' of policing (Bayley & Shearing 2001), and also justice-makers, the Russian vigilantes sometimes carry out all stages of judicial proceedings. This de-differentiation of the phases of a criminal investigation brings these groups closer to vigilantes observed in other contexts (Caughey 1960; Pratten & Sen 2007).

Vigilantism and profit

'What do you do that for?' is one of the most common questions addressed to vigilantes during their raids, as I observed during the numerous *Lev Protiv*'s raids I have witnessed. Discussions on social networks about vigilantes also deal with the hidden motivations of the self-proclaimed rule enforcers. The prospect of individual retribution needs to be integrated into the analysis of vigilantism in order to refute the facile notion that these mobilisations are simply answers to a security problem that the political authorities have neither the resources nor the desire to deal with. By fighting crime, Russian vigilantes make themselves a name, build their reputation and expect to make a profit. They are initially not paid to patrol the streets—as a private security company, for instance—but in some cases they progressively find sources of financing through grants, crowdfunding or advertisements (Favarel-Garrigues 2020b). Blossoming in the social-media age, Russian activists challenge the standard definition of vigilantism by combining citizenship, law enforcement and business venture in an innovative way.

[46]'Ya v tyur'mu ne khochu opyat', *Lenta.ru*, 18 September 2012, available at: https://lenta.ru/articles/2012/09/18/tesak/, accessed 25 November 2020.

[47]In 2018 Datsik was sentenced to three and a half years in prison for his anti-brothel raids. 'Natsionalistu Vyacheslavu Datsiku dali srok za "marsh golykh prostitutok"', *Novaya Gazeta*, 19 March 2018.

[48]According to Bayley and Shearing (2001), 'auspices of policing' are groups (and sometimes individuals) that explicitly and self-consciously take upon themselves the responsibility to organise their own protection.

The issue of personal retribution and remuneration seems to be a blind spot in the literature on vigilantism. The reasons to engage in this sort of activity are usually only examined at the level of a group. As a collective movement targeting crime or transgressive acts in its immediate environment, vigilantism brings to each member a feeling of inclusiveness (see for instance Shapira 2013). However, an individual-based approach can be productive (Fourchard 2016). No qualitative work has yet been carried out on the motivations of rank-and-file participants in raids or safaris. Two sources of information make it possible, however, to appreciate the potential benefits of vigilantism: the first is related to the leaders, their careers and how they communicate their activity; the second comes from critical investigations into vigilantism undertaken by bloggers and YouTubers on social media, seeking to reveal that personal interests are hiding behind the façade of altruism (Favarel-Garrigues 2020b).

The concern for notoriety is manifest and the supportive reactions of bystanders are included in online vigilante shows. When I observed *Lev Protiv* raids, the number of fans willing to take a selfie with the leader impressed me. One of them came from a provincial city especially to observe a raid in order to reproduce the idea in his hometown.[49] This popularity can be converted into income. Firstly, the pro-government groups enjoy public subsidies under programmes of support to civil society, often worth several million rubles over two or three years; for example, in 2013–2014, *StopKham* received a total of R10 million, *Khryushi Protiv* received R20 million in 2013–2016 and *Lev Protiv* received R12 million in 2014–2015. Such subsidies are part of a more general policy, as illustrated by the assignment of presidential grants to patriotic NGOs such as *Ofitsiery Rossii*.[50] Secondly, Russian vigilantes can expect to generate some revenue from their YouTube channels. Profit is difficult to estimate, but with more than 1.7 million subscribers on their main YouTube channels, and almost 470 and 270 million total views respectively in January 2020, *StopKham* and *Lev Protiv* are undoubtedly profitable businesses.[51] Both groups have opened second channels to show more videos.[52] In January 2019, *StopKham*'s monthly earnings from the ad revenue of its main YouTube channel were estimated to reach more than €2,600.[53] Furthermore, this revenue does not include the remuneration for all the products or services advertised during the videos. For instance, in addition to the advertisements chosen by YouTube, Lev Protiv runs its own advertisements at the beginning of raids—for pizza delivery, sports betting or gyms, targeting young males—and calls for viewers to sponsor its activity. As of this writing, *Lev Protiv* provided privileged access to its new videos for premium donors.[54] These

[49]Personal observation, *Lev Protiv* raid, Bolotnaya square (Moscow), 29 September 2017.

[50]See TI-Russia's *Prozrachnost' NKO* project, available at: https://transparency.org.ru/projects/prozrachnost-nko/, accessed 12 November 2020.

[51]On *Stopham*, see Gabdulhakov (2019); on *Lev Protiv*, see Favarel-Garrigues (2020b).

[52]In November 2020, Lazutin had created four channels around *Lev Protiv*: *Lev Protiv*, *Lev Protiv* 2 kanal, *Lev Protiv* LIVE and Mikhail Lazutin; *StopKham* had two channels, one in Russian and one in English.

[53]For estimated earnings, see the *StopKham* page on the Social Blade website, available at: https://socialblade.com/youtube/user/stopxamlive, accessed 2 December 2020.

[54]'Eksklyuzivnye materialy. Novosti Proekta Lev Protiv', Boosty, available at: https://boosty.to/mikhail_lazutin, accessed 12 November 2020.

sources of income explain why Mikhail Lazutin no longer presents *Lev Protiv* as a 'social project' but as a 'full-time job' (Lazutin 2019).

So far as the vigilantes' audience is concerned, it is perhaps best inferred from observing how the vigilantes present themselves. Stating clearly that they are acting because they cannot be 'indifferent' (*neravnodushnye*) to the cause they defend, the activists address a public that spends its evenings on a couch (*divanny plankton*, the Russian equivalent of 'couch potatoes') and not in the streets helping to maintain order. Given that the YouTube economy is a potential source of income, the most visible groups seek to attract web users in general, particularly the urban young. The comments made on the videos show clearly that male provincial adolescents are overrepresented and that the videos attract Russian-speaking youth abroad. However, only *StopKham* has reached beyond the borders of the Russian-language web by providing English subtitles for some of its videos on a special YouTube channel named 'Stop a Douchebag', with considerable success. In November 2020, this channel attracted more than 862,000 subscribers and almost 330 billion views.[55]

Groups without any access to government subsidies may try to find other sources of financing. Tesak, the head of Occupy Paedophilia project, is probably the best example of someone profiting from vigilante activity. Not only had he launched several YouTube channels and social-media pages (closed in 2014, when Tesak started to serve his prison sentence), but he also sold the right to attend a 'safari', organised anti-paedophile parties, wrote a book named *Restrukt*, delivered lectures around Russia about flirting, refusing to work, losing weight or bodybuilding,[56] and advertised bodybuilding gear and food. He even used his image to attempt to build a financial pyramid based on a Ponzi-type scheme (Emerina 2013).

Benefits are not strictly economic. A leader's popularity on the web may also constitute a source of political legitimacy. However, few cases correspond to this hypothesis: the leader of *StopKham*, Dmitri Chugunov, formerly commissar of the pro-Putin youth movement *Nashi*, had been appointed a member of the Public Chamber of the Russian Federation from 2014 to 2017. However, he failed to win election to the State *Duma* in 2016.[57] Anna Levchenko is another case of possible connections between rule enforcers and political power. Also with a background in *Nashi*, she gained renown with her project *Sdai pedofila* (Turn in a Paedophile), which did not espouse the use of violence. In the early 2010s, she criticised violent paedophile hunters and won several grants to support her own project. She claims to have helped prosecute 164 paedophiles and shut down 150 websites with child pornography content. She was an assistant to the Russian Federation's ombudsman defending children's rights from 2011 to 2016. In 2018, she became an assistant of Senator Elena Mizulina to strengthen legislation against paedophiles (Favarel-Garrigues 2020a).

[55]See Stop A Douchebag's channel on YouTube, available at: https://www.youtube.com/channel/UCMrKscEv_Ri1pvlRsLxsqJQ, accessed 12 November 2020.

[56]Tesak's seminars are still available on Youtube. See for instance: 'Ne ver'! Ne boisya! Ne rabotai! Seminar ot Tesaka', *YouTube*, 24 February 2014, accessed 12 November 2020.

[57]'Esery vydvinut v Gosdumu osnovatelya "Stopkhama" Chugunova', *Vek*, 14 April 2016.

Connections between vigilantes and politicians are also visible when political figures themselves take part in vigilante justice. Deputies from United Russia (*Edinaya Rossiya*) such as Vitaly Milonov have been involved in anti-paedophile raids organised by *Roditel'sky Kontrol'* (Parent's Control) in St Petersburg in 2012.[58] LDPR local deputies have appeared in several videos, for example, exposing drugstores in Moscow selling psychotropic drugs without a prescription or joining a local initiative aimed at throwing smokers and drinkers out of building courtyards (Fedorov 2015). In Moscow, LDPR municipal deputy Andrei Andreyev took part in several Occupy Narcophilia raids in 2014.[59] Dmitri Nosov, the head of *Antidiler*, was also an LDPR deputy in the State *Duma* from 2011 to 2016. In 2017, he was appointed a member of the Public Chamber of the Russian Federation.[60] At the local level, LDPR local deputies show their interest in vigilante activity by taking part in patrols (such as those of *Trezvye Dvory* in Chelyabinsk) (see Fedorov 2015). Former members of ultranationalist movements may join vigilante groups to change their image from that of skinhead troublemakers to public do-gooders. It does not always work: after having organised raids against two brothels in St Petersburg in 2016, Datsik was arrested and condemned in 2018 to three and a half years of prison for hooliganism, assault and home invasion.

Vigilantism and the state

Russian vigilantes raise one last problem with regard to the standard definition, which values 'autonomous citizenship'. Analysing these groups' relationship to the state is a challenge to observers for several reasons. First of all, the Russian vigilantes are not homogeneous according to this criterion. Some of them are opposed to the Russian government (in particular because they support National Socialism or other far-right ideologies), while others, on the contrary, claim to support the Russian president (for example, MAS), and are sometimes even funded by the government. In this sense, some groups are repressed, and others ignored, while others are explicitly encouraged and sponsored. Secondly, government support to a group varies over time, as illustrated by *StopKham* (Gabdulhakov 2019). Initial government support did not prevent it from being dissolved by court decision when its leader Dmitri Chugunov seemed less in official favour following a series of scandals, including a fight occurring during a raid with the gymnast and Olympic champion Alexei Nemov in 2016 (Lyutykh 2016),[61] and also conflicts with law-enforcement agencies at the local level.[62] Although they still exist on social media, their image in the pro-governmental media has changed after 2016 (Gabdulhakov 2019). Finally, each of these groups has developed a complex relationship to law-enforcement agencies. As mentioned above, despite the adoption of an ambitious reform in 2011, the

[58]'Vitaly Milonov i "Roditel'ski kontrol' vnov" poimali pedofila v sotsseti', *Gazeta.SPb*, 2 August 2012.

[59]See on Andrei Andreyev's Youtube channel, for instance, 'Okkupai Narkofiliyai #61 i LDPR Moskva, Tekstil'shchiki', *YouTube*, 18 September 2014, available at: https://www.youtube.com/watch?v=2us87O4csSM, accessed 12 November 2020.

[60]See his presentation on the Civic Chamber's web page, available at: https://www.oprf.ru/chambermembers/members/user/2333, accessed 12 November 2020.

[61]See also, Gabdulhakov (2019).

[62]'Stopkham byl vynuzhden zakryt' svoe otdelenie v Karelii', *Respublika*, 17 February 2016.

police as an institution has continued to be heavily criticised (Semukhina & Reynolds 2014). Like *Lev Protiv*, some vigilante groups also target the police during their raids, seeking out officers who dishonour the uniform. Rather than denouncing the state, they denounce the 'state's performance' (Abrahams 2007, p. 423), and it is therefore possible for a group to challenge the police while claiming to support the president and the regime. As a result, criticism of policy inactivity, ineffectiveness and bureaucratisation is a permanent feature of Russian vigilante shows. *Lev Protiv* revels in calling out police officers smoking in non-smoking areas with statements like: 'Next time, go and smoke somewhere else'; 'You should honour your epaulets by setting a good example'; or 'Given your behaviour, no wonder so many people say the police force sucks'.[63] However, *Lev Protiv* has not been suppressed by the authorities. On the contrary, their videos show—and my observations confirmed—that police forces respond to vigilante calls for enforcement and arrest the alleged wrongdoers. Sometimes police and vigilante groups even coordinate their actions, as in the case of some *Lev Protiv* raids in the centre of Moscow during the summer of 2019 (Kirpanova 2019).

Three patterns can be distinguished in the relationship between public authorities and Russian vigilantes: explicit delegation, implicit support, and more or less stated rejection. Explicit delegation concerns state-sponsored *StopKham*, *Lev Protiv* and *Khryushi Protiv*. Delegation in the case of *StopKham* was made explicit by a meeting of its leader with the president in 2013,[64] and, in the case of *Khryushi Protiv*, by the support of Vladimir Putin and an official appointment with the Minister of the Interior.[65] As previously indicated in connection with *StopKham*, this mode of delegation remains, however, ephemeral and basically fragile.

MAS provides a very enlightening case of implicit support. This group appeared in 2010 to fight the devastation caused among youngsters by a new synthetic drug called 'spice'. The authorities at that time were unable to stop sales of spice, which was not yet included in the official list of prohibited substances.[66] The raids carried out and filmed by MAS were particularly spectacular. Wielding pickaxe handles, hammers and axes, the activists immobilised and destroyed the pushers' cars while waiting for the police, forced them to leave their dealing areas with smoke bombs, tied them up and splashed them with paint.[67] Filmed and put online, these raids were rich in *ekshen* and therefore very popular. No information was available about MAS funding, but they clearly had a budget, as shown by the quality of their videos. MAS was not officially state-sponsored but did not hide its proximity to power. Its leader, Arkady Grichishkin, used to show on social media pictures of himself with Vladimir Putin[68] and attended the pro-presidential International Youth

[63]Lev Protiv, #29, 'Kurenie i rukoprikladstvo politsii', *YouTube*, 29 January 2015, available at: https://www.youtube.com/watch?v=1iKXacN0uCE, accessed 12 November 2020.

[64]'Putin podderzhal aktivistov "Stopkham"', *RIA Novosti*, 2 August 2013.

[65]'Glava MVD poobshchalsya s "Khryushami"', *NTV*, 1 August 2012.

[66]'Pravitel'stvo RF vklyuchilo komponenty spaisov v perechen' zapreshchennykh veshchestv', *Tass*, 13 December 2014.

[67]See for instance, 'Molodezhny antinarkotichesky spetsnaz. Reid', *YouTube*, 6 June 2013, available at: https://www.youtube.com/watch?v=3CaaWLrZ6Qw, accessed 12 November 2020.

[68]This picture is available at: http://combat.extreme.sportedu.ru/content/molodezhnyi-antinarkoticheskii-spetsnaz?theme=simply_modern, accessed 12 November 2020.

Forums *Seliger* in 2012 and 2013. His Facebook page was perfectly aligned with the official stance on developing healthy and patriotic youth. However, MAS stopped its activity in 2013, as soon as 'spice' was added to the list of prohibited narcotics. Grichishkin has since devoted himself to charitable work, combat sports and the promotion of patriotism. He has attempted to start new projects dealing with the denunciation of scams (for instance, fake diploma smuggling) but has not met with the same success as with MAS.[69] He has taken part in the *Antimaidan* movement denouncing US interference in the so-called 'coloured' revolutions in the post-Soviet space. Funded in 2015, *Antimaidan* aimed to prevent, through the use of force if need be, any attempt to destabilise the Russian political regime.[70] In contrast to other groups trying to use the legislative context to justify their activity, MAS intervened to bridge a legislative failure. This case shows the possibility for the state of managing, indirectly and for a limited amount of time, a security issue by entrusting the mission to volunteer citizens. The striking illegality of MAS raids seems to have been covered up by the authorities, since blatant violence committed during the raids and showed on social media have never been prosecuted (Favarel-Garrigues & Shukan 2019).

Such tolerance can be observed with respect to groups that develop forms of vigilantism focused on political or religious issues. Like MAS, the National Liberation Movement (*Natsional'noe Osvoboditel'noe Dvizhenie*—NOD), for instance, denounces foreign interference in Russian politics. This movement is not only hostile to liberal opponents like Aleksander Naval'nyi, but also to human rights NGOs partially financed by Western funds. The group's targets include, for instance, the well-known NGO *Memorial*, accused of serving US interests by painting a bleak picture of the Russian past, in particular by tarnishing Stalin's record. Other groups, such as Christian State (*Khristianskoe gosudarstvo*) and 40 × 40 (*Sorok sorokov*), have acted in the name of the values of Orthodox Christianity; they oppose abortion, 'decadent' art, 'propaganda of non-traditional sexual relations among minors' and blasphemy.[71] However, these reactionary groups call into question the boundaries of vigilantism: their autonomy is dubious; they maintain more or less public ties with factions of the political elite; and they are closer to supplementary forces, for instance, Cossack units, ready to combat regime enemies (Turovskii 2015).

Repression is mainly directed at those vigilantes who fight police corruption and hunt down paedophiles. The car-blogger Davidych was not prosecuted for his initiatives against corruption among road-traffic policemen until he launched a more ambitious investigation—denouncing senior officials' illicit enrichment through number-plate trafficking.[72] He was arrested on charges of 'large-scale fraud' in February 2016 and

[69]See the VKontakte page of the *Antilokh* project, available at: https://vk.com/antilohmsk?z=video-24199209_456254107%2F93a24cae322fec4c25%2Fpl_wall_-55037277, accessed 12 November 2020.

[70]See his VKontakte profile picture, in which he stamps on the US flag. He was interviewed on television as an 'Antimaidan movement activist' in February 2015, see: 'Lidery dvizheniya "Antimaidan" proveli pervuyu publichnuyu aktsiyu', *5 kanal*, 16 February 2015, available at: www.5-tv.ru/news/94187, accessed 12 November 2020.

[71]On 40 × 40, see Turovskii (2015).

[72]See Davidych's investigation, 'Okhota Davidycha. Udar Pervy', *YouTube*, 23 November 2015, available at: https://www.youtube.com/watch?v=XF-i9bba1nA&t=1609s, accessed 12 November 2020.

imprisoned for two years (Malyutina 2018).[73] Hunting down paedophiles is another area in which the most radical movements have been banned by the government, accusing them of 'extremism'. The above-mentioned neo-Nazi agitator Tesak sought to use his notoriety in a variety of commercial projects supported by *Restrukt*. The most popular was Occupy Paedophilia, but other initiatives were adopted to fight social ills such as drug trafficking and alcohol consumption. Tesak's activity was initially welcomed: many talk shows were devoted to him, and his attempt to rehabilitate his neo-Nazi image by targeting paedophiles was showing results. In some cases, his 'safaris' led to convictions for paedophile acts, as in the case of a top tax administration official in the Moscow region.[74] There were, nonetheless, scandals—as in the Kamensk-Uralsky case described above—when his ultra-violent supporters overstepped the mark. Although Tesak's last prison sentence—ten years, which he had been serving since 2014 until his death in 2020—was not directly related to his anti-paedophilia activity but to incitement to racial hatred, robbery and hooliganism, *Restrukt* as an organisation was dissolved in 2014 as part of the ruling against him. This decision has not prevented, however, some local branches from continuing to spread videos on the web.[75] Whereas each vigilante project monopolises a potentially profitable niche, the anti-paedophilia campaign encourages the formation of a competitive space in which moral entrepreneurs confront each other and seek to impose their definition of the boundaries of legitimate violence in the sector, as shown by the example of the state-sponsored *Sdai Pedofila* project (Favarel-Garrigues 2020a).

Conclusion

In 2010s Russia, vigilantes show a particular combination of references to civil society, law-enforcement practices and entrepreneurialism in the age of the internet. For the best-known groups, profit takes a central place in the enterprise. All vigilante groups share a common critique of the performance of Russian law-enforcement agencies; however, this critique in no way destabilises political order in Russia. On the contrary, Russian vigilante groups strengthen state legitimacy in two ways. Firstly, the groups I have scrutinised are not able to anticipate or predict the public authorities' attitude towards them. Such a situation, while being characterised by permanent instability, shows that the balance of power clearly tilts towards institutional actors that can profit from it, as these actors can either tolerate a group of 'useful activists' or liquidate groups of 'extremists'. The opening of a space for negotiation of the right to use force with impunity echoes a governmental message according to which it can be legitimate to break the law to maintain order or to defend a right cause. In a context wherein social movements as *Antimaidan* or the NOD are ready to defend the country against any insurrection promoted from abroad, the preference for order is dissuasive indeed. These unbalanced configurations feature two competing visions of policing. Vigilantes expect the police to enforce the law in an uncompromising way. Whereas police activity is usually defined by

[73]Davidych was released in December 2018.
[74]'Poimanny Tesakom pristav-pedofil poluchil 2,5 goda t'yurmy', *NTV*, 24 August 2014.
[75]The videos produced by Tesak, which were mostly banned, nonetheless reappear regularly on the web.

its discretionary nature, the activists I have observed differ because they are intransigent: any offence they notice must be stopped and the end justifies the means. Paradoxically, this radical conception of policing may improve the legitimacy of law-enforcement agencies, as many comments under raid videos suggest. Any police officer who appears professional and law-abiding compares favourably to the vigilantes in action, who unintentionally contribute to humanising the police, give credibility to the justice system and, ultimately, help to maintain political order.

References

Abrahams, R. (1998) *Vigilant Citizens: Vigilantism and the State* (Oxford, Polity Press).

Abrahams, R. (2007) 'Some Thoughts on Vigilantism', in Pratten, D. & Sen, A. (eds).

Bayley, D. & Shearing, C. (2001) *The New Structure of Policing. Description, Conceptualization and Research Agenda* (Washington, DC, National Institute of Justice).

Becker, H. (1963) *Outsiders. Studies in the Sociology of Deviance* (New York, NY, The Free Press of Glencoe).

Bennett, T., Holloway, K. & Farrington, D. (2006) 'Does Neighborhood Watch Reduce Crime? A Systematic Review and Meta-Analysis', *Journal of Experimental Criminology*, 2, 4.

Brown, R. M. (1975) *Strain of Violence: Historical Studies of American Violence and Vigilantism* (New York, NY, Oxford University Press).

Caughey, J. W. (1960) *Their Majesties The Mob: The Vigilante Impulse in America* (Chicago, IL, Chicago University Press).

Cheskin, A. & March, L. (2015) 'State–Society Relations in Contemporary Russia: New Forms of Political and Social Contention', *East European Politics*, 31, 3.

Daucé, F. (2013) *Une paradoxale oppression. Le pouvoir et les associations en Russie* (Paris, CNRS Éditions).

Elias, N. & Dunning, E. (1994) *Sport et civilisation. La violence maîtrisée* (Paris, Éditions Fayard).

Emerina, N. (2013) 'Narod zovut k Tesaku', *Gazeta.ru*, 11 September.

Favarel-Garrigues, G. (2011) *Policing Economic Crime in Russia. From Soviet Planned Economy to Privatisation* (London & New York, NY, Hurst/Columbia University Press).

Favarel-Garrigues, G. (2020a) 'Digital Vigilantism and Anti-Paedophile Activism in Russia. Between Civic Involvement in Law Enforcement, Moral Policing and Business Venture', *Global Crime*, 21, 3–4.

Favarel-Garrigues, G. (2020b) 'Moral Policing Under Critique in Russia. Controversies Around Lev Protiv in Moscow', in Trottier, D., Gabdulhakov, R. & Huang, Q. (eds).

Favarel-Garrigues, G. & Gayer, L. (2016) 'Violer la loi pour maintenir l'ordre. Le vigilantisme en débat', *Politix*, 29, 115.

Favarel-Garrigues, G. & Shukan, I. (2019) 'Perspectives on Post-Soviet Vigilantism. Introduction', *Laboratorium: Russian Review of Social Research*, 11, 3.

Favarel-Garrigues, G., Tanner, S. & Trottier, D. (2020) 'Introducing Digital Vigilantism', *Global Crime*, 21, 3–4.

Fedorov, P. (2015) 'Trezvye dvory—bandity ili geroi', *Live Journal*, 15 June, available at: https://pasha-vidik.livejournal.com/14681.html, accessed 12 November 2020.

Fourchard, L. (2016) 'Engagements sécuritaires et féminisation du vigilantisme en Afrique du Sud', *Politix*, 29, 115.

Gabdulhakov, R. (2019) 'Heroes or Hooligans? Media Portrayal of StopXam (Stop a Douchebag) Vigilantes in Russia', *Laboratorium: Russian Review of Social Research*, 11, 3.

Gabowitsch, M. (2018) 'Are Copycats Subversive? Strategy-31, the Russian Runs, the Immortal Regiment, and the Transformative Potential of Non-Hierarchical Movements', *Problems of Post-Communism*, 65, 5.

Galeotti, M. (2007) 'Private Security and Public Insecurity: Outsourced Vigilantism in Modern Russia', in Pratten, D. & Sen, A. (eds).

Galeotti, M. (2012) 'Purges, Power and Purpose: Medvedev's 2011 Police Reforms', *The Journal of Power Institutions in Post-Soviet Societies*, 13.

Gerber, T. & Mendelson, S. (2008) 'Public Experiences of Police Violence and Corruption in Contemporary Russia: A Case of Predatory Policing?', *Law & Society Review*, 42, 1.

Gorlizki, Y. (1998) 'Delegalization in Russia: Soviet Comrades' Courts in Retrospect', *The American Journal of Comparative Law*, 46, 3.

Gusfield, J. R. (1963) *Symbolic Crusade. Status Politics and the American Temperance Movement* (Urbana and Chicago, IL, University of Illinois).

Hemment, J. (2012) 'Nashi, Youth Voluntarism, and Potemkin NGOs: Making Sense of Civil Society in Post-Soviet Russia', *Slavic Review*, 71, 2.

Jaffrelot, C. (2019) *L'Inde de Modi. National-populisme et démocratie ethnique* (Paris, Fayard).

Jobard, F. & De Maillard, J. (2015) *Sociologie de la police* (Paris, Armand Colin).

Johnston, L. (1996) 'What is Vigilantism?', *British Journal of Criminology*, 36, 2.

Khodzhaeva, E. (2016) *Lokal'nye initsiativy okhrany obshchestvennogo poryadka v Rossii: ot narodnykh druzhin do munitsipal'noi militsii* (St Petersburg, Tsentr Strategicheskikh Razrabotok).

Khodzhaeva, E. (2019) 'Revival of the DND (People's Volunteer Squads) in Russia: A Case of Top-Down Social Mobilization', *Laboratorium: Russian Review of Social Research*, 11, 3.

Kirpanova, E. (2019) 'Lev? Lev ozveret', *Novaya Gazeta*, 15 June.

Kozlov, V. (2016) 'Skinkhedy, bortsy s sistemoi. Kto takie "primorskie partizany" i kakie prestupleniya oni sovershili', *Meduza*, 19 July.

Lapointe, M. (2014) *Nettoyer Montréal. Les campagnes de moralité publique 1940–1954* (Québec, Septentrion).

Lazutin, M. (2019) 'Otvety na voprosy', *YouTube*, 17 April, available at: https://www.youtube.com/watch?v=8hXTGfBVQXs, accessed 12 November 2020.

Le Huérou, A. (2012) 'Police Brutality and Police Reform in Russia and the CIS. Introduction', *The Journal of Power Institutions in Post-Soviet Societies*, 13.

Levo-Pravo (2020) 'Kameru uberi! Ili mozhno li snimat' cheloveka bez razresheniya?', 14 April, available at: https://zen.yandex.ru/media/duralexsedlex42/kameru-uberi-ili-mojno-li-snimat-cheloveka-bez-razresheniia-5e95c5ca984e257a197100b5, accessed 12 November 2020.

Lyutykh, S. (2016) 'Intelligent-provokatory', *Lenta.ru*, 17 February.

Malyutina, D. (2018) 'Srok dlya stritreisera: Davidychu ostalos' nedolgo', *Gazeta.ru*, 19 October.

Martsinkevich, M. T. (2014) 'Pravozashchita', *VKontakte*, 29 March, available at: https://vk.com/wall-67113019_1223, accessed 12 November 2020.

Moncada, E. (2017) 'Varieties of Vigilantism: Conceptual Discord, Meaning and Strategies', *Global Crime*, 18, 4.

Pfeifer, M. (2004) *Rough Justice: Lynching and American Society, 1874–1947* (Urbana, IL, University of Illinois Press).

Pratten, D. & Sen, A. (eds) (2007) *Global Vigilantes* (London, Hurst).

Roizman, Y. (2005) *Gorod bez narkotikov* (Ekaterinburg, Fond Gorod bez Narkotikov).

Romanov, D. (2013) 'Pokhorony "Aleny SS" vyzvali isteriku sredi natsistov', *MK.ru*, 16 October.

Rosenbaum, H. J. & Sederberg, P. C. (1976) 'Vigilantism: An Analysis of Establishment Violence', in Rosenbaum, H. J. & Sederberg, P. C. (eds) *Vigilante Politics* (Philadelphia, PA, University of Pennsylvania Press).

Semukhina, O. & Reynolds, K. M. (2014) 'Russian Citizens' Perceptions of Corruption and Trust of the Police', *Policing and Society*, 24, 2.

Shapira, H. (2013) *Waiting for José: The Minutemen's Pursuit of America* (Princeton, NJ, Princeton University Press).

Shnirel'man, V. (2011) *Porog tolerantnosti. Ideologiya i praktika novogo rasizma. Tom 2* (Moscow, Novoe literaturnoe obozrenie).

Solopov, M. (2020) 'Chem zapomnilsya Maksim Martsinkevich po prozvishchu Tesak—samy talantlivy mediamanipulator iz rossiiskikh neonatsistov', *Meduza*, 16 September.

Taylor, B. (2011) *State Building in Putin's Russia. Policing and Coercion after Communism* (New York, NY, Cambridge University Press).

Trottier, D. (2017) 'Digital Vigilantism as Weaponisation of Visibility', *Philosophy and Technology*, 30, 1.

Trottier, D., Gabdulhakov, R. & Huang, Q. (eds) (2020) *Introducing Vigilant Audiences* (Cambridge, Open Book Publishers).

Turovskii, D. (2013) 'Obraztsovo-pokazatel'noe unizhenie', *Lenta.ru*, 5 July.

Turovskii, D. (2014) 'Moya orientatsiya—eto amoral'no?', *Meduza*, 12 December.

Turovskii, D. (2015) 'Stroiteli oflain-gosudarstva', *Meduza*, 22 September.

Turovskii, D. (2020) '"Belaya sotnya": nasledniki Tesaka', *Meduza*, 20 October. https://meduza.io/news/2014/10/20/belaya-sotnya-nasledniki-tesaka, accessed 12 November 2014.

Volkov, V. (2002) *Violent Entrepreneurs: The Use of Force in the Making of Russian Capitalism* (Ithaca, NY, Cornell University Press).

Technological Solutions for Complex Problems: Emerging Electronic Surveillance Regimes in Eurasian Cities

ERICA MARAT & DEBORAH SUTTON

Abstract

This essay examines 'smart city' initiatives rapidly emerging across Eurasia that are aimed at the surveillance of disorderly and criminal behaviour in public spaces. They are a result of both locally driven demand to modernise law enforcement and global pressures to innovate. We specifically compare Kyiv, Almaty, and Bishkek. Each city differs in regard to who initiated smart city policies and under what conditions new technology was purchased from foreign vendors. Our essay contributes to the growing socio-legal literature on Eurasia by analysing how these electronic surveillance projects are used to manufacture an orderly, safe society and achieve modernity without the burden of deeper political change.

'SMART CITY' IS THE NEW BUZZWORD IN CITIES ACROSS Eurasia. Moscow's mayor, Sergei Sobyanin, has pledged to make the Russian capital among the most interconnected cities in the world, on a par with New York and London.[1] Kyiv's mayor, Vitali Klitschko, plans to expand the use of facial recognition cameras beyond the city's central zones (Kulesh 2020). The president of Kyrgyzstan has declared 2019 to be 'the year digital technology comes to daily life', and the country's first 28 smart cameras have been installed in Bishkek.[2] Most capital cities and large urban areas in the post-Soviet space have already embraced smart city technologies, and those that have not are in the process of finding smart technology solutions to persistent social problems. From Minsk to Dushanbe, state and local officials have joined the global trend of automating urban governance (see Figure 1). City plans differ in terms of creativity, level of public oversight, and even their understanding of what it means to be 'smart'; however, almost all smart city projects agree on the law-enforcement benefits of speed cameras and other forms of automated surveillance.

These socio-technological imaginaries (Jasanoff & Kim 2015) of automated methods of law enforcement in an urban setting aim at the most substantive change to date in the

[1] 'Sergei Sobyanin: Moskva ne ustupaet drugim mirovym stolitsam po urovnyu tekhnologii', *Mos.ru*, 13 September 2017.

[2] 'Prezident ob"yavil 2019 god "Godom razvitiya regionov i tsifrovizatsii strany"', *Kabar.kg*, 1 January 2019.

everyday work of police and criminal justice systems in Eurasia. This change takes power away from interior ministries in favour of technologies controlled by municipal authorities, other security structures, and international firms. Police are no longer the only enforcer of order on the streets; today, they complement the work of automated systems. Technologies also help police and municipal authorities to move towards results-oriented law enforcement by measuring success in terms of the number of interdictions, successful criminal investigations, arrests, and fines imposed thanks to documented violations. This use of technologies serves the larger ideal of a society in which even minor crimes are meticulously documented, a habit dating back to the Soviet tradition of criminological research (Solomon 1974; Shelley 1979). Using Jasanoff and Kim's (2015) 'dreamscape of modernity', a notion that describes a collective vision of technological advancement with concrete measurable sociological outcomes, this essay views the pursuit of smart cities in Eurasia as an imaginary of a more orderly society with fewer crimes, an ideal community that simultaneously strives to attain modernity without the burden of deeper political change.

Municipal and national authorities embarking on smart city innovations have also been influenced by global moves towards digital governance. Thanks to advanced computational powers and access to 'big data', political leaders have sought to harness artificial intelligence (AI) to drive behavioural change and economic growth (Horowitz 2018; Li 2018). The pursuit of AI has set off an innovation competition among the United States, Russia, China, and the European Union (Kania 2017; Cummings *et al.* 2018; Roff 2019). In Eurasia, an arena of intense competition between regional powers like Russia and China, the pursuit of expanded automated surveillance is presented as the answer to both local demands for greater public safety and national ambitions for the greatest digital governance. The result is a variety of new surveillance regimes: some feature local and national control over collected data, while in other cases firms linked to foreign governments have control. Countries with greater dependence on foreign vendors inevitably become part of global competition for data collection for AI purposes. These global firms skilfully adapt their product pitch to meet the safety needs of different cities (Söderström *et al.* 2014; McNeill 2015). Despite the spread of surveillance technologies in public spaces, the public knows (and inquires) little about data-collection methods, including exactly what and whom the new smart cameras are 'watching'. Meanwhile, the global and local spheres are becoming increasingly interconnected.

We review smart city initiatives rapidly emerging across Eurasia on two dimensions: first, local initiatives to modernise law enforcement and, second, global pressures to innovate fuelled both by smart city trends pursued by wealthy cities and transnational state-controlled firms promoting their own security products. This two-level analysis is necessary to understand the motivations for innovation that lead domestic and international government and private actors to ultimately pursue different goals. Domestic demand for smart technologies could not be supplied without access to expensive foreign products at favourable rates. And these transactions—albeit discounted—allow for state-controlled technology companies in China and Russia to increase their competitive edge on the international scene by entering new markets. Local and international incentives combine, but also collide, as these groups meet in a city space and collaborate on developing technology-based law-enforcement solutions.

Drawing on Susan Strange's (1996) theorisation of knowledge, governance, and the exercise of power in international political economy, we ask: who is watching whom? Is it the global and regional powers that furnish the equipment, the municipal authorities who purchase it, or the security agencies that have access to surveillance? We answer these questions by analysing the supply chain process in three cities: Kyiv, Almaty, and Bishkek. Each case study paints a different picture in terms of who initiated the smart city policies and under what conditions new technology was purchased from foreign vendors. The three cities' varying wealth is an important factor in determining their acquisition of innovative technologies and their relations with both foreign providers of technologies and international ideas of modernity. We find that the more a city depends on foreign investments for smart city projects, like Bishkek and Kyiv, the greater the involvement of foreign companies in local efforts to use smart technologies for results-oriented law enforcement. Wealthier cities like Almaty and Moscow are able to purchase competitive IT solutions from a more diverse set of providers and retain leverage over collected data. They are still, however, guided by global metrics of what constitutes 'smartness' within a city.

Of the three cities we examine, Kyiv and Bishkek have become dependent on foreign providers—China and Russia. Both cities have prioritised increasing law-enforcement capabilities in diverse neighbourhoods where newcomers mix with long-term residents. Bishkek, in particular, has deployed smart technology solutions to reduce disorderly behaviour and crime. Authorities have used statistics generated by technological solutions to declare reductions in criminal acts and disorderly behaviour. However, any gains may come at the expense of external access to data generated through smart cameras. Kyiv, Bishkek, and other cities collaborating with foreign technology vendors may be inadvertently sharing surveillance data with foreign governments.

By contrast, in Almaty, the mayor's office (*akimat*) has the means to procure whatever technologies administrators believe the city needs and to purchase from any provider. The city authorities view smart city concepts as a way to close the connectivity gap between Almaty and global technology pioneers such as Seoul and Singapore.[3] At the same time, city authorities are responding to local demands for a more orderly and convenient city life. The desire for improved aesthetics and uniformity coincides with growing population diversity, expanding economic opportunities, and an emerging urban middle class. As seen in other knowledge and legal regimes, the smart city concept in Almaty is a foreign import embraced and reinforced by local leaders.

This essay surveys the primary trends and consequences in the global rush to apply technological solutions to urban problems. While the demand for modernisation of crime control may originate locally, smart technologies built on a city level are increasingly part of hegemonic forms of knowledge production, as well as an emerging arena for geopolitical competition between China and Russia. The relationships between residents and public spaces and regional state-led tech firms are being gradually transformed as well. Some criminal and disorderly conduct is punished but without a deeper consideration

[3]'Almaty planiruet sotrudnichestvo s Singapurskimi kompaniyami v sfere "Smart city"', *profit.kz*, 20 February 2017.

of the circumstances causing such behaviour. Municipal officials do not deny that Chinese firms, such as HikVision and Huawei, and the Russian firm, Vega, collect intelligence data from foreign cities using their equipment.[4] On the contrary, the authorities seem resigned to the fact that geopolitical dynamics appear in the guise of urban innovation. None of the policy documents or statements referred to in our study touch upon the idea of surveillance or privacy concerns related to surveillance and focus, rather, on law-enforcement innovations.[5]

Surveillance and public space

A ubiquitous yet elusive term, 'smart city' signifies a space that measures, manages, and predicts human behaviour and social interactions (Batty 2013; Söderström *et al.* 2014; Angelidou 2015). First discussed in the early 1990s, the concept has taken on a broad range of variations, including 'intelligent city', 'knowledge city', 'ubiquitous city', 'sustainable city', and 'digital city' (Cocchia 2014). In the 2010s, the notion of 'smart' as applied to a city merged with neoliberal ideals of free markets, economic development, connectivity, secure spaces, and capital accumulation (Kitchin 2014; Datta 2015; Kitchin *et al.* 2019; Willis 2020). In the urge for connectivity, 'smartness' as a socio-technological imaginary depicts public spaces that allow free human activity but prevent or punish behaviours that impede economic exchange or social experiences. Smart city innovations combine surveillance as a tool for governance (Brayne 2017) with the idea that surveillance improves the lives of the urban public. As a result of smart city innovations, public spaces become zones of population control and expand local authorities' ability to profit from offensive behaviour (Frischmann & Selinger 2018).

Literature on smart cities in the Global South see rapid technological advancements within a city as a reaction to growing urban diversity fuelled by internal and external migration (Ghertner 2015; Watson 2016). Cities became centres of economic growth and are further cultivated by urban authorities to fully exploit their potential (Grossi & Pianezzi 2017). A growing economy inevitably produces crime and disorderly behaviour, followed by efforts to eradicate them (Garland 2001). Authorities turn to surveillance and urban planning to control unruly areas populated by economically less-desirable groups with varying legal status, language skills, wealth, and economic potential (Koskela 2000; Galdon-Clavell 2013). The migrant population and urban poor, who are not always able to participate in the formal economy, need to turn into civilised citizens. In other words, the socio-technological imaginary of a smart city presumes a place in which diverse groups peacefully coexist; their behaviour positively influenced by the presence of surveillance and automation. Combined with the neoliberal urge to quantify growth and accumulate competitive scores of market performance, 'smart city' becomes synonymous with creating a uniform urban space to achieve organised economic prosperity.

Whereas 'smart' is problematic in some contexts, 'safe' inevitably reflects political divides. Calls to improve safety presume the existence of dangerous individuals and

[4]Interview with a former member of Kyrgyzstan's prime minister's office, Bishkek, January 2019.
[5]Interview with a former member of Kyrgyzstan's prime minister's office, Bishkek, January 2019.

subgroups, including internal migrants, populations engaged in the shadow economy, and the urban poor, who threaten the wellbeing of others. Public spaces become formally privatised or informally dominated by wealthier populations and long-term urban residents, while newly urbanised groups find themselves relegated to poor urban neighbourhoods (Koskela 2000). According to the Habermasian argument of the dominant class developing institutions, privileged urban groups are allowed to decide which groups are 'nefarious' and require regulation of everyday behaviour (Habermas 2010). The urban middle class, which typically benefits from the increased surveillance, is likely to support smart city innovations. Technologies, as a result, function not only as law-enforcement tools but also to modernise entire groups. They become a supplement to migration-related functions performed by police officers, as well as order-maintenance and zero-tolerance law-enforcement practices.

If viewed from a post-Soviet perspective, state-driven modernity projects have popular support while enforcing the interests of the state. Nevertheless, government policies eventually extend regime control over diverse groups, just as Soviet-era practices of enforcing autocratic regimes did (Kassymbekova 2017). Aspirations for modernity for the society and the inclination to repress social groups may coexist in the state's promise to improve quality of life within a city. Technological advancement in cities like Almaty, for instance, reflects the combination of technologies to enforce social order with popular support for illiberal values of governance (Junisbai 2010; Laruelle & Royce 2019). According to a high-ranking employee of an Almaty city *akimat*, after extensive market deregulation in the 1990s and lopsided wealth accumulation in the 2000s, urban residents want to see a more organised urban space replace *samostroy* (jerry-rigged), street trading, and unregulated street advertising.[6] Following the initial rush to improve their private home spaces and accumulate material wealth (Bissenova 2012), Almaty residents are now looking to improve their public spaces. And the desire for aesthetics has led to the securitisation of public spaces.

The tension between ideas of modern urbanity and vernacular categories of 'backwardness' is well documented in studies of the urban middle class and migration in post-Soviet cities. As Schröder puts it, 'such identification habitually entails distinctive lifestyle aspirations of consumption and display, of sophistication and communication, of mobility and the attachment to multiple modernities' (Schröder 2016, p. 154). In most capital cities, market relations have led to more spontaneous interactions, at times blending populations with different incomes, as well as long-term residents and recent arrivals. Global cultural influences and commodity flows have transformed urban spaces (Schröder 2016). Shopping malls especially have become areas of socio-economic intermingling, and their heightened security measures, such as guards and CCTV, make them appear safer spaces for economic transactions than the open streets (Jäger 2016). Central squares, on the other hand, have become spaces mostly visited by tourists and new residents, associated with 'backwardness'. Such perceptions have been translated into specific law-enforcement initiatives by local and national authorities (Marat 2018). The demand for curated safety now extends to public spaces where long-term residents find

[6]Interview with an employee of the Almaty *akimat*, December 2018.

and fear the 'backwardness' of newcomers. 'Smart' and 'safe' are understood as the absence of disorderly and criminal behaviour through prevention, evidence collection, and punishment.

Range of local regimes

In the Eurasian context, the phrase 'smart cities' is typically used interchangeably with 'safe' and 'less corrupt' and comes with quantifiable metrics for both indicators. For this essay, we conducted discursive analysis of policy statements and published programmes promoting smart city initiatives during 2015–2020, along with several interviews with former and current municipal officials in Bishkek and Almaty. We also scanned all available reports in major new outlets of smart technologies installed across Eurasian cities and in the three cities researched here and triangulated these data with municipal programmes announcing smart city innovations.[7] We then reviewed statistics and statements published by either municipal authorities or law-enforcement agencies on crime and disorderly behaviour detected by the new technologies.[8] This methodology helped construct a picture of what aspects of technological innovation were politically more salient both for the public and state authorities. To analyse the geopolitical pressures to innovate, we reviewed the policies of both Russian and Chinese governments and the available literature assessing both countries' global ambitions in the smart technology sector. Finally, we discussed whether the decision for city innovation was made on a national or local level. We argue that when decisions are made on a national level, surveillance becomes a bigger priority for innovation. On the local level, smart technologies serve the role of more effective collection of fines in addition to enforcing public order.

Authorities in each of the three cities examined here emphasised that the revenue generated from smart city programmes can be used for economic development. In other words, smart city technology is justified by results-oriented, aspirational, and predictable outcomes. Data collected through an automated process facilitate the imposition of fines for violations. Revenue collected through fines is then incorporated into national or city budgets. In 2015, Almaty's authorities even predicted a specific amount of crime reduction over the next five years.[9] As reflected in policy statements by municipal authorities and national security structures, the three main dimensions guiding smart city innovations in Almaty, Kyiv and Bishkek are public safety, efficient revenue collection, and more convenient urban life. In other Eurasian cities, including Tbilisi and Tallinn, automation in medical emergency services and public Wi-Fi are also included and overlap with other categories. All three cities surveyed in our study seek to prevent and interdict disorderly

[7]See for example: 'Za kievlianami nablyudayut 7000 videokamer. Kakie dannye oni sobirayut i dlya chego?', *tech.liga.net*, 6 October 2019; '"Bezopasnyi gorod". Vyvody posle analiza polumilliona dannykh', *Kaktus Media*, 22 December 2019.

[8]For example, the official website of the Kyrgyz Interior Ministry (mvd.gov.kg) and the Official Portal of Kyiv (kyivcity.gov.ua) regularly publish official data on new technologies and crime statistics, while outlets like *Tengrinews.kz* and *tech.liga.net* publish the latest innovations in smart and safe city programmes in Kazakhstan and Ukraine, respectively.

[9]Almaty has the most detailed plan for smart city innovations: see, 'Programma razvitiya Almaty—2020', 10 December 2015, available at: http://smartalmaty.kz/docs/ADP_2020.doc, accessed 4 April 2019.

behaviour, reduce corruption, and increase tax revenue using technological innovations. However, we find that smart city innovations are unevenly distributed across the cities and, more broadly, across urban and rural areas within the country. For example, surveillance technologies in particular are focused on central parts of each city as well as in areas of high traffic.

First, the most popular smart city innovations, such as CCTV cameras, facial recognition software, and traffic and parking sensors, facilitate surveillance. The expanding international use of surveillance technology coincides with growing global demands for results-oriented policing of urban spaces. The urge to tame criminal activity in cities by monitoring everyday behaviour aligns with national efforts to embrace result-oriented policing. Smart city innovations thus often extend existing mechanisms of micro-control of behaviour, such as the increased presence of police officers, signs regulating behaviour ('No Littering', 'No Spitting'), and video surveillance used by businesses and gated communities. Cameras have appeared in central squares, intersections, shopping areas, parks, and public squares across Kyiv, Bishkek and Almaty. Surveillance technologies are concentrated in busy markets and areas prone to public littering or spitting.

Yet photographic evidence of disorderly or criminal behaviours conveys a narrow representation of the vast range of experiences lived within a city. Evidence based on surveillance footage presents only a selected reality and is more akin to eyewitness testimony, not the more scientific evidence derived from fingerprints and DNA (Evison 2015). Visual evidence of disorderly behaviour often replaces a more comprehensive police investigation and is unlikely to be contested in courts. CCTV cameras change the metrics of how crimes are counted, pre-empted, and punished with more emphasis on crime statistics derived from surveilled areas (Koskela 2000). Cities can pick and choose what to surveil from a menu of different behaviours, depending on their own policy priorities (Germain *et al.* 2011). In Russia, for instance, Rostelecom has released an 'intelligent video surveillance' product based on AI software that analyses CCTV footage and automatically flags disorderly conduct and violence. It is then programmed to recognise this behaviour and report it to the police.[10] Instances of disorderly conduct or crimes documented on surveillance video can, in turn, increase the need for law enforcement.

Second, smart city technologies that focus on the efficient, automated collection of fines eliminate two persistent problems: collecting fines remotely (for example, punishing road violations without deploying police personnel) and collecting fines inefficiently (for example, avoiding corrupt police officers or bureaucrats). For instance, the Almaty *akimat* reports that, as a result of automation, proceeds from traffic fines reached US$180–200 million within one year, significantly higher than previous years, and revenue from public transport fares increased from US$20 million to US$30 million within 2018.[11] This technology also eliminates the need for often-corrupt middlemen, usually police officers or public transport operators, who pocket a portion of the penalties and fares they collect. Kazakhstan's major cities embraced such technology of automated payments for services and fines even before 'smart city' became a shorthand for 'modernisation'.

[10]'Prezentatsiya platformy "Umnyi gorod" proidet na forume v Ekaterinburge', *Tass.ru*, 9 April 2019.
[11]Interview with an employee of the Almaty *akimat*, December 2018.

Finally, while smart city initiatives can make city life more convenient, all of the programmes examined here make convenience secondary to safety and revenue generation. Municipal authorities elsewhere in Eurasia (including Minsk and Moscow) have expanded public transit, improved street lighting, added online payment options, and created Wi-Fi hotspots. However, within the three cities researched here, such amenities are provided by private companies, not municipal authorities, and have advanced at a slower rate, if at all, compared to the expansion of video surveillance, with cameras spreading at a higher rate compared to public Wi-Fi connection, automated emergency services or automated payments in public transport.

These socio-technological imaginaries of a smart city are advocated by professional societies (municipal and national authorities), as well as by state-led transnational corporations. The imaginaries are formalised in a collective agreement between municipal and national authorities on what constitute a society's pressing ills, how members of society relate to each other, and what the future of a nation should look like. They are a part of the 'master narrative' of a nation's identity and its imagined bright future (Jasanoff & Kim 2015). In Kazakhstan, smart cities have grown out of the leadership's ambition to belong to the 'club' of the world's most developed countries.[12] In Ukraine, the goal is to reduce corruption and move towards EU integration (Geitsya *et al.* 2015). In Kyrgyzstan, the goal is to regulate the chaotic political life of a nascent democracy (Tokoeva 2018). What is neglected in these approaches is an analysis of the factors that drive individuals to engage in criminal or disorderly behaviour, including high levels of unemployment, unequal access to infrastructure, and physical mobility.

Using smart technologies to solve public safety concerns changes global sources of local law enforcement. It offers a rival—or even replacement—option for the Western-driven rule-of-law programmes that proliferated in the 1990s and 2000s. Western donors presented the rule of law as being key to economic development and political democratisation. With some exceptions, Western rule-of-law programmes shied away from expanding or modernising the material base of law-enforcement agencies. Instead, assistance was used to train and re-train police personnel. Chinese and Russian surveillance technologies, by contrast, offer the opportunity to change law enforcement by revolutionising the tools. These technologies are transforming how crime and disorderly conduct are detected, investigated, and punished. The implications for the rule of law in countries embracing technology from authoritarian countries could signify the failure of the decades-long Western effort to imbue a value-based approach to policing and local governance without creating accountability mechanisms. Authoritarian models that impose automated rule of law as envisioned by the ruling elites may succeed.

[12]'Kazakhstan's Way—2050: Common Aim, Common Interests, Common Future', Official Site of the President of the Republic of Kazakhstan, 17 January 2014, available at: http://www.akorda.kz/ru/special/speeches/internal_political_affairs/in_speeches_and_addresses/poslanie-glavy-gosudarstva-nursultana-nazarbaeva-narodu-kazahstana, accessed 26 September 2020.

Almaty

Smart city innovations are a city-level reaction to the national government's goal to modernise and move Kazakhstan into the ranks of wealthy countries by 2050. The city's development plan adopted in 2015 launched an ambitious and meticulously planned multi-step developmental agenda.[13] Urban innovations, especially in larger cities, take place amid the robust presence of police and pre-existing structures of public regulations. The municipal innovations in Almaty are not to fill in the gaps created by inefficient law enforcement, but to replace the corrupt practices of rank-and-file public administrators with legal forms of collection of fines. The authorities in Almaty know that skimmed fines and fees undercut the real potential of the mayor's office to contribute to the national economy. Smart technologies are thus a response to an ineffective state.

The Almaty city *akimat* adapted the 2050 agenda to produce the 'General Plan of the Development of Almaty 2020'.[14] It establishes metrics for making the capital city more comfortable and safer for the residents, as well as safe 'from' certain residents who may interfere with the city's aspirations for modernity.[15] The initiatives are driven by the *akimat*'s desire to unleash the city's full economic potential through creating a business-friendly environment and efficient collection of fines. According to the *akimat*, law-enforcement surveillance introduces facial recognition capacity and real-time monitoring to the city's most densely populated areas. The security aspect of the plan is quantified by specified target levels for crime, fatal traffic accidents, thefts per 100 people, and trust in the police.[16] The city claims that in 2018, video surveillance helped solve 1,543 crimes and recorded 530,677 traffic violations; as a direct result, fines of over five billion tenge were imposed.[17] The rates of both crimes recorded and fines collected have increased with the expansion of automation, while, according to the Almaty police, incidents of pickpocketing and theft have decreased (Utenova 2019). The city currently operates over 100,000 cameras, with plans for full coverage within the next few years. Almaty also uses Russian Vocord cameras with facial recognition technology at its metro and in other public spaces as well.[18] The *akimat* believes that changes in behaviour will take longer to achieve, so the current goal is to ensure that violations are punished.[19]

By driving these innovation projects in the late 2010s, the Almaty *akimat* gradually took over the traditional functions of the local office of the Interior Ministry (*Upravlenie Vnutrennikh Del*—UVD), specifically the traffic division. The *akimat* determines areas for surveillance and governance automation in the name of eradicating corruption and increasing economic activity, and then collaborates with UVD. Fine payments generated

[13]'General'nyi plan razvitiya', Almaty *akimat*, available at: https://almaty.gov.kz/mobile.php?page_id=3200&lang=1&parent_id=3152, accessed 4 April 2019.

[14]'General'nyi plan razvitiya', Almaty *akimat*, available at: https://almaty.gov.kz/mobile.php?page_id=3200&lang=1&parent_id=3152, accessed 4 April 2019.

[15]Interview with a former employee of the Almaty *akimat*, January 2019.

[16]'General'nyi plan razvitiya', Almaty *akimat*, available at: https://almaty.gov.kz/mobile.php?page_id=3200&lang=1&parent_id=3152, accessed 4 April 2019.

[17]'V obshchestvennykh mestakh Almaty ustanovyat eshche tysyachi videokamer', *Profit.kz*, 9 April 2019.

[18]'Proekt Sistema raspoznavaniya lits Vocord FaceControl pomogla poimat' zloumyshlennikov v metropolitene g. Almaty', *Tadviser.ru*, September 2014.

[19]Interview with an employee of the Almaty *akimat*, December 2018.

from high-tech policing are deposited into the city's coffers, whereas fines collected as a result of traditional, face-to-face policing go to the Interior Ministry. However, *akimat*–UVD relations are mutually beneficial. Thanks to smart technologies, in 2018 the UVD reported an increase in successful investigations of crimes (arrest rates), and a corresponding decrease in petty crimes in 2018 compared with 2017. The reported statistics for both parameters were confined to areas with surveillance regimes and were presented as evidence that smart city innovations were already improving public safety.[20] Video footage often provides the only evidence for the crimes committed and may miss the context in which criminal or disorderly behaviour took place.

Almaty authorities were able to reject ideas imported by the national government. Following a rise in protests in 2019 after Nursultan Nazarbayev resigned from the presidency, the Committee on Legal Statistics and Special Accounts of the General Prosecutor's Office, with the backing of the pro-regime *Nur-Oran* party, announced in early January 2020 an initiative to install facial recognition technologies in areas with high concentration of people in Almaty. Smart cameras would be able to 'identify faces, licence plates, inadequate movements of people or transport' to monitor pickpockets (*karmanschiki*) in large crowds thanks to a private Qamqor[21] project responsible for AI development. Political activists complained that technologies would serve as a deterrent to political activism in the city, while legal activists raised concerns about citizens' rights to privacy (Alhabaev 2020a). Following these public complaints, the Almaty Police Department declined the project (Alhabaev 2020b). However, the initiative showed that Nur-Sultan (formerly Astana) is increasing its own capabilities in both installing smart technologies in Kazakhstan's cities and developing artificial intelligence.

Almaty's approach resembles Moscow's more than any of its Central Asian neighbours. In both Almaty and Nur-Sultan, technological infrastructure is built by Kazakhtelecom, a state-run firm that collaborates with local start-ups. External firms are invited to bid on projects on a competitive basis. Kazakhtelecom collects and manages the recorded data.[22] Like South Korea, Brazil, and Russia, Kazakhstan is buildings its own smart city, Aqkol, near the capital, from the ground up.[23] In line with the national goal of joining the club of most developed countries, Almaty has its own plan to develop AI capabilities based on domestically collected data as well as 5G connectivity. The city government portrays these ambitious plans to reform urban policing as an internally deliberated, carefully planned innovation that will serve the needs of the population.[24]

[20]'Bezopasnyi i umnyi gorod: V Almaty ispol'zuyutsya vozmozhnosti svyshe 118 tys. kamer videonablyudeniya', *NewTimes.kz*, 20 September 2018.

[21]Qamqor is a privately owned company focused on the analysis of patterns of criminal and disorderly behaviour in Kazakhstan and is not to be confused with a government portal that collects law enforcement statistics. 'Sistemu raspoznavaniya lits vnedryayut v Almaty', *Tengrinews.kz*, 11 January 2020.

[22]'Kazahtelekom' predstavil Kazahstan na Mobile World Congress Shanghai 2019', *Tengrinews.kz*, 26 June 2019.

[23]'Kak zhivet pervyi umnyi gorod Kazahstana. Akkol' prevrashchaetsya v Aqkol', *Tengrinews.kz*, 19 January 2019.

[24]'Iskusstvennyi intellekt—yadro umnogo goroda Akkol', *Profit.kz*, 22 February 2019. Other smart technologies include an online healthcare system, education portal Kundelik, and a mobile application 'Open Almaty' that allows residents to report broken streetlights and road problems, apply for government services, and manage transportation cards.

The AI-based system will allow national and local governments to produce a myriad of new correlations between naturally occurring parameters—such as weather conditions and air pollution—and behavioural indicators, such as school performance. In Nur-Sultan, meanwhile, local developers produced a surveillance system 'Sergek' that reportedly helped reduce road accidents and, in 2018, resulted in the collection of one billion tenge in fines for the *akimat*.[25] Other projects include an automated collection of public transportation fares through facial recognition technologies. As in Russia, surveillance technologies are applied to everyday civic governance in Nur-Sultan and Almaty without any transparency. Analysis of the data collected by such surveillance technologies will reflect the needs of political elites and their aspirations for modernity, not the needs or desires of the broader population.

Almaty's 'smart city' policies reflect the *akimat*'s own socio-technological imaginary of a wealthy, modern city within a country with a bright economic future. Almaty is a prime example of the tensions that emerge when the economic benefits from urban growth go overwhelmingly to the urban middle class, not the new residents often living in the city's outskirts. The city contributes one-quarter of Kazakhstan's GDP and sets its own priorities in modernising public spaces. Almaty's *akimat*, not the national authorities, plans city development in line with the national agenda, global standards, and local needs.[26] The city's authorities prioritise the preservation of the ideal urban middle-class lifestyle and elevate it to international standards by concealing the 'backwardness' of the city's migrant population. Social order is enforced against the very people who come to cities seeking new opportunities for education and economic security. The 'dreamscape of modernity' does not include a revision of redistributive programmes or a more open collaboration between municipal authorities and Almaty residents.

Municipal authorities strike a balance between national development priorities and local aesthetic concerns. Almaty's effort to blanket itself with video surveillance is inherently driven by the mayoral administration's efforts which align with the national ambition of joining the most-developed countries in the world. Other cities with greater penetration of technology and high ratings in 'smart city' indexes, including Moscow, New York, and Singapore, have become the benchmark for Almaty authorities. Like the Soviet regime, the state's efforts at modernisation and progress aim to improve not the daily life of citizens, but how they perceive the state. Cities with large migrant populations, including Moscow and Almaty, now lead the post-Soviet space in the penetration of surveillance into public spaces.

Kyiv

A lack of effective law enforcement at the street-level drove smart city innovations in the Ukrainian capital. Kyiv turned to two Chinese companies, HikVision and Huawei, to supply and install new surveillance cameras and provide cloud data storage. Kyiv mayor, Vitalii Klitschko, presented the initiative as a way forward for the city's security without

[25]'Sergek has Brought to the State Budget more than 1 Billion Tenges', *Daynews.kz*, 29 October 2018.
[26]Interview with an employee of the Almaty *akimat*, December 2018.

explaining why these particular foreign vendors were selected.[27] By 2020 the number of surveillance cameras exceeded 10,000, a significantly smaller number compared to Almaty (Kulesh 2020). However, unlike Almaty, where authorities primarily focus on collecting fines, in Kyiv the authorities stress the valuable role of smart cameras in solving crimes in areas where the police are in short supply.[28] The financial aspect of increased collection of fines from the population is rarely mentioned. Instead, the justification for smart technologies is mostly focused on crime interdiction and investigation. Cameras—some visible, some concealed—are used in central public spaces, including roads, bridges, schools, bus stops and tourist attractions.[29] They are intended to regulate behaviour by enabling the imposition of significant fines and also by reminding individuals that they are always being watched. Some cameras have facial recognition capabilities, and most can read number plates. 'Smart cameras' monitor activities in the central square (the Maidan), major streets, and urban beaches. In central Kyiv, the cameras help law-enforcement agencies monitor crowds during large events. Kyiv's smart cameras can determine 'the age, the route of travel and even the emotional state' of an individual in a crowd.[30]

After the ouster of pro-Russian leader Viktor Yanukovich as a result of Euromaidan protests in 2013–2014, political fault lines were exposed between regions and also between those proud to belong to the Ukrainian nation and those who felt disenfranchised by the rapid political change (Kulyk 2016). Kyiv, the epicentre of the Euromaidan demonstrations, itself is divided. Alongside intellectual elites looking to build a 'new' nation are those who disagree with or are indifferent to the recent political changes in the country. These groups mostly live in the central part of the city and include economically disenfranchised and apolitical youth, and the elderly population. The areas in which they live are policed more intensely and the government specifically broadcasts its efforts to deploy order-maintenance methods against these groups (Marat 2018). Police reform became one of the few signs of a functioning government amid continuing criticism of the corruption of President Petro Poroshenko's administration of 2014–2019. Therefore, technological innovations for even more pervasive state surveillance in the name of fighting crime were easy to sell to both Kyiv authorities and the Interior Ministry.

Statistics on crime solving and specific cases have allowed both Mayor Klitschko and the Interior Ministry to highlight the specific contributions of smart technology to the safety and modernisation of the city. However, while the mayor and the ministry are eager to underscore the abundance of new data available on urban crime,[31] they do not accept that there is a wider criminal landscape beyond that captured on camera. In one case, the police justified the use of facial recognition cameras by citing the arrest of a fugitive who had been on the run for 15

[27] 'Vitalii Klitschko: "Mi planumo vstanoviti u Kievi 8 tisyach kamer videosposterezhenniya"', Official Portal of Kyiv, 1 October 2016.

[28] 'Za kievlyanami nablyudayut 7000 videokamer. Kakie dannye oni sobirayut i dlya chego?', *tech.liga.net*, 6 October 2019.

[29] 'Sledyat za dorogami, det'mi i metro: Chto umeyut umnye kievskie dorozhnye kamery', *Ubr.ua*, 27 July 2018.

[30] 'Rozumne misto—bezpechne misto: scho znayut' pro nas smart-videokamery?', *Hromadske.ua*, 6 July 2018.

[31] 'Za kievlyanami nablyudayut 7000 videokamer. Kakie dannye oni sobirayut i dlya chego?', *tech.liga.net*, 6 October 2019.

years until he was spotted on camera.[32] The Interior Ministry also reported that 2,500 crimes were solved thanks to surveillance footage.[33] In 2018, Kyiv's mayor claimed that after cameras were installed, the crime rate declined by 37% and more crimes, including theft and the abduction of a new-born baby, were prevented.[34] Officials repeatedly cite the case of the abducted infant to justify the pervasive video surveillance. Such an emotive story implies that a well-surveilled space can stop a criminal in the act. What this imagery omits is the reality that some crimes will still go unsolved despite extensive footage and that there will continue to be successful arrests in areas without surveillance.

In Kyiv and other Ukrainian cities, the Interior Ministry, Security Council, and National Guard control surveillance footage. In the early stages of the 'smart city' policy, both the mayor and Interior Ministry asserted that this footage would be used for reducing crime and solving criminal cases.[35] However, the security agencies are also tasked with internal intelligence collection. All three security agencies informally compete for authority on the streets and a monopoly on domestic intelligence collection (Oliker *et al.* 2016). These agencies allow municipal administrative authorities access to the data to monitor disorderly conduct, but national agencies' use of surveillance is far broader than that of the city. Thus, the introduction of smart cameras has elevated the role of municipal authorities in law enforcement, as well as the ability of power ministries to advertise their efficiency in criminal investigations.

Journalists have suggested that Kyiv's reliance on HikVision and, increasingly, Huawei indicates possible kickbacks between the mayor's office and Chinese companies.[36] Huawei and HikVision are banned by the United States, the United Kingdom, Australia and New Zealand. Japan and Canada are considering banning the firms as well (Hawke 2020).[37] The point of dispute is that these companies are creating technologies for the purpose of monitoring and social control inside China. Beijing's experimentation with technologies reportedly also extends to Xinjiang detention camps (Kynge 2019). Disagreement between Huawei and the Western tech industry intensified in the early 2010s when the company began hiring hundreds of engineers from leading Western firms (Jenkins 2012) and was accused of stealing Western designs (Yap *et al.* 2019).

In Ukraine, HikVision has created its own Russian-language website where it shares the latest global innovations and tries to soothe the fears about surveillance voiced by Ukrainian media outlets. For example, in response to the fears of 'Chinese control' in Kyiv, HikVision cites its successful expansion in the United States to counter allegations that it might collect intelligence in Ukraine.[38] Despite its attempts to mitigate public suspicion, HikVision

[32]'Kak rabotaet sistema videonablyudeniya s raspoznovaniem lits v Kieve', *Ain.ua*, 24 October 2017.

[33]'U Kyivi za rik za dopomogoyu kamer sposterezhennya 2,5 tisyachi zlochiniv—politsiia', *Hromadske.ua*, 31 October 2018.

[34]'Rozumne misto—bezpechne misto: scho znayut' pro nas smart-videokameri?', *Hromadske.ua*, 6 July 2018.

[35]'Za kievlyanami nablyudayut 7000 videokamer. Kakie dannye oni sobirayut i dlya chego?', *tech.liga.net*, 6 October 2019.

[36]Interview with an independent Kyiv journalist, January 2019.

[37]'US Government Ban of Dahua, Hikvision, Huawei Takes Effect Now', *ipvm.com*, 13 August 2019, available at: https://ipvm.com/reports/aug-13-2019, accessed 9 September 2020.

[38]'Politsya S.Sh.A. vybiraet Hikvision', *hikvision.org.ua*, 26 April 2016.

remains under intense Western scrutiny for enabling the Chinese government in socially and politically suppressing its people. Like HikVision, Huawei—whose founder and president, Ren Zhengfei, is a People's Liberation Army veteran[39]—has also opened a research and development office in Kyiv.[40] Despite being relative latecomers to the global technologies market, both HikVision and Huawei have made impressive advances onto the global stage and are rapidly expanding in Eurasia.

Kyiv has also installed GPS tracking on its public trams and buses so that citizens can track them in real time. Several bus stops have been updated to include 'smart' boards that show the bus or tram's exact time of arrival, and updates automatically if there is a delay. Citizens can also track city utility vehicles (also newly equipped with GPS), like rubbish collection or snow removal.[41] Thus, whereas in Almaty the dreamscape of modernity is focused on the 'smart' aspect of technological innovations that compensates for an ineffective state, in Kyiv both smart and safe imaginaries of the public space blend. The city and national authorities frame modern devices of law enforcement as a way of achieving a safer public space in addition to the regular police and surveillance work done by security agencies.

Bishkek

The law-enforcement aspect of smart city innovations is even greater in Bishkek, the capital city with the least resources to attract investors. While Bishkek's mayor Aziz Surakmatov, appointed in 2018, sought to generate economic exchange and growth, municipal authorities lack the funds needed to drive large-scale modernisation.[42] As a result, there is a sharp division between 'safe' and 'smart' city projects, mirroring, in turn, a division between the Interior Ministry and the municipal authorities. As a national institution, the Interior Ministry's projects are guided by the national political leadership. Unlike in Kyiv and Almaty, neither the mayor's office nor the Interior Ministry aspires to join the top ranks of global 'smart cities'. Instead they respond to local demands voiced by civil society and municipal elected officials to expand law enforcement (Marat 2018). The socio-technological imaginary in Bishkek is thus much simpler than in Almaty and Kyiv: the goal is to have motorists comply with basic traffic regulations. This dreamscape reflects the government's promise to deliver a more orderly society through foreign innovations. Technologies are imported because the state cannot enforce something as basic as traffic laws.

The first traffic cameras slowed down drivers far more than any attempts by police, yet the number of recorded violations exceeded expectations. On the first day of testing in February 2019, Bishkek accumulated fines of 9,000,000 soms (US$129,000), suggesting that there are

[39]'Does Huawei or Ren Zhengfei Have Ties to the PLA?', available at: https://www.huawei.com/en/facts/question-answer/does-huawei-or-ren-zhengfei-have-ties-to-the-pla, accessed 1 September 2020.

[40]'Huawei Opens R&D Center in Kyiv', *Ukraine Digital News*, 17 April 2017, available at: https://www.uadn.net/2017/04/17/huawei-opens-rd-center-in-kyiv/, accessed 9 September 2020.

[41]'Musornye mashiny v Kieve oboruduyut GPS-datchikami', *focus.ua*, 31 July 2019.

[42]'Mer A. Surakmatov ogorchen tempami tsifrovizatsii', *meria.kg*, available at: https://www.meria.kg/ru/post/19993, accessed 1 September 2020.

broader issues in play.[43] Problems like poor road infrastructure, insufficient public transport, and a dynamic labour market may contribute to rule violations on the roads. However, these issues fall outside the Interior Ministry's jurisdiction or Committee on Information Technologies' (CIT) functions; they are the responsibility of municipal authorities. In mid-2019, six months after the cameras were installed, the number of unpaid fines increased from 28% to 86%, showing that the new measures had failed to increase enforcement of the collection of fines. Authorities claimed that the number of accidents had decreased in areas covered with technologies.[44] Kyrgyzstan's then Prime Minister, Mukhammedkaly Abylgaziev, credited the presence of surveillance cameras as an effective deterrent to traffic violations;[45] the results were in fact attributable to improved evidence collection. However, the new cameras are focused on road violations such as crossing a double line or driving through a red light, but are not equipped to capture images when cars hit pedestrians or cyclists.[46]

Kyrgyzstan's government first brokered an agreement with Huawei to install surveillance cameras in 2017; however, the deal fell apart after the presidential election later that year (Chudubaeva 2018). In 2018, the CIT signed an agreement with Vega, a Russian radio engineering corporation, to install 28 smart cameras in Bishkek and a total of 90 across the country. The Interior Ministry of Kyrgyzstan was authorised to determine where they would be installed and to monitor them. While local programmers developed the software for the cameras, Vega's Prisma system collects, stores, and manages the data from its headquarters in Russia. The revenue from traffic violations caught on camera is distributed among Vega, Kyrgyzstan's power ministries, and city infrastructural projects (Talgatbek 2018). In 2019, CIT selected Chinese firm Shenzhen Sunwin to install another 314 cameras across the country. In the same year, the Interior Ministry brokered another deal with the Chinese firm CEIEC to install 60 facial recognition cameras in undisclosed locations across Bishkek (Kolbaev 2019). As part of the US$5 million contract, Kyrgyz authorities will gain access to facial recognition software, but the exclusive intellectual property rights associated with the software will belong to the Chinese side.[47] As in Almaty, smart cameras perform revenue collection functions, but, as in Kyiv, they also interdict disorderly and criminal behaviour, a police function.

Vega had no prior experience with smart- or safe-city technologies and has mostly serviced the Russian government's development telecommunications systems for military purposes. Company officials insisted that Vega had 'some activity in some African countries, [and its] equipment was tested just two weeks ago in Tashkent and in Russian regions'.[48] Vega is a division of Rostech, a Russian state corporation hit with US

[43]'"Bezopasnyi gorod": v pervyi den' kamery zafiksirovali bolee 14 tysyach narushenii', *rus.azattyk.org*, 13 February 2019.

[44]'"Bezopasnyi gorod". Vyvody posle analiza polumilliona dannykh', *Kaktus Media*, 22 December 2019.

[45]'Abylgaziev: Situatsiya na dorogakh Bishkeka uluchshilas; posle zapuska "Bezopasnogo goroda"', *kaktus.media*, 5 March 2019.

[46]'GUOBDD napominaet: S 12 fevralya startuet "Bezopasnyi gorod"', *kabar.kg*, 6 February 2019.

[47]'Komitet grazhdanskogo kontrolya vozmushchen ustanovkoi kamer po raspoznavaniyu lits iz Kitaya', *Kaktus Media*, 6 November 2019.

[48]'Kalmykov: "Bezopasnyi gorod" v Bishkek—eto pervyi krupnyi proekt kontserna "Vega"', *Azattyk.org*, 5 October 2018.

sanctions in 2018.[49] The firm's CEO, Viacheslav Mikheev, has been awarded several state honours, including one for the 'Return of Crimea'.[50] However, who exactly has access to Bishkek's data and how they are used, if at all, beyond imposing fines, remains opaque. Both the Interior Ministry and CIT have justified the use of smart cameras as a way to document and change the behaviour of citizens.[51]

Bishkek's IT community denounced the government's contract with Vega, arguing that the sector had enough competence to develop its own smart city innovations that would give Kyrgyzstan a sustainable informational independence. According to a member of 'Taza Koom' (Smart Nation), a policy developed under former president, Almazbek Atambayev, promoting development of a knowledge-based economy in Kyrgyzstan—local experts could use the smart city initiative as an incubator for future innovations.[52] With local control of data, he argued, the local IT community could generate its own AI capabilities within a decade. This would make Kyrgyzstan more like Estonia, a country that prioritised domestic technological innovations over imports.

The three cities offer three different paths of expanding urban surveillance in the post-Soviet space. The lower-capacity cities do not have the wherewithal to fund smart city initiatives and so they depend on foreign financing. They offer innovation through increasing law-enforcement functions and will likely rely on a single supplier of technology. National authorities contract with external firms with limited involvement of municipal authorities. Bishkek, with the least capacity, has essentially outsourced smart-camera management and oversight to a Russian firm. Even though these efforts are focused on local traffic issues, the push for innovation came from the national level. Other post-Soviet capitals, such as Dushanbe[53] and Yerevan (Atanesian 2019), have followed a similar model. Huawei will recoup its investment in Tajikistan and Armenia by collecting fines (Atanesian 2019). Vega's profit in Kyrgyzstan depends on continued crime: the firm will take a cut from all recorded fines. Cities pursue a dreamscape of modernity that imagines public spaces with minimal disorderly and criminal conduct, but discord and criminal behaviour benefits financially the city, state, and smart city corporations. These elite groups can reap monetary rewards with minimal changes to the existing city infrastructure and without any increase in the political accountability of local and national officials to the public.

In comparison, surveillance programmes in Kyiv are shared between city and national authorities, with the goal of improving public safety and order. However, the breadth of HikVision's access to the data collected by its equipment remains unknown and is not

[49]'Announcement of Expanded Treasury Sanctions within the Russian Financial Services, Energy and Defense or Related Materiel Sectors', US Department of the Treasury, 12 September 2014, available at: https://www.treasury.gov/press-center/press-releases/Pages/jl2629.aspx, accessed 9 September 2020.

[50]'Mikheev Viacheslav Alekseevich', available at: http://www.vega.su/about/management/gendir/index.php, accessed 4 April 2019.

[51]'MVD: Vveden v ekspluatatsiyu mobil'nyi apparatno-programmnyi kompleks fiksatsii narushenii PDD', Kyrgyzstan Interior Ministry, 28 September 2016, available at: https://mvd.gov.kg/index.php/rus/mass-media/all-news/item/2703-mvd-vveden-v-ekspluatatsiyu-mobilnyj-apparatno-programmnyj-kompleks-fiksatsii-narushenij-pdd, accessed 26 September 2020.

[52]'Kak Kyrgyzstan poteryal svoi "Umnyi gorod". Monolog byvshego chlena komandy "Taza Koom"', *Kloop.kg*, 25 September 2018.

[53]'Kitaiskaya Huawei realizuet v Dushanbe proekt "Bezopasnyi gorod"', *News.tj*, 24 December 2012.

publicly discussed. There is also little information about how or why HikVision was selected as the main supplier of smart city technology in Ukraine. Thus, even though the concept of a smart city is interpreted more broadly in Kyiv than in Bishkek and the involvement of the city authorities is greater, the control structure over surveillance in the city is obscured and likely involves HikVision as well.

In Kyrgyzstan and Ukraine, officials promoting smart technologies acknowledge privacy concerns, but they largely ignore the potential risks of using technology from Russian or Chinese firms and, by proxy, foreign governments. There is a sense of resignation among public officials that Chinese and Russian companies—in other words, Beijing and Moscow—will inevitably gather intelligence if they so desire.[54] All the same, they believe that the benefits of collaboration with foreign tech giants far outweigh the possible repercussions of foreign access.

In effect, both Bishkek and Kyiv use surveillance technologies supplied by companies that have been sanctioned by Western countries. Similar to countries in South Asia, Africa, and Latin America, Eurasian states now find themselves at a crossroads: do they open up to external influence or abstain from global trends in modernisation? China's superior technology may offer Beijing its first serious form of influence over governance in post-Soviet cities, a niche traditionally occupied by Russia. Smart city hardware offers an easy entry point into Eurasian cities. It may even be that there is not the domestic capacity to maintain equipment or to construct algorithms to process the data. Maximising the potential benefits of smart technologies requires, first, a specialised talent pool and skillset, second, data storage and processing capacity, and third, effective inter-agency and public–private cooperation.

The Almaty *akimat*, by contrast, was able to establish local control over surveillance. Kazakhstan's Interior Ministry is continuing to impose invasive law-enforcement regimes in cities across the country and most certainly has access to surveillance footage of daily life. The *akimat* had the economic capacity to attract various companies to bid for contracts to install surveillance technologies across the city. Moscow and Baku, with their greater financial independence, acquired advanced technologies with fewer strings attached and considered surveillance to be just one part of a menu of smart city-innovations. Almaty's authorities included urban middle class demands for aesthetics and economic growth, but the public has no oversight over the city's surveillance mechanisms.

Geopolitical regimes

Arguably, domestic demands for public order, aesthetics, and unconstrained market relations can be satisfied with a variety of policies not involving external technological solutions. However, the supply side of smart technologies exported by global companies in new markets may undermine locally driven governance solutions and technological innovations. Previous sections demonstrate that for wealthy cities like Almaty, global

[54]Interview with a former high-ranking government official from Bishkek, August 2018; interview with a Kyiv-based journalist who previously attempted to investigate the Kyiv mayor's relationship with HikVision, January 2018.

standards become the dominant force of measuring 'smartness', while cities with fewer resources, like Bishkek, become targets of geopolitical competition to provide smart services. Kyiv is driven by its ambition to resemble cities with a high penetration of smart technologies. Smart city innovations thus have two distinct geopolitical dimensions as well: global standardisation of what 'smart' means in a city and the expansion of state-controlled firms as part of geopolitical competition between states. One form of geopolitical and geoeconomic dominance may prevail over another, but both urban modernisation and global processes are intertwined (Hambleton & Gross 2007; Pierre 2014). Some literature on urban development goes as far as to view municipal authorities as managers of global capitalist influences as opposed to representatives of local needs (Smith 2002).

First, cities use these projects in an attempt to score well on international indexes of urban economic growth and innovation, including the UN Smart Cities for Sustainable Development index (Robin & Acuto 2018). In most automated cities, including Almaty, municipal authorities rationalise their smart city programmes as a way to emulate large urban centres in developed countries. Yet the value of these scores is debatable, as they compare cities with entirely different labour markets, criminal dynamics, and demographic indicators. The definition of what qualifies as 'urban' tends to prioritise economic growth as the leading criteria for global dominance. When city planners embrace this definition, they rely on a global understanding of urban efficiency and intentionally try to move cities closer to global standards of an elusive 'smart city' model irrespective of local social dynamics.

Robin and Acuto (2018) examine 28 databases that compare cities across 17 standardised indicators to define their manageability, growth prospects, and modernity. They predominantly measure physical aspects within a city, such as transportation infrastructure, economic development, ability to withstand disasters, and effective governance. Assessment of softer issues, such as access to education, civic participation, or universal rights to the city, are mostly descriptive and based on case studies (Robin & Acuto 2018, p. 82). These datasets still have a strong Western bias regarding what constitutes 'smart' within a city, with European cities dominating most datasets. However, Singapore and Seoul, which are both frequently invoked in smart city ideas in Eurasia, are exceptions to the rule. How cities are mapped and what makes an area 'urban' is another recurrent bias in global datasets, especially when applied to cities in the Eurasian context with high levels of internal migration and the recent emergence of a middle class. Quantitative and easy to visualise frames of 'smart' become entry points for cities like Almaty and Kyiv with ambitions to modernise by investing domestic resources. Neither city is included among the major ranks of smart city datasets, yet their city development programmes regularly cite better-known examples of smart cities. Smart initiatives in both cities are predominantly driven by easily quantifiable metrics, such as number of smart cameras, crime rates, and fines collected.

The second geopolitical dimension is whether state-owned companies in Eurasia are providing smart city hardware and software. In the emerging knowledge-based economy, the combination of centralised data processing and the availability of big data offers greater potential to develop artificial intelligence for economic expansion and military purposes (Li 2018). The IR literature has only begun to consider how global competition over new AI capabilities will unfold and their future strategic use. Previous debates on technological innovations show how leapfrogging allows countries with cheaper labour to take the lead in new technologies (Brezis *et al.* 1993) and how competition and the accumulation of power become ends in themselves (Organski 1958). While the United States still leads in AI innovations and conducts the largest AI research and development efforts, Chinese AI firms have been rapidly gaining ground since 2014 (Li 2018; Wang & Chen 2018). Premier Li Keqiang announced Beijing's 'Made in China 2025' strategic plan in 2015; it was subsequently led by the Ministry of Industry and Information Technology (Crawford 2019). In 2017, the Russian government announced a 'Russian Digital Economy Plan', and President Vladimir Putin declared AI to be the next frontier of global competition (Sneps-Sneppe *et al.* 2018). However, Russian companies still lack a competitive edge in Eurasia compared to Chinese firms. Russia's domestic market is only beginning to be saturated with Russian tech firms providing smart city technologies. Unlike the Chinese approach, where major urban areas were digitised first, Rostelekom launched its smart city projects in remote areas. Rostelekom's spread of smart city technologies is similarly state driven, but far slower than in China.

China's largest companies are expanding in South Asian, African and Latin American countries where desire for greater connectivity and innovations overshadow any privacy concerns of the populace (McKinnon 2019). By 2017, China had registered significantly more patent applications in the AI domain than the United States. In China alone, roughly 500 cities are implementing smart technologies in 2020 (Keegan 2020). Indeed, China issued 'A Next Generation Artificial Intelligence Development Plan' to emerge as a global power in AI development by 2030. This top-down approach to development includes China's efforts to create favourable conditions and financial support for AI research and development without regard to ethical implications and transparency (Wang & Chen 2018).

In Eurasia, Chinese and Russian firms broker deals directly with political officials, not the private sector. Figure 1 demonstrates how Western, South Korean, and Turkish companies occupy a smaller share of the Eurasian market compared to Huawei and HikVision. Major projects usually begin with the company inviting government officials to its headquarters to showcase their state-of-the-art facilities and their role in reducing crime in China. To promote its products, Huawei also carries out soft-power projects in the region. For example, upon securing a multi-year telecommunications project in Uzbekistan, Huawei sponsored a visit by ten Uzbek students to China to learn about Beijing's Belt and Road initiative.[55]

Figure 1 displays some of the major partnerships between city or state governments and private corporations. Depending on the smart city initiative, these corporations provide technical expertise, site-specific planning and evaluation, implementation and installation, software platforms, hardware devices, and, in some cases, database monitoring services. The map key gives the company's name and location of its headquarters.

[55]'Uzbekistan', Huawei, available at: https://www.huawei.com/en/about-huawei/sustainability/win-win-development/social-contribution/seeds-for-the-future/uzbekistan, accessed 4 April 2019.

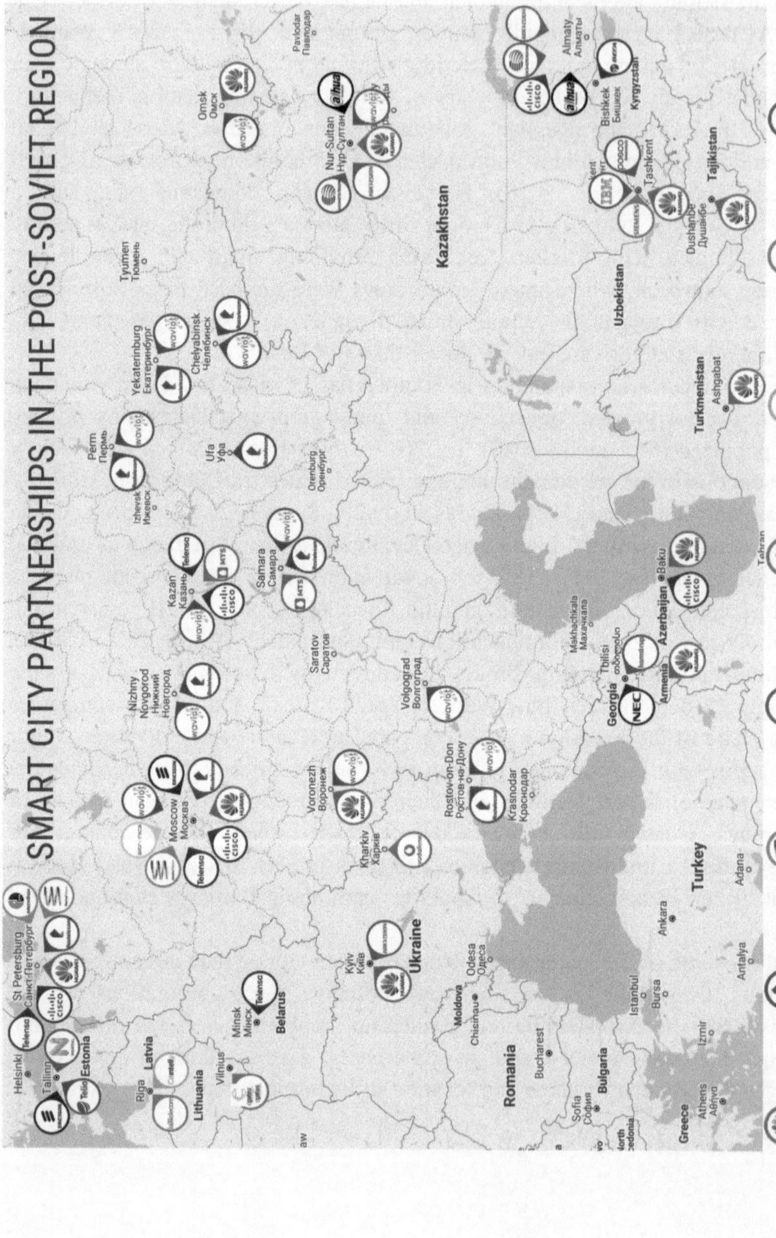

FIGURE 1. SMART CITY PARTNERSHIPS IN THE POST-SOVIET REGION

Russia's Rostelekom and Rostech, in turn, dominate the Russian market (Krinichansky 2019) and have supplied telecommunication products other than from smart technologies to government agencies in Kazakhstan, Tajikistan, Armenia, and Moldova.[56] Likewise, Rostech supplies equipment to border checkpoints across Central Asia. After Western and Chinese smart technologies proliferated in Russian cities, the Russian government developed its own smart city strategy based on the use of Russian providers. Starting in spring 2018, Rostelekom tested smart city technologies in 50 cities and created a 'Knowledge' (*Baza znanii*) of best practices across all smart city operations.[57] By 2018, Rostelekom had implemented a pilot project in Sakta and announced plans for digital programmes in Chelyabinsk, Taganrog, and Kursk, among other sites. The first project implemented in Sakta focused on safety issues, including surveillance in public (central parks) and private (condominiums) spaces. While described as 'smart', the project focused on improving safety by installing facial recognition cameras that collected and stored big data.[58] By the end of 2018, the Russian government had begun to centralise control over the implementation of smart city technologies and collecting big data from across the federation. Rostelekom frames the initiative as innovation in public life that also fosters economic growth. Russian state-driven smart city initiatives tend to focus on surveillance and collection of fines. In 2017, Deputy Minister of Communications, Sergei Kalugin, offered a neoliberal economic stance: 'cities are an integral part of the digital transformation of the economy. Occupying only 2% of the earth's surface, they account for 70% of world GDP and 50% of the population. In Russia, the urban population already makes up 74%'.[59] In effect, Kalugin's argument was that by turning 'smart', Russian cities would further generate greater economic output.

On a regional level, Russia is using its influence in post-Soviet space to standardise digital initiatives within the Eurasian Economic Union (EEU). In the face of Huawei and HikVision's rapid expansion in the post-Soviet region, Moscow introduced the 'Digital Agenda in the Globalisation Epoch 2.0: Eurasian Innovation Ecosystem' at the 2019 EEU meeting in Almaty.[60] Part of this initiative is to create a specialised venture fund and industry-specific digital platforms to harmonise standards across member-states. Igor Shuvalov, Russian first deputy prime minister, has encouraged interior ministries across the EEU, especially those that are more advanced in their use of technology than other member-states, to build horizontal ties within the union in addition to advancing their own national digital agenda.[61] The EEU presents the integration of digital innovations as a way of gaining a global competitive edge by 2025. Bishkek is a prime example of a market

[56] 'Rostelecom to Provide Integrated Telecommunications Services to the State Automated System "Justice"', *Company.rt.ru*, 14 February 2017.

[57] 'Rostelekom predstavil v Minstroe Rossi proekt dorozhnoi karty po napravleniyu "Umnyi gorod"', *Company.rt.ru*, 6 April 2018.

[58] 'Rostelekom prodemonstriroval pervye resul'taty proekta "Umnyi gorod" v Sakte', *Company.rt.ru*, 30 August 2018.

[59] 'V Rossii budet sozdana kontseptsiya pervykh "umnykh" gorodov', *Company.rt.ru*, 17 October 2017.

[60] 'Prem'ery pyati stran soberutsya v Almaty: chto obsudyat na Evraziiskom mezhpartsovete', *Sputniknews.kz*, 1 February 2019.

[61] 'Strany EAES mogut stat' zalozhnikami sobstvennykh programm po tsifrovizatsii ekonomiki', *Profit.kz*, 25 August 2017.

where Russian firms succeeded when Chinese companies were unable to dominate the market.

The declaration was the first of its kind, signalling the Kremlin's interest in guiding modernisation efforts within the union's market and possibly blocking or at least increasing barriers for external companies. The EEU is now interested in collaboration between 'digital ecosystems' across member states to 'stimulate innovation'. In early 2019, Russian Prime Minister Dmitry Medvedev focused on security aspects, stating that 'security, digital sovereignty and digital integration are the goals of the Eurasian Five'.[62] However, Chinese telecommunications companies still see Russia as a large market for potential expansion. Of the 160,000 cameras across Moscow, 15% belong to HikVision. Chinese companies make up 88% of the telecom import market in the Russian capital.[63] However, in 2018, the Moscow mayor Sergei Sobyanin declared his intention to incorporate more domestic smart city innovations in the coming years, including the collection of big data, reliance on AI in decision-making, and encouraging 'the internet of things'.[64]

Both Chinese and Russian companies have strong ties to their respective governments and are emerging as exporters of smart technologies that could be used to collect and store big data, as well as to develop artificial intelligence capabilities. Neither are overtly grabbing market shares but their presence exploded in the period 2017–2019. Thus, the common Western experience of automated surveillance and predictive analytics is coming to Eurasian cities thanks to regional powers who have joined the global competition for dominance in smart technologies.

Conclusions: implications for the rule of law

The spread of surveillance technologies in Eurasia shows how cities and countries aspire to follow global trends for smart city technologies. Mayors of all large cities have adopted some technological aspects under the aegis of 'smart'. While cities pursue 'smartness', the region has followed the Western path of expanding the crime-control industry in response to increasing economic activity in urban centres. Local leaders have also responded to requests from urban residents to increase aesthetics and safety in public spaces. In the three cases analysed in this essay—Almaty, Kyiv and Bishkek—as well as in most other post-Soviet cities, smart city innovations prioritising safety have primarily consisted of expanding surveillance technologies in public spaces. In all three countries, the socio-technological imaginaries include a modern 'dreamscape' in which drivers obey traffic laws, pickpockets fear the 'gaze' of smart cameras, potential trespassers are warned off, children are safe, fugitives are quickly arrested, police corruption is eliminated, and everyone pays their taxes.

However, in their pursuit of technological intelligence, cities are inevitably influenced by global forces that drive urban innovation in accordance with foreign (often Eurocentric)

[62]Dmitry Medvedev's Twitter account, 1 February 2019, available at: https://twitter.com/medvedevrussiae/status/1091247494414123008?s=21, accessed 4 April 2019.

[63]'Keep an Eye Out: Russia's Video Surveillance Market', *Securika-Moscow.ru*, 26 July 2018.

[64]'Sobyanin poruchil razrabotat' programmu "Umnyi gorod"', *Ria.ru*, 10 April 2018.

understanding of 'smartness'. They are also susceptible to the whims of technological giants that are working as part of their countries' geopolitical ambitions. Almaty in particular, with its goal to become one of the most developed cities in the world, is influenced by global rankings that define smart and safe ideals within a city. The city of Almaty is driving smart innovations in Kazakhstan on its own and within its national policy to rely on home-grown systems of surveillance. Where the global appeal of smart technologies has not been matched by domestic capabilities to innovate, Chinese and Russian state-controlled companies have stepped in. The quest for an efficiently modern crime control system in Kyiv and Bishkek has been satisfied by outside firms with foreign understandings of public safety that may expand surveillance opportunities both for national political elites and foreign governments. Given the pervasive absence of legislative oversight, the countries looking to leapfrog into the digital future are adopting a virtual authoritarianism that risks suppressing political dissent and further marginalising already disadvantaged groups.

The spread of smart city technologies in Eurasia raises the question of who is watching whom. Similar to what has been argued by Strange, the power struggle lies at the convergence of the varied domestic demand for surveillance technologies and the availability of Chinese and Russian state-controlled firms to provide products and services. Like most cities across the world looking to modernise public order, the three cities analysed here can afford new technologies thanks to subsidised products supplied by international firms who may have motives beyond revenue. Despite the risk, the merging of the global supply of technologies and local socio-technological imaginaries through state mediation has resulted in altered law-enforcement regimes in Eurasian societies. Surveillance technologies change behaviour without the participation of the police, allow the authorities to collect fines more effectively, and generate new ideas of public order. In distant ways, the foreign tech companies, national government, municipal authorities, and the urban middle class all benefit from a surveilled public space, while subsets of urban residents become more policed and order is enforced against groups committing disorderly or illegal conduct in surveilled public spaces.

References

Alhabaev, S. (2020a) 'Yurist raskritikoval sistemu raspoznavaniya lits v Almaty', *Tengrinews.kz*, 15 January.

Alhabaev, S. (2020b) 'Sistema raspoznavaniya lits v Almaty: politsiya ne podpisala memorandum', *Tengrinews.kz*, 16 January.

Angelidou, M. (2015) 'Smart Cities: A Conjuncture of Four Forces', *Cities*, 47, September.

Atanesian, G. (2019) 'Armenia Mulls Chinese Surveillance Firm', *Eurasianet.org*, 20 February.

Batty, M. (2013) 'Big Data, Smart Cities and City Planning', *Dialogues in Human Geography*, 3, 3.

Bissenova, A. (2012) *Post-Socialist Dreamworlds: Housing Boom and Urban Development in Kazakhstan*, PhD thesis (Ithaca, NY, Cornell University), available at: https://ecommons.cornell.edu/handle/1813/29225, accessed 25 May 2019.

Brayne, S. (2017) 'Big Data Surveillance: The Case of Policing', *American Sociological Review*, 82, 5.

Brezis, E. S., Krugman, P. R. & Tsiddon, D. (1993) 'Leapfrogging in International Competition: A Theory of Cycles in National Technological Leadership', *The American Economic Review*, 83, 5.

Chudubaeva, G. (2018) 'Sapar Isakov rasskazal o rastorzhenii dogovora s Huawei', *knews.kg*, 17 March.

Cocchia, A. (2014) 'Smart and Digital City: A Systematic Literature Review', in Dameri, R. P. & Rosenthal-Sabroux, C. (eds) *Smart City: How to Create Public and Economic Value with High Technology in Urban Space* (New York, NY, Springer).

Crawford, E. (2019) 'Made in China 2025: The Industrial Plan that China doesn't want Anyone Talking About', *pbs.org*, 7 May, available at: https://www.pbs.org/wgbh/frontline/article/made-in-china-2025-the-industrial-plan-that-china-doesnt-want-anyone-talking-about/, accessed 9 September 2020.

Cummings, M. L., Roff, H. M., Cukier, K., Parakilas, J. & Bryce, H. (2018) *Artificial Intelligence and International Affairs Disruption Anticipated* (London, Chatham House).

Datta, A. (2015) 'New Urban Utopias of Postcolonial India: "Entrepreneurial Urbanization" in Dholera Smart City, Gujarat', *Dialogues in Human Geography*, 5, 1.

Evison, M. P. (2015) 'The Third Forensics—Images and Allusions', *Policing and Society*, 25, 5.

Frischmann, B. & Selinger, E (2018) *Re-Engineering Humanity* (New York, NY, Cambridge University Press).

Galdon-Clavell, G. (2013) '(Not So) Smart Cities? The Drivers, Impact and Risks of Surveillance-Enabled Smart Environments', *Science and Public Policy*, 40, 6.

Garland, D. (2001) *The Culture of Control* (Oxford, Oxford University Press).

Geitsya, V. M., Danilenka, A. I., Libanovoi, E. M., Gritsenka, A. A., Makarovoi, O. V., Kizima, M. O., Egorova, I. Y. & Odotyuka, I. V. (eds) (2015) *Innovatsina Ukraina 2020: natsional'na dopovid* (Kyiv, Natsional'na Akademiia Nauk Ukraini).

Germain, S., Douillet, A. & Dumoulin, L (2011) 'The Legitimization of CCTV as a Policy Tool: Genesis and Stabilization of a Socio-Technical Device in Three French Cities', *The British Journal of Criminology*, 52, 2.

Ghertner, D. A. (2015) *Rule by Aesthetics: World-Class City Making in Delhi* (New York, NY, Oxford University Press).

Grossi, G. & Pianezzi, D. (2017) 'Smart Cities: Utopia or Neoliberal Ideology?', *Cities*, 69, September.

Habermas, J. (2010) 'The Public Sphere: An Encyclopedia Article (1964)', in Gripsrud, J., Moe, H., Molander, A. & Murdock, G. (eds) *The Idea of the Public Sphere: A Reader* (Lanham, MD, Lexington Books).

Hambleton, R. & Gross, J. (2007) *Governing Cities in a Global Era: Urban Innovation, Competition, and Democratic Reform* (New York, NY, Palgrave Macmillan).

Hawke, J. (2020) 'Britain Bans Huawei from its 5G Network and will Remove Existing Equipment by 2027', *abc.net.au*, 14 July, available at: https://www.abc.net.au/news/2020-07-14/uk-set-to-exclude-huawei-from-telecommunications-networks/12455930, accessed 9 September 2020.

Horowitz, M. C. (2018) 'Artificial Intelligence, International Competition, and the Balance of Power', *Texas National Security Review*, May, available at: https://tnsr.org/2018/05/artificial-intelligence-international-competition-and-the-balance-of-power/, accessed 8 June 2019.

Jäger, P. F. (2016) 'Where the Whole City Meets: Youth, Gender and Consumerism in the Social Space of the MEGA Shopping Mall in Aktobe, Western Kazakhstan', *Central Asian Survey*, 35, 2.

Jasanoff, S. & Kim, S. (eds) (2015) *Dreamscapes of Modernity: Sociotechnical Imaginaries and the Fabrication of Power* (Chicago, IL, University of Chicago Press).

Jenkins, H. W. (2012) 'What to do about Huawei? The Chinese Telecom-Equipment Maker may be No. 2 in the World, but it's still Distrusted by Uncle Sam', *Wall Street Journal*, 10 July.

Junisbai, A. (2010) 'Understanding Economic Justice Attitudes in Two Countries: Kazakhstan and Kyrgyzstan', *Social Forces*, 88, 4.

Kania, E. (2017) *Battlefield Singularity: Artificial Intelligence, Military Revolution, and China's Future Military Power* (Washington, DC, Center for a New American Security).

Kassymbekova, B. (2017) 'Understanding Stalinism in, from and of Central Asia: Beyond Failure, Peripherality and Otherness', *Central Asian Survey*, 36, 1.

Keegan, M. (2020) 'In China, Smart Cities or Surveillance Cities?', *USA Today*, 31 January.

Kitchin, R. (2014) 'The Real-Time City? Big Data and Smart Urbanism', *GeoJournal*, 79, 1.

Kitchin, R., Cardullo, P. & Di Feliciantonio, C. (2019) 'Citizenship, Justice, and the Right to the Smart City', in Cardullo, P., Di Feliciantonio, C. & Kitchin, R. (eds) *The Right to the Smart City* (Bingley, Emerald Publishing).

Kolbaev, B. (2019) '"Bezopasnyi gorod-2": chto izvestno o kompanii—pobeditel'nitse tendera', *rus.azattyk.org*, 19 September.
Koskela, H. (2000) '"The Gaze Without Eyes": Video-Surveillance and the Changing Nature of Urban Space', *Progress in Human Geography*, 24, 2.
Krinichansky, K. V. (2019) 'Smart Solutions for Smart Cities: A Snapshot of Russian Urban Life', in Sergi, B. S. (ed.) *Tech, Smart Cities, and Regional Development in Contemporary Russia* (Bingley, Emerald Publishing).
Kulesh, S. (2020) '"Tsentr upravleniia poletom": Mier Kieva Vitalii Klichko pokazal, kak umnye tekhnologii pomogaiut emu v upravlenii stolitsei', *itc.ua*, 4 August.
Kulyk, V. (2016) 'National Identity in Ukraine: Impact of Euromaidan and the War', *Europe-Asia Studies*, 68, 4.
Kynge, J. (2019) 'U.S. Pressure Building on Investors in China', *Financial Times*, 29 March.
Laruelle, M. & Royce, D. (2019) 'Kazakhstani Public Opinion of the United States and Russia: Testing Variables of (Un)favourability', *Central Asian Survey*, 38, 2.
Li, L. (2018) 'China's Manufacturing Locus in 2025: With a Comparison of "Made-in-China 2025" and "Industry 4.0"', *Technological Forecasting and Social Change*, 135, October.
Marat, E. (2018) 'Mimicking "Broken Windows" Policing in Post-Soviet Cities: Expanding Social Control in Uncertain Times', *Policing and Society*, 28, March.
McKinnon, A. (2019) 'For Africa, Chinese-built Internet is Better than no Internet at all', *Foreign Policy*, 18 March.
McNeill, D. (2015) 'Global Firms and Smart Technologies: IBM and the Reduction of Cities', *Transactions of the Institute of British Geographers*, 40, 4.
Oliker, O., Davis, L. E., Crane, K., Radin, A., Gventer, C. W., Sondergaard, S., Quinlivan, J. T., Seabrook, S. B., Bellasio, J., Frederick, B. & Bega, A. (2016) *Security Sector Reform in Ukraine* (Washington, DC, Rand Corporation).
Organski, A. F. (1958) *World Politics* (New York, NY, Knopf).
Peck, J. & Tickell, A. (2002) 'Neoliberalizing Space', *Antipode*, 34, 3.
Pierre, J. (2014) 'Can Urban Regimes Travel in Time and Space? Urban Regime Theory, Urban Governance Theory, and Comparative Urban Politics', *Urban Affairs Review*, 50, 6.
Robin, E. & Acuto, M. (2018) 'Global Urban Policy and the Geopolitics of Urban Data', *Political Geography*, 66, September.
Roff, H. M. (2019) 'The Frame Problem: The AI "Arms Race" isn't one', *Bulletin of the Atomic Scientists*, 75, 3.
Schröder, P. (2016) 'Urban Spaces and Lifestyles in Central Asia and Beyond: An Introduction', *Central Asian Survey*, 35, 2.
Shelley, L. (1979) 'Soviet Criminology: Its Birth and Demise, 1917–1936', *Slavic Review*, 38, 4.
Smith, N. (2002) 'New Globalism, New Urbanism: Gentrification as Global Urban Strategy', *Antipode*, 34, 3.
Sneps-Sneppe, M., Sukhomlin, V. & Namiot, D. (2018) 'On the Program "Digital Economy of the Russian Federation": How to Create an Information Infrastructure', *International Journal of Open Information Technologies*, 6, 3.
Söderström, O., Paasche, T. & Klauser, F. (2014) 'Smart Cities as Corporate Storytelling', *City*, 18, 3.
Solomon, P. H. (1974) 'Soviet Criminology: Its Demise and Rebirth, 1928–1963', *The Soviet and Post-Soviet Review*, 1, 1.
Strange, S. (1996) *The Retreat of the State: The Diffusion of Power in the World Economy* (Cambridge, Cambridge University Press).
Talgatbek, A. (2018) 'Shtrafy po "Bezopasnomu gorodu" khotyat razdelit' mezhdu MVD, GKNB i mestnymi vlastyami', *kloop.kg*, 23 November.
Tokoeva, A. (2018) 'Chto takoe "Umnyi gorod" i kak vlasti vnedryayuut ego v Kyrgyzstane?', *kloop.kg*, 7 May.
Utenova, Z. (2019) 'V Almaty stali men'she vorovat'—politsiya', *Tengrinews.kz*, 1 November.
Wang, Y. & Chen, D. (2018) 'Rising Sino–U.S. Competition in Artificial Intelligence', *China Quarterly of International Strategic Studies*, 4, 2.
Watson, V. (2016) 'New African City Plans: Local Urban Form and the Escalation of Urban Inequalities', in Datta, A. & Shaban A. (eds) *Mega-Urbanization in the Global South* (New York, NY, Routledge).
Willis, K. S. (2020) 'The Death and Life of Smart Cities', in Willis, K. S. & Aurigi, A. (eds) *The Routledge Companion to Smart Cities* (New York, NY, Routledge).
Yap, C., Strumpf, D., Volz, D., O'Keeffe, K. & Viswanatha, A. (2019) 'Huawei's Yearslong Rise is Littered with Accusations of Theft and Dubious Ethics', *The Wall Street Journal*, 25 May.

Index